The Power of the Church

The Power of the Church

The Sacramental Ecclesiology of Abraham Kuyper

MICHAEL R. WAGENMAN

◆PICKWICK *Publications* • Eugene, Oregon

THE POWER OF THE CHURCH
The Sacramental Ecclesiology of Abraham Kuyper

Copyright © 2020 Michael R. Wagenman. All rights reserved. Except for brief quotations in critical publications or reviews, no part of this book may be reproduced in any manner without prior written permission from the publisher. Write: Permissions, Wipf and Stock Publishers, 199 W. 8th Ave., Suite 3, Eugene, OR 97401.

Pickwick Publications
An Imprint of Wipf and Stock Publishers
199 W. 8th Ave., Suite 3
Eugene, OR 97401

www.wipfandstock.com

PAPERBACK ISBN: 978-1-5326-9765-4
HARDCOVER ISBN: 978-1-5326-9766-1
EBOOK ISBN: 978-1-5326-9767-8

Cataloguing-in-Publication data:

Names: Wagenman, Michael R., author.

Title: The power of the church: the sacramental ecclesiology of Abraham Kuyper / Michael R. Wagenman.

Description: Eugene, OR : Pickwick Publications, 2020 | Includes bibliographical references and index.

Identifiers: ISBN 978-1-5326-9765-4 (paperback) | ISBN 978-1-5326-9766-1 (hardcover) | ISBN 978-1-5326-9767-8 (ebook)

Subjects: LCSH: Kuyper, Abraham, 1837–1920. | Church. | Church and state—Netherlands. | Public theology.

Classification: BX9479.K8 W34 2020 (paperback) | BX9479.K8 W34 (ebook)

Manufactured in the U.S.A.   11/16/20

For Rev. Dr. Leith Anderson

ὅτι σοῦ ἐστιν ἡ δύναμις καὶ ἡ δόξα εἰς τοὺς αἰῶνας.

—Didache 8:2

Again I saw all the oppressions that are practiced under the sun.

Look, the tears of the oppressed—with no one to comfort them!

On the side of their oppressors there was power—with no one to comfort them.

—Ecclesiastes 4:1

The church is for the world

by providing the world with speech

that the world wouldn't have if the church did not exist.

—Dr. Stanley Hauerwas, Epiphaneia Conference
May 16, 2014, Toronto

Contents

Abstract		ix
List of Abbreviations		xi
Preface		xiii
1	Introduction: The Disappearance *Church, Power, and Abraham Kuyper*	1
2	Power *An Historical Survey of the Conceptual Landscape*	28
3	Disappearing No Longer *The Ecclesiology of Abraham Kuyper*	75
4	Sovereignty, Authority, and Power *Abraham Kuyper's Worldview*	108
5	The Ecclesial Sphere and Kerygmatic Power	144
6	The Nature of Ecclesial Power *Further Philosophical, Theological, and Biblical Investigations*	181
7	The Sacramental Nature of Ecclesial Power *Abraham Kuyper's Ecclesiology and Vatican Council II*	226
8	Conclusion	266
Appendix 1: A Chronology of Abraham Kuyper		279
Appendix 2: The Church in the Reformed Confessions		297
Bibliography		309
Index		329

Abstract

ABRAHAM KUYPER WAS RAISED in a nineteenth-century Dutch Reformed environment deeply influenced by the Enlightenment which concentrated civic power in the state which dominated civic life, the church included. In response, Kuyper re-articulated the power of the institutional church to address the resultant ills perceived in church, state, and society. This book analyzes the power of the institutional church in Kuyper's ecclesiology through an investigation of his primary works, historical-cultural context, and comparison with other theologians and philosophers of ecclesial power.

For Kuyper, the institutional church is structurally grounded in creation, emerging after the Fall as an institution of human society. It occupies an essential place as a societal sphere with its own direct accountability to Christ, independent from other spheres. The church exists bi-modally: as institution and organism. In both modes, the church is the bearer of the salt and light of the Christian Gospel of Jesus Christ to the world. But the institutional church does not accomplish its task with the same means or power as other cultural institutions. It is a unique sphere of public life with a unique form of power. This unique power of the institutional church emerges from Kuyper's comprehensive Calvinist worldview.

The power of the institutional church is its unique vocation, in vital union with Christ, to proclaim the comprehensive Word of God (through proclaimed Word, celebrated sacraments, discipleship, and diaconal acts of justice and mercy). This proclamation is oriented toward personal and public conversion, not directly through ecclesial cultural dominance but indirectly through public Christian witness.

This analysis is then brought into critical dialogue with others to highlight and clarify it for application to the church today. It is argued that Kuyper's insight has not been fully received, that it is deeply resonant with Scripture, and that it remains rich with potential for the contemporary world.

List of Abbreviations

AKCR	James D. Bratt, ed., *Abraham Kuyper: A Centennial Reader* (Grand Rapids: Eerdmans, 1998).
AKASPI	Richard Mouw, *Abraham Kuyper: A Short Personal Introduction* (Grand Rapids: Eerdmans, 2011).
AKMCCD	James D. Bratt, *Abraham Kuyper: Modern Calvinist, Christian Democrat* (Grand Rapids: Eerdmans, 2013).
ARP	Anti-Revolutionary Party
CCW	Peter Heslam, *Creating a Christian Worldview: Abraham Kuyper's Lectures on Calvinism* (Grand Rapids: Eerdmans, 1998).
CGKN	Christelijke Gereformeerde Kerk in Nederland (The Christian Reformed Church in the Netherlands, which originated in the *Afscheiding* of 1834 and later merged with Kuyper's GKN).
DCMA	James D. Bratt, *Dutch Calvinism in Modern America: A History of a Conservative Subculture* (Grand Rapids: Eerdmans, 1984).
FCHN	John Bolt, *A Free Church, A Holy Nation: Abraham Kuyper's American Public Theology* (Grand Rapids: Eerdmans, 2001).
FLP	Jacques Ellul, *On Freedom, Love, and Power* (Toronto: University of Toronto Press, 2010).
GD	John Halsey Wood, *Going Dutch in the Modern Age: Abraham Kuyper's Struggle for a Free Church in the Nineteenth-Century Netherlands* (Oxford: Oxford University Press, 2013).

GKN	Gereformeerde Kerken Nederland (Kuyper's *Doliantie* church, formed in 1892).
LC	Abraham Kuyper, *Lectures on Calvinism* (Grand Rapids: Eerdmans, 1943).
NHK	Nederlandse Hervormde Kerk (National Dutch Reformed Church).
NIV	The Holy Bible: New International Version (Grand Rapids: Biblica, 2011).
NRSV	The Holy Bible: New Revised Standard Version (Division of Christian Education of the National Council of the Churches of Christ in the USA, 1989).
PK	Jacques Ellul, *The Presence of the Kingdom* (Colorado Springs: Helmers & Howard, 1989).
R&G	Abraham Kuyper, *Rooted and Grounded: The Church as Organism and Institution* (Grand Rapids: Christian's Library, 2013).
VU	Vrije Universiteit Amsterdam (The Free University of Amsterdam, founded by Abraham Kuyper in 1880).

Preface

It dawned on me one day that in all the media reports and discussions of the church's abuse of power in the early years of the twenty-first century, few if any seemed to notice that the accusation of the church's misuse of power presupposed a shared understanding of the positive use of power within the church that had been violated. Rather than an interest in the sociological aspect of this question, I was drawn to the more ontological and normative aspects of it. That is, I wanted to investigate and discern the foundational theological framework of culture and society and the location and purpose of the church within them. As a cultural force and societal institution, what does the church constructively bring to the human community? This book is the result of the investigation that followed.

What I quickly discovered was that in order to fully address the question of the church's power, I needed to delve deeply into both the theology of the church (ecclesiology) and emerging theologies and philosophies of power. It was at the intersection of these two important concepts (the church and power) that little material existed. There are many theologies of the church, each ecclesial tradition having its own history of theological reflection on itself. I chose to focus on the Dutch Reformed tradition for a variety of reasons that I believe will become clear to the reader in the pages that follow. This tradition, especially the more focussed tradition that grew around the work of the late nineteenth and early twentieth-century theologian Abraham Kuyper, is one of the most recent examples of a theological tradition deeply and intentionally engaged in the cultural and societal aspects of the Christian religion in the modern and late modern era.

But when it came to considering theologies of power in the late twentieth century, I found a very different situation. Rather than being overwhelmed by a wealth of material, as I was with theologies of the church, I found a startling and disappointing lack. Yet, once again, Abraham Kuyper came to my rescue. For in his theology I found an implicit theology of power—it just hadn't been excavated for analysis yet, and especially not in English. Within the theological framework or worldview of Abraham Kuyper there is a rich and multifaceted understanding of the world as God's creation. This creation is not just limited to rocks and trees and human beings but includes the very cultural forces and societal institutions I was interested in exploring.

And so, what you will find in these pages is a general theological analysis of God's creation in Kuyper's worldview with particular focus on the unique power of the church. Of course, this theological understanding of God's creation needs to be extended to the other institutions of society (schools, governments, businesses, art guilds, etc.). But I must leave it to others to continue what I have only been able to begin here. This is a critically important task as the culture and society of western Europe and North America (what constituted, until relatively recently, Western Christendom) continues to undergo the transformations that began centuries ago with the Renaissance and Enlightenment (what we call modernity and for many today, post-modernity). The Christian church has functioned in a surprisingly consistent way in this part of the world for the last couple of millennia. Now that these cultural changes are well underway, I am convinced that if the church is to have on-going influence in our global world, it will only be possible through a rediscovery of what the church is and how it has been uniquely constituted by God to do something unique in the world. I believe this is a positive and constructive task; but without a fresh discovery of the church's theological nature and calling, many will only operate out of a reactive or pragmatic frame of reference, a reference point that too often contributes to the negative and restrictive modes of being in the world that are a sign of fear and a lack of faith. Instead, in Kuyper's theology of the church's power, we are invited to conceive of the church's nature as fundamentally sacramental. And in this way, Kuyper's theology of the church's power, while rooted in a specific time and place and tradition, opens up fresh avenues of dialogue with other Christian communities so that, in an ecumenical spirit, Christians of various denominations can rediscover their unity, purpose, and vocation in and for the world.

It is with gratitude and humility that I dedicate this work to Rev. Dr. Leith Anderson, pastor emeritus of Woodale Church in Minneapolis, Minnesota, and president emeritus of the National Association of Evangelicals.

I had the distinguished opportunity to be shaped by Leith's ministry for nearly two decades. He has been for me a contemporary example of Abraham Kuyper's grand theological vision of a church engaging all of life, culture, and society with the comprehensive and multifaceted message of love, joy, and hope in Jesus Christ.

    MICHAEL R. WAGENMAN
    Epiphany 2020

1

Introduction: The Disappearance

Church, Power, and Abraham Kuyper

THE DISAPPEARING CHURCH

EIGHTY KILOMETRES EAST OF Brussels, a church stands atop a small hill overlooking a pastoral vista. The church is constructed of rusty steel beams separated by gaps which make it very much unlike the nearby churches. It is an optical illusion. The building is nearly invisible when viewed from one angle but when viewed from another angle the church reappears. Depending on where one stands, it either appears or fades away from view. Even standing within the structure, one's view of the outside world may be entirely obstructed or virtually uninhibited. This ecclesial disappearing act is not only the artistic work of Pieterjan Gijs[1] but a deeply philosophical statement about the evanescent place of the church in contemporary Western society today. Depending on one's vantage point, the church as a cultural and societal institution is either deeply formative to one's identity or simply nonexistent.

---

1. Gijs is a Belgian architect and founding partner of the Gijs Van Vaerenbergh architectural firm. Since 2007, he has participated in the design and construction of several public art installations. For information on and additional photos of "Reading Between the Lines," see Gijs and Vaerenbergh, "Z-OUT." All images used with permission.

2   THE POWER OF THE CHURCH

From a critical and demographical perspective, the contemporary church in the Western world is marked by dwindling attendance, shrinking fiscal budgets, and evaporating cultural and social influence. The church buildings of earlier eras today have been transformed into museums, historical/cultural centers, restaurants, and private homes. Even in those churches that still operate as places of Christian worship, the empty pews can be matched by the theological vacuity of the pulpits. The churches that remain standing retain their outward appearance but their sacramental or devotional or cultural significance is waning. Whereas the steeples of centuries-old churches once functioned as geographic and theological points of reference for pilgrim and resident alike, today one is left wondering what of their former power remains. On the other hand, one cannot deny that the cultural institution of the church remains and continues to be a voice of piety, morality, hope, and virtue not only to the faithful but to the societies which surround them. As a cultural institution, the church continues to exert its power of influence over members and detractors alike through its very presence within society. In this way, the church remains present and visible. And yet, as with the eerie desolation of the see-through art installation in Belgium, whether or to what extent the church retains significance (religious, spiritual, historical, cultural, etc.) for the society in which it is located is another matter—often a matter of one's personal or subjective perspective. The church buildings may still be visible in the contemporary cultural landscape of the West but their power remains an open question. In this way, we can ask whether the church has "disappeared" from its previously held place of formative influence in the lives of peoples, cultures, and societies.[2]

One reason why the church has seemingly disappeared for some today may be the perceived or actually questionable exercises of power for which the church has been called to account. The early years of the twenty-first century have included reports that document a host of ills within the Christian church of one kind of another. The Roman Catholic Church is rocked by clergy abuse scandals on multiple continents. The Anglican Communion struggles to come to grips with widely divergent attitudes and practices on a host of theological, ethical, and liturgical issues and how those in positions of ecclesial leadership can respond in ways that promote harmony rather than friction for the communion as a global body. Independent Protestant churches in North America face social scorn after leaders are found guilty of embezzling funds from their ministries for lavish personal projects. Charismatic or Pentecostal pastors, believing they can avoid the notice of the twenty-four hour news media, preach outlandish messages to congregations

---

2. Jinkins, *Church Faces Death*, uses the category of "death" rather than "disappearance" to describe the situation of the church in contemporary Western society. I take him to be engaged in a provocative form of hyperbole and have attempted to more accurately capture the situation on the ground with my own term.

who, it is quite reasonable to say, should know better.[3] The church today clearly faces serious questions—questions often connected to the nature and exercise of ecclesial power. These questions demand an answer if the church is to avoid utter invisibility and remain positively constructive on the cultural landscape of modern society.

In these ways, the term "disappearance" is helpful for it carries within itself this very nuance: the church remains physically visible as a building within the institutional marketplace of our society; and yet the church has clearly been dislodged from its previously-held place of prominence and central significance in the cultural story of the West. This change has made possible the sociological study of the church's "disappearance" even while church buildings continue to dot urban and rural landscapes. Like "Reading Between the Lines," while the church remains present, it is nevertheless in danger of disappearing today.

DOCUMENTING THE CHURCH'S DISAPPEARANCE

Sociological studies have been published which attempt to chart, explain, and even correct the declining membership and influence of the church, primarily in western European and North American society. The Canadian sociologist Reginald Bibby regularly publishes research on the state of the church in Canada. His most recent work documents that the average weekly church attendance of Canadians has dropped from 60 percent to 25 percent in the 60 years from 1945 to 2005.[4] Bibby and others have also shown that the drop-off rates are much steeper when youth and young adults are considered as a sub-demographic instead of the general population.[5] The Evangelical Fellowship of Canada's study, *Hemorrhaging Faith: Why and When Canadian Young Adults are Leaving, Staying and Returning to Church*, shows that "by young adulthood only one in ten respondents raised in Catholic and Mainline traditions reported attending religious services at least weekly—compared to four in ten raised in Evangelical traditions."[6]

---

3. For example, on January 28, 2013, a news agency published a story about Valdeci Sobrino Picanto, an Evangelical Brazilian pastor who proclaimed to his congregation that the Holy Spirit resides in his penis. See "Pastor Arrested for Raping His Faithfuls."

4. Bibby, *New Day*, 5. The drop-off is even sharper for Roman Catholic and mainline Protestant bodies specifically.

5. The work of American sociologist Christian Smith is also helpful here. See Smith, *Soul Searching*; *Souls in Transition*.

6. Penner et al., *Hemorrhaging Faith*, 22.

Despite stories of renewal and revival of the church occasionally,[7] this research shows that not only is the church struggling today but the vitality of tomorrow's church may appear grim. This sociological data is one example of the cultural shifts that have taken place in Western societies that have had a marginalizing effect on the church's place within culture and society. While occasional reports suggest otherwise, the case of Canada is similar to the larger North American and European context: the church in Western culture and society is indeed disappearing from the landscape of many.[8]

James Davison Hunter has chronicled how Christians individually, communally, and as institutional church bodies have been responding to the various deep cultural changes making an impact on the church.[9] Hunter highlights the tragic ways the American church has attempted to reassert its cultural influence—tragic, he argues, because these attempts are rooted in narratives of power that are alien to the Christian faith.[10] Though the reasons are more complex than he allows, he focusses on church leaders' efforts to re-create or re-establish a Constantinian cultural matrix in which

---

7. R. R. Reno suggests that despite the claims that the church is losing touch with the surrounding culture and "dying," the church can have hope as it faces the future because "most types of religion, even mild ones, engage people at deep levels. The communal aspect of religion creates powerful bonds of loyalty. Religious rituals carve convictions into the soul" (Reno, "Religious Freedom," 7). That is, even rudimentary faith practices form us as human beings, a shaping influence that is difficult to shed from our lives in later years.

8. One reason why Canada is a compelling example of this trend is because it sits nicely between the US and European situations. Johnson, "Swedish Syndrome," quotes Peter Berger as having commented that if India is the most religious country in the world and Sweden the most secular, then the US is a nation of Indians ruled by Swedes. Canada has fewer Indians than the US. Europe has even fewer Indians than Canada. This is not to deny the vibrancy of European Christianity, as evidenced by the Taizé community of rural France, the resurgence of evangelical Anglicanism in Britain, or the energetic flocks of young Roman Catholics in southern Europe. Neither is it meant to paint all American political leaders with the same faith-less brush, as D. Michael Lindsay has reminded us in Lindsay, *Faith in the Halls of Power*. Despite these nuances, *Hemorrhaging Faith* does capture actual cultural shifts taking place that are discernable over time.

9. Hunter, *To Change the World*.

10. As we will observe in a subsequent chapter, if we are to determine both the internal and external causes of the church's marginalization, then the cultural analysis must go much deeper than Hunter, *To Change the World*, 40–43, allows for. One example *inter alia* which Hunter does not engage but is vitally important is the Enlightenment's introduction of the fact/value distinction. As a result, facts are scientifically verifiable. Religious belief, which cannot be scientifically verified as fact, is consequently relegated to the category of personal, subjective value. This, too, has contributed to the ecclesial (self-)marginalization which Hunter explores and may in fact have a greater effect that he imagines.

the church might once again play a central and leading role in society. These attempts, he argues, are often carried out through collusion with forms of political power which are rooted in inherently flawed theological and/or cosmological visions and incapable of generating the sociological or politico-cultural change they are intended to produce for the church specifically or the Christian faith generally.[11] As a result, equipped with the broader culture's methods, the American church has participated in its own ideological capitulation and cultural marginalization.[12] Not only is the church in the West facing significant challenges within her various denominational communities, but there are also signs that the church's responses to its cultural marginalization are producing external challenges that consequentially exacerbate the very dilemma they seek to address.[13]

THE POWER OF THE CHURCH

This project does not attempt to add to the plethora of suggestions or methods to strategically maneuver the church out of these challenging waters in any kind of programmatic or utilitarian way—in neither neo-Constantinian nor neo-Anabaptistic fashion. Rather, this project seeks to analyze the church theologically and to explore as-yet un-mined theological resources that may help clarify the true challenges the church faces today in the West, particularly in terms of the root issue of power. In order to accomplish this, a concept rich with problematic potential, which Hunter uses in his own study, will form the core of our question: What is the true power of the institutional church? If the Western church is being accused of abuse(s) of power, as it regularly is, it very well might be the case that the Western church is not only unclear about issues of power within her own life but also about the nature of ecclesial power foundationally. Failures of ecclesial power are due to failures of theology. Questions of the church's

---

11. Hunter does not question the apparent "power from above" posture inherent in his argument.

12. This is the claim made in Hauerwas and Willimon, *Resident Aliens*. Two examples from their work must suffice: "We believe both the conservative and liberal church, the so-called private and public church, is basically accommodationist (that is, Constantinian) in their social ethic. Both assume wrongly that the American church's primary social task is to underwrite American democracy" (32); and, "We argue that the political task of Christians is to be the church rather than to transform the world" (38).

13. Bacote, "Beyond 'Faithful Presence,'" argues that Hunter's concept of "faithful presence" is too weak for faithful Christian engagement. His suggestion is that a more biblical engagement of the church with its culture is possible from within the Kuyperian vision that avoids falling into the trap of triumphalism.

cultural influence, societal position, as well as relationships with other civic institutions and people raises the question of what the church's power really and truly is. This is the central question of this project. Admittedly, it is a question fraught with difficulties on many levels. And by stating positively what the church's power is, we will also simultaneously be addressing *via negativa* what the power of the church *is not*, which may help re-orient the church theologically for constructive ways of engaging in future ministry.

While Sykes and Percy argue that there exists a "modern theological reluctance" to address the concept of power, we will begin by acknowledging how church and power are connoted in the general cultural milieu of twenty-first-century Western culture.[14] Some uncritically assume that the concepts of church and power, if they can be appropriately considered together at all, are in an inverse relationship with each other: as the church's power increases, it is believed that its authenticity as the community of Jesus' disciples decreases. Likewise, as the church divests itself of power, it is assumed by others to be more in tune with the early church, the New Testament, and the person of Jesus himself.[15] Because of these active, widespread, and simplistic assumptions, clarity of key terms like "church" and "power" is therefore needed. We must remember, with Karl Rahner, that power has an inherent ambiguity and names "multiple realities, each manifold in itself . . . power is not a univocal concept."[16]

---

14. Sykes, *Identity of Christianity*, 53. According to Percy, *Words, Wonders, and Power*, 40, there is also a reluctance to deal with power theologically: "Power has been a neglected, even despised, concept. . . . Theology has been reluctant to find a legitimate place for it in its doctrine. Embarrassment over the reality of power often leads to the concept being cloaked or misrepresented through the use of terms like 'authority,' 'Lordship,' or 'headship.'"

15. Many have made note of this assumption in the general population. Dooyeweerd, *Roots of Western Culture*, 66–67, notes: "Many equate power with brute force. Today many Christians, misled by this identification, consider it unchristian to strive for the consolidation of power in organizations that aim at applying christian principles to society. They believe that power may play no part among Christians. Especially theologians in Barth's circle. . . . A Christian may speak of love and justice with an unburdened conscience, but as soon as power comes into his purview he has probably lent an ear to the devil." As Tillich, *Love, Power, and Justice*, 11, puts it: "Love and power are often contrasted in such a way that love is identified with a resignation of power and power with a denial of love. . . . This, of course, is unavoidable if love is understood from its emotional side and power from its compulsory side. But such an understanding is error and confusion." Crouch, *Playing God*, names and attempts to discredit this popular assumption—held by those within and outside the church's membership. Macaulay, "Influence of the Church of Rome," also acknowledges this common assumption which is set within the American context and denominational struggles for public attention in Hart, "Church Not State," 32.

16. Rahner, *Theological Investigations*, 4:391.

To achieve this clarity, the question "What is the power of the church?" turns out to be unhelpfully vague even though at first it appears promising. For example, theologians from the Roman Catholic tradition will approach such a question of the church and power very differently than an anabaptist would. Also, speaking of the "church" does not offer clarity as to whether the church as an institution of bricks, mortar, cultural influence, and official representatives and pronouncements on the one hand or the church as the people assembled for worship or Christian persons or voluntary Christian associations dispersed into the whole of life on the other hand are in view. What do we mean by "the church" in this question of the power of the church?

The same sorts of questions could be raised about what we mean by "power." Whether we conceive of power as a spectrum of influence ranging from "softer" forms of power such as persuasion and suggestion at the one end to the "harder" forms of power such as coercion and manipulation at the other end, our analysis would proceed quite differently. Indeed, when we ask about power and the church, do we have divine power or human power in view, or both, or neither?

In addition to these complications, a unique scholarly contribution has been made over the past century on what has come to be known as "the powers."[17] When we consider the "power" of the church, do we have in mind these supernatural, suprahuman phenomena or something else? As such, focus through clear definition of terms is required. So, while the question of the church's power appears at first glance to be rather straight-forward, some of these various probing questions reveal that this is not the case. In fact, there is even a long history of theological reflection on the power of the church related to the "keys of the kingdom."[18] What this project will uncover and explore is actually something quite different yet. Exactly what this is will emerge over the next few chapters. In the meanwhile, further introductory examinations must take place before we are prepared to fully consider the unique alternative we will present from the theological contributions of Abraham Kuyper.

---

17. For example, see Heuvel, *These Rebellious Powers*; Wink, *Engaging the Powers*; *Naming the Powers*; *Unmasking the Powers*. In its own way, Aulén, *Christus Victor*, also addresses this topic but from a history-of-dogma point of view.

18. On this subject, see the excellent study by Hans von Campenhausen, *Ecclesiastical Authority and Spiritual Power*.

ABRAHAM KUYPER AND THE POWER OF THE CHURCH

The landscape in the theological sub-discipline of ecclesiology (the theology/doctrine of the church) is complex and diverse.[19] Attempting to analyze the concept of power within the generic field of ecclesiology would prove to be unmanageable. Therefore, this project will provide a creative theological answer to the question of the power of the church by working out of and analyzing power within the ecclesiological worldview of Abraham Kuyper, an ecclesiology which is creative within the (Dutch) Reformed tradition of Protestant Christianity and which contributes a unique and positive perspective to questions of ecclesial power and authority. The reasons for making this particular foundational selection are numerous and deserve extended discussion.

Kuyper's Sensitivity to Power

First, Abraham Kuyper (1837–1920) lived and worked during a period of significant cultural transition as the Enlightenment's influence spread across nineteenth-century Europe. His expressed goal was to address the question of the church in the emerging modern era—an era marked by expressions of power in multiple ways. As such, power was not a foreign concept to Kuyper. He was attentive to power operative in multiple arenas of human life: within the state, the church, church hierarchies, the power of "first principles" or worldview,[20] the power of culture, the power of prayer, nature, the arts, etc. Through his attentiveness to power generally, Kuyper's ecclesiology also addressed the unique cultural, societal, and theological issue of power. Because of its engagement with the intellectual currents of the day, Kuyper's ecclesiology thus offers significant opportunity for theological dialogue mindful of power. As a result of Kuyper's dynamic and evolving theological method, his ecclesiology contains unique and creative formulations that are even held in unresolved tension, tensions we will highlight and analyze in future chapters.

We can illustrate Kuyper's sensitivity to issues of power and authority generally by briefly looking at four of his works that span his most active

19. A classic introductory ecclesiology text, Kärkkäinen, *Introduction to Ecclesiology*, gives only an overview of twentieth-century developments in ecclesiology without an overarching theological argument towards a coherent doctrine of the church. Even a recent work, Garcia and Wood, *Critical Issues in Ecclesiology*, ranges far and wide and lacks a unifying conceptual framework for the study of ecclesiology.

20. An overview of Kuyper's worldview can be found in McGoldrick, "Claiming Every Inch."

thirty-four-year public career which spanned from 1870 to 1904. Within this timeframe, Kuyper moved from pastoral posts in Utrecht and Amsterdam, to academic and administrative roles at the Free University of Amsterdam, to Princeton University where he delivered the Stone Lectures in 1898, to his political responsibilities as the leader of the Anti-Revolutionary Party, the Netherlands' first national democratic political party, and to eventually becoming Prime Minister of the Netherlands in 1901. In all of these cultural roles, his keen attention to power is evident.

1870

We begin with Kuyper's farewell sermon from the church in Utrecht (1870), "Conservatism and Orthodoxy: False and True Preservation."[21] As the title suggests, in this sermon Kuyper attempts to navigate a path between static repetition of past theological shibboleths (what he calls "conservatism") and the dynamic-yet-faithful application of Calvinistic or biblical first principles to the historical, cultural, and ecclesial exigencies of one's day (what he calls "orthodoxy"). Kuyper refers to various forms of power on nearly every page of this sermon. He contrasts the dead power of conservatism with the regenerating and living power of orthodox Christianity.[22] He distinguishes between "the magical power" of enforced unity and agreement with the true power that emerges from faith active in one's whole life.[23] He speaks of the destructive power of unbelief versus life-giving biblical faith once given and tended throughout the generations. Kuyper argues that the Word of God, the gospel, and the glory of God are all forms of power.[24] Cultural change does not happen, argues Kuyper, through the articulation of hollow ideas (Christian or otherwise) but by the exercise of real animating power that becomes foundational in particular historical and cultural contexts and needs to be identified, developed, and applied with sensitivity.[25]

Kuyper's goal is that rather than operating out of a defensive posture and merely conserving the faith as it was formulated, understood, and articulated in the past, each generation of Christians is called to actively and proactively live and discern how to articulate and embody the orthodox

---

21. *AKCR*, 65–85.
22. Kuyper, "Conservatism and Orthodoxy," 68–69.
23. Kuyper, "Conservatism and Orthodoxy," 73. By "magical power" [his words], Kuyper means a simplistic or "mechanical" operation that requires little commitment from those involved.
24. Kuyper, "Conservatism and Orthodoxy," 84–85.
25. Kuyper, "Conservatism and Orthodoxy," 79–81.

Christian faith afresh so that the gospel might be presented with dynamic and persuasive power. And in this sermon, he argues that this task of tending to the fresh articulation of Christian orthodoxy is one of the responsibilities of the institutional church so that the church, as it exists in its organic mode of being,[26] might be equipped for addressing the gospel to all of life. In these various ways, Kuyper demonstrates himself attentive to various forms of power at work in the culture around him. Yet, what we do not find in this sermon is a clearly developed or unique theological understanding of power ontologically. Throughout this sermon, one repeatedly gets the impression that Kuyper is just about to clearly state what he means by the nature of power. Yet, he never delivers to his hearer/reader his explicit understanding of power's ontology, a point we will return to below.[27]

1886

If Kuyper was not prepared to define power in 1870, he had every reason to do so sixteen years later in a speech (in all respects a sermon except that it couldn't be called that for reasons which will become clear) given in the Frascati Auditorium in Amsterdam on Sunday evening, July 11, 1886. The historical context is that ten days earlier, on July 1, 1886, after a lengthy conflict with the local Amsterdam church council, the classical (regional) judiciary church board had deposed Kuyper as an ordained minister, along with a host of his colleagues, from ministry in the NHK, effectively setting the stage for the formation of the GKN by Kuyper and his supporters. "It Shall Not Be So among You" was Kuyper's first "sermon" given after this occasion and, as Bratt notes, Kuyper had to bring "abstract principles down to a very concrete situation" and "wrestle with issues of power." In this case, the main issue was that of the institutional church's power which had been exercised in Kuyper's deposition from ecclesial office. In Kuyper's mind, this was a clear example of the church's abuse of power.[28] Being of such a personal nature, we would naturally expect this incident to elicit from Kuyper

---

26. Kuyper's distinction between the "institutional" and "organic" modes of the church's being will be addressed in a later chapter. We can say at this point that the institutional church is the church gathered under appropriate ecclesial leadership while the organic church is the church (primarily of the laity) sent into the whole of the world, in the totality of their lives as followers of Jesus Christ.

27. By "ontology," I mean a clear explication of power's "being-ness" or "created-ness." That is, in giving a comprehensive analysis of ecclesial power, we not only need to know about ecclesiology but also how power is part of reality.

28. *AKCR*, 125–26.

a non-reductionistic critique of power. But while his thoughts on power generally are clearer, the details remain disappointingly implicit.

Kuyper begins by saying that "having betrayed its holy calling, the [NHK] church has been conformed to the world by lust for power."[29] This constant concern for the dynamics of power permeates this speech, possibly being that single work of Kuyper's in which the word occurs most frequently. This is rather understandable since Kuyper felt that he had been treated unjustly by the "lust for power" within the institutional NHK hierarchy.[30]

While we would have expected this to be the occasion when Kuyper would offer a detailed elaboration of his understanding of the nature of specifically *ecclesial* power, he does not go that far. Kuyper outlines the historical establishment of the institutional church's hierarchy, a hierarchy consisting of bureaucratic or administrative distinctions at the congregational, regional, and national levels. Kuyper contends that unfortunately these hierarchical institutional "powers" have "been conformed to the world by a lust for power."[31] The church, consequently, has become a haven of corrupt powers under which the membership of the church must dutifully, and sometimes begrudgingly, render obedience. The result, for Kuyper, is that "a hierarchy of power in both church and state" has taken shape in which "the sin of power-lust" on the part of the church mimics the state.[32] But, he warns, the church's lust for power is worse than an "unoriginal" and benign power at work equally in both the church and the state for the "rulers of the world might trample on the people in their lust for power but certainly the political arena always has restraints on these lusts. . . . But in the church these guarantees [are] totally lacking."[33] While citizens of the state may have recourse to abusive political power, the church is rendered impotent in the face of ecclesial abuses of power at the hands of those who assume for themselves divine-like infallibility through the lack of a court of appeal.

Immediately following this denunciation of the NHK's abuse of power, Kuyper issues a strikingly forceful Christological account of power and the church. Rather than the church trying to "copycat"[34] the power of the state and its abuses, without any court of appeal beyond itself, he asserts that the root error of the NHK hierarchy's "power-lust" was that it forgot that

---

29. *AKCR*, 126.

30. As Bratt says about this episode in Kuyper's life, "If Kuyper disagreed with Modernist theology, he detested church hierarchy" (*AKCR*, 125).

31. Kuyper, "It Shall Not Be So among You," 126.

32. Kuyper, "It Shall Not Be So among You," 127, 130.

33. Kuyper, "It Shall Not Be So among You," 130.

34. Kuyper, "It Shall Not Be So among You," 136.

"*All* power in the church of Christ must forever be traced back to Christ. He and He alone is our King. To Him alone is given all power in heaven and on earth."[35] After providing a variety of Scriptural texts to support this theological assertion, Kuyper enters into a deeply polemical critique of the false power of the NHK hierarchy which had deposed him (which he refers to as the power of sin) versus the true power of the church which Kuyper believes he and his supporters are exercising in the establishment of the GKN. For, rather than these "ungodly powers that [have] invaded the church," Christ the King gives "*the power of the Spirit that belongs in the church* reawakened."[36] Where Kuyper believes the Spirit of God to be truly active is quite clear!

Kuyper then outlines the various manifestations of true spiritual power in the church: rather than dominating others, true spiritual power causes Christians to embrace weakness over obtrusive forms of power and power-lust through a recognition of the sheer powerlessness of violence. True spiritual power draws people to Christ, bringing about their regeneration, producing faithfulness and perseverance in Christians. True spiritual power, Kuyper says, enables Christians to discern the spirits of the age and reject the false spirits that encroach upon the church. It provides the ability to comfort the sad and depressed and ease their pain, as well as controlling one's tongue, triumphing over temptations of the flesh. True spiritual power leads to prayer, even praying for one's enemies. These are the manifestations of the true power at work in the church, Kuyper says, for "Scripture never takes exception to power, but only to the wrong kind of power."[37] And thus Kuyper closes with an eye toward the imminent formation of his new, albeit small, denomination whose suffering, meagre membership, and lack of power will be blessed by the Lord of the church.

These are sharply polemical words flowing from Kuyper. He expends a considerable amount of energy critiquing the abuses of power he perceives. Yet, he contrasts this with a rather heart-warming account of God's spirit of power manifesting upright character and actions in faithful Christians' lives. And Kuyper has also made himself more explicit about the root and manifestations of the power of the church. All power in the church, he says, finds its foundation in Christ and this Christocentric power is mediated to the church from Christ by the Holy Spirit. But, we are still left with important areas where clarity is lacking, especially regarding exactly how Christ's power is mediated to the church through the spirit, the exact relationship

---

35. Kuyper, "It Shall Not Be So among You," 131.
36. Kuyper, "It Shall Not Be So among You," 136.
37. Kuyper, "It Shall Not Be So among You," 138–39.

between the essence of power and other forms or manifestations of power, the interests or subjects of power generally or ecclesial power specifically, and the means by which this positive power is mediated to or through church leadership. In short, Kuyper assumes an understanding or definition of power, which he relates to the church Christocentrically, but he still is not explicit about it. After sixteen years, there has been development in Kuyper's thought on power but we still do not find in him a systematic treatment of the concept.

1898

We leave Kuyper on the stage of the Frascati Auditorium on July 11, 1886, and catch up with him across the Atlantic at Princeton Theological Seminary twelve years later, in October of 1898, delivering his famous Stone lectures.[38] We also pick up one of the questions we were left with from before: what are the means by which the Christocentric power of the church is mediated by the Holy Spirit to or through the church? In his opening lecture, Kuyper displays his concern once again with power generally in the culture, military, state, and other arenas of human life. He captivatingly explores how they exist in the present and how he foresees them taking shape in the future.[39] But Kuyper addresses the topic of power relative to the church more pointedly in his second lecture where he is much more focused on religious life and the church as the institutional center of religious life. Themes which we will explore in more detail later present themselves here: election,[40] the world-engaging nature of Calvinism,[41] the destructive power of sin in the post-lapsarian world,[42] humanity's immediate relationship with God via Scripture and the Holy Spirit,[43] and the church as God's chosen agent in redemption and in the renewal of creation.[44]

It is precisely at this point in discussing the church that Kuyper invites his American audience to, with him, "turn our attention to its [the

38. See also Molendijk, "Neo-Calvinist Culture Protestantism." On the subject of Kuyper's Stone Lectures and their enduring American receptivity, see Bolt, "From Princeton to Wheaton." For Kuyper's American receptivity more generally, see Bratt, "In the Shadow of Mt. Kuyper."

39. LC, 39, 43–44, 45.

40. LC, 55. At a later point in the lecture, Kuyper will contrast election with chance, "a fatal imaginative power" (93).

41. LC, 62–63.

42. LC, 66.

43. LC, 69.

44. LC, 75.

church's] form or manifestation here on earth."[45] Countering many competing conceptions, he says that the "Church on earth is not an institution for the dispensation of grace, as if it were a dispensary of spiritual medicines."[46] Rather, he argues, the church exists "to preach the Word, to administer the sacraments, and to exercise discipline, and in everything to stand before the face of God."[47] To engage in these activities is to come under "Church power" which "originates in Heaven, in Christ" who "rules, governs his church by means of the Holy Spirit," with this power "descending directly from Christ Himself."[48] The power of God in Christ is mediated directly to Christians by the Holy Spirit, not the institutional church hierarchy,[49] for according to Kuyper there is "no other church[-institution]-power superior to the local churches, save only what the churches themselves constituted, by means of their [free, voluntary] confederation."[50]

Kuyper's Stone lectures were not the occasion for detailed theological argument even though the audience was generally receptive to his Calvinist convictions. What is of interest for our purposes is how Kuyper has equated the traditional Calvinist "marks of the true church" (pure preaching of the Word, proper administration of the sacraments, and the practice of church discipline[51]) with his understanding of ecclesial power. The Christocentric power of God is mediated to the church membership democratically by the Holy Spirit by means of the preaching of Scripture, celebration of the sacraments, and church discipline. (It is important to note Kuyper's emphasis that the institutional church's power is distributed democratically and immediately by the Holy Spirit rather than being mediated through the church's institutional hierarchy. The church's office-bearers have a role to play but they are the instruments, rather than the direct sources, of God's grace distributed to his people.) And this is for the purpose that God's people might stand before God, *coram deo*, in the totality of their lives. As we've noted already, as we follow Kuyper's career he continues to offer a fuller and more detailed account of his understanding of ecclesial power. But, simultaneously, Kuyper still has not offered what we could classify as a fully-formed systematic theological explication of his understanding of

---

45. *LC*, 75.
46. *LC*, 76.
47. *LC*, 76.
48. *LC*, 77.
49. *LC*, 78.
50. *LC*, 78.
51. See Calvin, *Institutes of the Christian Religion* 4.1.

power, ecclesial or otherwise, with clarity. One last stop on this tour offers the hope of discovery.

1902–1904

Finally, we turn to *Common Grace*, first appearing as newspaper articles which ran in two instalments in *De Heraut*, first between April 20, 1879, and June 13, 1880, and secondly between August 29, 1880, and October 23, 1881. They were eventually published in two volumes in 1888 and 1889 before being compiled, in final form, into Kuyper's three volume *De Gemeene Gratie* (*Common Grace*) in 1902, 1903, and 1904. Unfortunately, if we were hoping that this would be the point at which Kuyper would spell out his thoughts on ecclesial power in their fullest and most explicit detail, we will be disappointed. Nonetheless, Kuyper does offer instructive comments on his understanding of power relative to the church.

Kuyper touches upon an impressive range of ecclesial and extra-ecclesial topics that he deemed necessary to elaborate upon if the Reformed theological tradition were to plausibly relate to the concerns of the modern era.[52] Kuyper also addresses the place and role of the church in society as a key means by which God's grace is extended toward the whole of creation. "Christ's church," Kuyper argues, "and its means of grace cover a broader field than that of special grace [for the salvation of God's elect] alone."[53] How does God's grace minister to both the church and the world? Kuyper doesn't use the word "power" at this point, but the idea is implicit in his argument. God's grace, ministered to the world through the church, he says, "does two things: (1) it works *directly* for the well-being of the elect [in the church]; . . . but (2) it works *indirectly* for the well-being of the whole of civil society, constraining it to civic virtue."[54] This is Kuyper's distinction between special and common grace which parallels his distinction between the church as institution and the church as organism, a key distinction which will be addressed below.

This is another polemical passage in which Kuyper is arguing that his separated GKN denomination is not a sect, withdrawn from civic and social life through its desire for an orthodox confession of faith from its members. Rather than the GKN being withdrawn from the world, "the expectation [is]

---

52. Bratt notes that Kuyper's critics didn't see him "elaborating" the Reformed Christian faith; rather, they saw him "inventing" his own theological tradition (*AKCR*, 165). See also Lonkhuyzen, "Abraham Kuyper."

53. Kuyper, "Common Grace," 189.

54. Kuyper, "Common Grace," 190.

that the comparatively small circle of the church will radiate influence upon civil life outside the church."[55] For Kuyper, the fact of ecclesial organizational or hierarchical separateness does not equate with sectarianism for "a group is a *sect* only when it puts itself outside the context of human life."[56] Since God's grace is for the whole of creation (working directly in the church as special grace through office-bearers and indirectly in the world outside the church as common grace through lay Christians), then the church also must be related to the whole of life somehow. For Kuyper, this influence of the church on the whole of life is to be effected "indirectly" through the church as an organism rather than via the church directly through its hierarchy or as an institution.[57]

It makes sense that within the institutional church God's grace is mediated directly. But what does Kuyper mean by saying that the church as an organism mediates God's grace to the world "indirectly"? This is where Kuyper's distinction between the church as an institution and the church as an organism is relevant (to be addressed in greater detail later). For Kuyper, the church as an institution exists, as noted above, to be the official means of grace operating directly through preaching, sacraments, and church discipline. And these institutional ecclesial activities are geared toward equipping the church as an organism (the people of God in the whole of life) to be "the influence that should impinge upon the world outside" the church institution.[58] This is how the institutional church has *indirect* influence on society: it is mediated by the church existing as an organism.

But we ought not to distinguish these two modes of the church's existence too sharply. They both refer to a single entity and are related to each other by each mode providing what the other requires for the church to carry out its vocation faithfully and fully. As Kuyper says, it is through the brightly shining lamp of the gospel within the church as an institution that empowers the people of God in the whole of life, the church as an organism, which "is not circumscribed by a certain number of people listed in church directories, and does not have its own office-bearers but is interwoven with the very fabric of national life . . . in society."[59] It is this "influence" of the church as an organism which

> must begin by arousing a certain admiration for the heroic courage. . . . Next it must inspire respect for the earnestness

---

55. Kuyper, "Common Grace," 190.
56. Kuyper, "Common Grace," 190.
57. Kuyper, "Common Grace," 197.
58. Kuyper, "Common Grace," 194.
59. Kuyper, "Common Grace," 194–95.

and purity of life lived in church circles. It must further excite feelings of sympathy by the warm glow of love and compassion in the community of faith. And finally, as a result of all this, it must purify and ennoble the ideas in general circulation, elevate public opinion, introduce more solid principles, and so raise the view of life prevailing in state, society, and the family.[60]

In short, the church as a means of indirect grace in the world must, by its example, make Christian faith plausible for the world by being "a city set on a hill" or "a leaven."[61] The indirect influence of the church to the world occurs *inter alia* through the inherent persuasiveness of the sanctified Christian lives of the church's members, a life-formation (traditionally called church discipline) that takes place within the institutional church's means of official and direct grace.

Summary

In all these ways, Kuyper shows himself to have an extended concern with power (in the church, state, culture, etc.) throughout his career. Yet despite this brief survey, we have achieved little systematic clarity from Kuyper regarding the nature of power as it exists and functions generally or within the church. In fact, as we've observed, every time Kuyper discusses power he resorts to a phenomenological catalogue of power's manifestations rather than a systematic ontological or theological argument. Kuyper's treatment of power is much too occasional for us to find a detailed treatment of the topic in a single place. As such, while one might be impressed with Kuyper's attentiveness to power dynamics generally, we are left with a number of unanswered questions regarding the theoretical framework out of which he is operating: What is power's ontology? How is the power of the state ontologically similar to or uniquely different from the power of the church? Would Kuyper consider the nature of human power to be the same as the nature of God's power? If so, how? If not, why not? How does the nature of a worldview's ideological power relate, in Kuyper's mind, to the nature of the power of a cultural institution? These questions are just the beginning when it comes to the sorts of questions that remain unclear in Kuyper.

Therefore, we have observed Kuyper's extended concern with both power and ecclesiology. Yet, due to a number of factors mentioned, there is a significant lack of clarity when it comes to understanding the origin and manifestation(s) of power or the specifically unique nature of *ecclesial*

---

60. Kuyper, "Common Grace," 195.
61. Kuyper, "Common Grace," 196.

power, a concept that he clearly has in mind but does not explicitly or fully address. At best, there is a kind of implicit assumption that Kuyper and his readers have a mutually-shared understanding of power. But given Kuyper's deep commitment to proceeding from first principles, the lack of a clear explication of his understanding on such an important topic is surprising.[62]

Power as Lacuna in Kuyper's Ecclesiology

As we have seen, Kuyper is attentive to issues of power and the church throughout his career. And this represents a second reason for drawing on Kuyper to discern the power of the church: while ecclesiology occupied the span of Kuyper's varied career, and issues of power were part of the contextual matrix of his work, the specific issue of *ecclesial* power is only implicit within Kuyper's work. In fact, in the above section we could hardly separate Kuyper's attentiveness to power generally from the specific form of *ecclesial* power and yet nowhere did Kuyper achieve explicit description of power's nature. Therefore, seeking to make this aspect of Kuyper's ecclesiology more explicit and to bring it into constructive dialogue with the rest of his ecclesiology addresses a lacuna in Kuyper's ecclesiology as it currently exists.[63]

As we observed above, within Kuyper's concerns about power, the specific issue of *ecclesial* power is, at best, implicit in his thought and work. In this regard, we turn to his speech given at the founding of the Free University of Amsterdam in 1880. This speech is significant because Kuyper's reasoning for the academic legitimacy of a distinctly *confessional* university strikes at the core of the issue of the power of the church within liberal (and post-Revolutionary Dutch) society. George Harinck notes the historical and cultural context of this speech in which the church and a confessional orientation to life had been marginalized by the secular academic, political, and cultural elites of the day.[64] As such, Kuyper was viewed as an "outcast" by

---

62. Bratt, "Passionate About the Poor," 36–37, observes that "Kuyper liked comprehensive political platforms, hierarchically organized under absolute principles, strong on clarity and controls," and yet, these "principles" were dynamic rather than static and Kuyper "often invoked such principles, not least to bolster his authority or his followers' sense of security. But Kuyper argued that he practiced 'inductive' in contrast to his opponents' 'deductive' social thinking."

63. As we will discover in a later chapter, ecclesiologies are intimately connected to worldviews. This means this project will not only address the question of the power of the church in Kuyper's *ecclesiology* but also the unresolved question of Kuyper's unique understanding of these matters within his *worldview*. For a brief overview of the main issues, see Koyzis, "Neocalvinist Ecclesiology"; Zwaanstra, "Abraham Kuyper's Conception of the Church."

64. Harinck, "Historian's Comment."

such elites who judged him to be uncivilized in his old-fashioned religious views and combative methods.[65] Because of this, Kuyper was seen "as a modern Moses" who "outraged the Pharaoh of his days [the secular cultural elites] and liberated his people."[66] The symbolism wasn't missed as Kuyper delivered his *apologia* for a confessional university which would compete with the state universities from "the New Church . . . on Amsterdam's principal square, next to the royal palace—thus at the symbolic center of national life."[67] Kuyper was arguing for the creational grounding and cultural legitimacy of faith and the church at the center of cultural power which was the main force of marginalization Kuyper sought to counter.

Kuyper used the occasion of this speech to redefine "sovereignty" or cultural institutional *power* from within a religious or confessional framework. The reason for this is that in the wake of secularizing and revolutionary worldviews, the common notion of sovereignty had shifted from being grounded in the church to being grounded in the state and from being a component of belief/faith to a component of reason/science. Kuyper observed that Enlightenment-influenced state-sovereignty or worldly power meant that the state could orchestrate society as it saw fit.[68] From within Kuyper's worldview and confessional orientation, sovereignty (read: power) belonged to God alone and within creation God had ordered or normed a variety of cultural spheres of human activity and life, each with sovereignty delegated directly to it from God. These cultural spheres existed in pluralist fashion, each responsible to pursue their cultural vocation in allegiance to Christ alone. The cultural spheres that Kuyper mentions are those of the personal, the family, the university, the church, and the state. In this framework, the state has a minimalist responsibility that is "the power that protects the individual and defines the mutual relationships among the visible spheres, [it] rises high *above* them by its right to command and compel. But *within* these spheres that does not obtain. There another authority rules, an authority that descends directly from God apart from the State. This

---

65. Harinck, "Historian's Comment," 278. Woltjer, *Dr. A. Kuyper*, 35, notes at Kuyper's funeral that the Dutch Royal Academy never "opened their doors" to Kuyper and he was never considered an academic peer by the scientific community. The larger problem of Christian faith in a diverse public society is addressed by Perry, "Weight of Community."

66. Harinck, "Historian's Comment," 279.

67. *AKCR*, 461. See also Molendijk, "Mine." The enduring relationship between the Kuyperian tradition and educational endeavors is addressed by Plantinga Jr., *Engaging God's World*.

68. Kuyper, "Sphere Sovereignty," 468.

authority the State does not *confer* but *acknowledges*."⁶⁹ As such, rather than the tyrannical encroachment of the liberal secular state into all of life, the state's power is properly limited and a plurality of intermediate institutions and organizations are placed between the individual and the state to make up civil society.

While Kuyper's audience would have understood his point, his worldview-based mapping of a creational and cultural landscape which included a variety of institutions, including the church, does not approach the theoretical specificity one would expect or desire. Having argued for the cultural legitimacy of religion and the societal legitimacy of the church and a confessional university, all this was rooted in a worldview in which there are "as many spheres as there are constellations in the sky and that the circumference of each has been drawn on a fixed radius from the center of a unique principle . . . each with its own *domain*."⁷⁰ The reader is left to discern what exactly Kuyper means by "circumference," "radius," or "domain" even though the general point is clear enough. As Harinck notes, "Kuyper formulated the idea of sphere sovereignty, repeated it once or twice . . . but . . . he never developed the idea. . . . In Kuyper's hands, sphere sovereignty was mainly an instrument to make his point."⁷¹ We will return to this theory later but for our purposes here it is important to highlight how Kuyper connected this with issues of power.

Kuyper's point was that at the heart of life there was a confrontation between "two credos [which] stand squarely against each other."⁷² The one credo was rooted in revelation and emerged in society as sphere sovereignty. The other credo was rooted in reason and emerged in society as "State sovereignty."⁷³ But as we have seen, how the socio-political theory of sphere sovereignty demarcated the "circumference" of the ecclesial sphere, the normative "center" of the ecclesial sphere, or the unique sovereignty or power of the institutional church is more assumed than argued.⁷⁴ As such, a significant theoretical lacuna exists in Kuyper's ecclesiology.

In conclusion, despite the fact that Kuyper made numerous significant contributions to Reformed-Calvinist ecclesiology, especially equipping his own church to theologically respond to ideological and cultural challenges

---

69. Kuyper, "Sphere Sovereignty," 468.

70. Kuyper, "Sphere Sovereignty," 467.

71. Harinck, "Historian's Comment," 279. For another perspective, see Mouw, "Some Reflections on Sphere Sovereignty."

72. Kuyper, "Sphere Sovereignty," 468.

73. Kuyper, "Sphere Sovereignty," 469.

74. A review of the exhaustive Kuyper bibliography shows no single work which directly addresses ecclesial power. See Kuipers, *Abraham Kuyper*.

from within and without, Kuyper does not fully develop the specific concept of ecclesial power even though he was keenly attentive to issues of power and authority generally. It is important to note this gap and highlight it before delving into an analysis of his ecclesiology proper or bringing our two lines of reflection, on power and the church, together constructively in future chapters.

Ecclesial Power as a Lacuna in Kuyper Scholarship

A third reason for drawing on the work of Abraham Kuyper is that, while Kuyper scholarship has been extensive over the last century, the focus of this body of work has not primarily addressed his ecclesiology, though it was of primary concern to Kuyper himself. The examination of ecclesial power in Kuyper scholarship is a significant area of academic need. In fact, as Bratt rightly summarizes, "Kuyper is best known in English-speaking circles for his theology of *culture*" rather than his theology of the church.[75] This may be why one accusation levelled against Kuyper is that he has a higher view of the organic mode of the church's being which has resulted in an anti-institutional church tendency within the Kuyperian tradition.[76] Where Kuyper scholarship has addressed his ecclesiology, it has not addressed the issue of power. This project seeks to contribute to the growing body of Kuyper scholarship specifically in the area of his ecclesiology and power and thus addresses a lacuna in Kuyper scholarship more broadly.

When it comes to secondary literature, the Abraham Kuyper bibliography maintained at Princeton Theological Seminary is the primary database (not limited to the English language) for Kuyper scholarship to date.[77] Out of a total of approximately fifteen hundred entries, it has forty-nine sources listed which address Kuyper's ecclesiology generally (3 percent of the total bibliography). A review of these works reveals that they examine the specifics of Kuyper's church polity, his church reform efforts, the question of the church and its relationship to the state, and the creative distinction Kuyper developed between the church as an institution and the church as an organism. None address what we are attending to here: the nature of *ecclesial* power. In fact, a bibliographic search using only the English keyword "power" returns zero results. Even searching for the three Dutch words which can be rendered into English as "power" (Dutch: *macht*,

---

75. *AKMCCD*, 194 (emphasis added).

76. See Bratt, "Abraham Kuyper." The classic text is Machen, *Christianity and Liberalism*.

77. See "Abraham Kuyper Bibliography."

kracht, and *vermogen*) returns only results related to political power and questions of the state responding to mass or popular movements (other than the church). This is most curious, coming from the most exhaustive database on Kuyper scholarship to date.

If we turn to the most recent Kuyper scholarship that has attempted to bring Kuyper and Kuyper scholarship into conversation with contemporary issues and questions, there are three major works which are relevant and which draw upon the breadth of Kuyper's varied publications as well as Kuyper scholarship from the early-twentieth century to the present.[78] But while these three works extensively analyze Kuyper's ecclesiology, none address the specific issue of ecclesial *power*, its nature, or its authority. While possibly surprising, we can safely state that there is, in fact, a lacuna in Kuyper scholarship on this very topic of ecclesial power.

Kuyper's Positive View of Power

A final reason for choosing to focus our attention on Kuyper is that while Kuyper shows critical sensitivity to issues of power, including its negative and/or destructive potential, he also offers a uniquely positive and constructive view of power. Not only does Kuyper provide a positive view of power which counterbalances prevailing theological tendencies which conceive of power in almost exclusively negative terms,[79] but Kuyper works out of an alternative theoretical framework or worldview for understanding the multiple manifestations of power, the very problem which episodic theories of power have not resolved.[80] Kuyper's positive contribution, therefore, has the potential to not only clarify contemporary debates about church and

---

78. See *GD*; *FCHN*; *CCW*.

79. This is further addressed later. Here, for example, we can cite Streufert, "Affinity for Difference," whose understanding of power never quite escapes from a negative cast. Even Sykes, *Power and Christian Theology*, 7, claims that power is "an essentially contested concept" at best. Liberation theologies, which might be assumed to have a positive view of power for correcting political injustice, see power as an ambiguous concept. Power's abuse is critiqued and power's potential for good is acknowledged; but the temptation to exercise power for one's or one's group's benefit versus others' is always present and casts suspicion on power's potential for good. One thinks of Bossuet's pithy remark somewhere that "One is not powerful who cannot resist the temptation of power." In any case, most of the work in liberation theology arises from within the Roman Catholic tradition rather than the Reformed or neo-Calvinist traditions. For a provocative analysis of power and the institutional church from a Roman Catholic liberation theology perspective, see Boff, *Church*.

80. This is also addressed further below.

power and open a way for ecclesial renewal but also contribute to the larger discourses on power currently taking place.[81]

TERMINOLOGY

Before concluding this introduction with an overview of the chapters ahead, an explanation must be given about the ambiguous term "church." Since at least the fourth century, theologians have wrestled with the multiple "ways of being in the world" evidenced by the church. In a number of places, Augustine makes the distinction between the church as a cultural institution and the church as the mystical body of Christ.[82] This distinction between the church as a gathered institution and the church as the dispersed people of God living by faith in union with Christ is even evident in the New Testament writings themselves. For example, the Apostles refer to the churches in particular far-flung locations (Paul writes to the churches in Rome, Galatia, Ephesus, etc., including those followers of Jesus among the Jewish *diaspora* in James 1:1 and 1 Peter 1:1). At the same time, the Apostles (and evidently these dispersed Christians themselves) recognize the central institutional importance of the church in Jerusalem and its Council (Acts 15) with the Apostle Paul even successfully collecting financial donations from churches around the Roman empire he had visited to support this central ecclesial institution during a time of crisis.

As we will see in later chapters, to this distinction between the church as an institution and the church as the people of God, Kuyper will make further important distinctions. The most important for our purposes will be the distinction between the church as an institution and the church as an organism. As noted briefly above, by organism Kuyper means the church existing as Christians and Christian organizations "sent" into the whole of life to bear witness to the gospel in their everyday affairs. By the institutional church, Kuyper means the hierarchically-organized church, gathered under duly ordained leadership, for official functions. While Kuyper devotes much attention in his work to equipping Christians for faithful activity in the world as the sent church (organism), the focus of this project is on the

---

81. On this important subject, see Wolterstorff, *Divine Discourse*.

82. See Augustine, "Sermon 341," art. 11–12; *Confessions* 8.2; *City of God* 15.1. Grabowski, *Church*, 2, summarizes Augustine's ecclesiology as having three components: "the mystical body of Christ," "a hierarchical institution," and "a social organization." Thus, Kuyper's distinction between the church as an institution and the church as an organism isn't entirely new and unique. Though, to be fair, Kuyper's use of the organic metaphor is influenced by the organicism of his own day which would have been foreign to Augustine in his time.

institutional church. As such, references to the church throughout the following chapters should be read as referring to the institutional or gathered church. When the organic or sent church is in view, specific mention will be made. While this is a somewhat arbitrary and scholarly distinction, it is important for gaining clarity on Kuyper's view of the power of the institutional church as a civic institution among, and related to, others.

OVERVIEW

By this point, the various questions have emerged which must be addressed in order to formulate a response to the question of Kuyper's view of the power of the institutional church. Our analysis will therefore proceed along the following lines. First, a survey of the philosophical and theological approaches to power prepares us for Kuyper's unique contribution to this history. This is the aim of Chapter 2.

Then, we must acknowledge that Kuyper himself and the Kuyperian tradition are relatively unknown outside of a relatively small group of devoted followers.[83] As such, we must uncover the person of Kuyper and the tradition that follows him, particularly relative to the church. Neither Kuyper nor the Kuyperian tradition can be understood apart from their context. And the unique contributions Kuyper makes to Reformed ecclesiology are deeply embedded in the historical and cultural matrix of Kuyper and his era. To this end, Chapter 3 is devoted to Kuyper's cultural and ecclesial context and Kuyper's ecclesiology that emerges from within this context. In addition, Kuyper's biographical timeline can be found in appendix 1 and the confessional contours of the Reformed theological tradition in which Kuyper worked can be found in appendix 2.

As we have begun in this way, we must continue to draw primarily from Kuyper's works (and the most important secondary sources from within the Kuyperian tradition) on the important issue of ecclesial power. This should take place in two stages: on the one hand, a non-reductionistic, multi-dimensional analysis of power generally is needed; on the other hand, disclosing and drawing out Kuyper's unique view of *ecclesial* power specifically is required. An important part of this process is to compare and contrast what others have argued about power theologically and in the related fields of philosophy and sociology. While this sociological background is important to the context of this question it is not crucial to the argument and therefore has been set aside for the sake of clarity and focus. Chapter 4 turns to charting the contours of Kuyper's worldview which shapes his

83. This is the argument made in *CCW*, 1.

unique view of power's nature and manifestation(s). And, Chapter 5 brings these various lines of inquiry together to present Kuyper's understanding of the power of the institutional church.[84] This will conclude the first part of our investigation.

The second part of our analysis represents a critical engagement of Kuyper's view of the power of the institutional church. With Kuyper's view of ecclesial power before us, we must consider whether it is justifiable in light of Scripture. This is an important element for our study because Kuyper's stated life aim was to submit all of life to Christ as revealed in Scripture.[85] Considering the highly pragmatic and functional nature of Kuyper's cultural endeavors, we must judge whether Kuyper's understanding of the power of the institutional church was deeply and authentically theological or merely utilitarian for his view of the church as an organism. In order to accomplish this first stage of our critical engagement with Kuyper, our key interlocutor will be Jacques Ellul whose work raises the question of whether Kuyper's view of power is sufficiently biblical. This will be the task of Chapter 6, which will conclude with a detailed analysis of Acts 10 as a Scriptural example of ecclesial power in action in the early church's missionary encounter with the Roman empire.

Finally, one recent interpreter of Kuyper's ecclesiology has argued that Kuyper's is a *sacramental* ecclesiology.[86] This is not only an important question in terms of correctly categorizing Kuyper's ecclesiology but it is also critical as we look to the implications for further research that emerge from Kuyper's ecclesiology today. Partly, this will mean bringing Kuyper into ecumenical dialogue since the foundational and most important treatment of sacramental ecclesiology comes to us from Vatican Council II and the Roman Catholic tradition since then. This will take place in Chapter 7 and will prepare us to conclude our analysis of our findings

---

84. One of Kuyper's creative ecclesiological distinctions, which we will address below, is between the church as an institution and the church as an organism. In order to make this project manageable, I have made the choice to focus entirely on Kuyper's view of the power of the *institutional* church. I take comfort in the argument of Gary Badcock: "[What] we confess in the great ecumenical creed . . . *can* be seen in space and time as an ordinary human institution. Though we may draw Augustinian [or (neo-) Calvinist] distinctions between the visible and invisible church, mainstream Christian theology is committed to the view that the one, holy, catholic, and apostolic church is, in the final analysis, what we can actually see. There is in ecclesiology no final escape into otherworldliness. . . . The church that we say we believe in is also a 'place' we can attend physically on Sundays and, if we are observant, on other days of the week as well" (Badcock, *House Where God Lives*, 8).

85. LC, 23–24.

86. See GD.

along with their importance for the Kuyperian tradition, ecclesiology, a host of other sub-disciplines within theology, and the ongoing study of the contemporary church. Let us now begin by charting the theoretical landscape of power.

2

Power

An Historical Survey of the Conceptual Landscape

Lord Emerich Edward Dalberg Acton (1834–1902) was a life-long student of power in history. Born into a wealthy and eminent family, he not only had the connections but also the means to devote his life to political service and academic study despite the barriers that stood in his way as an English Roman Catholic. As a highly esteemed historian at Cambridge University, he dedicated his life to studying personal freedom and the power dynamics that hinder that freedom in all of its social, political, and theological aspects. When he died at the dawn of the twentieth century, Lord Acton was widely regarded as the most learned man of his age. And based on his personal experiences and his study of universal history from antiquity through the nineteenth century, he famously quipped that "power tends to corrupt, and absolute power corrupts absolutely."[1]

Lord Acton has not been the only one to address such a profound topic as power. It is a perennial human question, a question that Acton found

---

1. For background on Lord Acton, see Chadwick, *Professor Lord Acton*; Himmelfarb, *Lord Acton*; Acton, "Introduction." Various other works are available from the Acton Institute, a North American study center which seeks "to promote a free and virtuous society characterized by individual liberty and sustained by religious principles" (Acton Institute, "About"). Coincidently, the Acton Institute is currently engaged in the first-ever project to translate and publish the entirety of Abraham Kuyper's three-volume *De gemeene gratie* (*On Common Grace*) in English. See Kuyper, *Noah–Adam*.

irresistible: What is power? This is the very question which this chapter puts into historical perspective.

INTRODUCTION

What is power? The reason why this question is important for our analysis of Kuyper's view of power generally and *ecclesial* power specifically is because Kuyper's view of power offers a unique alternative to the typical approach(es) to power in the mainstream philosophical and theological treatments of this concept. Kuyper's view of power is unique both due to definition and evaluation. In terms of definition, we will see that most theories of power start from either a theoretical-reductionist point of view or an episodic-phenomenological point of view. Kuyper attempts to transcend this divide. And in terms of evaluation, throughout the modern and postmodern periods, power has become more and more suspect to the point that many contemporary theorists struggle to escape from assuming power to be nothing more than a categorically negative force of domination and/or coercion. Kuyper, on the other hand, offers a thoroughly positive view of power's nature as something rooted in God's creation, without neglecting the ways in which power can become distorted through human agency.

Therefore, the focus of this chapter is to engage in a survey of philosophical and theological reflection on the nature of power. This is an important task because, as we shall see, power is a highly complex and debated concept. Power is deeply embedded in ideology and context. And despite the wide-ranging work that has been done up to the present, there is little to no consensus regarding power's definition or how to approach or understand power's various manifestations. Our purpose in surveying the history of reflection on power is neither to achieve a comprehensive theoretical view of power nor to resolve the many divergent views among theorists but rather to discern power's scholarly landscape for considering and developing Kuyper's formidable contribution to this debate as well as how it relates to the civic institution of the church

OUTLINE

Theories of power stretch back at least two and a half millennia. This theoretical history is rich and highly diverse. It would be impossible to capture every nuance in thought, emphasis, or articulation that has been made regarding power. But through careful and representative selection, a narrative can be presented which summarizes this history in illuminating and descriptive ways. Therefore, this chapter will present an historical survey of significant works and theorists who have contributed to our present-day understanding(s) of power. In particular, the contributions of philosophy, theology, and sociology are most relevant, from both Christian and non-Christian sources.

Before we embark on this survey, some general comments about this entire question, What is power?, will help us frame the task. We must begin by acknowledging that the concept of power resists clear definition despite the fact that it is an inherent dynamic in human life and human interactions. Kearsley observes that "Though 'power' seems to have a vaguely common meaning to all speakers, in reality its varied deployment is far from simple or consistent. Muddling of categories easily occurs."[2] As an object of study, therefore, power spans multiple disciplines, each discipline having its own interest in the concept and its own methodology for examination. Whether we reflect on power biblically, historically, or linguistically, one consistently encounters a certain ambiguity about the word and its usage.[3] The term "power" is utilized in a wide variety of ways and contexts and within a number of different classification systems. Power has been analyzed via a host of distinctions, arenas, and types. As such, the scholarly literature is marked by "sheer quantity" and a fundamental "lack of unanimity."[4] One of the beneficial outcomes of our survey in this chapter, in addition to preparing us to consider Kuyper's view of power generally and ecclesial power specifically, will be to demonstrate that reductionistic oversimplification of one kind or another is a foundational reason for this wide diversity of perspectives on power.

THE ANCIENT PERIOD

The first occurrence of power (Greek: δύναμις) is most probably from the Greek philosopher Parmenides in his *Poem*. Parmenides lived around the late sixth or early fifth century BC and was to have a strong influence on Plato over a century later. Stanza 9 of his *Poem* reads:

> Yet since all things have been named Light and Night
> and these according to their powers [have been assigned] to one
> and the other

---

2. Kearsley, *Church, Community, and Power*, 5.

3. Sykes notes that "the problem in the case of power is not merely that in ordinary usage it is imprecise; it is also that there is no general agreement about how it should be defined with precision" (Sykes, *Power and Christian Theology*, 5).

4. Sykes, *Power and Christian Theology*, 93.

> all is full of Light and obscure Night together,
> both equally, since nothing has a share in neither.[5]

The philosophical sense of "power" here is ontological: it is used as a criterion for being; that is, a thing which has being (rather than merely the appearance of being) is a thing which acts on another being. Each thing that has being exists because it has a unique, irreducible power which makes it what it is, whether "light" or "night." Barnes says, reflecting on this passage from Parmenides, that "power [here] is the fundamental category of existence."[6] The power of one thing which acts on and effects another thing transforms that thing by its own power. As Barnes says, "The effect of a *dunamis* is identical with the *dunamis* itself: a *dunamis* acts by manifesting itself, thereby replacing (or dominating) the previously manifested *dunamis*."[7] Simply put, this is "*like* from *like* causality."[8] For example, as fire exerts its power on wood, it transforms the wood into fire.

From this "like from like causality" in Parmenides, the mathematical or geometrical understandings of power came to dominate the ancient period. The mathematical or geometrical conception of power captured the way in which a thing had its own unique type of being. It denoted the type of being a thing was, the characteristics of its being. Two examples will suffice:

> The lines, or sides, which have for their squares the equilateral plane numbers, were called by us lengths or magnitudes; and the lines which are the roots of (or whose squares are equal to) the oblong numbers, were called powers or roots.[9]

> The formula of the circle does not include that of the segments, but that of the syllable includes that of the letters; yet the circle is divided into segments as the syllable is into letters.—And further if the parts are prior to the whole, and the acute angle is a part of the right angle and the finger a part of the animal, the acute angle will be prior to the right angle and finger to the man. But the latter are thought to be prior; for in formula the parts are explained by reference to them, and in respect also of the power of existing apart from each other the wholes are prior to the parts.[10]

---

5. This is the translation of Hermann, *To Think Like God*, 155–62.
6. Barnes, *Power of God*, 40.
7. Barnes, *Power of God*, 29.
8. Barnes, *Power of God*, 31.
9. Plato, *Theaetetus*. Theaetetus is speaking here.
10. Aristotle, *Metaphysics* 7.10.

Barnes says about this second usage of "power" that it describes "the causal capacity of a material entity."[11] Or, "the fundamental level of [a thing's] existence is an irreducible unit of powers."[12] That is, the specific combination of power(s) which "determines the identity or nature of an existent, and it is the action of these powers upon other mixtures that determines all the causal relations that we perceive and know . . . the concept of power(s) describes everything that really exists."[13] Power, in this second sense, is the identifying nature of something which exists. The powers inherent within a thing make it what it is.

The Ancient period also witnessed the development of a medical understanding of power. The powers of physical human existence were believed to regulate life and health. Physical health resulted from the powers existing in proper balance with their opposites. Disease resulted from one power becoming dominant with the resulting medical treatment consisting of the restoration of a balance of the powers. Here the cosmological (the balance of the powers in the natural world) and the bodily intersected in ancient belief. This understanding of power originated with Hippocrates and continued through Plato and beyond. Barnes classifies this type of power as "the causal capacity of a material entity."[14] Some examples which illustrate both the manifestational and causal aspects of medical power are the following:

> And each of those which are accompanied by a rational formula is alike capable of contrary effects, but one non-rational power produces one effect; e.g., the hot is capable only of heating, but the medical art can produce both disease and health. The reason is that science is a rational formula, and the same rational formula explains a thing and its privation, only not in the same way; and in a sense it applies to both, but in a sense it applies rather to the positive fact. Therefore such sciences must deal with contraries, but with one in virtue of their own nature and with the other not in virtue of their nature; for the rational formula applies to one object in virtue of that object's nature, and to the other, in a sense, accidentally. For it is by denial and removal that it exhibits the contrary; for the contrary is the primary privation, and this is the removal of the positive term.[15]
>
> For there is in man the bitter and the salt, the sweet and the acid, the sour and the insipid, and a multitude of other things

---

11. Barnes, *Power of God*, 7.
12. Barnes, *Power of God*, 8.
13. Barnes, *Power of God*, 8.
14. Barnes, *Power of God*, 7.
15. Aristotle, *Metaphysics* 9.2.

having all sorts of powers both as regards quantity and strength. These, when all mixed and mingled up with one another, are not apparent, neither do they hurt a man; but when any of them is separate, and stands by itself, then it becomes perceptible, and hurts a man.[16]

A fourth way in which "power" was understood in the Ancient period was in the context of human virtues, faculties of mind, or artistic abilities developed through practice. These are immaterial causal "powers" which not only produce a duplication of themselves but which produce and bring into being some external result that is not identical to the cause but is still dependent on it for its being. They can exist either as potencies or as actualized powers. As Aristotle says,

> As all potencies are either innate, like the senses, or come by practice, like the power of playing the flute, or by learning, like artistic power, those which come by practice or by rational formula we must acquire by previous exercise but this is not necessary with those which are not of this nature and which imply passivity.[17]

Aristotle did not limit himself to reflection on human power alone, on the horizontal level. He also turned his mind to the vertical, to divine nature, and therefore to divine power. In his *Metaphysics*, Aristotle considers the human instinct to philosophize and, he says, "when almost all the necessities of life and the things that make for comfort and recreation had been secured," then human nature turns its thought not only to human power, or to "the greater matters, e.g., about the phenomena of the moon and those of the sun and of the stars, and about the genesis of the universe," but also to "divine power."[18] In fact, Aristotle says, "divine science is . . . [the] most honorable," a subject we will return to in the next section.[19]

In summary, the ancient philosophers viewed power as a fundamental category of being. First, it was seen as causal: it was able to effect itself in relation to other things (power which creates itself from the other and power which creates the other from itself). Second, power was seen as ontological: it identified and/or described the unique thing that something is. Third, powers were forces (along with their opposites) which regulated human life,

---

16. Hippocrates, *On Ancient Medicine* 14.
17. Aristotle, *Metaphysics* 9.5.
18. Aristotle, *Metaphysics* 1.2.
19. Aristotle, *Metaphysics* 1.2

bodily and cosmologically. And fourth, powers were abilities that human beings had or were able to develop through discipline.

THE PATRISTIC PERIOD

During the Patristic period, the early church was heavily involved in one Christological controversy after another. Many of these debates were about the humanity and/or deity of Jesus as the divine Son and thus related to divine power, an issue stretching back to Aristotle, as noted above. Picking up the themes we explored in the previous section, we could phrase these Christological questions as follows: Is the Son the result of the Father's generative power or the same as the Father's power? That is, is the Son's power equal to or subordinate to the Father's power? Is the generation of the Son a consequence of the Father's divine nature or the result of his works of creation? Each theologian intersected these questions from their own understanding of power: power which creates itself from the other, power which creates the other from itself, power which categorically identifies and/or describes the unique thing that something is.

Hippolytus of Rome

The church father Hippolytus of Rome (170–235 AD) is one from among a handful of writers after the New Testament authors to address this debate. In his work, *Against Noetus*, he uses the shorthand "two powers, and one power" to explain his understanding of the relationship between the Father and the Son.[20] Hippolytus argues that since there is only one divine power and one God,[21] which the Father and the Son both share by nature, divinity must be ascribed to the Son equally as to the Father. He goes on to argue this based on God's lack of a contemporary at creation:

> God, subsisting alone, and having nothing contemporaneous with Himself, determined to create the world. And conceiving the world in mind, and willing and uttering the word, He made it; and straightway it appeared, formed as it had pleased Him. For us, then, it is sufficient simply to know that there was nothing contemporaneous with God. Beside Him there was nothing;

---

20. Hippolytus, *Against Noetus* 7.
21. Hippolytus, *Against Noetus* 8.

but He, while existing alone, yet existed in plurality. For He was neither without reason, nor wisdom, nor power, nor counsel.[22] And thus there appeared another beside Himself. But when I say another, I do not mean that there are two Gods, but that it is only as light of light, or as water from a fountain, or as a ray from the sun. For there is but one power, which is from the All; and the Father is the All, from whom comes this Power, the Word.[23]

Origen

In like manner, Origen (c. 184–254) also makes an argument for the Son's equal divinity with the Father by an appeal to power. In his *De Principiis* ("On Principles"), Origin draws upon Wisdom of Solomon 7:25–26[24] to define God's power as "that by which He is strong; by which He appoints, restrains, and governs all things visible and invisible; which is sufficient for all those things which He rules over in His providence; among all which He is present, as if one individual."[25] Origen then equates the breath of power spoken of in the Wisdom of Solomon with an emanation from the Father's power, which he says was "never at any time non-existent . . . that breath of God's power always existed, having no beginning save God Himself. . . . And according to the expression of the apostle, that Christ 'is the power of God,' it ought to be termed not only the breath of the power of God, but power out of power."[26]

In Hippolytus and Origen, we can observe a shift in the understanding of power from the ancient philosophers before them. Whereas power for Aristotle and other ancient authors was a causal property of things which exist in the world and which exert themselves on other objects, in the Patristic period we can observe that an understanding of power emerges that finds its ultimate being in God's creative and providential power. As such, Barnes observes that "There are thus two powers: the first is the unbegotten

22. Hippolytus, *Against Noetus* 10.
23. Hippolytus, *Against Noetus* 11.
24. "25 ἀτμὶς γάρ ἐστιν τῆς τοῦ θεοῦ δυνάμεως καὶ ἀπόρροια τῆς τοῦ παντοκράτορος δόξης εἰλικρινής, διὰ τοῦτο οὐδὲν μεμιαμμένον εἰς αὐτὴν παρεμπίπτει. 26 ἀπαύγασμα γάρ ἐστιν φωτὸς ἀιδίου καὶ ἔσοπτρον ἀκηλίδωτον τῆς τοῦ θεοῦ ἐνεργείας καὶ εἰκὼν τῆς ἀγαθότητος αὐτοῦ" (LXX); "For she is a breath of the power of God, and a pure emanation of the glory of the Almighty; therefore nothing defiled gains entrance into her. For she is a reflection of eternal light; a spotless mirror of the working of God, and an image of his goodness" (NRSV).
25. Origin, *De Principiis* 1.2.9.
26. Origen, *De Principiis* 1.2.9. Origen's scriptural reference is 1 Cor 1:24.

power [of God] from which arises the second power [in creation]."[27] Origen assumes but does not elaborate upon the relationship between these two powers (first and second) within the created world over which the power of God acts as providence. For Origen, power is a divine attribute as well as a characteristic of the relationship between God and his creation. As with Hippolytus and other early church fathers, Origen's contributions to Christology remained helpful through to the conclusion of the Christological controversies.

Gregory the Great

One final (late) Patristic author we will introduce is Gregory the Great (540–604). In Gregory's polemical dogmatic treatise, *Against Eunomius*, we can observe the same argument for the Son's equal divinity with the Father through an appeal to a sharing in power in addition to sharing also in divine royalty, wisdom, glory, wisdom, and love.[28] In all these ways, the Son "is not in Him [the Father] in one respect only, but He [the Son] is in Him [the Father] altogether, in respect of all that the Father is conceived to be. As, then, being in the incorruptibility of the Father, He is incorruptible, good in His goodness, powerful in His might, and, as being in each of these attributes of special excellence which are conceived of the Father, He is that particular thing, so, also, being in His eternity, He is assuredly eternal."[29] And, in addition to the inseparability of the Father and the Son, Gregory also argues for the inseparability of the attributes from God himself. In Book 9 of his argument in *Against Eunomius*, we can see that it was Eunomius's position that (as Gregory quotes Eunomius) the Father "'has dominion over His own power.'"[30] Gregory's response borders on severe when he responds:

> Tell me, what is He? over what has He dominion? Is He something else than His own power, and Lord of a power that is something else than Himself? Then power is overcome by the absence of power. For that which is something else than power is surely not power, and thus He is found to have dominion over power just in so far as He is power. Or again, God, being power, has another power in Himself, and has dominion over the one by the other. And what contest or schism is there, that God should divine the power that exists in Himself, and overthrow

27. Barnes, *Power of God*, 116.
28. Gregory the Great, *Against Eunomius* 1.24.
29. Gregory the Great, *Against Eunomius* 8.1.
30. Gregory the Great, *Against Eunomius* 9.1.

one section of His power by the other. I suppose He could not have dominion over His own power without the assistance to that end of some greater and more violent power! Such is Eunomius's God: a being with double nature, or composite, dividing Himself against Himself, having one power out of harmony with another, so that by one He is urged to disorder, and by the other restrains this discordant motion.[31]

Rather than God's nature being an endless conflict of warring powers, which would result in a creation inherently at war with itself, Gregory argues for a peaceful and harmonious unity of God with his attributes and characteristics, power included. For Gregory, the root cause of the conflict of powers within creation is sin and does not find its origin in the nature of the creator God. As he says, "He Who bestowed on all things that are, the power of being, is the God and overseer of what He has Himself produced. But since, by the wiles of him that sowed in us the tares of disobedience, our nature no longer preserved in itself the impress of the Father's image, but was transformed into the foul likeness sin."[32] Gregory attributes this sin to the religious rebellion of humanity against God, not in our physical, bodily existence. For, Gregory argues, if sin was inherent in physical bodily existence, then the Son of God would have become sin and lost his divine power in his Incarnation.[33]

Summary

Whereas in the Ancient period, power was a property of things that exist and a causal property of things which interact with other things in the world, the Patristic period grounds this ontological and causal understanding in the ultimate power of God in both creation and providence, an important aspect of which is the Christological debate about the Father's relationship to the Son. Since power is singular (a crucial commitment of all theologians through this period, and a view which is severely challenged in later periods) and since the Father and the Son both share in that power, then they also share in divinity. The singular existence of power, rooted in the Triune God, also functions to explain the relationship between a holy God and a sinful world. This is not due to a plurality of powers which are in inherent tension with each other in God's nature. Rather, this is due to humanity's sin of rebelling against God, creating a world of chaos out of

---

31. Gregory the Great, *Against Eunomius* 9.1.
32. Gregory the Great, *Against Eunomius* 12.1.
33. Gregory the Great, *Against Eunomius* 12.3.

harmonious relationship with God and God's providence, and necessitating the Son's Incarnation, suffering, and death to make the world right again.

THE MEDIEVAL PERIOD

Due to limits of space, we must jump ahead to the Medieval period and the two figures who tower over the rest and have given theological guidance for nearly a millennium, Thomas Aquinas (c. 1225-1274) and his *Summa Theologica* and John Calvin (1509-1564) and his *Institutes of the Christian Religion*.[34]

Thomas Aquinas

Like the authors before him, Aquinas covers the range of topics we've already noted above: power as a divine attribute,[35] power in the sense of a human faculty (and the relationship between the human faculty and the divine attribute),[36] and power as a way of addressing the "Equality and Likeness among the Divine Persons."[37] Where Thomas goes beyond what we have addressed thus far is his attention to the following theological topics: power as a human object of desire for the purpose of securing happiness,[38] the relationship of power, as an object of desire, to human pain or sorrow,[39] the relationship between power and the habits of virtue,[40] power and original sin,[41] whether God's grace in redemption is available to humanity through natural power or only as divine gift,[42] whether "Christ's Judiciary Power" is due to his divine or human nature,[43] and the question of power relative to the debates of the time surrounding the sacraments.[44]

---

34. Calvin, *Institutes of the Christian Religion* [Battles]. See also the excellent English translation of Calvin's 1541 French edition, Calvin, *Institutes of the Christian Religion* [McKee].
35. Aquinas, *Summa Theologica* I.8.3; I.25.1-2.
36. Aquinas, *Summa Theologica* I.12.4; I.77-82.
37. Aquinas, *Summa Theologica* I.42.6.
38. Aquinas, *Summa Theologica* II.2.4; II.5.5; II.11.1; II.15.1.
39. Aquinas, *Summa Theologica* II.36.4; II.37.1.
40. Aquinas, *Summa Theologica* II.54.1; II.56.1-5.
41. Aquinas, *Summa Theologica* II.83.2-4.
42. Aquinas, *Summa Theologica* II.109.3-4.
43. Aquinas, *Summa Theologica* III.59.
44. Aquinas, *Summa Theologica* III.62-64, 78.

But where we can observe the most important development in the history of reflection on power is when Thomas brings power to bear in his reflections which are of a more political or legal nature. For example, in Part II, Question 96, of his *Summa*, "The Power of Human Law" (both divine and human) comes into view. Here, Thomas considers six different aspects of the power of human law: "(1) Whether human law should be framed for the community? (2) Whether human law should repress all vices? (3) Whether human law is competent to direct all acts of virtue? (4) Whether it binds man in conscience? (5) Whether all men are subject to human law? (6) Whether those who are under the law may act beside the letter of the law?"[45] These more political concerns of power are also picked up again when Thomas considers "Whether one who is under another's power can give alms?"[46] or "Whether those who are subject to another's power are hindered from taking vows?"[47] The significance of Aquinas here is that by incorporating political-legal discussions (of a more horizontal nature), he anticipates the shift in direction that we will see in the modern period's discussions of power which have a decidedly political nature.

A second area of significance in Aquinas's discussion of power in his *Summa* relates to his discussion of the "keys of the Kingdom."[48] This is a particularly *institutional* topic in ecclesiology (since only those who have been ordained to institutional church offices are typically regarded as having the authority of the keys) and will surface again at a later point as we discuss the institutional power of the church in Kuyper. As Campenhausen has persuasively shown, the topic of the keys of the kingdom was present in theological discussions from the very earliest days of the church and among the earliest theologians. So, while Thomas's inclusion of this topic is not unique, we can observe that in the medieval period's increasing nationalism and in the lead-up to the Reformation, this aspect of power comes to receive greater attention. In Thomas's understanding of the power of the keys, the Ancient period's causal understanding is drawn upon even as he explicitly references Aristotle:

> I answer that, According to the Philosopher (*De Anima* ii, text. 33), "powers are defined from their acts." Wherefore, since the key is a kind of power, it should be defined from its act or use, and reference to the act should include its object from which it

---

45. Aquinas, *Summa Theologica* II.109. This important set of questions also relates to "Whether Christians are bound to obey the secular powers?" (II-II.104.6).

46. Aquinas, *Summa Theologica* II-II.32.8.

47. Aquinas, *Summa Theologica* II-II.88.8.

48. Aquinas, *Summa Theologica* III-II.17–20.

takes its species, and the mode of acting whereby the power is shown to be well-ordered. Now the act of the spiritual power is to open heaven, not absolutely, since it is already open, as stated above, but for this or that man; and this cannot be done in an orderly manner without due consideration of the worthiness of the one to be admitted to heaven. Hence the aforesaid definition of the key gives the genus, viz. "power," the subject of the power, viz. the "ecclesiastical judge," and the act, viz. "of excluding or admitting," corresponding to the two acts of a material key which are to open and shut; the object of which act is referred to in the words "from the kingdom," and the mode, in the words, "worthy" and "unworthy," because account is taken of the worthiness or unworthiness of those on whom the act is exercised.[49]

Let us now turn to a specific example of Aquinas tackling the topic of power. In Part I, Question 25 of his *Summa*, he addresses the question of the power of God. Here we find Aquinas's view of both power generally and divine power specifically. In terms of power generally, Aquinas distinguishes between the powers of persons versus non-persons. In the case of non-persons, if certain conditions are met, the power will be exercised. In the case of persons, though, even if the conditions are met, the person can still choose to exercise the power or not. This is where Aquinas introduces his distinction between active and passive power (Latin: *potentia*). Various objects and people in the world exhibit at various times either active or passive capacities for power. But then, turning to the specific question of God's power, Aquinas argues that God's power is always active because "God is pure act. . . . Whence it most fittingly belongs to Him to be an active principle, and in no way whatsoever to be passive."[50] For God to be passive would contradict his perfection, actuality, and completeness in and of himself. For God to have passive power would mean that he was capable "of being acted upon by something else" outside of himself. Someone or something could force God's hand when it is passive.[51]

Kelly notes that, for Aquinas, "God's power is not a principle or source of [God's] action" separate from his being but that "God's power is identical with His action" in a perfect unity of being.[52] Thus, Aquinas's view of power means that it "can be a capacity for action, or a source or principle of an effect, namely, the action or activity of a thing which can be productive of

---

49. Aquinas, *Summa Theologica* III-II.17.2.
50. Aquinas, *Summa Theologica* I.25.1.
51. Aquinas, *Summa Theologica* II.25.1.
52. Kelly, "Power in Aquinas," 476.

an effect."[53] Now we observe a second distinction Aquinas introduces to the question of power. Not only is power active or passive but there are also two kinds of active power. On the one hand, there is the active power which is not identical with its effect (Kelly provides the example of a man who is powerful enough to lift a weight but decides not to: he is still powerful enough to lift the weight even if he doesn't put that power into action). On the other hand, there is the active power which is identical with its effect (the man picking up the weight). Aquinas argues that God has both kinds of active power: the active power of potency and the active power of actual effect.

The result is that Aquinas continues to work out of the received understanding of power as effecticity: power is a capacity of being which produces or causes an effect.[54] For objects, when the conditions are met, the power effects an action. When persons are in view, though, the conditions alone are not sufficient to produce the effect. There must also be a change in the willingness of the person which in turn produces the effect (i.e., the man who is powerful enough to lift the weight must willingly decide to move his body to pick up the weight). And, finally, when God is in view, Aquinas's view of power provides a space in which God's will to put his power into action and produce an effect (the power and the effect are one) is mediated by his disposition or will. God can have the power to do something but God must decide whether to do that something or not. In either case, God remains active.

Thomas Aquinas serves as an example from the medieval period in which theological reflection on power in the Ancient and Patristic periods is supplemented by two additional topics of interest: the political-legal nature of power in human (and divine) community and the power of the increasingly institutional nature of the church. As we will see in the modern period, where attention to power dramatically increases, it is exactly these two areas of human life which receive the greatest share of attention: power in the state and the institutional church.

John Calvin

A few centuries later, the French church reformer also addressed the topic of power in the state and institutional church. As a second example of this Medieval period, we will consider Calvin's most notable work, *The Institutes*

---

53. Kelly, "Power in Aquinas," 476.

54. I am indebted to Dr. Jonathan Chaplin for this term who used/coined it in our personal correspondence on the nature of Kuyper's contribution to political theology.

of the Christian Religion, in which Calvin also articulates a view of ecclesial power. This occurs in Book 4, Chapter 8, when Calvin picks up the topic of "The Power of the Church in Articles of Faith" and "The Unbridled Licence of the Papal Church in Destroying Purity of Doctrine." In this chapter, Calvin argues, first, that ecclesial power is for service, for the ministers of the church are "servants of Christ and at the same time, servants of the people in Christ."[55] But Calvin makes a distinction here between the ecclesiastical office held and the person holding the office for, he says, ecclesiastical office "given to Church-officers is not given to themselves, but their office."[56] In addition, the calling and duties of ecclesiastical office, that is "The power of the Church, therefore, is not infinite, but is subject to the word of the Lord."[57] The "word of the Lord" not only limits the power of those in ecclesial office but guides the activity of those called to that office. There is a power which resides in the offices of the institutional church, not powers for the person who has been called to that office, and this is for the good of the church and the glory of God. As Calvin says,

> Here is the supreme power with which pastors of the Church, by whatever name they are called, should be invested—namely, to dare all boldly for the word of God, compelling all the virtue, glory, wisdom, and rank of the world to yield and obey its majesty; to command all from the highest to the lowest, trusting to its power to build up the house of Christ and overthrow the house of Satan; to feed the sheep and chase away the wolves; to instruct and exhort the docile, to accuse, rebuke, and subdue the rebellious and petulant, to bind and loose [keys of the kingdom language]; in fine, if need be, to fire and fulminate, but all in the word of God.[58]

Calvin returns to this point again in the next chapter when he reminds his readers that the authority of those in official positions of the institutional church's hierarchy can only come from the word of God, otherwise the creature comes to have an element of ultimate power and authority over the Creator.[59]

We can now observe the foundation from which Calvin's close relationship between church and state can be understood. Whereas the Roman Catholic view of the time was that both ecclesial and political power found

55. Calvin, *Institutes of the Christian Religion* 4.8.1.
56. Calvin, *Institutes of the Christian Religion* 4.8.2.
57. Calvin, *Institutes of the Christian Religion* 4.8.4.
58. Calvin, *Institutes of the Christian Religion* 4.8.9.
59. Calvin, *Institutes of the Christian Religion* 4.10.6, 24.

their earthly source in the Petrine office[60] and the Lutheran view of the two kingdoms greatly reduced the power of the church through a "rupture" between these two spheres, "Recovering ecclesiastical power allowed Reformed church communities of a Calvinist stamp to take on a proactive role alongside the State and helps explain the eventual difference between the Lutheran and Calvinist models of Church-state relations. . . . Calvin progressively abandons the Lutheran doctrine of the Church in favor of an institutional Church that reasserts part of its old powers."[61] In future chapters, we will observe how Kuyper's understanding of the church's relationship with the state (among other civic institutions) bears this distinctly Calvinist stamp.

THE MODERN PERIOD

Modern interests in power all take their lead from the framework presented by the German sociologist Max Weber (1864–1920), a contemporary of Kuyper's. Due to the formative influence of Weber on subsequent theories of power (and authority) in the modern and post-modern periods, it is worth presenting his thought as a representative example of this period. Following a presentation of Weber's analysis of power, we will conclude by paying specific attention to those theologians who grapple with power in modernist fashion from a theological point-of-view before concluding with an extended discussion of the unanswered questions highlighted by the modern period: namely, that which *authorizes* power.

Max Weber

In Weber's classic text, *Theory of Social and Economic Organization*, he defined power as "the probability that one actor within a social relationship will be in a position to carry out his own will despite resistance, regardless of the basis on which this probability rests."[62] This power is evident within social, political, economic, and legal relationships based on authority. Weber classified authority into three basic types: legal, traditional, and charismatic.[63] In Weber's lecture, "Politics as Vocation," he offers this condensed

---

60. Avis, *Authority, Leadership, and Conflict*, 3, remarks in this regard that the Roman Catholic Church was/is a church with "an excess of authority."
61. García-Alonso, "Calvin and the Ecclesiastical Power of Jurisdiction," 138.
62. Weber, *Max Weber*, 152.
63. Weber, *Social and Economic Organization*, 382–92.

definition of these three basic authority types with the only qualification that "these types rarely occur in their pure form in reality."[64]

> There are in principle three grounds that *legitimate* any rule. First, the authority of "the external past," of *custom*, sanctified by a validity that extends back into the mists of time and is perpetuated by habit. This is "traditional" rule, as exercised by patriarchs and patrimonial rules of the old style. Second, there is the authority of the extraordinary, personal *gift of grace* or charisma, that is, the wholly personal devotion to, and a personal trust in, the revelations, heroism, or other leadership qualities of an individual. This is "charismatic" rule of the kind practiced by prophets or—in the political sphere—the elected warlord or the ruler chosen by popular vote, the great demagogue, and the leaders of political parties. Lastly, there is rule by virtue of "legality," by virtue of the belief in the validity of legal *statutes* and practical "competence" based on rational rules. This type of rule is based on a person's willingness to carry out statutory duties obediently. Rule of this kind is to be found in the modern "servant of the state" and all those agents of power who resemble him in this respect.[65]

The (rather pessimistic) assumption Weber utilizes in both his definition of power and his understanding of the three bases of authority is that "Whoever is active in politics strives for power, either power as a means in the service of other goals, whether idealistic or selfish, or power 'for its own sake,' in other words, so as to enjoy the feeling of prestige that it confers."[66] Or, as he puts it later in his lecture, power is "the probability that one actor within a social relationship will be in a position to carry out his own will despite resistance, regardless of the basis on which this probability rests."[67] This is a decidedly zero-sum (winner-loser) scenario.

Weber's is an episodic notion of power, an understanding of power in which there is a (relatively) harmonious status quo which is interrupted by an occasional assertion of will or power (authorized or not) through influence, control, or domination towards a particular end.[68] This means that there are winners and losers in confrontations involving power. As a sociologist, Weber can be credited with the strong sociological character in

---

64. Weber, *Vocation Lectures*, 34.
65. Weber, *Vocation Lectures*, 34.
66. Weber, *Vocation Lectures*, 33–34.
67. Weber, *Vocation Lectures*, 152.
68. Weber, *Vocation Lectures*, 34, notes that this is often achieved by the more powerful party tapping into the hopes and/or fears of the party with less power.

much theorizing about power in the modern period, a methodology which not only reflects the growth of the discipline of sociology but also the way in which theological discourse has been marginalized in modern culture.[69] Because there are those with greater power and those with lesser power in socio-political relationships, this has resulted in power being seen generally by many as a suspect force—not only in human relations but also as power becomes embedded in institutions and patterns of communication.[70] Power then becomes something viewed primarily as a negative entity, even an abusive means of controlling others according to one's (assumed, sinister) agenda.[71] We will observe this in more detail below, for it is precisely this aspect of power which has lead to the eventual diversity of post-modern theories of and approaches to power.

Modern Theologies of Power

Can theology offer anything additional to the modern understanding of power as presented by Weber's theory? In addition to Weber's foundational sociological work, Christian theology makes at least three important contributions to the study of power in this period: (1) theology expands the scope of consideration, (2) theology questions the faulty assumption that power is an inherently negative force, and (3) theology contributes exceptionally gifted multidisciplinary theologians who combine the best political, sociological, and philosophical thought with the best Christian theological reflection on power.[72]

69. See Habermas, "Religion in the Public Sphere."

70. Hannah Arendt addresses the communicative aspect of power. She views power as emerging not only from "power centers" of strong individuals within communities but also from the margins of social groups, in the forms of suggestion and participation in corporate decision-making processes, which can also be used to subversively yet intentionally sway group dynamics to achieve desired outcomes without resorting to more traditional, direct, or explicit forms of coercion of dominance. See Habermas, "Hannah Arendt's Communications Concept of Power." Fairclough, *Language and Power*, iix, also addresses how language functions in maintaining and changing power relations in contemporary society. For him, power is embedded in ideologies (2), which are expressed in language (5), which have their meaning within a particular context (21). The context of discourse is made up of economic and political class (26–27) which eventually give rise to class/social struggles (28). The topic of power within discourse is a burgeoning field of study presently.

71. Kearsley, *Church*, 28, notes that modern views of power tend toward viewing power as embedded in a kind of strategic game which could only rarely end in a draw. The winner in the contest is clearly assumed in such a framework.

72. There is a tendency within modern theology to collapse the phenomenon of "power" into the quasi-supernatural and/or suprahuman concept of "the powers" which

Theology Expands the Field of Scope

In particular, theological accounts of power are helpful because they introduce a previously methodologically-excluded divine (i.e., "vertical") dimension to the field of scope. Mackey approaches power in a way that honors its profound mystery and complexity but in a way that not only focusses on the church as a site of power-dynamics but also by including the church as a moral community in society which morally limits the negative manifestations of power as raw or coercive force. He recognizes that power "name[s] something that will not go away, something endemic in the human condition" and as such is "not a simple thing."[73] He reflects that "Power is that which achieves the realization of one's intentions and will, affecting to that end one's own behaviour and that of others, and overcoming resistance in both cases."[74] The hesitancy he acknowledges in this potential definition is that "power seems inherently inclined, in the human condition at least, to emerge as raw force," resulting in an understanding of power that consistently tends toward the negative.[75] Given this challenge, he resorts to a thin definition of power as that which "effects things, or . . . enables states of affairs to come about" through its being "deployed along a range of

---

a number of New Testament authors refer to cryptically. What exactly Paul is referring to by the "κοσμοκράτορας" (Eph 6:12), the "κυριότητες" (Col 1:16), or the "ἀρχὰς" (Col 2:15) is an open debate. Reflection on this has come to be referred to as "the powers." Walter Wink has written a landmark three-volume work in which he defines "the powers" as "the inner and outer aspects of any given manifestation of power. As the inner aspect they are the spirituality of institutions, the 'within' of corporate structures and systems, the inner essence of outer organizations of power. As the outer aspect they are political systems, appointed officials, the 'chair' of an organization, laws—in short, all the tangible manifestations which power takes" (Wink, *Naming the Powers*, 5). He uses as examples common phenomena like a team spirit or a mob mentality. Additionally, in the Dutch Reformed theological tradition, see Heuvel, *These Rebellious Powers*; Berkhof, *Christ and the Powers*. Leslie Newbigin also addresses this in his work. See, for example, Newbigin, *Gospel in a Pluralistic Society*, 198–210. See also Wolters, "Creation and 'The Powers,'" which addresses this topic, Newbigin's treatment of it, and a Kuyperian response. We will distinguish between "power" and "the powers" and leave this at-times speculative topic of "the powers" unaddressed in order to focus our attention more pointedly on the creational phenomenon of power as approached by theology. While Wink's work has drawn attention to and made a contribution toward understanding the interpretive choices relative to the New Testament references to ἀρχή, ἐξουσία, and δύναμις, an over-reliance upon his work would lead us toward a reductionist understanding of the dynamics present in human communities and cultural institutions, such as the church. On the reductionistic tendency of Wink's approach, see Lynch, "How Convincing Is Walter Wink's Interpretation?"

73. Mackey, *Power and Christian Ethics*, 2–3.
74. Mackey, *Power and Christian Ethics*, 2–3.
75. Mackey, *Power and Christian Ethics*, 7.

appearances of which raw force is one extreme and pure authority another."[76] Because, for Mackey, power is too often deployed as raw force, "it then constantly needs the control and conscious corrective of operative moral values in order that it should cease to be destructive of the freedom and dignity of human persons."[77] One of those sources or moral values is the Christian church which exerts its influence (authority) on the use of force (power). But, as Mackey asserts, "the essence of power is the same in church and state."[78] That is, while power may have a variety of manifestations, its nature or essence is singular. Power is a single entity which comes to expression along a spectrum of types ranging from positive to negative and within a variety of institutional arenas of life, the church included.

Mackey's most significant contribution for us, though, is the way he outlines the multiple foundational questions an analysis of power ought to answer, questions which are theological or otherwise: What is the "locus" of power? What are power's "interests"? What are power's "outcomes"?[79] To these questions of power's means and ends, we will add, "What is power's "nature"? These questions will form the skeleton of our analysis of ecclesial power in the worldview and ecclesiology of Abraham Kuyper in the following chapters.

Another theologian who shows the potential of Christian theology for extending the field of scope when considering power is Baptist theologian James E. Wood. In 1971, Wood delivered a paper on "A Theology of Power" at the Baptist World Alliance Commission on Religious Liberty and Human Rights at Acadia University in Nova Scotia, Canada. In that paper, Wood observed that "We live in an unprecedented age of power" and he defined power as "the ability to do or act, the capacity of doing or accomplishing something."[80] This ability is distinguished from "the exercise, let alone the abuse, of power" for, conceptually, "Power is a morally neutral concept."[81] He argued that power has its ultimate source in God, "who is the omnipotent, the Almighty One"; in fact, "Power is bound up with the very essence of God."[82] But God is not the only agent of power in the universe for "God shared his power with men."[83] Yet because God is the absolute source of

---

76. Mackey, *Power and Christian Ethics*, 13.
77. Mackey, *Power and Christian Ethics*, 7.
78. Mackey, *Power and Christian Ethics*, 18.
79. Mackey, *Power and Christian Ethics*, 2.
80. Wood Jr., "Theology of Power," 107.
81. Wood Jr., "Theology of Power," 107.
82. Wood Jr., "Theology of Power," 109.
83. Wood Jr., "Theology of Power," 111.

power, this precludes absolute human power within creation. Human power is of a limited, delegated nature. Recognizing that the world is a place of distorted power, God's renewal of creation means that "any theology of power . . . [must recognize that] it is ultimately through his [God's] power that his Kingdom will come."[84] The distorted power of limited human agents will be made right through the redemptive power of God's omnipotent grace.

Wood's approach to power is similar to that of Paul Avis, who names the irony of Christian theology studying power. Avis writes: "It is one of the supreme ironies of Christianity that, while in its daily prayer it ascribes 'the power and the glory' to God alone, it is itself deeply implicated in the pursuit, the retention and the exercise of power. . . . As a human and social institution, the Christian Church cannot be exempt from the law that all social activity involves the distribution of power."[85] But "the central paradox of authority" is the "fact that obedience to legitimate authority is regarded as voluntary and is based on consent rather than coercion, yet at the same time is felt to be mandatory or obligatory, in contrast to persuasion which can be legitimately resisted. . . . It is this paradox that is at the center of contemporary ferment regarding authority in the church."[86] As we will see in a later chapter, Christian reflection on power is rich with resources for a healthier and more sustainable approach to power than we often see worked out in our corporatized, globalized world. But by including often neglected aspects of power in modern understandings of it (i.e., the divine and the institutional church), theologians working in this period and/or from this framework assist us in achieving a wider view of power's nature and manifestations.

Theology Questions the Faulty Negative Assumptions about Power

We noted above that many theorists in the modern period view power with suspicion, especially when the institutional church is involved. This has resulted in some theological approaches to power which tend to be plagued by negative connotations and which in turn preclude a comprehensive analysis which considers power's potential as a good or for good.[87] Mary Streufert is an example of a theologian who attempts to provide a balanced theology of power but whose methodology and work is so focussed on militaristic, economic, political, and ideological abuses of power that the possibility of

---

84. Wood Jr., "Theology of Power," 123.

85. Avis, *Authority, Leadership, and Conflict*, 16–17.

86. Avis, *Authority, Leadership, and Conflict*, 25.

87. Koyzis, *We Answer to Another*, 19–20, acknowledges "a general tendency to assume that power manifests itself primarily as [negative] coercive force."

a positive view of power becomes eclipsed from view.[88] This can be seen most clearly when Streufert turns her attention to power dynamics within churches. She claims that "None of us exists with complete power or with a total lack of power" but then opts for a synthesized view of individual power in which everyone is rendered guilty to some extent as being "simultaneously privileged and oppressed."[89] Applying this view to how "Jesus re-organizes the power dynamics of the meal table," the power of Jesus comes off not as an alternative to power but as a kind of affirmative-action (or retributive) power in which the powerful and the powerless merely exchange places around the table.[90] There is no radical critique of power's status quo, stemming from an unclear ontology of power in the first place. But her attempt towards balance, even if she doesn't successfully avoid the negative shadow completely, is noteworthy.

This negative tendency has resulted in a lack of scholarly commitment even to address power theologically. It is viewed as a kind of theological boogieman. As Sykes notes, there is a "modern theological reluctance" to deal with the culturally and theoretically challenging concept of power.[91] These assumptions and lack of commitment, while unfortunate, have made possible a renewed commitment on the part of some to name this tendency and to re-examine and reframe theological approaches to this taboo subject. Andy Crouch's recent book, *Playing God: Redeeming the Gift of Power*, is one such recent example.[92] In his account of power, a detailed examination of the opening chapters of Genesis is leveraged to form a Judeo-Christian understanding of divine creative power in opposition to a coercive Nietzschean understanding of power. Divine power, which finds its parallel in human creative cultural power, is a power which, when shared or delegated, not only brings about human flourishing but also increases the total power within a given system. The Nietzschean power of coercion or force is less generous, a universal zero-sum game which explains why those with access to coercive forms of power are reluctant to share it with others.

While this distinction between "creative" and "coercive" power is helpful for addressing and counterbalancing the negative connotations of power as inherently abusive, it is subject to a number of logical weaknesses. First, Crouch's approach assumes in dualistic fashion that creative power is good and coercive power is bad. This assumption cannot be maintained when we

88. These are the categories named by Streufert, "Difference," 29.
89. Streufert, "Difference," 29.
90. Streufert, "Difference," 32.
91. Sykes, *Identity of Christianity*, 53.
92. Crouch, *Playing God*.

consider parental responsibility in keeping young children safe from danger (sometimes necessitating physical, coercive force to protect the good of the child) or the ways in which anti-social or illegal behaviour spreads through the sharing of power and authority in street gang relationships or the illicit drug trade. Simply put, not all creative power is morally praiseworthy and not all coercive power is morally suspect.

Additionally, when it comes to God, this creative-coercive dualism would imply that God is always creative in relation to power and only because of the human fall into religious rebellion is coercive human power extant, being rooted in sin (another unfashionable theological term!). A brief examination of Scripture or the Christian theological tradition reveals that this distinction cannot be maintained. While there are many instances of God sharing power with his covenant people, God is also recorded as being utterly unique in his power and authority as the universe's creator and supreme law-giver.[93] Because of these two weaknesses, Crouch's distinction is not as helpful as one might have initially hoped, though it has sparked a renewed discussion of power at the popular level. Therefore, we must look elsewhere for a framework that is not only distinctly theological but which is also able to wrestle with the inherent nuances of power. This is exactly where Kuyper will be insightful and helpful.

Exceptional Theologians on Power

The list of contributions which theology has made to theories of power would be incomplete without briefly mentioning the work of those significant theologians who have engaged in broad, interdisciplinary thinking that has attempted to bridge the academic fragmentation which has also affected the modern study of power.[94] We will mention here two representatives among many: one from the Roman Catholic tradition and one from classical Protestantism.

---

93. On Scripture's record of God's use of coercive or forceful power, see, e.g., Exod 9:14; Deut 4:32; 2 Sam 7:22; Jer 10:6. Regarding the Christian theological tradition, the incommunicable divine attributes traditionally include God's omnipotence and sovereignty which result in God's unique creative (*ex nihilo*) and judging power.

94. The literature on the state of the contemporary university is massive. One example must suffice for this large body of work: Côté and Allahar, *Lowering Higher Education*.

Karl Rahner

Karl Rahner's "Theology of Power" represents a phenomenological approach to power, offering a spectrum along which the different manifestations of power can be arrayed.[95] Rahner roots the need for a theology of power in the fact that as Christians "we use the concept of power in the very first articles of the primitive Christian creed, when we call God the 'almighty.'"[96] Granting this divine origin of the manifestation of power within creation, he argues, "Power is clearly something which comes from God and testifies to him in the world."[97] And yet, though power in creation reflects the Creator, power as a temporal phenomenon has an inherent ambiguity to it, making it impossible to come to a succinct definition of power because "power is not a univocal concept."[98] In short, "There are very many nuances in the Christian understanding of power."[99]

Rahner's theology of power then names one specific manifestation of power, "brute force," which he argues is "the lowest form of power" even though "often enough [it] is popularly supposed to be the only form of power."[100] Rahner says that there are two theological statements which can be made about brute force. The first is that brute force is a result of the Fall. Brute force gives the one with greater physical power the ability "to interfere in the sphere of another, disregarding his will and the justice of such an intervention."[101] Had the Fall not occurred, Rahner concludes, "power would exist as a possibility of physical effectiveness, societies would be formed and hence there would be superiors and inferiors, direction and law. But all power would address itself to the free decision in an appeal to insight and love."[102]

The second theological statement Rahner makes about power is that "power, including physical force, is (although stemming from sin, manifesting it and tempting to it) is not itself sin but a gift of God, an expression of his power, an element of the reflexion of God in the world."[103] In language similar to Crouch's noted above, Rahner sees power as a divine *gift* to

---

95. Rahner, "Theology of Power," 391–409.
96. Rahner, "Theology of Power," 391.
97. Rahner, "Theology of Power," 391.
98. Rahner, "Theology of Power," 391.
99. Rahner, "Theology of Power," 409.
100. Rahner, "Theology of Power," 393.
101. Rahner, "Theology of Power," 393–94.
102. Rahner, "Theology of Power," 394.
103. Rahner, "Theology of Power," 395–96.

humanity to effect positive change in the world. This is to say, power, as one dynamic creational phenomenon, is ambiguous. It is part of God's creation but it is subject to human perversion and misuse as well as faithfulness. "Of itself it [power] is good . . . [but] capable of being perverted."[104] Rahner's theological approach to power sees power as a good creational phenomenon with the potential to be perverted into coercion and brute force: something capable of violating the freedom and dignity of another which is rooted in humanity's historic Fall and ongoing rebellion against God and humanity.

For Rahner, then, power "is one of the existentials of man's existence, which cannot be eliminated from the nature of man on earth."[105] It is an inherent aspect of creation. But while "not intrinsically evil," it "can be perverted to serve sinful [ends]."[106] This is where Rahner is helpful for us: while not intending to provide a comprehensive statement on power's definition, he roots power (using the example of brute force) as a dynamic structure of God's creation which is able to be utilized in ways that either promote or detract from God's creational intentions according to the free agency of humanity. Rahner's theological view of power has many similarities with Kuyper's multi-dimensional view of power which we will present in a subsequent chapter.

Jürgen Moltmann

Whereas Rahner is interested in a phenomenological approach to power in creation which has the potential of being perverted through sinful human agency, Moltmann views power Christologically: true power is the reality of Christ who is the critical antithesis between the fallen creation and the emergence of God's renewed creation through the Holy Spirit. For Moltmann, the most basic distinction one can make about reality is not "between soul and body or between persons and structures, but between the powers of the world as it decays and collapses into ruin, and the powers of the Spirit [of God] and of the future."[107] This antithesis between the powers of the world in rebellion against God and the powers of the Spirit of God is manifest "in every sphere of life [where] the powers of the coming new creation are in conflict with the powers of a world structure which leads to death."[108] Moltmann says that this is "the inevitable tension of the Christian

---

104. Rahner, "Theology of Power," 396.
105. Rahner, "Theology of Power," 396.
106. Rahner, "Theology of Power," 397, 402.
107. Moltmann, *Crucified God*, 24.
108. Moltmann, *Crucified God*, 24.

faith. Christian identification with the crucified Christ means solidarity with the sufferings of the poor and the misery both of the oppressed and the oppressors."[109] And it is human unwillingness to live in this tension which leads either to an unorthodox attempt to assimilate into one these opposing forces of life and death or to a sectarian withdrawal from what is alien into a social ghetto in order to maintain one's undefiled (and unchallenged) identity in Christ.[110] Rather, for Moltmann, what is important is sustained attention to the dialectical nature of power.

The dialectical nature of power (which creates the oppressed and the oppressor) is dependent upon human will. For those who choose to align themselves with the power of the fallen world, the result is the coercive power of death which leads to "the will for political power and world domination" whereas through alignment with the "powerless and crucified" Christ, liberation from "this desire to have power and domination over others" is possible.[111] Moltmann employs a counter-intuitive or ironic view of power: the true power of human flourishing "is contained in the weakness and folly of the crucified God."[112] For Moltmann, true life is found through death to the fallen world,[113] the riches of God's kingdom are found through human poverty,[114] joy is found in submissive suffering,[115] and divine power is revealed in the weakness and death of Jesus.[116] Though Moltmann does not use the term specifically, we could call this God's *kenotic* power, a self-emptying power which is more effective and life-giving than all other wills-to-coercive-power which seek to achieve some benefit for one's self or group as opposed to one's neighbor. It is "the suffering of Christ as the power of God and the death of Christ as God's potentiality"[117] which Moltmann sees as the true power to be reckoned with in reality. We will observe later that Moltmann and Ellul's views of power are strikingly similar.

Moltmann then applies this dialectical understanding of power to the church living in the "power of the Spirit."[118] It is this power of the Holy Spirit, which is the power of God's renewed creation or the power of God's

---

109. Moltmann, *Crucified God*, 25.
110. Moltmann, *Crucified God*, 28.
111. Moltmann, *Crucified God*, 69.
112. Moltmann, *Crucified God*, 70.
113. Moltmann, *Crucified God*, 72–73.
114. Moltmann, *Crucified God*, 131.
115. Moltmann, *Crucified God*, 146.
116. Moltmann, *Crucified God*, 205.
117. Moltmann, *Crucified God*, 215.
118. Moltmann, *Church in the Power of the Spirit*.

kingdom, which is the power of freedom and liberation breaking into the fallen world under the lordship of Christ.[119] And, for Moltmann, just as Christ is the dividing line between the powers of death in the world and the power of renewed and liberated life in God's kingdom, so the church becomes that agent in the world which presents the world with an alternative to the pseudo-powers marketed and idolized by the fallen creation. Unfortunately, Moltmann observes, churches sometimes collude with the pseudo-powers of the world in "presenting themselves as the power of order against enlightenment, emancipation and revolution" rather than through faithful obedience to the power of God's renewed creation which liberates humanity from these alternative and counterfeit powers.[120]

But Moltmann does not conceive of the power of the Holy Spirit, who gathers the church, as a sectarian force of world-withdrawal and ghettoization. The kingdom of God is not a select club for the few. Rather,

> Where the kingdom is at hand, the people gather together for the kingdom and free themselves from the power of slavery. . . . The church of Christ is hence simultaneously the people of the kingdom. It is not "the non-world"; it is the world which is now already turning anew to the future of God because it follows the call of freedom. . . . This does not mean the "emigration of the church" from society into the ghetto; it means the exact opposite: the departure from exile and ghetto into freedom.[121]

In fact, Moltmann sees the renewing power of God's kingdom working through liberated believers and effecting the ultimate conversion of destructive power through powerlessness. "Only the person who through Christ has been snatched from the powers of this world wins the freedom and the strength to make these powers powerless."[122] Ultimately, this counter-intuitive, kenotic power for Moltmann is a power of hope. Everything which might lead to death has been addressed in the sacrificial powerlessness of Christ's death in which ultimate liberation occurs through resurrection.[123] This is then mediated through the ministries and sacraments of the church.[124] In the end, for Moltmann, the church is a sacramental presence in the world, pointing the fallen and deathly world to the liberating and

---

119. Moltmann, *Church in the Power of the Spirit*, 5.
120. Moltmann, *Church in the Power of the Spirit*, 16, 34.
121. Moltmann, *Church in the Power of the Spirit*, 83.
122. Moltmann, *Church in the Power of the Spirit*, 104.
123. Moltmann, *Church in the Power of the Spirit*, 166, 191–92.
124. This is the lengthy argument Moltmann begins in *Church in the Power of the Spirit*, 225, and extends for approximately one hundred pages.

renewing grace of God and the powers of life in the kingdom of God, an eschatological presence which is coming into the present through the work of the Holy Spirit.[125]

Moltmann offers a deeply Christocentric view of power, theologically and dialectically understood. It is a theology of power fused with a theology of suffering. Moltmann's approach to power begins with the suffering, death, and surprising resurrection of Christ, a kenotic power which is the loving power of God's kingdom, a power of liberating life, which is mediated through the church to the world by the Holy Spirit.[126] This is a conception of power which takes the power of sin (as rebellion against God) seriously as life-destroying in its orientation toward death. And yet his approach to power is a firm conviction of hopeful anticipation that the life of God's creation, through the renewing gift of the Holy Spirit, is the hope of the world.

Summary

We can summarize the theological contributions to analyzing power by referring to former Archbishop of Canterbury Robert Runcie. Theology expands the field of scope beyond the merely sociological (the "horizontal"). In Runcie's words, that is, "some form of authority is necessary to sustain life" because power and authority are part of God's creation.[127] By rooting power and authority in God, therefore, the assumed negative definition of power is challenged. Runcie puts it this way: "Once we see authority in this enabling way, we are able to see why 'authoritarianism' is the evil it is. False forms of authority do not result in such freedom and flourishing; they create an immature form of dependence."[128] The divine source of power and authority, in turn, give guidance in evaluating power and authority in creation, whether within or between communities or as a theoretical construct. As Runcie says rather playfully, "Authority is rarely claimed or asserted until it is well on the way to being lost."[129] The reason for this is that authority and power are relational and "authority always properly refers to a moral

125. This is Moltmann's concluding argument in *Church in the Power of the Spirit*, 342–61.

126. It is worth noting that there is a connection, though an oblique one, between Moltmann and the post-Kuyper Dutch Calvinist tradition. Richard Bauckham notes the influence that A. A. van Ruler and J. C. Hoekendijk had on Moltmann's "eschatological perspective of the church's universal mission towards the coming kingdom of God" (Bauckham, *Theology of Jürgen Moltmann*, 2).

127. Runcie, *Authority in Crisis?*, 17.
128. Runcie, *Authority in Crisis?*, 18–19.
129. Runcie, *Authority in Crisis?*, 25.

relationship, freely bestowed and accepted, between free and rational agents. In contrast, the concept of power often refers to merely physical and material mechanisms."[130] These are the insights that the exceptionally grand visions of the Christian tradition offer to the broader task of understanding power.

Unanswered Questions about Power in the Modern Period

The modern period sought to define power exhaustively, separate from religious dogma.[131] In the process, modern approaches to power only raised further questions about power that could not be resolved within the inherited paradigms of the Enlightenment that blocked certain avenues of inquiry. We will raise two of these questions which in turn fuel the post-modern approaches to power: (1) What legitimates the use of power? and (2) Is there a favored field for studying this phenomenon? We will briefly address each below.

What Legitimates Power?

If power is the use of (a position of) strength to obtain a desired outcome, then what is the norm by which power is made legitimate? As noted above, Weber outlined three bases for power's authorization (legal, traditional, and charismatic) but he also confessed that those with power desire greater power. The thorny question then arises: When does accomplishing something (possibly against another's will) go from influence to coercion? Many theorists after Weber have sought to address this question. Could the empirical setting in which authority and power are exercised (the moral life, political life, religious life, etc.) offer assistance in this regard? Or could the various forms of authority which ground power as legitimate (reason, revelation, social compact/consent, etc.) solve this? Whether one views authority as norms-based or rights-based, the question over and over again is: What *authorizes* power?[132]

One approach is to offer a list of possible authorizations, similar to Weber. Kim's approach is most similar to Weber's in offering three options: (1) "the right (or ability) to issue commands and/or to expect or exact obedience" and this right can be derived from "the *position, office* or the *source*

---

130. Runcie, *Authority in Crisis?*, 25.

131. The role of the Enlightenment in questions of power during this period will be addressed in the next chapter for it is a key contextual issue for Kuyper's view of power.

132. Ineson, "Language and Authority in Christian Worship," 3, observes that the question of authority in the church "has come to a point of crisis."

from which a command is issued."[133] This, he says, is his rendering of Max Weber's kind of *legal* authority in which the authority is "institutionalized," making authority "a special kind of influence, legitimate influence."[134] Or, (2) "the *voluntary* nature of command acceptance," as in "the faculty of inducing voluntary consent."[135] Authority in this case is the willing and voluntary acceptance of another's (persuasive or compelling) authority rather than authority's coercive or influential exacting of obedience. And (3) "the dimension of *acceptance* with or without special reference to the reasons for compliance" and is based on a prevailing "feeling... that it must be accepted as binding upon oneself."[136]

Willer goes beyond Weber and Kim's three-fold categorization of authority and introduces a fourth acceptable ground for authority: a values-based authority in which an action is authorized if it is grounded in a deep commitment to its absolute worth or moral legitimacy.[137] What sets this apart from Weber's three types is that it introduces a highly individualistic approach to authority. No longer is the community's legal tradition, the community's history, or the community's recognition of special gifting required. Rather, what is required is an individual feeling obligated, due to *personal* values, to pursue a course of action. One can see here the shift from a communal to an autonomous individual orientation which will mark later approaches to power.

Others, rather than trying to categorize various forms of authority instead have sought a synthesis of types into a systematic legitimation. Mackey takes this approach which takes Willer's individualistic values-based approach and seeks to retain the communal nature of values. For Mackey, authority is grounded in a synthesis of these types: "a system of law" in which power "is itself legitimated and validated."[138] And these laws are the reflection of a community's moral system. "Authority," he says, "refers in the first instance to the operative influence of certain values—order, freedom, or something as diffuse and evocative as 'the common good'—in the activity of those who rule and are ruled, values which legitimise or validate" power's exercise. It is in this way that "Power refers to the operative influence of a system of law in the activities of rulers and ruled."[139] Community values/

---

133. Kim, "Authority," 223.
134. Kim, "Authority," 224.
135. Kim, "Authority," 225.
136. Kim, "Authority," 225.
137. Willer, "Max Weber's Missing Authority Type."
138. Mackey, *Power*, 4.
139. Mackey, *Power*, 5.

morals give rise to a community's laws which in turn give rise to authority structures within which certain actions are evaluated.

Yet another approach is to root authority in cosmological factors of one kind or another. Vos approaches the question of authority from a biblical-exegetical perspective and roots the concept of power and authority in humanity's covenantal relationship with God and the rest of creation. We might call his a hierarchical-servanthood approach that sees power as authorized "when there is genuine concern for that over which one exercises authority."[140] Authority, he argues, is typically understood only from a hierarchical point of view (i.e., the strong over the weak), but this is a "warped sense of authority," he says, and "has had its blighting influence on every sphere of life: political, ecclesiastical, domestic, educational, and so on."[141] After reviewing the biblical witness to God's relationship to creation, one he describes as servanthood, he concludes that "as the Lord calls on us to exercise authority in a serving manner, He has not left us without an example—His own. We are indeed made in His image, after His likeness. His Word and His law are not a burden, but they give life."[142] Here, rather than authority having an objective (Weber) or subjective (Willer) basis, power is authorized when it arises out of a desire to serve another's good within a theological matrix of meaning.

Vos then goes on to address how the concept of authority relates to ecclesiology. He says about this hierarchical-servanthood authority that "Both the proclamation and the program of the church should be patterned after that likeness."[143] In fact, it is through selfishness that we come to see the devastating effects of human sin, says Vos:

> Sin is wanting to exercise authority in an unrestricted way, being answerable to no one. The situation is further complicated by the fact that this man who wants to represent himself is not dismissed from the role of representing God. He continues to represent Him only to misrepresent Him. The result of all this is that whoever comes into contact with this misrepresentation of God will be prone—wittingly or unwittingly—to curse God rather than to bless Him. This is particularly relevant with respect to the exercise of authority. As man misuses authority, he is misrepresenting God.[144]

---

140. Vos, "Authority," 214.
141. Vos, "Authority," 215.
142. Vos, "Authority," 217.
143. Vos, "Authority," 217.
144. Vos, "Authority," 217–18.

This servanthood concept of authority, Vos claims, is exactly what is missing from many Christologies in which "the servanthood of Christ is discussed only in conjunction with the suffering of Christ. This leaves the impression that the servanthood of Christ is a temporary phase of Christ's ministry through which He had to pass. . . . The servanthood of Christ, in my judgment, must be viewed as permanent, not temporary."[145] This is also the approach taken by Runcie, that not only is authority "*inevitable*" but it is to be oriented toward "service" and "love" which creates "a common life."[146]

Another way to approach authority from a cosmological point of view is to distinguish between internal and external authority. This is the practice followed by Richardson and Bowden in their entry on "authority" in *A New Dictionary of Christian Theology*.[147] By "external authority," these authors mean that authority attaches "to a person as an official or to an office as an office."[148] By "internal authority," they mean "the authority residing in convincing argument or weighty moral or spiritual example or experience."[149] In Christian history, they judge that "In the NT [New Testament] almost all authority is internal," meaning that the "ultimate authority (which is the word of God) is expressed through preaching or through miraculous occurrences, or found in meditation or prayer or inspired vision and dream or in reading the (OT [Old Testament]) scripture."[150] They go on to apply this as an interpretive lens which results in a problematic redaction of church history, explaining that "the twelve apostles do not hold authority because they have been invested with an office, but because they are in a position to witness what Christ did in the days of his flesh and to his appearances as risen Lord."[151] Rather, it was "As the centuries passed, [that] more and more external authorities came into being. . . . By the end of the Middle Ages the church was supported by a vast system of external authority."[152] But then, due in part to the Protestant Reformation, "Today . . . internal authority is now widely regarded as the only authority in matters religious."[153] This is a problematic historical interpretation because the apostles, by being named "apostles," bear a particular office even within the early church. It

---

145. Vos, "Authority," 222.
146. Runcie, *Authority in Crisis?*, 24.
147. Richardson and Bowden, *New Dictionary of Christian Theology*.
148. Richardson and Bowden, *New Dictionary of Christian Theology*, 58.
149. Richardson and Bowden, *New Dictionary of Christian Theology*, 58.
150. Richardson and Bowden, *New Dictionary of Christian Theology*, 58.
151. Richardson and Bowden, *New Dictionary of Christian Theology*, 58.
152. Richardson and Bowden, *New Dictionary of Christian Theology*, 59.
153. Richardson and Bowden, *New Dictionary of Christian Theology*, 59.

also represents a historical oversimplification: there have always been both institutional and non-institutional forms of Christian spiritual vitality. One is left wondering as well whether the very duality between internal/external is due more to inspired or scriptural insight or to post-Enlightenment categories of rational proof.

The Canadian political scientist David Koyzis[154] relies heavily on the work of Yves Simon[155] and sees authority connected directly to the holding of office, similar to Vos above. This would fit Weber's/Kim's first authority type above, that of legal authority. For Koyzis, power is legitimately utilized when it is the kind of power which a given office within the structure of creation/society entails and authorizes for the purpose inherent within that sphere. Koyzis relies heavily on Kuyper's theory of sphere sovereignty, understanding each cultural role as having a particular office which it has been given by Christ for its own unique cultural contribution to human life. Each cultural sphere constitutes its own unique office with its own unique form of authorized power.

Is There a Privileged Discipline for Studying Power?

In the previous section, we observed the many different ways which have been offered to legitimate power. A second contentious question in modern theories of power is which academic discipline is best suited to study power. As we have seen, Weber's own sociological methodology bequeathed to subsequent scholars an assumed privileged status to sociology for this task. But about this there is much debate as political theorists, philosophers, and theologians have also addressed this important concept with unique contributions from their various fields.

On the one hand, there are those who believe that the study of power as a manifestational aspect of human social/communal life is, therefore, best studied by sociology. Kearsley, for example, summarizes a number of

---

154. Koyzis, *We Answer to Another*, 226, cautions against the equating of power with authority (contra Kuyper), saying: "All human authority derives from God's sovereignty, as Romans 13:1 affirms. This authority is not to be confused with ability—with the mere power to do something. Nor should it be opposed to freedom, which itself has no meaning apart from divinely-instituted authority. Authority is not an arbitrary principle legitimated only through consent, but has a divine origin. Authority is a lofty office given to all human beings, who exercise it in diverse ways according to their respective callings. Only by living in grateful obedience to God's call can we truly know his love for us and hope to fulfill the divine image perfected and redeemed in Christ Jesus our Lord."

155. See, for example, Simon, *Nature and Functions of Authority*; *General Theory of Authority*.

twentieth-century figures who propose a number of different "power plus prepositions" schemes to make sense of power's different relational forms.[156] According to Kearsley, these take three primary forms: First, a coercive kind of "power over," in which one party seeks to use their influence or control to move another closer to one's own position against the other's will. The second is a more complementary kind of "power with," in which multiple parties seek to pool their resources in order to achieve a common purpose in concert with each other. The third is a utilitarian form of "power to," in which the cooperative nature of multiple parties working together is secondary to the primary purpose of achieving an intended effect cooperatively.

Viewing power as the achievement of intended effects has given rise to another kind of modern approach to power in which results-oriented paradigms are used for categorization and/or evaluation. Kearsley summarizes these power-effected results as (1) power to achieve life versus death, (2) power to empower versus disempower, and (3) power to produce community versus isolation.[157] Both the "power plus prepositions" and "power-effected results" categorizations are largely due to Lukes and Clegg, who we will introduce in the next section as they serve as segues into the post-modern period. The point here is that if power is studied as a manifestational reality, then sociology (or political science) is a prime discipline for addressing it.

But there are those who disagree. Roscigno, for example, is a sociologist who believes that the typical sociological study of power is too limiting. He says that "There is perhaps no construct in sociology as theoretically ambiguous . . . as power."[158] While power is "integral to understanding core social processes . . . power, although an abstract and useful construct, is relatively hollow."[159] He, therefore, advocates "not simply 'widening the scope.' . . . Rather, serious consideration of power requires, even dictates, a fundamental reconsideration of assumptions—assumptions about inequality, agency and constraint, and the interplay of human actors, social structure and culture."[160] It is curious to note that, while Roscigno recognizes some of the limitations in sociology's methodology and working assumptions, he still assumes that power rightly falls within the purview of sociology for its study.

---

156. See Kearsley, *Church, Community, and Power*, 25–50, for "power's various meanings." This chapter also contains a recent history of definitions of power.

157. See Kearsley, *Church, Community, and Power*, 34–37.

158. Roscigno, "Power, Revisited," 349.

159. Roscigno, "Power, Revisited," 349–50.

160. Roscigno, "Power, Revisited," 350.

Even a moment's reflection on this question should reveal that the complexity of power necessitates a complex and multidisciplinary approach to defining and understanding it. Just as there is a diversity of manifestations of power, there are multiple and varied approaches to power helpfully provided by a variety of academic disciplines. This is not a justification for oversimplification or resignation in the face of complexity. Rather, this is acknowledged in order that each discipline might be liberated to intersect with the phenomenon of power in a methodologically rational and authentic and constructive way.

Multiple disciplines from sociology to psychology to political science to philosophy have grappled with power and authority. Theology must do likewise. As we will see in the next chapter, Kuyper gives strong reasons why theology should not be discarded as a worthy discipline that is able to bring serious critical engagement to the theoretical and practical questions of power. But there are multiple reasons why, unfortunately, theology has been unsuccessful in a more *theological* analysis of power.

First, theology is often burdened by the expectation that its methodology mirror that of other social sciences or the humanities (sociology, political science, or philosophy in the main). Many theological treatments consider power as a philosophical or sociological phenomenon only. These methodologies are then used as a lens through which to look at the relations within the church or between the church and other cultural institutions, effectively side-stepping a distinctly *theological* or biblical engagement with power.[161] The problem with these kinds of approaches is not that political science or philosophy have nothing to contribute to theology but that political science or philosophical inquiries and insights are assumed, but never argued, to be synonymous with theological inquiry or insight. The result is that the analysis becomes theologically vacuous.

Sykes is an example of a theologian studying power with a sociological methodology at the core. He maintains that "the study of sociology enhances and deepens a theological understanding of power."[162] Possibly because of this dependence upon sociology, Sykes utilizes the biblical narrative pattern of creation, redemption, and consummation in his theological analysis of power. Curiously, this pattern leaves out the important biblical and

---

161. For example, Bruggemann, "Negotiating the Meaning of Power," is a purely *sociological* study of power published in a reputable *theological* journal. John Bolt argues that there is a "drawback, from a theological point of view . . . [when] theoretical models are sociologically oriented. . . . While these *sociologically* oriented typologies are helpful to the theologian, they do need to be complemented by specifically theological models" (Bolt, "Church and World," 5–6).

162. Sykes, *Power*, 81.

theological motif of human rebellion against God and the resulting Fall which provides an important explanation of the abuses of power we must wrestle with theologically.[163] Again, the problem is not that sociology has nothing to contribute to our understanding of power and the church. Rather, it is the same methodological problem of assuming a *sociological* account of power *qua* sociology results in a *theological* analysis *qua* theology. Why does theology not step into this discussion with its own methodology on full display and in full force?

It is true that "Christians both need and have the resources to understand and cope with power in [its] many forms, other than violence."[164] The argument here is not that philosophy and sociology have nothing to contribute generally, or even to contribute to a specifically *theological* project. Rather, philosophy and sociology do not exempt one from the uniquely *theological* work which must also take place. If a theological account of power and authority is desired, the resources which can be found within the theological discipline must be utilized, rather than searching among a variety of other disciplines, some being theological and others being from neighboring disciplines, for a theologically coherent result. There is social or philosophical theology or theology related to the social or philosophical dimensions of human life but one need not leave the theological discipline and enter the realm of sociology or continental postmodern philosophy in order to obtain these insights and smuggle them back into, and pass them off as, theology.[165] Each discipline must contribute the resources of their unique methodological study of power to the larger conversations taking place.

Summary

What we can say after reviewing the modern period's scholarly literature on power and authority is that authority is the moral/ethical/legal framework

---

163. Sykes, *Power*, 20, argues that "creation, redemption, and last things are, so to speak, the beginning, middle, and end of God's story. They are each involved in any attempt to do justice to the range of the power of God." This is quite curious since God's redemption and renewal of creation are directly related to the Fall, an alien power in God's creation. Sykes offers no explanation for this omission.

164. Sykes, *Power*, 83.

165. Even though this project will not engage in sociological reflections on the church and power, for an extended discussion on the move toward sociology within the recent study of Christian theology, see Kearsley, *Church, Community, and Power*, 8–10. Even Berkhof, *Christian Faith*, 348, observes that "a predominantly sociological approach to the problem of the church is gaining ground."

which grounds, legitimates, or validates a system of human organization, relations, or actions of power. Authority can exist extrinsically in a codified legal form which governs those who are subject to power in a particular (political) jurisdiction. Or, authority can exist intrinsically in the values and common orientations shared within a community, tradition, or other social group which is entered into on a voluntary basis. In either case, authority is that which provides justification for the appropriate exercise of power. Until the mid-twentieth century, these modern approaches to power went largely unchallenged from radical critique. But with the arrival of a number of post-modern theorists, the coherence of the modern view of power was broken. New questions began to shape reflection on power: Is it true that the natural status quo of human relations is relatively neutral or peaceful until interrupted by overt instances of coercive power? Likewise, where do minority voices and persons fit into a community whose values produce its legal codes, which give rise to its normative basis for personal actions? Is not majority (but not unanimous) status inherently coercive? These questions gave birth to a plethora of new approaches to power. It is to this last period of consideration that we will now turn.

POST-MODERN THEORIES OF POWER

Beginning in the late-twentieth century, the Weberian framework within which power and authority were understood, studied, and evaluated began to show signs of wear. Whereas philosophy had initiated the long history of reflection on power in the ancient period, it had become marginalized by sociology and political theory. The same was the case for theology, though for different reasons, as we've seen. At the twilight of the second millennium AD, a significant number of scholars began to enter the study of power with a diversity of interests and perspectives that broke the dominance of an episodic, causal view of power. This has ushered in a bewildering array of sub-disciplines which have rendered the modern meta-narrative of power effectively powerless.[166] In the remainder of this chapter, space permits us only a cursory view of this post-Weberian, post-modern scene.

---

166. Clegg, *Frameworks of Power*, xvii, lists some of the sub-specialties in the post-modern period: power has become incorporated into "literary, film, and textual criticism, feminist analysis, social history, organization analysis, penology, sexology, and so on."

Lukes and Clegg

Sociologists Steven Lukes and Stewart Clegg ought to be considered together. This is because their work has attempted to (1) summarize theories of power within the modern period and (2) raise important, critical questions which show the limitations and/or weaknesses of modern approaches to power. It is their work that bridges the modern and post-modern periods and serves as an excellent introduction to the questions raised by post-modern theories of power, an example of which we will see in Michel Foucault below.

After considering Weber's view of power and authority as well as the numerous questions Weber's theory is unable to account for, Lukes wonders whether "the very search for such a definition [of power] is a mistake."[167] Why does he say this? Because "the variations in what interests us when we are interested in power run deep . . . and what unites the various views of power is too thin and formal to provide a generally satisfying definition, applicable to all cases."[168] The four critical issues Lukes lists for Weber's view of power and authority are illustrative: (1) the relationship between power and responsibility, (2) how power's various ways of distribution affects our understanding of power, (3) what are the sources of power?, and (4) how to evaluate power in light of alternatives, what *could have been*.[169]

These questions form Lukes's argument for the "need to think about power broadly rather than narrowly . . . [and] we need to attend to those aspects of power that are least accessible to observation."[170] The problem that Lukes then identifies with this problem (and need) is the incredibly vast "conceptual terrain that power occupies."[171] Is it even feasible, given the "unending disagreements about how to define [power] and study it, [that] we need the concept of power at all"?[172] A potential pathway forward in this maze is the recognition Lukes encourages us to make: that "how much power you see in the social world and where you locate it depends on how you conceive of it."[173] Though Lukes doesn't use this term, we might call this the worldview aspect in studying power. That is, one's view of power arises from "a particular moral and political perspective."[174] This means that while

---

167. Lukes, *Power*, 4.
168. Lukes, *Power*, 4–5.
169. Lukes, *Power*, 13–17.
170. Lukes, *Power: A Radical View*, 1.
171. Lukes, *Power: A Radical View*, 12.
172. Lukes, *Power: A Radical View*, 12.
173. Lukes, *Power: A Radical View*, 12.
174. Lukes, *Power: A Radical View*, 29–30.

actual instances of power usually appear in a causal form (what Lukes refers to as the "basic common core to, or primitive notion lying behind, all talk of power is the notion that A in some way affects B"[175]), our abstractions and conceptualizations of these instances, once "defined, when interpreted and put to work, yields one or more views of power—that is, ways of identifying cases of power in the real world."[176] Therefore, the views of power that we have will run along our pre-existing worldview tracks.

Clegg sees the same problems at work with Weberian analyses of power—where "the first major conceptual puzzle concerning power . . . [is] its definition."[177] The reason for this is that power is normally handled conceptually, abstractly. But, he says,

> Power is not a thing like a cat or a dog which we can point to and correctly identify as "cat" or "dog" and be sure we are right. We can not do this because power is not something animal, vegetable or mineral which we can sample, and compare against communally agreed criteria of what a thing is. . . . Power cannot be thought to be a thing, or species of thing, which has a definite being in the world, that comes wagging its tail, recognizably dog-like in a way that a particular dog might correspond to our concept of dogs in general.[178]

The most significant way in which power is most unlike a dog or a cat is the way in which "normal" states of affairs function as "the most potent type of power . . . which is rarely, if ever, exercised."[179] The reason why this type of power is rarely exercised and yet still so powerful is because

> There is little need for it to be so. Normal states of affairs, meanings and conventions routinely appear to be natural, as if they were without interest. What might once have been called "legitimate authority" prevails. In such instances all that the conventional attribution of meaning will do is to exhibit the dominant "theorizing power" which conceals the relation of meaning and social interest. To believe what people tell us, or to accept it as the standard of what we judge people to mean, is to make of the socius a quite arbitrary logos. It is the replacement of an

---

175. Lukes, *Power: A Radical View*, 30.
176. Lukes, *Power: A Radical View*, 30.
177. Clegg, *Power, Rule, and Domination*, 1.
178. Clegg, *Power, Rule, and Domination*, 2.
179. Clegg, *Theory of Power and Organization*, 21.

undialectical logocentrism with an undialectical sociocentrism. It is a suspension of judgment and the negation of wisdom.[180]

The end result for Clegg, like Lukes, is that "There is no such thing as a single all-embracing concept of power."[181] All the student (or agent!) of power is left with are endless choices of options, perspectives, and interests. The move from modern to post-modern approaches to power, then, is a realization (rooted in one's worldview) that "thick" definitions of power are either elusive or forms of power themselves. This raises the question: if we change the worldview through which we view power, could a "thick" definition come into view?

Elias Canetti

Elias Canetti (1905–1994) approaches power from a unique worldview. He was born in Bulgaria to Spanish-Jewish parents. He moved to London (UK) at the start of World War II. He was a successful writer, winning the Nobel Prize for literature in 1981. Though not often considered in studies of power, he makes an important distinction between power and force. This distinction is helpful in understanding the power of the church as a civic institution, a distinction which arises from his war-time context.

Force, Canetti says, is "something close and immediate in its effect."[182] He uses the illustration of a predator capturing the prey in its mouth. Power, on the other hand, "is more general and operates over a wider space than force; it includes much more, but is less dynamic. It is ceremonious and even has a certain measure of patience."[183] Then Canetti uses the example of a cat and mouse to illustrate the difference between force and power. The illustration is beautifully written, intellectually stimulating for our consideration of power and authority, and is therefore worth quoting at length:

> The cat uses force to catch the mouse, to seize it, hold it in its claws and ultimately kill it. But while it is *playing* with it another factor is present. It lets it go, allows it to run about a little and even turn its back; and, during this time, the mouse is no longer subjected to force. But it is still within the power of the cat and can be caught again. If it gets right away it escapes from the cat's sphere of power; but, up to the point at which it can no longer

---

180. Clegg, *Theory of Power and Organization*, 21.
181. Clegg, *Frameworks of Power*, xv.
182. Canetti, *Crowds and Power*, 327.
183. Canetti, *Crowds and Power*, 327.

be reached, it is still within it. The space which the cat dominates, the moments of hope it allows the mouse, while continuing however to watch it closely all the time and never relaxing its interest and intention to destroy it—all this together, space, hope, watchfulness and destructive intent, can be called the actual body of power, or, more simply, power itself. . . . Inherent in power, therefore, as opposed to force, is a certain extension in space and in time.[184]

Canetti then brings this distinction to bear on religious life. There are, he suggests, those for whom God's power (general and diffuse) is not enough. They desire God's nearness, his presence, for God's *force* to lay hold of them. They live in a constant state of expectation, waiting to hear an immediate word from God which they can receive and obey. "It is as though they were already in God's mouth, to be crushed in the next instant. But they have to live their whole lives in this terrible place, undaunted by it and still striving to do right."[185] Calvinism (along with Islam), Canetti says, is a religion of God's *force*. We will see in future chapters how Kuyper's Calvinism exemplifies Canetti's distinction. What we should observe here, though, is that power and/or force are not necessarily causal in nature as they are normative. They describe a state of being in relationship with an other. This is precisely what Foucault sought to illumine about the nature of power in his work.

Michel Foucault

Michel Foucault (1926–1984) has been described as an "ultra-radical" with "massively influential writings about power"[186] and as someone who is "cavalier"[187] in his post-structuralist approach to power. He attempts to escape the modern categorization of instances of power as episodic or one-directionally causal. On the contrary, his approach sees power as a constant matrix in which human life is inexorably embedded. As Sheldon Wolin says about him, "Perhaps no writer of the last half of the twentieth century has done more to illuminate the nature of power than Michel Foucault."[188]

For Foucault, power is not the intrusion of a coercive force into a neutral status quo. Rather, power is the status quo itself. Foucault understood

---

184. Canetti, *Crowds and Power*, 327.
185. Canetti, *Crowds and Power*, 328.
186. Lukes, *Power: A Radical View*, 12.
187. Clegg, *Frameworks of Power*, 2.
188. Wolin, "On the Theory and Practice of Power," 179.

power as the institutional and social matrix through which society creates knowledge, normality, and socially-acceptable behaviour.[189] Rather than power being objective, occasional, and oppressive, Foucault sees power as un-/sub-conscious, pervasive, and unavoidable. It is pre-critical and shapes the consciousness, values, priorities, biases, and norms not only of individual persons but also of whole communities and societies. Power, for Foucault, is so pervasive, yet subtle, that it masquerades under forms of "knowledge" or "facts" that communities uncritically or pre-critically believe to be true apart from proof. Power doesn't rear its ugly head, do something painful to us, and then leave. For Foucault, Western society has created systems of discipline ("disciplinary power") through which communities willingly, even eagerly, embrace constructions and networks of power so as to internalize social or cultural norms which they see it as their duty to defend and abide by.

Foucault's interest is in "power, right, [and] truth."[190] From his perspective, the way that Western societies have historically controlled their citizens is through what Foucault calls "sovereign power," that is, discourses and techniques that legitimate hierarchical power structures with the attendant legal obligations of mass obedience.[191] With the rise of industrial capitalism, this sovereign power was oriented toward the creation and maintenance of an economically productive community through systems and relationships of domination, surveillance, and punishment.[192] There are similarities here between Foucault's view of power as a "net-like organization" and Friedman's psychological systems theory for communities.[193] The resultant social norms and "knowledge" are what Foucault calls "disciplinary power." Disciplinary power seeks to create norms through repression of unwelcome actions or desires.[194] In this way, power operates at the level of worldview, frameworks of knowledge and acceptability, as opposed to intentional and cognitive will. As Wolin summarizes him, "Foucault's world is suffused with power. There is no social space undefined by power relationships and no socially significant form of power which is not housed. It is a social world totally dominated by power but not necessarily a totalitarian world."[195]

---

189. Kearsley calls this the power to produce "a well-behaved and prosperous society" which is produced through the "shaping [of] universal norms and values for individual persons" (Kearsley, *Church, Community, and Power*, 52).

190. Foucault, "Disciplinary Power and Subjection," 229.

191. Foucault, "Disciplinary Power and Subjection," 231.

192. Foucault, "Disciplinary Power and Subjection," 231–32.

193. Friedman, *Generation to Generation*.

194. Kearsley, *Church, Community, and Power*, 53–55, summarizes Foucault well on "disciplinary power."

195. Wolin, "On the Theory and Practice of Power," 186.

There is significant debate concerning Foucault and his approach to power, including significant resistance.[196] A main area of critique is whether Foucault's division of power between "sovereign power" and "disciplinary power" sufficiently transcends the objections to modern conceptions of power.[197] Wolin calls the downside to Foucault's view "the same error of totalistic thinking" that plagued classical or modern understandings of power, the very drawback which Foucault sought to counter with his own approach. But while

> Foucault's conception of power seemingly depended on a thoroughgoing rejection of the proudest achievement of modern theory, the conception of the sovereign state as the center of power and authority, the ultimate source of rules, and the final arbiter of social conflicts . . . Foucault's conception is flawed by a narrow construction of state power as essentially negative and preventative . . . parasitic rather than grounded.[198]

Thus, Foucault's view of power ends up being too pessimistic as it

> offers no hope of escape. Every discourse embodies a power drive and every arrangement is repressive. There is no exit because Foucault has closed off any possibility of a privileged theoretical vantage point that would not be infected by the power/knowledge syndrome and would not itself be the expression of a Nietzschean will-to-power.[199]

As such, "Foucault has come to a dead-end, the consequence of having accepted an unqualified Nietzschean conception of knowledge as generated by power drives that leaves no room for conceptions of theoretic vocation and civic commitment."[200] That is, Foucault's post-modern deconstruction of power is all too easily deconstructed itself to show the antinomian intentions behind his pursuits to dethrone supposedly dominating forms of knowledge, normality, and socially-acceptable behaviour. That is, in Foucault's attempt to unmask power dynamics in society, his theory of power is itself just another mask.

---

196. Kearsley, *Church, Community, and Power*, 59–60, outlines the implications of Foucault's view, implications which Kearsley assumes will make many church communities uncomfortable.

197. Kearsley, *Church, Community, and Power*, 38–50, summarizes Foucault's contributions to philosophies of power.

198. Wolin, "On the Theory and Practice of Power," 182.

199. Wolin, "On the Theory and Practice of Power," 186.

200. Wolin, "On the Theory and Practice of Power," 196.

POWER   71

It is this selfishness which resides in Foucault's theory of power which Smith critiques. Smith questions whether Foucault must necessarily be so pessimistic or anxious as he seems to be about power. Smith agrees that "There is no claim to truth that is innocent; there is no knowledge that simply falls into our minds from the sky, pristine and untainted. What might be claimed as obvious or self-evident is, in fact, covertly motivated by other interests—the interest of power."[201] But, simultaneously, even if Foucault's sovereign power is pervasive, is it not necessarily the case that all forms of power are to be feared and rejected as totalitarian? For example, speaking of discipline, a matter about which the Christian faith speaks of in the language of discipleship: Smith argues that the Christian practice of discipleship does not negate the liberty of the individual under a Foucauldian "exercise of a power of normalization."[202] Instead, Smith suggests, it could very well be the case that "Christians should understand discipline [as a form of power] positively, precisely because Christians should not be liberals in the classical sense.... Christians should eschew the very notion of an autonomous agent who resists any form of control. By rejecting Foucault's liberal Enlightenment commitments, but appropriating his analyses of the role of discipline in formation [of individuals in society], we can almost turn Foucualt's project on its head."[203] As such, sovereign power does not necessarily exist as *power over* in the sense of domination. Formation and discipline do not necessarily negate individual identity or willingness. Not acquiescing to being formed according to the non-Christian power operative in the world is not avoided by a wholesale non-conformity (if that is even possible); one can willingly, voluntarily opt for a counter-formation in Christianity even though it is still a form of power. It depends on the *telos* of the formation: *what* or *who* one is being formed to be as much as the worldview in which power is understood. On this score, Foucault appears to be reductionistic or, as Wolin claims, totalistic. In the end, the post-modern understanding of power falls under the same judgment as classical views of power. Or, to put it another way, power appears, and functions, differently from within different worldviews or points of view.

DOES POWER DEFY DEFINITION?

In this chapter, we have surveyed a wide variety of philosophical understandings of power by following the broad contours of the history of

201. Smith, *Who's Afraid of Postmodernism?*, 86.
202. Smith, *Who's Afraid of Postmodernism?*, 94.
203. Smith, *Who's Afraid of Postmodernism?*, 99.

reflection on this complex topic. The diversity we have encountered makes defining power a significant challenge. One path we must refuse to take is to say that power is too elusive as a philosophical or practical concept to be pinned down by definition. This is the path advocated by Steven Lukes in an otherwise very helpful anthology on the topic of power.[204] The reason Lukes takes this path is because, he says, once one begins studying power, as it has been reflected upon over the centuries, it "turns out to be far from simple."[205] After reviewing many possible definitions of power, Lukes wonders whether "these various insights" can be brought "together into a single picture?" He answers his own rhetorical question agnostically: "Perhaps, but I doubt it. It is more likely that the very search for such a definition is a mistake."[206] If one wonders why, in the face of so many divergent definitions of power, the only result is to throw up one's hands and surrender, Lukes does not explain his position. The various views on power's interests, intentions, means, goals, forms of resistance, and outcomes (intended or not) is indeed complex, as we have readily seen. This is why so many attempts at defining power end up being reductionistic, even though theorists set out with a strategy to be (somewhat or apparently) comprehensive. It is assumed, in the end, that mere description is all that is possible. "Perhaps this explains why," Lukes comments, "in our ordinary unreflective judgements and comparisons of power, we normally know what we mean and have little difficulty in understanding one another, yet every attempt at a single general answer to the question [of power] has failed and seems likely to fail."[207]

But is it not possible to avoid "thin," reductionistic definitions of power but also approach a greater degree of comprehensiveness? It seems that the task of finding a "thick" definition must still be possible. True, as we have seen, every definition of power offered, which seeks to be comprehensive, fails to address all the varied aspects which the phenomenon presents to us. And there is the risk, Foucault would remind us, that a comprehensive definition of power is merely a will to power for a particular agenda. This may, in fact, be where Lukes is most helpful: he reveals the inherent weakness of seeking comprehensive definition through reductionist strategies, something which does not satisfy in the end.

What can be the pathway forward? In the following chapters, we will acknowledge that "Clearly power occurs in many and varied forms"[208]

---

204. Lukes, *Power*. Mackey, *Power*, 3, says about Lukes that this approach "will not do."
205. Lukes, *Power*, 1.
206. Lukes, *Power*, 4.
207. Lukes, *Power*, 17.
208. Percy, *Words, Wonders and Power*, 42.

because "Power is not a single concept, but a multiple reality."[209] But by looking to the worldview level, in which we find Kuyper's view of power, we will be able to engage in a multi-dimensional understanding of power, something which both approximates greater comprehensiveness and also avoids reductionism. By going through the doorway of worldview, the faulty assumptions Lukes brings to his engagement with power, the very assumptions which make definition an unreachable goal for him, will become clear and avoided. At this point, it is enough to say that there are worldview assumptions at work in Lukes's approach to power, assumptions about the nature of power, which prohibit the very goal he assumes to be possible: that of a single comprehensive definition of power which will cover all of its manifestations into a single definitional category. Our analysis of Kuyper's multi-dimensional understanding of the nature of power will illuminate this pathway forward. For, as Percy said, power "demand[s] a multi-dimensional appreciation."[210]

CONCLUSION

As we have seen, over the centuries, when one asks the question, What is power?, the answers are diverse and far from approaching consensus. Power, whether approached philosophically, sociologically, politically, or theologically, resists simple definition. There are as many theories of power as there are theorists. In fact, what is often the case with power is that its ambiguous nature is accepted as all one is able to state authoritatively on the subject. If not, then a phenomenological approach is adopted which only achieves a categorization of power's diverse manifestations in the world. As Christine Pohl summarizes and illustrates about this kind of resignation to power's dynamic nature, "There are many different forms of power that can be used for good or evil."[211] James Skillen wonders whether the problem of definition arises from the fact that power, theologically approached, is an abstraction separated from Scripture and interpreted into human and historic actions. As such, power is open to various interpretations, depending on the perspective of the interpreter, ranging from faithful responsibility (as in covenantal stewardship) to dominating coercion.[212] Power is a perennial

---

209. Percy, *Words, Wonders and Power*, 143.

210. Percy, *Words, Wonders and Power*, 45.

211. Pohl, *Living into Community*, 128.

212. This is based on personal correspondence with James Skillen. I am indebted to his willingness to dialogue with me on the theological issues of power, especially as they relate to the political process. I am grateful for his generosity and insights.

question, probably not as inherently corrupt as Lord Acton remarked, but at least as problematic in most of its human manifestations. Power is deeply embedded in the human condition and for this reason it is conceptually familiar without being easily given to succinct theoretical definition. We, therefore, turn now to a fuller exploration of the man and the thought of Abraham Kuyper who devoted his life to making sure the church didn't disappear from either the hearts and minds of the Dutch people or the secularizing Dutch culture which was so intent on marginalizing him, his confessional worldview, and the power of the church.

3

Disappearing No Longer

The Ecclesiology of Abraham Kuyper

TWO GREAT NINETEENTH-CENTURY CHURCHMEN

CHARLES H. SPURGEON (1834–1892) was arguably England's greatest Victorian era churchman.[1] Abraham Kuyper was arguably Holland's greatest Victorian era churchman. The two are remarkably similar. Both were ethnically Dutch, committed Calvinists, the sons of Christian ministers, and raised in families of meagre economic means. Both showed an uncanny religious sense at very young ages (Spurgeon read the great Puritan theologians and Kuyper evangelized sailors, both at the age of seven) and were converted to Christian orthodoxy as young adults through the persuasion of poor, uneducated Christians. Both were widely regarded for their oratorical gifts, voracious reading habits, rigorous daily disciplines, exceptionally large public audiences, and prolific publications. Both were pastors of denominations they regarded as falling under the dangerous sway of theological liberalism and modernist historical-critical hermeneutics resulting in both of them advocating ecclesial secession and the founding of new church communions. Both spawned cultural institutions to address the perceived needs of their day. Both were plagued by psycho-somatic illnesses throughout their active careers. And, in response to their faith-based endeavours,

---

1. For biographical background on Spurgeon, see Barclay, "Men and Affairs," 128; Ratiner, *Encyclopedia of World Biography*, 402–5; "Spurgeon, Charles Haddon," 57–58.

both Spurgeon and Kuyper were regularly criticized in the media by the cultural elites.

But given these contemporaries' exceptional similarities, there is one striking difference for our purposes. While Spurgeon continued to preach and pastor at the same church for nearly forty years, Kuyper resigned his ministerial credentials in 1874 to enter national politics and would go on to serve as the long-time leader of one of Holland's first national democratic political parties, the Anti-Revolutionary Party.[2] Spurgeon's Calvinism rooted him in the institutional church.[3] Kuyper's sent him from the church into the world. And rather than this being a temporary move, Kuyper's career from 1874 onwards, while never disconnecting from the institutional church completely, took on a greater public focus in the academy, media, and government. Kuyper remained active in the Amsterdam church council, taught theology at the VU, wrote theological articles and books for both popular and academic audiences but, increasingly so over the years, Kuyper the theologian and churchman became Kuyper the national culture reformer and politician-statesman.

Their similarities could be readily explained by the influence of nineteenth-century culture. But what might explain their difference, especially their significant difference relative to the institutional church and the wider culture?[4] Both Spurgeon and Kuyper agreed with the mainstream Calvinist ecclesiology of Calvin's *Institutes*, the lordship of Christ over the church, the sovereignty of God in salvation, the work of the Holy Spirit in personal and corporate sanctification, and the centrality of the preached Word in both church and personal life. Yet, it is the unique elements of Kuyper's ecclesiology within Calvinist Dutch Reformed Christianity that resulted in his departure from institutional church ministry and his uniquely public life as compared with Spurgeon. We might say that whereas Spurgeon sought to reform England through preaching, Kuyper sought to reform the Netherlands through civic institutions of higher education, national media, grassroots democratic organizing, and political statecraft.

What might explain why Kuyper contextualizes his Calvinist ecclesiology so uniquely? In particular, there are differences between Kuyper's

---

2. On the history of the Dutch Anti-Revolutionary Party, see Dyke, "Abraham Kuyper," 7–26.

3. On Spurgeon's socio-political views, see Smith, *Transforming the World?*

4. One would not want to underestimate Spurgeon's cultural endeavors (founding a preacher's college in 1855, opening an orphanage 1866, and starting a religious literature publishing company). The point here is that while Spurgeon's cultural projects were consistently based in the institutional church, Kuyper's were organizations within civil society which were officially independent from the institutional church.

and Spurgeon's religious, political, and cultural contexts that shed light on the forces which motivated Kuyper to formulate the unique elements of his ecclesiology as he did. This context becomes clear when we consider Kuyper and the tradition that bears his name to this day. Having considered Kuyper's context, we will then be prepared to analyze the two most significant contributions he made to Reformed ecclesiology before concluding with a reflection on the historical irony of Kuyper's legacy.

CONTEXTUALIZING ABRAHAM KUYPER

We are analyzing the power of the institutional church in the ecclesiology of Abraham Kuyper. In this chapter, therefore, we turn our attention to the Dutch theological renaissance of the late-nineteenth and early-twentieth centuries in which Abraham Kuyper played a significant leading ecclesial and cultural role. In the introductory chapter we outlined the reasons for this choice. Abraham Kuyper's ecclesiology specifically and the Kuyperian tradition more generally contain significant resources for understanding ecclesial power. In this chapter, we present the person of Abraham Kuyper, the tradition he birthed within Western Protestant-Reformed Christianity, and the relevant elements of his ecclesiology. We will see that Kuyper's unique contributions to Calvinist/Reformed ecclesiology guided his life and work in ways quite different from others of his time or tradition. But rather than attempting to provide a comprehensive analysis of Kuyper's ecclesiology or life project of bringing Calvinism up to date, either of which would take us far afield of our main focus, the purpose of this chapter is to present and analyze the two most unique contributions Kuyper made to Calvinist/Reformed ecclesiology which bear upon his understanding of ecclesial power. This will then serve us well as a suitable preparation for our analysis and development of the power and authority of the institutional church in Kuyper's worldview, a more constructive project we will begin in the next chapter. In order to contextualize Kuyper, we will reflect on his unique methodology, his central concerns, and his significant contributions despite the suspicion with which he was viewed.

KUYPER'S METHODOLOGY

Kuyper's historical and cultural context as well as his own personal theological methodology impact the way in which he goes about his work. In light of prior scholarship on Kuyper's ecclesiology,[5] we need only briefly note here the historical and cultural background of nineteenth-century Holland that exerted its formative influence on Kuyper. This was a period of great sociocultural and political change as well as institutional reconfiguration, the church included, in the emerging modern Dutch era. Kuyper's ecclesiology is embedded within his immense project of engaging every aspect of Dutch culture from Christian first principles.[6] Kuyper was compelled, to the point of psycho-somatic breakdown at least three times during his life, to achieve what may in fact be impossible for one person in a single lifetime: the nonviolent reform of every aspect and cultural institution of society, indeed, an entire country, for the glory of God.[7]

But Kuyper develops his thought and engages in this monumental project in the most occasional way. His ecclesiology matured organically over four decades of painstaking work as pastor, journalist, university founder, theology professor, political leader, and church reformer. His published work on most topics, ecclesiology included, often followed this pattern: (1) ideas would be presented first in public addresses and sermons, (2) these ideas would then be developed in print as daily newspaper editorials or weekly meditations, (3) these newspaper articles would then be combined (often unedited) into published book volumes, and (4) in later years Kuyper would edit these volumes and publish them in final form.[8] It is this occasional methodology that makes Kuyper such a fascinating but challenging study.

---

5. Wood analyzes Kuyper's ecclesiology from an historical perspective (see *GD*). Bolt analyzes Kuyper's ecclesiology for application towards a renewed American public theology (see *FCHN*).

6. Wood observes that for some Kuyper represents a "revolutionary departure" from mainstream Calvinism (*GD*, 141); for others "his [Kuyper's] thought reveal[s] undeniable tensions" (*GD*, 24). Heslam observes that Kuyper states on other occasions that he only sought to modernize the "*application* of Calvin's theology" (*CCW*, 260). For Kuyper's own understanding of his intention, see his speech to the delegates of the seventeenth national assembly of the ARP in Utrecht on April 24, 1909, as proof of Kuyper's personal commitment to the orthodox Calvinist tradition, contra his critics, see Kuyper, "Wij, Calvinisten." Bratt situates Kuyper within the Victorian period and ethos and how this shapes his perspective (*AKMCCD*, 244–50). His approach was inspired by the Dutch Christian-Historical school of thought. For background on this period, see *AKMCCD*, 137; Harinck, "Abraham Kuyper's Historical Understanding." Dooyeweerd, *Roots of Western Culture*, 42–44, offers a brief explanation of historicism and its influence on cultural development from a Kuyperian perspective. For a brief introduction to German Historicism generally, see Dooyeweerd, *Roots of Western Culture*, 49–55; Beiser, "Historicism"; Clouser, "Critique of Historicism."

7. Bratt, "Raging Tumults of Soul."

8. At least four of Kuyper's works appeared in this manner: *De Gemeene Gratie*; *Work of the Holy Spirit*; *Nabij God te Zijn*; *Asleep in Jesus*. Even his *Lectures on Calvinism* went through a similar process before being delivered at Princeton Theological Seminary in the Fall of 1898.

KUYPER'S CENTRAL CONCERNS

Even though Abraham Kuyper and the tradition that follows him are not that well or broadly known, his thought continues to resource an international network of scholars.[9] Kuyper has been recognized as being of significant historical, theological, and cultural importance.[10] This came about through his unique blend of abilities as pastor, journalist, politician, theologian, institution-builder, and cultural critic, a blend that was unique in the cultural milieu of late-nineteenth-century Holland.[11] And yet it was a *theological* vision that animated all of Kuyper's work. In the words of B. B. Warfield, president of Princeton Theological Seminary from 1887–1902, Kuyper was a "theologian of genius."[12] His genius was not only limited to the field of theology, though, for Kuyper was also the founder of the Free University of Amsterdam, two national newspapers, and long-time leader of Holland's first national democratic political party, eventually serving four years as the Prime Minister of the Netherlands (1901–1905).

In addition to his strong public impulse, Kuyper's life was bookended by a focussed and sustained concern for the church. At the beginning of Kuyper's career, his doctoral thesis compared the church polities of John Calvin and the Polish church reformer John á Lasco (Laski).[13] And at the end of his life, the newspaper announcement of Kuyper's death was published alongside the sixty-eighth installment in his series "Concerning the Church" (November 14, 1920).[14] Kuyper was convinced that the problem of relating the church to modern society was "none other than the problem of Christianity itself"[15] if it had any hope of avoiding cultural marginalization.[16] In fact, for some scholars, the core of not only Kuyper but also the Kuyperian tradition after him is the church.[17] This is not to suggest that Kuyper was the

---

9. *CCW*, 1. Wells, "Until the Trumpet Blows," 25, also notes that "Abraham Kuyper [is] a person known to some in the Presbyterian and Reformed community, but perhaps not so much elsewhere."

10. *CCW*, 4.

11. *CCW*, 56.

12. Warfield, "Calvinism."

13. For background on Kuyper's conversion which produced his interest in the church, see *GD*, 20–21. On Kuyper's work comparing Calvin and á Lasco (Laski), see *GD*, 68.

14. *GD*, 155. Kuyper's "Van de Kerk" articles ran in *De Heraut* from 1919 to 1920.

15. Kuyper, "Conservatism and Orthodoxy," 68.

16. For related studies on Kuyper's desire that the church not become obsolete, see *GD*, 26.

17. For example, *GD*; *FCHN*.

only theologian at the time wrestling with ecclesial questions. Numerous others in the NHK and beyond sought to address this same challenge, albeit from different starting points or via different means.[18] And sometimes these theologians viewed each other and their contributions unfavourably, including Kuyper who was viewed sometimes as a radical, sometimes as a conservative; sometimes as a reformer, sometimes as a revolutionary; sometimes as dangerous to church and state, sometimes as faithfully carrying the Calvinist tradition forward in new and creative ways.[19]

KUYPER'S PRODIGIOUS LIFE AS AN OUTCAST

From his numerous cultural achievements, one might judge Kuyper to have been a popular figure. While Kuyper was viewed positively by many, they were not those who mattered on the public stage. In the eyes of the cultural elites, Kuyper's problem was exactly his popularity among the "little people" (Dutch: *kleine luyden*).[20] Without attempting a psychological analysis of Kuyper's inner motivations, an interest in the reasons behind his keen attention to the marginalization and disappearance of the church within late-nineteenth-century Dutch society is more than simple curiosity. This is an historical question and we can formulate an impression of Kuyper's reasoning by putting the known historical pieces together. Consider the following series of observations as they relate to Kuyper's reception among the Dutch upper-class. First, we reflect on Kuyper the academic scholar. As noted in the previous chapter, Kuyper earned his doctorate in theology, founded the VU, and served there as professor of theology from 1880 to 1901. Yet, despite this, we noted that Prof. Woltjer remarked at Kuyper's funeral that Kuyper was never admitted to the Royal Dutch Society, the premier academic guild in the Netherlands.

---

18. One important example is Foppa M. Ten Hoor (1855–1934), who eventually immigrated to the United States, where he served as professor of dogmatics at Calvin Theological Seminary, Grand Rapids, MI, from 1900 to 1924. He was a staunch opponent of Kuyper's, particularly critical of Kuyper's distinction between the church as institution and organism as well as Kuyper's *Doleantie* formation of the GKN. An excellent summary of Ten Hoor's theological differences with Kuyper can be found in Pronk, "F. M. Ten Hoor."

19. *GD*, 17–18. See also the detailed history of and controversy surrounding Kuyper and the Kuyperian tradition in *FCHN*, 443–64.

20. Himmelfarb, "Methodism," 116–30, makes a similar observation of John and Charles Wesley and the early British Methodist movement: it was deeply connected to the disadvantaged working classes, an important insight to which we will return in a later chapter.

Second, turning to Kuyper's political career, we observe that not only did Kuyper found and lead the ARP from 1879 to just before his death in 1920, but he was also a member of the Dutch legislature from 1874 to 1877 and 1879 to 1919, even serving as Prime Minister from 1901 to 1904. Yet, in spite of this significant political career, Queen Wilhelmena viewed him with deep political suspicion and personal dislike and was all too eager to see him defeated in the election of 1905.[21] Harinck, therefore, correctly summarizes the situation when he says that Kuyper "had not been accepted in the political culture of his days."[22]

Thirdly, we must consider Kuyper's ecclesial career, especially in light of his deposition from ministerial office in the NHK. The mid-1880s saw Kuyper's church reform efforts reach their highest (and for his detractors, most annoying) pitch. In 1883 he had published his *Tract on the Reformation of the Churches*. It was a scathing attack on the intrusion of the state into church affairs, a clear violation of his principle of sphere sovereignty, a principle we will analyze further below. But Kuyper saved his most damning critiques for the NHK hierarchical structure and its domineering control over the wills of local congregations and councils. This erupted into an all-out ecclesial war in January of 1886, when Kuyper, his supporters, a team of lawyers, some VU students, and a locksmith and carpenter literally sawed their way through the locked council room door of the New Church in Amsterdam. As if this was not enough to enrage his ecclesial foes, Kuyper positioned armed students loyal to him and his cause outside to guard his occupation of the council room. Not only was this a highly controversial move but also one loaded with symbolic significance on Amsterdam's main square. It was this event that finally lead to the NHK's deposition of Kuyper and his allies that summer.[23] To say the least, Kuyper had an uneasy relationship with the church.

Finally, we must reflect on Kuyper's general cultural reception. One might think that Kuyper the theologian, the institution-founder, the professor, and the politician and prime minister would be cut off from the mass population who did not or could not achieve such impressive public credentials. This is the surprising element of Kuyper's project: he was intimately connected to and sacrificially supported by poor, uneducated, working class Christians who saw him as their hero.[24] But while Kuyper enjoyed the sup-

21. For Kuyper's relationship with Queen Wilhelmena, see *AKMCCD*, 302, 322, 346.

22. Harinck, "Historian's Comment," 278.

23. This period is covered well in *AKMCCD*, 149–71; Wood begins his historical analysis of Kuyper's ecclesiology with this "panel-sawing" event (*GD*, 1).

24. I am drawing on personal interviews with numerous Dutch immigrants to

port and favour of the lower classes, the upper class saw him very differently. For the cultural elites, Kuyper was an embarrassment and it did not sit well with them that he had such strong democratic support among the commoners, many of whom could not even vote![25] Kuyper was regarded as a brilliant organizer and polemicist but he was still viewed as old-fashioned and out of date with the liberal mindset of the upper class. The political cartoons aimed at Kuyper illustrate the disdain with which he was viewed.[26]

In all these ways: academically, politically, religiously, and culturally, Kuyper was an outcast. Harinck's summary of Kuyper's context supports this: "Kuyper . . . was an outcast; Kuyper was an outcast in politics, in academia, and he soon would be an outcast in the Church as well."[27] From this historical standpoint, it is entirely reasonable to believe that if Kuyper knew that he was an outcast among the cultural elites, and he must have had more than a vague sense of this, he also knew that the Christian faith and the Christian church were also in the process of being cast out from Dutch society and culture caught up in revolutionary and secularizing forces. It doesn't take much historical imagination to believe that Kuyper must have felt to some extent that he represented the orthodox and confessionally Reformed Christian faith, which through his efforts had one last chance of cultural survival before being irreparably marginalized by Modernity's sweep. Because of Kuyper's deep commitment to the church, the only means Kuyper must have imagined for regaining a place for the church once again in Dutch society was to reformulate the received Calvinist ecclesiology[28] to meet these marginalizing forces that were threatening to make the church disappear from the cultural landscape of his beloved country. When compared with someone like Spurgeon whose English context meant that he was received more positively, Kuyper's ecclesiology, particularly the two most important contributions he makes, becomes intelligible as an attempt to stem the church's cultural ostracization and social marginalization from the point of disappearing.

Canada who, fifty or eighty years later, remember their families saving their pennies and fervently praying daily to support Kuyper's VU, labor union, and ARP. This is also confirmed in *GD*, 20, with the added observation that it was Kuyper's own poor minister-family upbringing that endeared him to the *kleine luyden*.

25. It was actually through Kuyper's political work that Dutch enfranchisement was extended to one vote per household in 1896. See *AKMCCD*, 228–34.

26. Albert Hahn was probably the best political cartoonist who captured this discrepancy especially well. The best resource for Kuyper cartoons is *Kuyper in De Caricatuur*.

27. Harinck, "Historian's Comment," 278.

28. For a history of the history of the Dutch Revolution and the nationalization of the Dutch Reformed Church, see *AKMCCD*, 5.

THE KUYPERIAN TRADITION

Despite his critics, Abraham Kuyper is credited with the translation of a renewed Calvinist theology to the modernist world of late-nineteenth and early-twentieth-century Holland. Through his prodigious publications and widespread public speaking, Kuyper is acknowledged as the founder of the Kuyperian branch within the Reformed theological tradition, a unique form of Christianity marked by a commitment to the church's comprehensive world-engagement.[29] This world-engaging vision of Christian faith sparked a tremendous shift in the posture of the church towards culture and society.

This adjusted self-understanding of the church has contributed, from Kuyper's day to the present, to push the church into the whole of the world missionally, "to establish the sovereignty of Christ in the world."[30] As Heslam has observed, "For Kuyper, Calvinism represented a kind of centrifugal force that moved outwards in ever-widening circles—from its initial influence in the sphere of religion—to encompass the whole of human existence. The same outward-moving force was also evident within the sphere of religion itself"—i.e., the church.[31]

This renewal within the Calvinist tradition of the Reformed/Evangelical branch of Western Protestant Christianity which Kuyper bequeathed to his successors around the world took root in Holland in the mid- to late-nineteenth century, reached its height of influence in the first half of the twentieth century, and continues to exert its influence in a variety of cultural arenas today.[32] As one has said, this is a tradition "so broad in its scope, dis-

---

29. Nicholas Wolterstorff rightly observes "that at the heart of the Reformed tradition is a passion for totality, for wholeness, for integrity, for not allowing life to fall into bits and pieces, for constantly asking, 'What does my faith—what does the gospel of Jesus Christ—have to do with this and what does it have to do with that?' And then never being content with the answer 'Nothing!' . . . The heart of the tradition is not theology but a certain, difficult-to-describe, way of being in the world before God, in which the notion of totality and wholeness is central" (Wolterstorff, *Hearing the Call*, 415–16). In fact, Wolterstorff, *Until Justice and Peace Embrace*, 3, refers to the Kuyperian tradition as "world-formative Christianity." Garber, *Fabric of Faithfulness*, uses the Kuyperian tradition to address the topic of vocation as a version of "world-formative Christianity." For a brief introduction to the Dutch neocalvinist tradition, see Dennison, "Dutch Neo-Calvinism."

30. *CCW*, 132–33.

31. *CCW*, 113. For Heslam's commentary on Kuyper's second Stone lecture, see *CCW*, 113–41.

32. Heslam states that the Kuyperian "school of thought . . . exercises considerable influence today" (*CCW*, 5).

tinctive in its emphasis, lasting in its influence, and successful in its practical consequences, that it deserves ongoing study and reflection."[33]

While it is Kuyper's name that is attached to this modern renewal of Calvinism, to be fair to Kuyper's historical predecessors, he did stand on the shoulders of some significant others. Groen van Prinsterer, a jurist who served King William I of the Netherlands as secretary, was significant in laying the "anti-Revolutionary" foundation upon which Kuyper would later build. This Dutch "anti-Revolutionary" spirit was in direct conflict with the ideology and social consequences of Enlightenment ideals that were spreading through northern Europe during this period, resulting in drastic and violent upheavals in society, revolutions that were supposed to be for the sake of equality, fraternity, and liberty.[34]

Despite the suspicion and outright derision he faced, Kuyper disseminated his theological vision through journalism, teaching, politics, and volumes of theological and devotional works that continue to be read and studied to this day. Attempting to articulate a world-encompassing Calvinist framework that saw "the doctrine of God's sovereignty . . . [as] the fundamental principle," Kuyper also brought this vision to bear on a renewed Calvinistic "ecclesiological paradigm"[35] which started with God rather than humanity.[36] "Modernism had exchanged divine for human sovereignty, with disastrous consequences," observes Heslam.[37] In fact, all the "radical changes that took place in the field of theology during Kuyper's career concerned in particular the relationship between the church and the world."[38]

The influence of Kuyper's theological insights has provided a significant contribution to the mid- to latter-twentieth-century Western Protestant-Reformed church for the proclamation and embodiment of the Christian gospel in every aspect of life and in all institutions of culture, not

---

33. *CCW*, 270.

34. Wood, in his introduction to *R&G*, lists those problems as "the problem of the human and the divine," "disestablishment and democratizing trends," "the [cultural] givenness of the church," "how the church could be simultaneously a divine and a human institution," "the question of belonging versus belief," and "Christianity's, and especially the church's, public role" (*R&G*, xviii). Wolterstorff, *Hearing the Call*, 335, notes in this regard that "it was not so much the theology of the Reformers that led them to new views but that the old views no longer looked plausible given the society that had emerged." Kuyper was now doing the same in his own changing context.

35. *R&G*, xviii.

36. *CCW*, 114, 97. It is Wood's argument that according to Dulles, *Models of the Church*, Kuyper's ecclesiology fits the sacramental model (*R&G*, xviii). It is this claim we address below.

37. *CCW*, 115.

38. *CCW*, 118.

only those directly ecclesial. These themes have influenced the work of successive Dutch theologians such as Herman Bavinck and G. C. Berkouwer as well as, to a lesser but still important extent, British figures such as the late John Stott, N. T. Wright, Elaine Storkey, Jonathan Chaplin, Peter Heslam, and Jeremy Begbie.[39]

The mid-twentieth-century, post-war Dutch diaspora exported this Kuyperian Christianity far and wide. In North America, it fuelled the widespread cultural enterprises of the Dutch immigrants to Canada following the Second World War. Bringing this Kuyperian mindset to civic institution-building, the Canadian wing of the bi-national Christian Reformed Church in North America was instrumental in forming hundreds of congregations across the country, a coast-to-coast network of private Christian elementary and secondary schools, Christian tertiary colleges and universities (the Institute of Christian Studies, University of Toronto, 1967; the King's University, Edmonton, Alberta, 1979; and Redeemer University, Ancaster, Ontario, 1982), a Christian labor union (Christian Labor Association of Canada, 1952 numbering about thirty thousand members), and a Christian political party (Christian Heritage Party, 1986). Kuyper birthed a movement that propels the church into the world through civically-engaged Christian faithfulness.

This movement has also been widely influential during the twentieth century in the United States. Stemming from Kuyper's 1898 Stone lectures at Princeton Theological Seminary, given at the height of Kuyper's career,[40] he offered his Calvinistic theological vision to an American audience that despite also being Calvinist in theological orientation was of a more pietistic strain. Heslam observes that Kuyper and his presentation of a renewed Calvinism was enthusiastically welcomed, even if there were vocal critics at occasional points.[41] George Marsden even speaks of the eventual "triumph—or nearly so—of what may be loosely called Kuyperian presuppositionalism in the evangelical [academic] community."[42] It was this comprehensive vision of the Christian faith and its implications for the whole of life that helped to expand the mission of a number of Christian liberal arts colleges beyond theological training for Christian ministry to include Christian intellectual pursuits across the academic spectrum.[43] Recent publications have helped

39. CCW, x. For a more detailed catalogue of scholars working from or influenced by Kuyper, see CCW, 5–8, including footnotes. See also Berkouwer, Church; Begbie, "Creation, Christ, and Culture."

40. CCW, 9.

41. CCW, 258.

42. Marsden, "State of Evangelical Christian Scholarship," 14.

43. See Boonstra, Our School; Hofman, Canadian Story of the CRC; Kromminga,

to highlight these insights and contributions for both academic and popular audiences.[44]

In the theological realm, the Kuyperian tradition is recognized to be a robust and inspiring theological system often identified by worldview studies[45] and a redemptive-historical approach to Scripture.[46] Within the Christian Reformed Church, which still maintains strong theological and cultural ties to Kuyper specifically and Holland generally, Kuyper has been one of the main theological voices which has animated the church to reach out into the wider world, to work out the social, ethical, and political implications of the gospel, extending the influence of the kingdom of God into the world beyond the boundaries of the church or Christian sub-cultures.[47]

While this cultural and theological history was documented in the mid-twentieth century, few original or creative works have been published which would continue to further develop this theological tradition systematically, and particularly in relationship to ecclesiology, until very recently.[48] Yet even these recent publications have sought to place Kuyper within his historical and cultural context rather than expanding and developing Kuyper's thought constructively for the present. As such, this project seeks to examine Kuyper's ecclesiology from a theologically systematic point of view with an eye to further theological developments relative to power and authority which can assist the church today in appreciating and implementing its identity and mandate in culturally constructive ways for human and cultural flourishing.

Before we turn to Kuyper's ecclesiology proper, a note about terminology is in order. This chapter is focused on the person of Abraham Kuyper with an acknowledgement that he stands at the head of a tradition that goes by several roughly synonymous names. What to call this "broad

---

Christian Reformed Church; Schaap, *Our Family Album*; Beeke, *Living for God's Glory*. This tradition is heavily influenced, theologically, by Berkhof, *Systematic Theology*.

44. *FCHN*; *AKMCCD*; *AKASPI*; Mouw, *Calvinism in the Las Vegas Airport*.

45. See Middleton and Walsh, *Truth is Stranger*; Walsh and Middleton, *Transforming Vision*; Wolters, *Creation Regained*; Goheen and Bartholomew, *Living at the Crossroads*.

46. Bartholomew and Goheen, *Drama of Scripture*; Goheen, *Light to the Nations*. These more recent works arise from the earlier Kuyperian tradition of Ridderbos, *Redemptive History*; Vos, *Biblical Theology*.

47. Kuyper is specifically named as an important part of the Christian Reformed Church's history on their website. See CRC, "History."

48. The most significant and ground-breaking exception in systematic theology is Spykman, *Reformational Theology*. Receptivity is noted by Haas, "Reformational Theology." In terms of ecclesiology specifically, Heyns, *Church*, is notable. Most recently, the resurgence in attention to Kuyper is seen in *GD*; *AKMCCD*; *DCMA*.

tendency in Western culture"[49] which Kuyper embodied is a difficult question. Heslam observes that "in order to avoid too close an association between his [Kuyper's] ideas and those of Calvin and traditional Calvinism he [Kuyper] sometimes preferred the term 'neo-Calvinism.'"[50] Yet Heslam also observes that this "term [neo-Calvinism] was first used by Kuyper's *critics* ... and may well have been influenced by the designation 'neo-Catholicism' to refer to the nineteenth-century school of liberal Catholicism."[51] Thus, many of Kuyper's critics also used this term to sharply critique the liberalization of Calvin and the Calvinist tradition that they perceived in Kuyper. Kuyperianism or Reformational Christianity are often used today instead of neo-Calvinism which in North America is often confused with "new Calvinism" as a uniquely twenty-first-century American phenomenon sparked by John Piper, Mark Driscoll, and others.[52] Here, the term Kuyperian or the Kuyperian tradition will be used for the worldwide ecumenical theological, political, philosophical, aesthetic, and social tradition that most closely follows Kuyper's original vision.

THE ECCLESIOLOGY OF ABRAHAM KUYPER

With this brief introduction to Kuyper and the tradition that bears his name, we now turn specifically to Kuyper's ecclesiology. While I have written elsewhere on this subject,[53] here it is important that we focus on the two most distinctive aspects of Kuyper's understanding of the church for in these we can discern most clearly Kuyper's understanding of the power of the institutional church. In this chapter, we grant the historical, occasional, and developmental nature of Kuyper's thought noted above and analyze these two elements of Kuyper's ecclesiology, both of which have particular relevance

---

49. *CCW*, 86.

50. *CCW*, 87.

51. *CCW*, 87n6 (emphasis added).

52. On the "New Calvinist" movement in North America, see George, "John Calvin"; Hansen, "Young, Restless, Reformed"; Billings, "Calvin's Comeback?"; Biema, "#3 The New Calvinism." Even the New Calvinist movement is concerned with the institutional church, as seen in DeYoung and Kluck, *Why We Love the Church*. Michael Horton has attempted to mediate between the various Reformed branches through his *Christless Christianity*; *Gospel-Driven Life*. Pennings, "Whole and Heart," suggests that the term "neo-Puritan" is preferable to the easily confusing "new-Calvinist" though neo-Puritan and neo-Calvinist are two discernable traditions within evangelical Reformed churches.

53. See Wagenman, *Engaging the World with Abraham Kuyper*; "Abraham Kuyper and the Church."

to our larger study of ecclesial power: (1) the church is grounded in creation, and (2) the church is both an institution and an organism.[54] These two ecclesiological insights, in the end, propelled Kuyper from the church to the world. Both his theory of "sphere sovereignty" (Dutch: *souvereiniteit in eigen kring*) and his distinction between the church as an institution and the church as an organism are essential for coming to a clear understanding of Kuyper's view of the power of the institutional church.

The Church Is Grounded in Creation

As noted above, for Kuyper, the church's posture is oriented toward the world. His own life displays a deep commitment to extra-ecclesial civic institutions such as universities, newspapers, political parties, and the state. So, how does he theologically conceive of and support Christian engagement in the extra-ecclesial or "secular" world? How does Kuyper reconcile church and world that exist in tension with each other, even in the New Testament?[55] We shall see that for Kuyper, the key for unlocking his vision on this question is his worldview epistemological understanding of the way the church (along with other cultural institutions) is knit together in the social and cultural fabric of God's creation. Kuyper's doctrine of the church grows out of his doctrine of creation.

Kuyper believed human beings were created, among other things, to worship and serve God in the totality of their lives. This created impulse within humanity for worship manifests itself historically, culturally, and organizationally (i.e., institutionally) in the church as a temporal social institution. Thus, for Kuyper, the church is grounded in creation, as a necessary consequence of the potentials built into creation's structure as well as the religious capacity of human nature made in the image of God rather than only as a means for human redemption post-Fall.[56] Kuyper utilized a variety

54. Venema, "Abraham Kuyper," 82, argues that the "key elements" of Kuyper's ecclesiology are "the church's freedom from inappropriate hierarchicalism and governmental interference in its distinctive area of competence [what I will refer to as 'sphere sovereignty' or the groundedness of the church in creation], the distinction between the church as institute and as organism, and the 'pluriformity' of the church." I do not address the pluriformity of the church here because it is a logical consequence for Kuyper of the church being grounded in a creation which is inherently pluriform. Otherwise, Venema gives a good overview and fair treatment of the critics of Kuyper's ecclesiology.

55. For example, in John's Gospel the "world" is the object of God's love (John 3:16) whereas in 1 Corinthians, Paul chastises the church for being too "worldly" (1 Cor 3:1 NIV).

56. Roy Clouser, *Myth of Religious Neutrality*, 228, argues that the church, as a social institution, is defined by three characteristics: "(1) their members are united to an

of metaphors and arguments to communicate this, some of which came to mark not only his ecclesiology as unique within Calvinism but his entire public theology. We will begin with an early look at how Kuyper communicates this belief metaphorically. Then we will examine Kuyper's concept of "sphere sovereignty" as his most enduring and salient way of asserting his belief about the institutional church's place in society.

Ecclesiology, Metaphorically-Speaking

Kuyper's inaugural sermon upon his appointment as pastor in Utrecht, preached on November 10, 1867, was entitled, "The Incarnation of God: The Life Principle of the Church."[57] In this early sermon, we find Kuyper speaking metaphorically about the issues and concepts he found significant, was wrestling with, and would shape his ecclesiology in the years ahead.[58] This sermon is an early example of Kuyper's desire for the church to be in relevant dialogue with the intellectual currents of the day. Drawing upon John 1, Kuyper uses the Incarnation as an ecclesial metaphor, insisting that the church "is not just a collection of Jesus' followers," but is "the Body of Christ, the rich organism in which not just his spirit but Christ himself is in a full sense . . . where a new power reveals itself and that new life works."[59]

This "power" and "life" of Christ in the church is the analogue to the Incarnation of the Son of God in the history of the world. But how does this church "organism" become a civic institution? Kuyper argues that there is both an internal/invisible and an external/visible aspect to the church. On the one hand, Christ is "the hidden life of the internal, invisible church, the true body of the Lord."[60] But, on the other hand, "the no less important

---

intensive degree; (2) membership carries the intention of being life-long; (3) membership is (at least partly) independent of the member's will." By "social institution," Clouser is showing the normative nature of the church in human culture, as opposed to "organization," which are less durable and more subject to change.

57. The text of this sermon has not yet been translated from the original Dutch to English. All references to this work are from *De Menschwording Gods*, from the online collection of Kuyper's works provided by the Neo Calvinism Research Institute (sources.neocalvinism.org). English translations are my own.

58. Wood rightly describes this sermon as giving "a trajectory to Kuyper's career" (*GD*, 54).

59. Kuyper, *De Menschwording Gods*. Dutch: "De Kerk is dan niet maar een verzameling van Jezus' volgelingen . . . het rijke organisme waarin niet maar zijn geest, maar Christus zelf voortleeft . . . waar die nieuwe kracht zich openbaart en dat nieuwe leven werkt."

60. Kuyper, *De Menschwording Gods*. Dutch: "het verborgen leven van die inwendige, onzichtbare kerk, die het waarachtige lichaam des Heeren is."

question, which can be derived from the same principle—the principle of the incarnation of God—is the visible, external church, endlessly varied in form and shape."[61] We observe here Kuyper's life-long concern with how the internal and external aspects of the church will relate theologically, how the church will be temporally manifest as an institution in society, and how the institutional church will be related to the other institutions of human society. A concise summary of Kuyper's view on this, which we will be exploring in greater detail below, is that the organic church gives rise to the institutional church while the institutional church serves the organic church.[62]

This incarnational metaphor makes Kuyper's point clear: the faithful institutional church may not promote a posture of sectarian world-withdrawal by over-emphasizing its internal or invisible aspect as opposed to its external aspect as an open-postured world-oriented church. This is apparent in two ways. First, the way in which Kuyper relates the internal and external aspects of the church reveals that he believes in the necessity of the external or visible church institution in society. He says that

> the principle of God's incarnation-action of the church demands a visible form. . . . The divine life only in the heart flowing along an inward way remains a latent force . . . a precious germ, but it can not grow. . . . [But] the external church is the continuation of Christ's historical appearance. . . . Without her [the external or institutional church] Christianity gradually withdraws until it . . . mourns and languishes, loses its clarity and awareness, and the history of more than one sect provides sufficient evidence that the abandonment of the external church means we also forget Christ and finally is actually a denial of God's incarnation in us [the church]. We must have an external church, as long as its shape coincides with the shape of the kingdom of God.[63]

---

61. Kuyper, *De Menschwording Gods*. Dutch: "de niet minder gewichtige vraag geleid, wat uit datzelfde beginsel—het beginsel der menschwording Gods—is af te leiden voor die zichtbare, uitwendige kerk, die eindeloos geschakeerd naar vorm en gestalte."

62. While Bavinck, *Reformed Dogmatics*, 4:330, concedes the institutional/organic distinction, he places this within the larger distinction between the visible and invisible church. The institutional/organic distinction belongs to the visible church.

63. Kuyper, *De Menschwording Gods*. Dutch: "het beginsel van Gods menschwording een optreden der kerk in zichtbare gestalte eischt . . . Het goddelijk leven alleen langs inwendigen weg in het hart gevloeid, blijft een sluimerende kracht . . . een kostbare kiem, maar die niet uitspruiten kan . . . Een uitwendige kerk als voortzetting van Christus' historische verschijning is . . . Zonder haar trekt het Christendom zich allengs geheel op het gebied des innerlijken levens terug, treurt en verkwijnt, verliest zijn klaarheid en bewustheid, en de geschiedenis van meer dan ééne secte levert het voldingend bewijs, dat het prijsgeven der uitwendige kerk ook den Christus buiten ons

As the Incarnation was God's presence within the world in the historical person of Jesus Christ, so the institutional church is Christ's on-going, visible, and world-oriented presence in the world. The internalized church, the church of sectarian world-withdrawal, is a practical negation of the theology and purpose of Christ's Incarnation.

Second, this is also apparent when Kuyper concludes this particular sermon by calling for the institutional church to equip and send the organic church into society as a visible presence of Christian influence through Christian individuals pursuing their vocations and voluntary Christian associations contributing to civil society. His concluding exhortations call upon Christian scientists, laborers, artists, musicians, and academics to "testify" like prophets "from the fullness of the Holy Spirit against the profane spirit of the world and prophesy with holy enthusiasm of the triumph of the kingdom of God that awaits . . . in all fields of life."[64]

The key to this sermon is how it allows us to perceive the trajectory of Kuyper's ecclesiology: it captures Kuyper's initial wrestling with questions of how the institutional church will address the social realities of its day, not by withdrawing as a sect from society but by being grounded as an objective institution among the various other institutions of civil society and by sending Christians individually and grouped together in voluntary associations into the world as the equipped organic church. From the very beginning, Kuyper was concerned that the institutional church not be sectarian and world-withdrawing. The institutional church, since it is grounded in creation, must be tended so that it will not disappear from the cultural or societal landscape of human life. And it must also be correctly related to the church as an organism.

Sphere Sovereignty

In 1867, Kuyper could articulate the reasons why the church is grounded in creation through a theological metaphor taken from Scripture but his theological argument was not going to persuade the Dutch intellectual and political elites who saw religion as out-dated and divisive. Kuyper would need to develop his incarnational model into a truly *public* theology to argue effectively for the church's welcome participation in society. By 1880,

---

al meer vergeten doet, en als laatste gevolgtrekking feitelijk een loochening van Gods menschwording na zich sleept. Een uitwendige kerk moeten we dus hebben, maar zoo lang haar gedaante met de gestalte van het koningrijk Gods niet samenvalt."

64. Kuyper, *De Menschwording Gods*. Dutch: "getuig dan uit de volheid des Geestes tegen den ongoddelijken geest der wereld en profeteer met heilige geestdrift van den triomf die het Godsrijk wacht . . . over alle velden des levens."

Kuyper was able to accomplish this at the founding of the VU. His speech provides a theoretical or worldview framework in which he publicly argues for the church's place in the institutional fabric of human civic society. Those embarking upon Kuyper's thought as a whole or in any subject will invariably encounter his concept of "sphere sovereignty" which is his unique socio-political theory, an explanation of the ordinances of human life and society which leads to human flourishing in all its multiformity.[65]

Kuyper believed that in God's creation human society is comprised of multiple realms or "spheres" of life (creational institutions such as the family, the state, the school, the arts, etc.).[66] Each of these spheres has its own independent authority, delegated to it directly in pluralist fashion by God rather than via the state or any other intermediary sphere. Each sphere, therefore, has a measure of independent yet relativized and cooperative sovereignty or authority over its unique domain of creational life, all refereed by a neutral state. All together, these multiple spheres make up the richness of human cultural and societal life. And for Kuyper the institutional church is one of these creational structures or spheres in which the unique aspect of "ecclesiastical" or "confessional" life becomes manifest within history and institutionally within society, first as an organic movement of people and then as a public institution.[67] The institutional church is not merely a human social construction that may or may not "fit" depending on the changing winds of cultural or intellectual mood.[68] It is, rather, one of the potential structures of creation, as he says,

65. There are similarities and differences between Kuyper's "sphere sovereignty" and the Roman Catholic social theory of subsidiarity which is addressed in Pope Leo XIII's encyclical *Rerum Novarum* (1891) and Pope Pius XI's encyclical *Quadragesimo Anno* (1931). For a good discussion of these two theories, see Van Til, "Subsidiarity and Sphere-Sovereignty." Jonathan Chaplin has worked to uncover common ground between them in "Subsidiarity and Sphere Sovereignty"; "Subsidiarity"; and his unpublished essay, "Concept of 'Civil Society.'"

66. Heslam argues that "the way in which Kuyper expounded his doctrine of sphere-sovereignty was an area of particular inconsistency" (*CCW*, 20). The main contour of the theory is represented here, as it relates to the church's groundedness in creation. In terms of the main contours of Kuyper's theory of sphere sovereignty and its relationship to John Calvin, see Calvin, *Institutes of the Christian Religion* 3.10.6. Clouser, "Puritanism on Authority," 18, also notes this passage from Calvin as foundational to Kuyper's theory of sphere sovereignty.

67. Eglinton, *Trinity and Organism*, contains significant excavation of Kuyper's use of the organic motif which is compared and contrasted with Bavinck. Eglinton argues that Kuyper's use of the organic metaphor emerges from the Calvinist tradition and not German Idealism. Botha, *Sosio-kulturele metavrae*, 143–46, provides a detailed analysis of the philosophical nature of Kuyper's organic corporate view of humanity and the church, especially in relationship to Herman Dooyeweerd.

68. As Wood correctly captures: "Kuyper argued that though the invisible church

> That perfect and absolute Sovereignty of the sinless Messiah at the same time contains the direct denial and challenge of all absolute Sovereignty on earth in sinful man; because of the division of life into spheres, each with its own Sovereignty.... Thus there is a domain of nature ... also a domain of the personal, of the domestic, of the scientific, of the social, and of the ecclesiastical life; each of which obeys its own law of life, and each subject to its own head.... Now in all these spheres or circles the cogwheels engage one another, and it is precisely because of the mutual interaction of these spheres that there is an emergence of that rich, many-sided, multi-formed human life.[69]

Kuyper is arguing that divinely created human life has an inherent multiformity of capacities which necessitates a plurality of cultural institutions for their expression, each uniquely suited to the various aspects and agencies of human life, but each with an independence which guards the boundaries of each sphere against intrusion from the others. It is this rich social fabric that contributes to human flourishing and functions to safeguard a just society through a middle realm of social institutions between the state and the individual (often called civil society).[70]

Kuyper's argument for the institutional church's place within society, therefore, is based on this framework. It is rooted in a conviction that God has instituted a plurality of creational potencies which give rise to a plurality of societal institutions to mediate the various arenas of human activity. And each of these spheres has its own unique creational norm or mandate or life/root-principle especially suited to it.[71] The church, consequently, has its own structural place in society apart from the permission or authority granted to it (or not) by any other sphere. This means that theoretically the church is inherently free from intrusion from a neighboring sphere and

---

had existed since creation, the church institution had not" (*GD*, 145).

69. Kuyper, "Sphere Sovereignty" (*AKCR*, 467).

70. Bacote, "Abraham Kuyper's Rhetorical Public Theology," 413–14, argues this same point—that Kuyper's theory of sphere sovereignty creates a structural pluralism in which humanity can flourish.

71. Wolters, *Creation Regained*, 15–16, discusses what to call the divine laws that norm creation. On this, see also *AKASPI*, 28–49. Wolterstorff, *Hearing the Call*, 275, critiques this legal emphasis in the Reformed tradition by saying that "among those philosophical frameworks which have emerged within the Reformed tradition in our century, the most prominent has spoken much of law, of creation ordinances, and of cultural mandates, but has said nothing about a liberation mandate.... In our century the Reformed tradition *has* often been oppressive in practice." This will be an important observation when we later consider the appropriation of Kuyper's thinking in the twentieth century in other parts of the world beyond the Netherlands.

is not required to justify its existence, ministry, or mission before another sphere. Only in cases where one sphere oversteps its legitimate boundary and impinges upon the authentic functioning of another might the state be justified in stepping in and limiting the functioning of a particular sphere so as to allow another sphere to also have the necessary freedom to function. This means that the church is a structurally-given component of human culture and society with an integrity of its own. In its own sphere, it has been delegated a certain sovereignty that may not be infringed upon by any other sphere.

This is the framework within which Kuyper grounds the church in the potentials of creation, becoming manifest as an institution historically under God's providence and human agency. The church is neither alien nor dispensable but a creational structure of human life and society for a particular confessional purpose.[72] What we begin to discern here is that while the mandate or function of the ecclesial sphere within creation is suited to the confessional aspect of human life, this is not an aspect of human life sequestered to the private margins of cultural life or human subjectivity. Rather, the confessional aspect (or as Kuyper sometimes refers to it, the "religious sphere") of human life is public and universal.[73] Consequently, the church has an open and constructive posture toward the other domains of civic life. The institutional church, while having a unique role, is nonetheless an integral part of civil society alongside a host of other equally-valid institutions.[74]

Summary

Kuyper's ecclesiology orients the church toward the world by grounding the church structurally in God's creation as a sphere with its own divinely-given authority. Akin to the Incarnation of Jesus Christ, the church is the manifestation in human society of the renewing life force of God. As a part of human culture, the church is a legitimate institution of human society. It is not a privileged realm nor the only important realm, but neither is it

---

72. According to Wood, Kuyper at one point considered the institutional church dispensable though his later ecclesiology emphasized the necessity of it (*GD*, 89). Again, this is an example of Kuyper's inconsistency related to the occasional nature of his work.

73. Dooyeweerd, *Roots of Western Culture*, 44–46, refers to this as "sphere universality." Venema, "Abraham Kuyper," 87, 91, also addresses this topic.

74. Sphere Sovereignty provided the impetus for the development of a unique way of viewing the plural structure of civil society, a topic a number of Kuyperian authors have addressed. For an excellent survey, including both primary and secondary source material, see Skillen and McCarthy, *Political Order*, 227–354.

a dispensable or an unnecessary realm. In this way, Kuyper lays a foundation for the church embedded in and responsible to its historical and cultural context. As a Calvinist, Kuyper confesses the church as a unique institution for God's redemption of creation and the official transmission of God's special grace. Yet for Kuyper, this is not achieved through withdrawal from the fallen world. The church accomplishes its redemptive mandate by being directly suited for humanity's universal religious impulse, an institution grounded in the fabric of society, unfolding in history, and having an independent sovereignty while simultaneously being woven into the social fabric of human culture. God in Christ is interested in more than the redemption of individuals; God is also concerned with the creational flourishing of communities and human society as a whole.

But, clearly, the church has a complex nature. One can refer to the church as a building or a hierarchy with official pronouncements. One can also refer to the church as a people, a movement, an historical community. This brings us to Kuyper's second most important ecclesiological contribution: the distinction between the visible church as both an organism and an institution, a distinction we've already touched upon but to which we now turn with special attention.

The Church Is an Organism and an Institution

Kuyper believed that the church is ontologically part of creation and therefore must always be existentially embedded in the public structure and multiform fullness of creation. This is his point in his theory of sphere sovereignty. The church is one sphere among many in the structure of God's creation of human society. We now turn to his distinction between the church as an organism and as an institution, which is possibly one of the most theologically creative and important developments within Calvinist/Reformed ecclesiology.[75]

In terms of Kuyper's church reform efforts and eventual secession from the NHK, consider the historical question Kuyper faced with the NHK's loss of cultural privilege in Dutch society as well as the resulting plurality of church bodies during his lifetime: How could the church be both an objective societal institution (in Kuyper's case, based on personal confession of orthodox faith in Jesus Christ) as well as a voluntary community exerting its moral force for the good of Dutch culture (again, in Kuyper's case, that

---

75. Wood connects this distinction to a "harmonizing" which took place in Kuyper's ecclesiology once the GKN had been formed out of the NHK in the mid-1880s (*GD*, 27).

does not withdraw from the public arena into personal piety, mysticism, or other-worldly sectarianism)? That is, how can the church maintain public universality as well as doctrinal purity in the midst of democratizing forces? Is it possible for the church to be culture-engaging as well as voluntary in the pluralistic and democratic modern world? For Kuyper, the answer was emphatically in the affirmative. And his career would personally embody this theological distinction between the church as an institution and an organism.

It is at the nexus of these crucial ecclesial, societal, and cultural questions where we begin to see the degree to which Kuyper's ecclesiology was truly world engaging.[76] But this posture of the church towards the world would not be at the cost of doctrinal purity. Kuyper advocated for a strong institutional church of sacraments and the ministry of proclamation of the Word, the church's institutional mode-of-being. But Kuyper also argued that the church exists as the people of God, formed as a voluntary community, and sent into the whole of the world to be the continuing presence of Christ in every occupation, institution, and way of life in a culture, the church's organic mode-of-being.[77] In order to achieve this, however, Kuyper needed to find a way to theologically support these two modes of the church's existence as well as to work out how they related to each other.

Kuyper would formulate this solution ecclesiologically by the time he reached Amsterdam in 1870: the essence of the church was its organic life in mystical union with Christ and this organic essence of the church comes to necessarily visible temporal expression in the institutional church.[78] By emphasizing this essential organic core of the church, Kuyper would be able to advocate for the doctrinal purity of the organic church. And by

---

76. Heslam rightly captures that "Kuyper's concept of the church was . . . a wide one, encompassing all Christian activity and influence in the world. The world was the church's sphere of activity and the church was called to establish the sovereignty of Christ in the world" (*CCW*, 132–33).

77. Wood points to this as the "improvisation" which Kuyper engaged in by which he was to "reconcile the internal and external aspects of the church . . . in a reciprocal relationship" (*GD*, 4).

78. As we noted above, Kuyper does allow for a mediating expression of the "visible organic" church which includes voluntary associations of Christians in the various spheres of life (Christian labor unions, Christian art guilds, Christian university faculties, etc.), independent from the institutional church. Wolterstorff argues against Kuyper here by wanting to hold the organic and the institutional together more equally: "The church is to gather for the celebration of the liturgy, and when it is dispersed it is to practice and struggle for justice and to spread the word about its Lord. When one of these is thought to be closer to the essence of the church than the other, aberration has set in; and that aberration always shows itself in distortion of that very activity that was thought to reveal the essence" (Wolterstorff, *Hearing the Call*, 40).

emphasizing the necessarily visible temporal expression of the institutional church, Kuyper would be able to advocate for the world engagement of the institutional church. Heslam argues that it was through this distinction that Kuyper was able to advance both his cultural-political agenda as well as his church-reformist strategies.[79] While Heslam might appear at first glance to be imputing subversive or utilitarian motives to Kuyper's ecclesiology, he is correct that through Kuyper's prioritization of the organic essence of the church, he was able to theologically articulate the link between the church institution (which, on its own, tends toward sectarianism) and the church organic (which, on its own, tends toward the obsolescence of the institutional form of the church within society) and fully achieve both an orthodox and a universal church.[80] Kuyper himself was a prime example of this in action, not only through his move into politics but also in his church reform/secession advocacy.

Justifying Ecclesial Secession

Kuyper challenged the cultural and political privilege that the NHK enjoyed even after the dissolution of the Dutch Republic in 1795 and the official disestablishment of the Dutch Reformed Church.[81] In Kuyper's mind, even though the NHK was never an officially-established state church, the problem with the NHK was that because of the cultural privilege given to it as a national (though not established) church with an establishment history, it had an ambiguous character. Was it an orthodox church of genuine Christian believers or the cultural/ethnic expression of the Dutch nation as a religious institution? The answer depended on one's prior commitments, it seemed. Thus, Kuyper's church-renewal project necessitated him navigating the multiple ecclesiological agendas being set before the NHK prior to the GKN's secession/formation in 1886.

There were three main alternatives, all related to this question of how to balance the church's universality versus the church's confessional holiness (or, the church's cultural dominance versus its doctrinal purity). First, the modernist (or spiritualist) option saw the church as a temporary historical

---

79. *CCW*, 134.

80. *CCW*, 135; Venema, "Abraham Kuyper," 84.

81. Wolterstorff rightly observes that Kuyper and those "who stand in the line of the Reformers cannot follow them but must engage in serious rethinking. For one thing, the Constantinianism that medieval and mainline Reformers both assumed has collapsed—I mean, that arrangement whereby the company of the baptized was coterminous with the company of the citizens. And second, in almost all areas of the world the church itself is deeply fragmented" (Wolterstorff, *Hearing the Call*, 343–44).

and institutional phase with the state gradually taking over the role of providing society with authority and meaning in life that had previously been provided by the church.[82] Christian faith would become completely voluntary, making it thereby ethical, individualistic, and subjective. A second alternative was the impulse to organize and control the institutional and organizational structure of the church more tightly along the lines of the hierarchical model of the Roman Catholic church. A third option, the option for which Kuyper advocated, was to set the church free from hierarchical state control and subsidy, allowing the church the freedom to come to authentic expression organically and independently, with the resulting need of discerning how to hold together both the organic and institutional aspects of a democratic free church in this new dynamic life-phase. A free church, rather than being a separatist, sectarian body of Christian withdrawal from society, Kuyper argued, would be a universal culture-engaging church, addressing the gospel to all areas of cultural life through its organic mode of being while simultaneously remaining a community of pure orthodox doctrine and lifestyle in its institutional mode of being.

We ought to remember that Kuyper was raised in a struggling minister's family and trained in theological modernism that together meant that he was ambivalent about the institutional church when he began his own ministry. It was the organic church, the church of ethical or mystical subjectivism, to which he was committed. But it was his exposure to the Anglo-Catholic Oxford Movement through Charlotte Yonge's novel *The Heir of Redclyffe* and his early encounters in the Dutch village of Beesd with the pious conventicles of the ordinary country folk rooted in orthodox Calvinism which impressed upon Kuyper the importance of subjective conversion, personal faith, and holy congregations.[83] And it was his church reformist intentions, after witnessing the destructive influence of theological modernism, which impressed upon Kuyper the need to tend faithfully to the institutional manifestation and life of the church in civic life. As such, up until the *Dolientie* secession from the NHK to form the GKN, Kuyper had numerous reasons to be committed to the church as an organism. But by the mid-1860s, Kuyper would be forced to become more attentive to and

---

82. Kuyper's main Modernist opponent was Joannes Henricus Scholten at the University of Leiden who was deeply committed to Kantian German philosophy. See Berkhof, *Two Hundred Years of Theology*, 98–103. For background on Kuyper's attacks on Modernism, see *AKMCCD*, 28–33.

83. For accounts of Kuyper's personal experience of Christian conversion and how this affected his theological orientations, see his autobiographical account in Kuyper, "Confidentially." See also *GD*, 22–25, 42; *AKMCCD*, 38–41; Wagenman, *Engaging the World*, 11–26.

concerned about the institutional church as well. It would not be until 1870 when Kuyper would be fully able to explain how the church as organism and institution existed as unique aspects of the church's being and also in relation to each other. It is through the use of two sets of metaphors that Kuyper would go on to elucidate his ecclesiology regarding the church's two modes of being: the church is rooted and grounded; and the church is the bearer of the light and salt of the gospel into the world.

The Church Is Rooted (Organism) and Grounded (Institution)

After leaving the church in Utrecht, it is Kuyper's inaugural sermon in Amsterdam (1870) wherein he clearly sets forth the distinction between the church's organic and institutional modes of being. Kuyper argues that, theologically, one must not give into "surrendering either the church as an organism or the church as an institution, [but] we must unite them both in the free church."[84]

Basing his argument on a unique interpretation of Ephesians 3:16-17 ("I pray that, according to the riches of his glory, he may grant that you may be strengthened in your inner being with power through his Spirit, and that Christ may dwell in your hearts through faith, as you are being *rooted and grounded* in love" [NRSV][85]), Kuyper argues that the church's "rootedness" is its organic life in mystical union with Christ and its "groundedness" is its institutional life within a particular history, culture, and society. The organic life of the church is its "natural [divine] growth . . . a force that comes to outward expression from the inside."[86] But, he explained, "The church not only grows, but [it] is also *built*" by human hands—this is the church's institutional life.[87] Yet these are not two churches or a church within a church. Rather, Kuyper explains that these are the two modes of the single church's being, tied inextricably together in a dynamic relationship, which is "not accidental but normative."[88] The "church of the Lord is one loaf, dough that rises according to its nature [organism] but nevertheless [is] kneaded with human hands, and baked like bread [institution]."[89] Like yeast, the organic life of the church is that which "operates instinctively . . . [coming]

84. *R&G*, 3.
85. Kuyper's emphasis. Kuyper's interpretation of this passage is especially allegorical and, therefore, open to criticism.
86. *R&G*, 4-5.
87. *R&G*, 5.
88. *R&G*, 6.
89. *R&G*, 5.

automatically into being" under divine providence in history with the family, the life of society, and the state being other examples besides the church of this creational phenomenon.[90] And in the case of the church, "eternal election is the heart blood of her life, and God's Word the foundation that cannot be dislodged."[91]

The institutional side of the church's being, on the other hand, comes to temporal manifestation when this divine life-force "awakens in self-consciousness" within history, taking on a "regulating" role "by means of ideas" and human progress.[92] It is the role of the institutional church "to give form to this [organic] life" like a body gives to a soul, a judicial institution gives to justice, that which the nation of Israel gives to God's revelation in the Old Testament, or which the Incarnation gives to the Second Person of the Trinity.[93] The institutional mode of the church's being is that necessary legal manifestation that safeguards the organic life of the church from degenerating into chaos and confusion. The institutional nature of the church provides "an organization that regulates the mandate for everything that happens."[94]

Being two modes of the single church's being, these two modes interpenetrate and reciprocally influence each other. As Kuyper says, "*From* the organism the institution is born, but also *through* the institution the organism is fed."[95] Drawing on Calvin's metaphor of the church as the mother of believers,[96] Kuyper says that the organic and institutional aspects of the church work together: as her "womb granted us life, her care nurtures us."[97] In other words, "The organism is the essence, the institution is the form."[98] But rather than the institutional side of the church being primary, even though the "church cannot lack the institution" and the institutional structure of the church provides necessary nurture to Christian believers, it is rather the organic life-force of the church which is of utmost priority for Kuyper.[99] Should the church find its primary identity in its institutional

90. *R&G*, 8. For the similar ways in which other scholars of Kuyper's era viewed and applied the concept of the organic, see *AKMCCD*, 239–58.

91. *R&G*, 33.

92. *R&G*, 8.

93. *R&G*, 13, 14.

94. *R&G*, 14.

95. *R&G*, 15.

96. Calvin's discussion of the church as the mother of Christian believers can be found in his *Institutes of the Christian Religion* 4.1.4–5.

97. *R&G*, 15.

98. *R&G*, 17.

99. *R&G*, 14.

manifestation, this, for Kuyper, would be equal to placing human efforts to build the church before God's sovereign and electing grace which must always be affirmed as a priority. Thus, it is eternal divine election in which the church is rooted, "or as the apostle expresses it here [Eph 3:17], she is rooted in [God's] *love*" which is "the heart of the church."[100] "The institution alone never constitutes the church.... A church cannot be manufactured; a polity, no matter how tidy, and a confession, no matter how spotless, are powerless to form a church if the living organism is absent."[101] As Wood nicely summarizes Kuyper on this point, "the institution... [is] the tangible expression of the organism."[102]

Bearer of the Light and Salt of the Gospel into the World

If we follow Kuyper as he makes this ecclesial distinction between the church's organic and institutional modes of being, a question should immediately form in our minds: if the church is a dynamic unity of its organic and institutional modes of being, the organic mode of the church having the priority and the institutional mode serving the organic, then how does the church truly orient itself to the world without compromising its orthodox essence and identity? Or, to put the question another way: if the organic essence of the church becomes manifest as a public institution of Christian orthodoxy, then how does this distinction move the church toward universal world-engagement without sacrificing its orthodoxy? That is, how can you have both civic universality and confessional orthodoxy? On its own, this distinction between institution and organism doesn't appear to serve Kuyper's larger cultural aim of the church being oriented toward the world. It still appears to leave the door open to the institutional church moving toward world-withdrawal and sectarianism or the organic church moving away from confessional orthodoxy.

The answer Kuyper offers is that not only is the church simultaneously rooted and grounded, given and built, organism and institution, but the church, as both organism and institution united together, has a redemptive telos: it is the bearer of the light and salt of the gospel to the world. The church in Kuyper's ecclesiology is orthodox, universal, and only as such is it

---

100. *R&G*, 11.

101. *R&G*, 11–12.

102. *GD*, 63. Kuyper also addresses the church as institute and organism in Kuyper, "Common Grace," 187–201. *FCHN* contains a good summary of the issue as well; Bolt argues that "Kuyper's use of this distinction is not entirely consistent and without ambiguity" and that it is "a highly abstract distinction" anyway (*FCHN*, 427).

therefore able to be God's agent of renewal in the world. Kuyper argued this in his second Stone lecture:

> To be sure, there is a concentration of religious light and life in the Church, but then in the walls of this church, there are wide open windows, and through these spacious windows the light of the Eternal has to radiate over the whole world. Here is a city, set upon a hill, which every man can see afar of. Here is a holy salt that penetrates in every direction, checking all corruption.[103]

These words capture the inherent dynamic between the two modes of the church's being in the world, as both organism and institution, and it relates as well to Kuyper's understanding of the intention built into the nature of the church. In the way Kuyper utilizes the metaphor of light and salt, in relation to the nature of the church, it is not the bricks and mortar of the church building nor the offices of its hierarchy (institution) in the midst of society which effect God's gracious influence in the world. Instead, it is the believing and worshipping community assembled in the church's institutional building for worship, equipped and discipled by the institution, which is then sent into the whole of the world in Christ's name as an organism.

Kuyper doesn't mean that the church influences the world as a passerby on the sidewalk outside the church building on a Sunday morning might hear the singing of a hymn of praise to God or hear a sentence or two of the sermon rooted in Scripture as the preacher's voice carries out the window. Rather, what Kuyper has in mind here is the way in which the church as an institution, the assembled congregation, believing, worshipping, being discipled, is formed through preaching, sacraments, and discipline and then blessed and sent into the world as the church in its organic mode of being by which the church will organically spread throughout the whole of humanity to accomplish this influencing work. To state it again, this is the institutional mode of the church's being serving the organic mode of the church's being so that the organic church can have universal Christian influence. But once again, while we see here Kuyper's prioritization of the organic over the institutional mode of the church's being, we also observe how both aspects of the church (institution and organism) are both oriented to the world. The institutional church is indirectly oriented toward the world while it is the organic mode which does this directly.

This is what Kuyper is illustrating when he uses the word "concentration" when speaking "of religious light and life in the Church." This light is concentrated in corporate worship (the church as an institution) and then dispersed and refracted during the rest of life, in the whole of life, through

---

103. *LC*, 63.

the various callings and occupations of each Christian as they go about their regular weekly routines or in the free associations (guilds and societies) of Christians banded together corporately in particular occupational or cultural arenas (the church as an organism). Thus, it is this gathering (institution) and sending (organism) dynamic which Kuyper then applies to the "city, set upon a hill" whose light radiates throughout the world or the "salt that penetrates in every direction."[104]

Kuyper is picking up on the dynamics inherent within both biblical metaphors of light and salt and through them is making explicit the church's foundational orientation to the world. The church is a concentration (gathered as institution) that is then dispersed throughout a larger space, penetrating the whole from the center (sent as organism). The light of the city shines in the darkness to the most remote distance. And the arresting power of the salt, once spread through the entirety of the meat, does its "checking" work against "all corruption." This is a dynamic that breaks down if either aspect of the dynamic is eliminated, either the gathering or sending or, by implication, the institution or organism. If the light remains hidden within the city walls or if the salt remains in the shaker, it is of no effect. Likewise, if the source of the light is extinguished, its rays may travel but will soon fade away; if the storehouse of salt runs empty, the salt that has been used up will lose its saltiness and no longer perform its necessary function. Therefore, both concentration (gathered institution) and extension (sent organism) must take place in a living, dynamic rhythm for the metaphor to function and the meaning to remain intact. The church in both of its modes of being, as an institution and as an organism, are equally important, though, as we've already observed, there is a logical and *theo*logical priority given to the organic mode of the church. But such a church, a church that bears the light and salt of the Christian gospel, is a church that is not only embedded in but also engaged with its context. What we observe here is Kuyper's redefinition of what is meant by the church's universality. The modernist camp had understood universality as the church's incorporation all members of Dutch society into the church's institutional membership with the resulting loss of doctrinal purity. Instead, Kuyper means that the church is that elect *gathering* of orthodox Christian believers as an institution which is apostolically *sent universally* into all the world as an organism.

---

104. Wolterstorff, *Hearing the Call*, uses the metaphor of respiration (19) and heartbeat to explain Kuyper's point here: "The best image I have for expressing the connection is the image of a heartbeat: systolic and diastolic. The church assembles and it disperses. In both its assembling and its dispersing it is living before the face of God, but in two different ways.... You can't have a heartbeat without having both the systolic and the diastolic phases" (417).

Summary

This is Kuyper's second main ecclesiological contribution which prepares us for analyzing the power of the institutional church. The church is an observable public institution within society as well as an organism universally spread through the culture. The church is that holy concentration (assembled for corporate worship) and universal extension (apostolically sent into the whole of the world) of God's grace, through which "God regenerates us,—that is to say he rekindles in our heart the lamp sin had blown out."[105] In the rapidly evolving cultural context of Kuyper's day, this distinction between the church as organism and institution was the way in which Kuyper could advocate for a free church of voluntary participation following personal profession of orthodox Christian faith and doctrinal purity without sliding into sectarian withdrawal from the world. A free church gathered for the proclamation of God's Word, celebration of the sacraments, and church discipline would be equipped and universally sent as an agent of God's redeeming and renewing grace in the world. The church is a theologically pure and orthodox institution for the worship of God and the discipling of Christian believers in the faith as well as a universal organism that penetrates every aspect of culture with Christian influence.[106] Such an ecclesial understanding helps us to understand the reasons for Kuyper's move from official church ministry to his other cultural pursuits in which he sought to influence his culture with the resources of the Christian faith. And through Kuyper's various efforts, theologically and personally, the church in Holland would be safeguarded from disappearing from the cultural landscape. This was Kuyper's intention. Did he accomplish this task? This raises the question of Kuyper's legacy and its historical irony.

CONCLUSION: THE HISTORICAL IRONY OF KUYPER'S LEGACY

What was the historical-cultural result of Kuyper's many cultural endeavours? Did the institutional church, due to Kuyper's reforms, remain visible and influential or did it disappear? How would one even decide how to answer such a question considering the numerous factors involved (ecclesial, political, academic, cultural, etc.)? Legacy is an ambiguous and deeply

---

105. *LC*, 69.

106. Wood refers to this as Kuyper's strategy to influence the broader culture for Christ through "the hearts of individuals, that is, the members of the congregation, not through the church as an [official civic] institution" (*GD*, 51).

subjective concept.¹⁰⁷ Does one point to his political legacy and the six ARP Prime Ministers in the Netherlands after Kuyper?¹⁰⁸ Or, does one look to his legislative legacy in which equal state funding for confessional and public schools (the issue which brought Kuyper into politics initially) became law? Or, does one look at Kuyper's immediate theological legacy in Herman Bavinck, J. H. Bavinck, and G. C. Berkouwer? Or yet again, do we point to the numerous Christian cultural institutions that, as noted above, were exported to North America (among other locales) in the mid-twentieth century and flourished there for a time? Kuyper made significant and positive contributions in a number of cultural arenas. But considering only these positive effects would ignore the others: the progressive decline of Kuyper's ARP which never garnered more than 20 percent of the legislature after his leadership of the party, the rapid secularization of Dutch society in the mid-twentieth century, and the near-disappearance of the institutional church in the popular Dutch imagination during the mid- to late-twentieth century. Would one not have assumed that following Kuyper's tireless cultural influence and the spawning of diverse Christian institutions that the church he strove to bequeath to his nation (or the world) would have had a different history in its home soil?¹⁰⁹

This is the historical irony of Kuyper's legacy: that following apparently effective Christian cultural work, Kuyper's GKN was unable to stem the tide of secularizing change within a single lifetime. And for our purposes, this only heightens the tension surrounding our question. What *is* the power of the church if it does not result in rising church attendance or membership statistics, lasting Christian political influence, or sustained godly cultural

---

107. After considering a number of possibilities, Bratt writes in a blog post that Kuyper's legacy can best be described as offering to his day a "faithful witness" to Christianity in the public arena, even though he does not "think we can capture Kuyper's purpose or legacy in one image" (Bratt, "Kuyper's Legacy").

108. The seven ARP Prime Ministers in the Netherlands (prior to the ARP merging with other parties to form the Christian Democratic Appeal in 1974, who produced the three Prime Ministers of Jan Peter Balkenende [2002–2010], Ruud Lubbers [1982–1994], and Dries van Agt [1977–1982]) were Barend Biesheuvel (1971–1973), Jelle Zijlstra (1966–1967), Pieter Sjoerds Gerbrandy (1940–1945), Hendrikus Colijn (1925–1926, 1933–1939), Theo Heemskerk (1908–1913), Abraham Kuyper (1901–1905), Aaneas Mackay (1888–1891).

109. Kennedy, "Problem of Kuyper's Legacy," contains a fair evaluation of Kuyper's political legacy, considering the historical and ideological context of mid-twentieth-century Europe. He not only argues that Kuyper's personality and the zeal of his overbearing followers alienated Kuyper from the following generations, but also that Kuyper's efforts had created an institutionalized conservative Calvinist sub-culture which had become disconnected from its ideological and confessional roots and no longer fit with the ecumenical and global mood of fifty years later.

change? Kuyper's ecclesial vision is one in which the institutional church is robust and has a significant position of cultural prominence through its influence on the academy, the state, and the media. And yet, from our historical vantage point, this sort of prominence doesn't seem to be very powerful, at least not in the longer term. These kinds of reflections only serve to make our question of the power of the institutional church even more poignant and necessary. In addition, this raises the critical question of whether Kuyper's ecclesiology has truly been received by the tradition that bears his name, even to this day. Kuyper's legacy may be phenomenal but it must be *received* to remain alive and effective.

In his day, Abraham Kuyper witnessed the beginnings of the near disappearance of the church from Dutch culture and popular imagination. In response, he took the received Dutch Calvinist tradition and adapted it to meet the challenges presented by modernism, liberalism, and the growing secularized power of the state over all the arenas of human cultural and societal life. He did this by theologically grounding the church within the doctrine and fabric of creation in his theory of sphere sovereignty. And he made a distinction between the two modes of the church's being: the church as a civic institution and the church as an organism or movement of Christians spread through the whole of life so that the Christian faith might have a comprehensive influence in every aspect of society. Up until 1886, Kuyper had focused his attention on the reform of the institutional church to meet these challenges. Then, around this time, Kuyper must also have begun to believe that the disappearance of the church's influence was not only an ecclesial problem to be addressed but a socio-political problem as well. The Christian faith's marginalization was being aided by *state legislation*. And so, Kuyper entered, slowly at first and then with great energy, the political arena to secure for the church, for the Christian faith, and for Christian people an enduring place within the culture.

The historical irony of Kuyper's ecclesiology and personal efforts is that while his ecclesiology aims to equip the church to be an institution able to respond to the challenges of its particular context, Kuyper's personal efforts after the late 1870s flow almost entirely out of the church as an organism. Kuyper's connection to the institutional church after 1886 is slim.[110] It is an open historical question but one which makes our analysis of the power of the institutional church all the more urgent: could it be that, because of Kuyper's focus on the organic church and the consequent lack of attention to the church as a civic institution, he was undermining his own

---

110. According to Bratt, at some point, Kuyper even stopped attending public worship on Sunday mornings. He would often send his wife and children to church without him so he could remain at home and write in peace and quiet (*AKMCCD*, 129).

efforts of public Christian influence? Maybe the older Kuyper immersed in politics needs to remember what the younger Kuyper of the pulpit, like Spurgeon, knew the power of the church to truly be. In order to wrestle with just this question, the power of the institutional church, it is to the landscape of Kuyper's worldview, in which we find his thoughts on the power of the church to lie, that we turn now.

4

Sovereignty, Authority, and Power

Abraham Kuyper's Worldview

IN 1924, THE FIRST (also known as The Peoples') Methodist Church of Chicago was built. It stretched 568 feet (173 metres) into the air and was (and still is) the tallest church building in the whole world, not to mention the Windy City. It towered over the Chicago City Hall, the center of Chicago's political life, just across the street. In fact, it remained the tallest building in all of Chicago for almost seventy-five years until 1949 when a series of expansive post-war building projects took place across the United States, mostly in New York and Chicago. Today, nearly a century after its construction, the First Methodist Church of Chicago is dwarfed by three of the world's tallest buildings nearby (the John Hancock Center, the Amaco Building, and the Willis/Sears Tower), all imposing structures of insurance, oil, and retail corporations.

Interpreting and commenting on this architectural history, Clinton Stockwell says that today the "modern corporation has superseded not only cathedrals of ecclesiastical traditions, but even the authority and power of nations and states. . . . In short, the modern corporation has redefined the whole question of power in modern society."[1] These giant buildings which dot our urban mega-centers are more than displays of architectural or financial success. Rather, they evoke something ominous. He argues that

---

1. Stockwell, "Cathedrals of Power," 81.

the general population today views institutions, especially institutions with sizeable cultural power, as displayed in the size of their buildings, as working *against* people rather than *for* people.[2] The contemporary West's corporate buildings are the cathedrals of yesteryear. "Cathedrals, secular or religious, are institutional manifestations of power and authority. Many people are afraid, or timid, about power. But power is an omnipresent reality."[3]

One question that Stockwell doesn't address is *how* a building's size relates to its popularly perceived power. What is the mechanism by which people view the corporate Willis/Sears Tower (standing at 1,729 feet, or 527 metres) as having more cultural power than the First Methodist Church (less than a third the height)? Or, a related question: what makes the size of a corporate structure equate to the degree of its evil? Craig Bartholomew points to *worldview* which functions to interpret our place in the world for us. Worldview, he says, is "a person's or community's . . . pretheoretical orientation toward life which interprets the world and prescribes how to live in it."[4] It is one's worldview that makes sense of the spaces in which we live, distinguishing taller from tallest buildings and the consequent relative cultural importance or power they have. It was assumed within the medieval worldview that higher meant closer to God just as it is assumed within the modern worldview that taller means more successful which means more powerful.

Worldview is an important concept in the Kuyperian tradition.[5] Wolters has defined worldview as "the comprehensive framework of one's basic beliefs about things" which "functions as *a guide to our life*."[6] Bratt concludes that Kuyper would define it as an interpretive "framework set by our answers to ultimate questions."[7] Heslam's definitive study of Abraham Kuyper's *Lectures on Calvinism* captures the importance of worldview in Kuyper's life and thought by incorporating the term into the title of his text.[8] Kuyper himself may have obtained the concept from James Orr whose Kerr lectures were published in 1887, just a few short years before Kuyper made the trip from Holland to Princeton in 1898 for his Stone lectures.[9] In his first lecture, Orr defines the German *Weltanschauung* in

2. Stockwell, "Cathedrals of Power," 84–85.
3. Stockwell, "Cathedrals of Power," 85.
4. Bartholomew, *Where Mortals Dwell*, 185.
5. See Walsh and Middleton, *Transforming Vision*.
6. Wolters, *Creation Regained*, 2, 5.
7. *AKMCCD*, 341.
8. See *CCW*.
9. Orr, *Christian View of God*. On Kuyper's knowledge or possession of Orr's work leading up to the Stone lectures, see *AKMCCD*, 207; *CCW*, 92–93.

English as "the widest view which the mind can take of things in the effort to grasp them together as a whole from the standpoint of some particular philosophy or theology."[10] Worldview is an interpretive framework, both for thinking and for living.

Therefore, if one desires to know how one views and understands the world and everything that makes up their world, one will need to attend to their pre-critical worldview. In other words, for our purposes, in order to discern Kuyper's understanding of power generally as well as the power of the church, attention to his worldview, and the place of power within that worldview, is critically important.[11]

In light of the previous chapters, we must now analyze the formative influence of worldview in Abraham Kuyper's approach to the topic of power, both generally as a creational phenomenon and specifically as an ecclesial concept. Not only does Abraham Kuyper's ecclesiology emerge from his worldview but his understanding of sovereignty, authority, and power are also deeply rooted in his Calvinist view of God and the world. In this chapter and the next our analysis must proceed, therefore, by specifically discerning the power of the church in Kuyper's worldview and ecclesiology. In this chapter, we begin with Kuyper's worldview generally in which we discover his view of sovereignty, authority, and power. Then, in the next chapter, we will turn to the specific matter of *ecclesial* power in Kuyper.

UNRESOLVED QUESTIONS ABOUT POWER

In light of the history of philosophical and theological reflection on power (Chapter 2), one observation that we can make is that the general tendency of the various conceptual approaches to power conceive of power as a single episodic entity which becomes manifest in human life in various observable ways. In response to the question, What is power?, most theories tend towards abstraction or reductionism to view power as a generic singular force which is causally effective or normative despite challenges or obstacles.

This ontologically unitary starting point raises a number of difficult and unresolved questions for theories of power.[12] For example, is the most

---

10. Orr, *Christian View of God*, 3.

11. Farrow, *Ascension and Ecclesia*, 41, argues convincingly that "Cosmologies and ecclesiologies are linked." I take cosmology and worldview to be synonymous for our purposes.

12. Koyzis concurs, arguing: "The assumption is that power is a single, continuous entity subject to a zero-sum distribution or competition. If someone increases her possession of power, it must be at another's expense. Yet, this masks the genuine complexity in the distribution of what should more properly be called *powers* (in the plural) throughout an ordinary society" (Koyzis, *We Answer to Another*, 97).

salient distinction truly between manifestations of power that are creative versus those which are coercive?[13] Is the power utilized by the state essentially the same as the power of a school or a church or a family, except for its differences in manifestation due to each particular context? Does neutral effective force (i.e., power) exist prior to its actual manifestation in willing action? In short, does "power," stripped of its particular existential manifestations, even exist or have theories treated power merely as an abstraction without close attention to its various unique manifestations? Could it be possible that the tendency towards theoretical agnosticism on the nature of power is due to the abstract way in which power is conceived apart from its actual existence in a variety of different arenas?

As we begin our analysis of the worldview of Abraham Kuyper as it relates to power and authority, two initial claims can be advanced which begin to set the stage for how worldview functioned for Kuyper. First, we ought to reject the singular ontological understanding of power in favour of a creational multiform approach. Kuyper argued that it was the false view of "Modernism, which denies and abolishes every difference . . . putting every distinction on a common level, kills life by placing it under the ban of uniformity. One type must answer for all, one uniform, one position and one and the same development of life."[14] Opposed to this anti-creational uniformity, Kuyper's worldview envisions a multiformity of powers within the diverse spheres and institutions of creation. And because various powers are active and become manifest in different arenas of human life, one must attend to the essentially multiform nature of the powers in creation.[15] While in common discourse, "power" is often spoken of as a naked and neutral force prior to its actual manifestation, this theoretical abstraction is unhelpful in critically distinguishing between the various arenas and forms of power within creation. Rather, as we shall observe in Kuyper's worldview approach, there are different powers at work in different ways in different spheres of life. And this multiform manifestation of creational powers flows from God who is the ultimate source of power's multiform reality. In this way, rather than "power" in abstraction, Kuyper more often prefers to speak about the multiform "powers" of creation (but not in the suprapersonal or supernatural manner of the late-twentieth century, as noted previously).

13. Crouch, *Playing God*.

14. *LC*, 26. Kuyper, "Uniformity," is also an excellent window into Kuyper's argument for creational multiformity.

15. Koyzis, *We Answer to Another*, 82, supports this Kuyperian argument by saying that in the social realm of life "every authoritative claim made upon us is itself subject to higher authority. We are embedded in a pluriformity of overlapping communal contexts, each of which makes an authoritative claim on us."

Second, unitary approaches to power can only work by engaging in reductionism, dualism, or theoretical agnosticism. Theoretical abstractions are examples of reductionist approaches. Crouch's distinction between creative power and coercive power is a form of dualism. And as I addressed in Chapter 2, Lukes's approach is an example of theoretical agnosticism in which power is assumed to be too mysterious or complex as a concept to penetrate too deeply.[16] In the end, all one is left with is a catalogue of power's diverse manifestations. Kuyper advocated an "architechtonic critique" which eschewed reductionism, dualism, or theoretical agnosticism.[17] No matter the topic, Kuyper refused to settle for scholarly resignation in the face of theoretical challenges. When it comes to power, as we shall see, even though Kuyper's theory of power is not as explicit as one might like,[18] it is deeply embedded in his worldview which allows us to interpret his views on power in a way far more clearly than his limited explicit statements on the concept would show. But before analyzing the contours of Kuyper's worldview, and power's place within it, some comments on terminology are in order.

ABRAHAM KUYPER ON SOVEREIGNTY, AUTHORITY, AND POWER

As we observed in Chapter 1, Kuyper is sensitive to issues of power. Prior to embarking on an analysis of his worldview, in which his understanding of the powers in creation is rooted, we need to acknowledge the different ways Kuyper refers to the concept of power. The reason for this is because within Kuyper's worldview, sovereignty, authority, and power are conceived of synonymously even though these terms are typically distinguished from each other in more scholarly works.

We can see this terminological synonymy by returning to Kuyper's "Sphere Sovereignty" address at the founding of the VU in Amsterdam in 1880, a speech introduced earlier. He raises the question of sovereignty's

---

16. One thinks of Martin Luther's reflections about justice: that we make God unjust when we claim to be able to explain his justice with our human concepts of justice. See Luther, *Bondage of the Will*, 65–67. Jacques Ellul summarizes this by saying that "In other words, the more we explain justice the more we obscure it" (*FLP*, 140). Kuyper would not agree, neither regarding justice nor power.

17. Abraham Kuyper introduced this phrase in his *Problem of Poverty*, 50–51. Wolterstorff, *Justice and Peace*, 23, defines "architechtonic critique" as an "analysis and critique of our society, that is, an analysis and critique of its structure and dynamics."

18. Peter Heslam argues that "Kuyper was more prone to characterize intellectual ideas by using broad brush strokes than to subject them to detailed theoretical criticism" (Heslam, "Prophet of a Third Way," 11).

definition directly and in his own response weaves together sovereignty, authority, and power seamlessly:

> What is Sovereignty? Do you not agree when I define it as the authority that has the right, the duty, and the power to break and avenge all resistance to its will? Does not your indestructible folk-conscience tell you too that the original, absolute sovereignty cannot reside in any creature but must coincide with God's majesty? If you believe in Him as Deviser and Creator, as Founder and Director of all things, your soul must also proclaim the Triune God as the only absolute Sovereign. Provided—and this I would emphasize—we acknowledge at the same time that this supreme Sovereign once and still delegates his authority to human beings, so that on earth one never directly encounters God Himself in visible things but always sees his sovereign authority exercised in human office.[19]

We also can observe Kuyper blending these three terms together in his third Stone lecture on "Calvinism and Politics" (1898), when he charts in general the leading functions of each of the various cultural spheres of human activity (addressed further below). Even though he uses different terms, he is clearly referring to the same concept of power:

> The University exercises scientific dominion; the Academy of fine arts is possessed of art-power; the guild exercises a technical dominion; the trades-union rules over labor;—and each of these spheres or corporations is conscious of the power of exclusive independent judgment and authoritative action, within its proper sphere of operation. Behind these organic spheres, with intellectual, aesthetical and technical sovereignty, the sphere of the family opens itself, with its right of marriage, domestic peace, education and possession; and in this sphere also the natural head is conscious of exercising an inherent authority,—not because the government allows it, but because God has imposed it.[20]

Dominion, power, sovereignty, and authority, in Kuyper's mind, all refer to the same core concept. Even Chaplin's summary of Kuyper's theory of sphere sovereignty elides the terms sovereignty and power: "The sovereignty of God issues forth in the diverse laws for each aspect [sphere] of creation. By concentrating a part of his power in each creature God endows it with its

---

19. Kuyper, "Sphere Sovereignty" (*AKCR*, 466).
20. *LC*, 123.

own unique nature and value."[21] As we will see in detail below, these passages contain significant insight into Kuyper's worldview, especially regarding the theocentric nature of power and the differentiation of various powers in creation within a multitude of cultural arenas. But what we must observe at this point, though, is the way in which Kuyper uses the various English words (sovereignty, authority, and power) in his addresses to refer to the same concept. For him, sovereignty is authority and authority is power and power is sovereignty. They are deeply interrelated. How can this be?

Wolterstorff's interpretation of Kuyper on this point recognizes that "Kuyper usually calls this sort of institutional authority 'sovereignty'; on occasion he calls it 'domination' or 'power.'"[22] Wolterstorff reminds us that the Latin *potestas* combines both what English-speakers consider "authority" as well as "power" and therefore Kuyper's practice in this regard is not necessarily a kind of conceptual or terminological imprecision.[23] Rather, Kuyper is giving a normative or cosmological account of a core reality, rooted in his worldview, and utilizing the terms sovereignty, authority, and power to describe how they function within human authority structures and institutions. George Harinck notes that part of the reason behind Kuyper's blending of these three concepts was that "Kuyper wanted to restore the religious interpretation of sovereignty in a post-revolutionary society."[24]

From this vantage point, we must realize the worldview reasons behind Kuyper's unique terminological blending of sovereignty, authority, and power to describe the normative *power structures* within creation's spheres. For example, the *sovereignty* granted to a family by God *authorizes* parents with the right to utilize formative nurturing *power* for the raising of children. Or, the *sovereignty* granted to an educational institution *authorizes* a university professor the *power* to assign grades to student essays. These are the normative authority structures at work within these different institutionalized arenas of human cultural activity. And in this way, Kuyper's references either to sovereignty or to authority or to power are references to a core concept of power which is structured in the multiple spheres of creation. This note on terminology will be important to bear in mind when we turn to the contours of Kuyper's worldview and the place of sovereignty/

---

21. Chaplin, *Herman Dooyeweerd*, 139–40.
22. Wolterstorff, *Mighty and the Almighty*, 161.
23. Wolterstorff, *Mighty and the Almighty*, 161.
24. Harinck, "Historian's Comment," 280. The reason for Kuyper's strategy on this point is that "the object of the French Revolution was to destroy this bond [between God and humanity]. Sovereignty was no longer seen as a religious matter; it was a purely rational matter."

authority/power within it. But first we must consider a key contextual factor in the shaping of Kuyper's worldview on power.

THE ENLIGHTENMENT AS CRITICAL CONTEXT OF KUYPER'S WORLDVIEW

Before we begin our analysis of the contours of Kuyper's worldview, the importance of the ideologies of the Enlightenment, which fuelled the French Revolution, provide the critically important context for understanding Kuyper's view of power.[25] From Holland, Kuyper viewed the events in nearby France as a disaster. There were a number of factors that gave rise to the Enlightenment. Goudzwaard[26] lists seven: (1) rapid advances in science and medicine, (2) economic and geographic expansion, (3) the split between earth (physical) and heaven (spiritual), which meant this earthly existence was the only realm for human self-realization along with the rejection of the church's authority/faith, (4) the overthrow of providence and fate and an intervening God, which made room for human self-direction/destination, and the re-interpretation of doctrine to fit Enlightenment purposes (original sin and total depravity don't engender confident notions of progress),[27] (5) the emergence of "a profound confidence in the possibilities of [humanity's] own rational insight and critical ingenuity"[28] and "This integral and all-encompassing faith in progress on the part of the Enlightenment thinkers can be explained only in terms of their acceptance of the infallible guidance provided by man's critical reason in which all the threads of human existence come together,"[29] (6) the acceptance of the idea of the perfectibility of humanity—not just society—such that Paradise lost can be regained through perfected human activities, leading not only to a perfected humanity but a perfected world, and (7) the result was that a consciousness of progress became a faith in and a plan for further progress—all the ills of the world could be fixed through determined and sustained human effort.[30]

25. We will focus on theological, cultural, and political modernity in this section. But Kuyper also felt that the worldviews of "pantheism," Catholicism, and evolution were dangerous to orthodox Christian faith (*AKMCCD*, 245, 287).

26. See Goudzwaard, *Capitalism and Progress*, 36–44.

27. On the matter of Enlightenment religion, Goudzwaard, *Capitalism and Progress*, 44, notes that "French Enlightenment religion is not a religion in a positive sense of that word. It is in the first place an antireligion, as it attempts to break radically with the Christian religion and with everything dependent on the latter."

28. Goudzwaard, *Capitalism and Progress*, 37.

29. Goudzwaard, *Capitalism and Progress*, 38.

30. Goudzwaard, *Capitalism and Progress*, 43, notes that the overthrow of existing

All of these currents came together to fuel the emergence of the Enlightenment worldview, which Goudzwaard describes as a parody of the Christian faith point by point.[31]

Hendrikus Berkhof provides a summary of the Enlightenment's influence on theology under seven headings: (1) the turn to general revelation instead of special revelation in which the Christian faith is turned into merely an advanced form of human religious consciousness,[32] (2) the introduction of critical approaches to Scripture which erodes Scripture's infallibility and/or authority, making the Bible merely a religious book that is approached using a hermeneutic of suspicion,[33] (3) instead of humanity's relationship to creation being that of steward, creation is seen as a resource to serve humanity's endless desires,[34] (4) instead of a hereditary understanding of original sin in an objective and theocentric sense original sin is personalized to a common awareness of the human failure to utilize freedom responsibly,[35] (5) Old Testament interpretation could no longer serve New Testament dogma but could only be exercised through "historical-literal exegesis,"[36] (6) previous understandings of Jesus "from above" were exchanged for those "from below" which discarded assumptions of divinity, pre-existence, or Chalcedonian doctrines,[37] and (7) the split between church and world and rather than the church seeking to "save" the world the world is seen as a great teacher from whom the church has much to learn.[38]

---

social structures and their replacement with a new political system, a new social order, and a new spiritual ethic were imperative.

31. Goudzwaard, *Capitalism and Progress*, 53.
32. Berkhof, *Christian Faith*, 83. See also Berkhof, *Christ, the Meaning of History*.
33. Berkhof, *Christian Faith*, 96.
34. Berkhof, *Christian Faith*, 171.
35. Berkhof, *Christian Faith*, 210.
36. Berkhof, *Christian Faith*, 231.
37. Berkhof, *Christian Faith*, 271, 292.

38. Berkhof, *Christian Faith*, 416. These seven points are nearly identical to those of Bosch, *Transforming Mission*, 264–67. They are (1) Reason, (2) Subject-Object scheme, (3) Elimination of purpose [telos/eschatology], (4) Progress or Modernization, (5) Knowledge was factual, value-free, and neutral, (6) All problems are in principle solvable, and (7) People as emancipated, autonomous individuals. Schaeffer, *How Should We Then Live?*, 121, summarizes the "utopian dream of the Enlightenment" with the following "five words: reason, nature, happiness, progress, and liberty. It was thoroughly secular in its thinking. The humanistic elements which had risen during the Renaissance came to flood tide in the Enlightenment. Here was man starting from himself absolutely. And if the humanistic elements of the Renaissance stood in short contrast to the Reformation, the Enlightenment was in total antithesis to it. The two stood for and were based upon absolutely different things in an absolute way, and they produced absolutely different results."

The Enlightenment's secularizing influence, based on autonomous human reason and a mechanical approach to fixing the perceived ills of human society, were making their way through Western Europe during Kuyper's lifetime. This influence affected the whole of society, introducing a hermeneutic of suspicion to biblical scholarship, demythologized materialism to theology, liberal State-centrism to politics, and a general mood of licentiousness to culture, etc.[39] Jeffrey Alexander has described modernity as the wedding together of the authority of autonomous reason with the belief that a Golden Age can be manufactured through humanity's technical competence. He writes:

> All complex societies have had myths about the Golden Age. Only in the West, however, did people seriously begin to think that such a new age might occur in this rather than some other fantastical world. . . . The Enlightenment translated these religious and secular strands of perfectionism into the vocabulary of rational progress. . . . Perfectionism is the belief that the human world can become the mirror of the divine. This possibility has defined the idealized essence of modernity. To be modern is to believe that the masterful transformation of the world is possible, indeed that it is likely.[40]

It is this modern combination of reason and technology which stems from the Enlightenment desire to usher in a utopia, he argues, and which bequeathed to the twentieth century the bittersweet juxtaposition of increased comfort and efficiency (for example, mass journalism, mass political enfranchisement, emerging higher education, surprising medical advances, etc.) alongside the disappointment and tragedy of total (and in the twenty-first century, constant) war. Bratt summarizes modernity's basic assumptions: that humanity "had climbed aboard the train of material power drawn by the engine of technological innovation. Its track was said to be laid out by unalterable laws of historical development, and its destination was promised to be a land of unprecedented liberty, plenty, and—consequently—happiness."[41] As such, the Enlightenment is a worldview about the progress of an alternative power and authority—an alternative to the power and authority of religious belief, of the institutional church, of human

---

39. Bratt summarizes the modernism of Kuyper's day by saying that it posed "a wholesale challenge to the established cultural order—an order to which Kuyper too had fundamental objections" (*AKMCCD*, 240). He also acknowledges that theological, cultural, and political modernism were both birthed by the Enlightenment but had differing results, all of which Kuyper sought to address (251, 253).

40. Alexander, *Dark Side of Modernity*, 6.

41. *AKMCCD*, 246.

community within a tradition—to address the lack of knowledge and power perceived to be a barrier to happiness. Alexander charts how the Russian, French, and Chinese revolutions all turned to alternative and revolutionary forms of power in order to correct intractable problems within their societies. Unfortunately, these corrections introduced horrors greater than the original problems.[42]

Max Weber, introduced in Chapter 2, also acknowledged the broken dreams of the Enlightenment worldview. He remarked that "a naïve optimism had led people to glorify science, or rather the techniques of mastering the problems of life based on science, as the road to *happiness* . . . After all, who [still] believes it—apart from some overgrown children in their professorial chairs or editorial offices?"[43] He made the same assessment elsewhere that "the rosy blush of its laughing heir, the Enlightenment, seems . . . to be irretrievably fading."[44]

Therefore, as a Dutch cultural observer (alongside others) at the end of the nineteenth century, Kuyper's worldview inevitably came to perceive and reject this modern alternative,[45] even though Kuyper admits that some Enlightenment cultural developments were positive and even though his life displays some ways in which the Enlightenment had an effect on him.[46] As a Christian seeking to remain faithful to God in the whole of life, in every sector of society, Kuyper addressed a confessionally-rooted view of sovereignty,

---

42. Alexander, *Dark Side of Modernity*, 1, believes that "To say that modernity has been a disappointment would be understating horrors that continue to endanger the very existence of humankind." Likewise, Bosch, *Transforming Mission*, 274, remarks that "the Enlightenment has not solved all our problems. It has in fact created unprecedented new problems, most of which we have only begun to be aware of during the last two decades or so. The Enlightenment was supposed to create a world in which all people were equal, in which the soundness of human reason would show the way to happiness and abundance for all. This did not materialize. Instead, people have become the victims of fear and frustrations as never before." Even Weber, *Protestant Ethic and the Spirit of Capitalism*, 182, remarked that "the rosy blush of its laughing heir, the Enlightenment, seems also to be irretrievably fading."

43. Weber, *Vocation Lectures*, 17.

44. Weber, *Protestant Ethic*, 182.

45. Bratt puts it even more strongly; that "Kuyper attacked nothing so often or strenuously" as modernity (*AKMCCD*, 246).

46. Alexander, *Dark Side of Modernity*, 45–47, comments that Max Weber's larger concerns were that modernity would turn the human being into a depersonalized thing that, via one way or another, would seek to engage in world-flight. In contrast Weber (and Kuyper as well) believed that the human person, "repulsed by world-flight," must discover a vocation that is highly this-worldly. It is interesting in this regard that Kuyper's first public institution founded to counter the influence of the Enlightenment was a university. See Kuyper, "Modernism," 92–96, for his positive evaluation of the Enlightenment's "tragic beauty."

authority, and power to every aspect of culture. He accomplished this by applying his worldview to the perceived issues of his day.

THE CONTOURS OF KUYPER'S WORLDVIEW

We are now ready to engage Kuyper's worldview epistemology.[47] In order to discern Kuyper's understanding of the power of the church, we must first come to an understanding of how Kuyper conceives of power generally. In Chapter 1, we noted the many ways in which Kuyper displays his sensitivity to issues of power, addressing its diverse manifestations repeatedly throughout his career. In addition to the Enlightenment context described above, another reason why power was of such concern to Kuyper is because Kuyper's worldview is a component of his doctrine of creation. This means that Kuyper is chiefly concerned with how the world is in reality rather than in theoretical abstraction or ideological projection.[48] Therefore, by analyzing the contours of Kuyper's worldview we will be able to discern his view of power.[49]

In good Calvinist fashion, Kuyper insists that a worldview that is both true and effective in addressing the issues of life is one that is also comprehensive in scope. Thus, Kuyper's worldview is not limited to a particular view of the church or what might be called "spirituality" but a unique view of the whole of life in all of its diverse interrelatedness. We can see this in Kuyper's first Stone lecture on worldview in which he argues that Calvinism is rooted in a specific kind of consciousness which gives rise not only to a particular doctrine or church polity but also to a particular alternative view of socio-political life, moral values, and the vast array of arenas of human life.[50] He argued that "Calvinism made its appearance, not merely to create a different Church-form, but an entirely different form for human life, to

---

47. Bratt calls worldview Kuyper's "trademark" (*AKMCCD*, 248) and "cornerstone" (341), something which has been preserved more in North American than in Europe (278). In addition to *CCW*; *AKMCCD*, 204–11, contains a good but brief summary of the worldview concept as it functioned for Kuyper.

48. Harink, "Historian's Comment," 281, rightly notes: "When Kuyper explained his idea of sphere sovereignty, he did not talk about *right*, but about the order of *creation*. . . . [For Kuyper] sovereignty has more to do with *responsibility* than with *right*."

49. As *CCW*, 88; *AKMCCD*, 207; Naugle, *Worldview*, note, Kuyper's use of "worldview" is indebted to the work of the Scottish Presbyterian theologian James Orr. The first edition of Orr's Kerr lectures (given in 1891) were published as *The Christian View of God and the* World (1893), just prior to Kuyper's Stone lectures (1898) and very well might have motivated Kuyper to make worldview such a prominent component of his lectures.

50. *LC*, 12.

furnish human society with a different method of existence, and to populate the world of the human heart with different ideals and conceptions."[51] Kuyper's Calvinism is concerned with the *whole world*.

It is this alternative vision of human life and existence in the world that Kuyper names a worldview. And his Calvinist worldview "provides us with such an unity of life-system" which "is such an all-embracing system of principles."[52] In this way, Kuyper's Calvinism is not only a system of dogma, a creedal interpretation, or a denominational marker, but he also calls it a "science" in the philosophical and political sense: "that system of conceptions which, under the influence of the master-mind of Calvin raised itself to dominance in the several spheres of life."[53] As a comprehensive account of reality, then, we can already begin to anticipate the complexity of Kuyper's Calvinistic worldview in which power is embedded. The contours of Kuyper's worldview, particularly as it relates to power, will be presented and analyzed under the following six headings:

- God is the sovereign creator.
- Creation is multiform.
- Creational powers are delegated into separate spheres of the multiform creation.
- Humanity's calling is to develop and steward the multiform powers of creation.
- Each sphere's power has a unique character which norms its action.
- Each sphere limits the powers of the other spheres.[54]

God Is the Sovereign Creator

Kuyper's worldview begins with the Triune God who has ultimate and absolute sovereignty—i.e., power—over his creation by virtue of being the Creator. We can see this foundational belief in two of Kuyper's primary public addresses. In his first Stone lecture, Kuyper firmly places himself not only within the broad sweep of Protestantism but specifically in a Calvinist worldview in which "the general cosmological principle of the sovereignty

---

51. *LC*, 13.
52. *LC*, 16.
53. *LC*, 7.

54. These six headings are rooted in Kuyper's doctrine of creation. The distorting effects of sin are addressed below.

of God" is fundamental.⁵⁵ Kuyper undercuts any claim to supremacy from either prince or bishop, state or church, placing all created persons and institutions under the objective and absolute sovereignty of God, the Creator. The sovereignty of the creator God was also a main focus of Kuyper's 1880 speech on "Sphere Sovereignty" introduced earlier. In that address, Kuyper rhetorically asked, "Does not your indestructible folk-conscience tell you too that the original, absolute sovereignty cannot reside in any creature but *must* coincide with God's majesty? If you believe in Him as Deviser and Creator, as Founder and Director of all things, your soul must also proclaim the Triune God as the only absolute sovereign."⁵⁶ In Kuyper's worldview, the absolute, original power of the Creator God was of utmost importance and was non-negotiable.⁵⁷ This first point is not at all unique, for Kuyper shares this conviction with the broad sweep of Christian theological orthodoxy. But what is unique is how Kuyper deploys this belief in the rest of his worldview.

Creation Is Multiform

Kuyper's worldview begins as one would expect from a Christian theologian: with the sovereign creator God. But then we must consider Kuyper's view of the nature of God's creation, a significant aspect of his worldview. For Kuyper, the nature of God's creation is that it is endlessly diverse or "multiform." This is Kuyper's direct response to his perception that modernity seeks to impose an unnatural and alien uniformity on God's multiform creation. Rather than seeing creation as a static given by God, open to human manipulation and construction according to ideology, Kuyper believes that "multiformity [is] the undeniable mark of fresh and vigorous life" within creation.⁵⁸ This multiformity can be seen in the diversity of both the inanimate and animate natural world as well as in human persons, cultures, and temperaments, a multiformity which must be respected and honored.⁵⁹ Wherever one looks, Kuyper says, the world is filled with

---

55. *LC*, 20.
56. Kuyper, "Sphere Sovereignty" (*AKCR*, 466).
57. Wolterstorff, *Mighty*, 163, argues this same point.
58. Kuyper, "Uniformity" (*AKCR*, 25).

59. Kuyper speaks of "the differences of climate and of nation, of historical past, and of disposition" which "exercise a widely variegating influence" on creation (*LC*, 78). Heslam correctly notes that by emphasizing the manifold nature of creation, Kuyper was bringing "his Calvinistic worldview into conformity with the social and intellectual circumstances of the late-nineteenth century, created largely by the rapid democratization and diversification of Dutch society" (*CCW*, 139).

diversity. "Uniformity in God's creation! No, rather infinite diversity, an inexhaustible profusion of variations that strikes and fascinates you in every domain of nature."[60] God is the sole and sovereign creator but God's creation is structurally multiform. And the multiformity of creation extends to the multiple spheres of human society.

Creational Powers Are Delegated into Separate Spheres of the Multiform Creation

If God is sovereign and creation is multiform, what is the nature of this relationship between power's unitary source and power's multiformity within creation? As we noted above, within Kuyper's worldview, sovereignty, authority, and power are used synonymously. This means that he could just as easily have used "power" to describe God: God is the ultimate source of power and power within creation is multiform. What we are seeking, therefore, is to discern the relationship between God as the source of power and creation's multiformity of powers in a diversity of spheres. The answer is that, within Kuyper's worldview, God has delegated sovereignty/authority/power to human beings and human society in a variety of official ways.[61] Out of the superabundance of God's power, there is a multiformity of powers that come to expression within creation. Not only is creation multiform in its animal life, human cultures, and individual personalities, but the multiformity of creational powers is a structural and normative part of human life in society and is "the glorious principle of Freedom" that Kuyper speaks of by saying that "This perfect Sovereignty of the *sinless* Messiah at the same time directly denies and challenges all absolute Sovereignty among *sinful* men on earth, and does so by dividing life into *separate spheres*, each with its own sovereignty" delegated to it directly by God.[62] Thus, rather than God mediating his power to creation in a singular, uniform way (for example, through the institutional church or the state), God has delegated his power to creation through the differentiation of powers in the diverse spheres of human cultural life in society.

60. Kuyper, "Uniformity," 34.
61. This is the same interpretation of Kuyper as that of Mouw, "Culture, Church, and Civil Society." It is this diversity which produces a "healthy, God-honoring [human] culture." Koyzis, *We Answer to Another*, 23–24, also equates the various "human capacities" in the various spheres of creation with "the various forms of power" because "Power itself comes in many diverse forms" because "Everything has a power-related aspect." Though, for Koyzis, power is equated with human ability while office confers authority.
62. Kuyper, "Sphere Sovereignty" (*AKCR*, 467).

This raises a crucial interpretive question: What does Kuyper mean by a "sphere"? Kuyper himself lists the following as the spheres he has in mind: "Just as we speak of a 'moral world,' a 'scientific world,' a 'business world,' the 'world of art,' so we can more properly speak of a 'sphere' of morality, of the family, of social life, each with its own *domain*. And because each comprises its own domain, each has its own Sovereign within its bounds."[63] By sphere, Kuyper means normatively specific, identifiable, and unique arenas of human cultural activity. And each sphere has its own unique power to engage in that unique cultural activity.[64] These differentiated or multiform spheres of creation, taken together, constitute "an infinitely complex organism" of human life in which "each [sphere is] animated with its own spirit."[65] The specific spheres that Kuyper lists in this address are the personal (moral), the family, civil society, education, church, and state, though we can clearly see that he was aiming at illustration and not exhaustive delimitation with this list.[66]

His point is that each cultural arena or sphere is uniquely suited to its own particular aspect of human life and activity.[67] Each sphere has its own delegated power to conduct its unique activities. And each sphere is directly responsible to Christ who delegated its power to it.[68] As Kuyper says, "There is a domain of nature in which the Sovereign exerts power over matter according to fixed laws. There is also a domain of the personal, of the

---

63. Kuyper, "Sphere Sovereignty" (*AKCR*, 467). *AKASPI*, 40–49, contains an excellent summary of Kuyper on the spheres of creation and the biblical basis for the notion.

64. Kuyper is using "sphere" in ways similar to some of Max Weber's work. For example, see Weber, *Vocation Lectures*. Wolterstorff, *Mighty*, 169n10–11, argues that Weber uses "sphere" similarly to Kuyper only in these *Vocation* lectures. Elsewhere, Weber's usage differs from Kuyper's.

65. Kuyper, "Sphere Sovereignty" (*AKCR*, 467).

66. As we noted in Chapter 1, while Kuyper lists these spheres, the occasion did not allow him to be comprehensive. There are spheres of life which he fails to mention and he wasn't exact in fleshing out the unique "center" or "circumference" that give each sphere its unique identity and place in the world. As Harinck, "Historian's Comment," 282, reminds us, Kuyper "neither defined the sphere nor the principle of each sphere." In these ways, Herman Dooyeweerd develops Kuyper's theory in more philosophical specificity. See Dooyeweerd, *New Critique of Theoretical Thought*.

67. On the relationship between the various spheres of creation and the multiple aspects of human life and activity, see Skillen, "Development of Calvinistic Political Theory."

68. On this point, Harinck observes that "the main contribution of Kuyper . . . was to remodel the old, religiously rooted idea of sovereignty. Sovereignty, for Kuyper, was no longer linked either to the king or to the people. No, sovereignty was something delegated to different spheres in society. This is considered to be Kuyper's most original contribution to social and political thought" (Harinck, "Historian's Comment," 281).

household, of science, of social and ecclesiastical life, each of which obeys its own laws of life, each subject to its own chief."[69] But, as Wolterstorff notes, "whereas for the most part Weber employed the idea [of sphere] descriptively, Kuyper employed the idea normatively."[70] That is to say, as Mouw put it, "Mediating structures are not merely to be valued for their functions of shaping character and curbing the powers of the state. God built these patterns of associational diversity into the very fabric of creation . . . and no human power has the right to inhibit their proper functioning."[71] The spheres, and the powers which operate within them, are normative, governed by divine law.

Against the historical and political background of Kuyper's day, the insistence upon ultimate divine power and directly delegated multiform human powers within the various arenas of human life were direct counterclaims to both the movements towards state-power and popular-power in the Netherlands, fuelled by the French Revolution.[72] For Kuyper, God's power over all creation and delegated human power in the multiple intermediary spheres of civic life make up the normative structure of God's multiform creation. This also functions as a safeguard for human liberty in the face of monopolistic tendencies in various times and places from various spheres.[73] Just as the rule of the church over all of life in the medieval period was a distortion of God's intention for creation, so too in the modern era the rule of the state over all of life is an equal distortion.

This is where Kuyper's worldview discloses his organic rather than mechanical view of the world. Kuyper believed that modernism generally envisioned the world and its processes in mechanical fashion, open to human manipulation and control, in a way that was alien to the world's true organic (i.e., liberated) nature. By seeing human life divided up into various spheres, Kuyper believed that "Our human life . . . constitutes an infinitely

---

69. Kuyper, "Sphere Sovereignty" (*AKCR*, 467). Kuyper, *Problem of Poverty*, 29–30, also refers to the powers within nature and art.

70. Wolterstorff, *Mighty*, 169.

71. Mouw, "Culture, Church, and Civil Society," 56.

72. Heslam, "Prophet," 15, correctly observes that for Kuyper both popular-sovereignty and state-sovereignty "were antitheistic, removing authority from God and placing it in the hands of human beings"—either the political leader or the popular masses. In response to this, Chaplin, "Sphere Sovereignty," notes that that idea of sphere sovereignty "did not drop from the sky into the neocalvinist movement of that time, nor did it leap straight out of the pages of Calvin's writings into the lap of Abraham Kuyper. It was, rather, a recognisably Calvinist response to the unique circumstances and challenges of modern European capitalism and secularism."

73. Heslam, "Prophet," 12, makes this same point, that "All authority," including that of the state, is "derived from the authority of God alone."

complex organism."[74] Kuyper's understanding of delegated human power in the various spheres of life arises from "the order of creation, [sphere sovereignty is] in the structure of human life."[75] This is why Chaplin calls Kuyper's doctrine of "sphere sovereignty" a social ontology of "differentiated communitarianism."[76] Within the differentiated communities that make up human culture, differentiated powers are at work. In analyzing Herman Dooyeweerd's development of Kuyper's theory of sphere sovereignty, Chaplin writes, "For example, the state's pursuit of justice is different from that of a church, family, business, and so on, because it is, uniquely, backed up by coercive power, as distinct from the faith power of a church, the moral power of a family, the economic power of a business, and so on."[77] Unto each sphere, God has bestowed a unique form of power.

Humanity's Calling Is to Develop and Steward the Multiform Powers of Creation

God is sovereign. Creation is multiform. And the relationship between the two is that God delegates and distributes differentiated powers to the various spheres of human cultural activity. This is a normative and purposive action on God's part because Kuyper's worldview entails a particular view of humanity's *telos*: humanity's vocation is to unfold, develop, and steward the rich potentials (powers) placed by God in every sphere of his creation.[78] In other words, humanity's task is to "discover the treasures and develop the potencies hidden by God in nature and in human life."[79] Kuyper honored every legitimate career of investigating, stewarding, and serving creation and neighbor for in all these ways human beings were unfolding and responsibly using the potentials of creation. He says that "human art [the human work of unfolding the potentials of creation which is not limited to the aesthetic] acts on every part of nature, not to destroy it or simply to impose another structure alongside it, but to unlock the power that lies hidden within it or to regulate the wild power that springs from it. God's ordinances require this."[80] Thus, the various powers that God has delegated to the spheres of

74. Kuyper, "Sphere Sovereignty" (*AKCR*, 467).
75. Kuyper, "Sphere Sovereignty" (*AKCR*, 469).
76. Chaplin, "Sphere Sovereignty."
77. Chaplin, *Dooyeweerd*, 89.
78. This is the same argument made earlier by Augustine, *Handbook on Faith, Hope, and Love*, 8.
79. *LC*, 33.
80. Kuyper, *Problem of Poverty*, 30.

creation are not obvious but must be sought out, discerned, and harnessed faithfully. Once discovered, the various powers inherent in the differentiated spheres of human life can be developed and utilized.

Kuyper employed a number of metaphors to communicate this teleological or vocational notion. Similar to the discovery of a treasure noted above, or the agricultural image of a plant growing from a seed, or the development of a particular entity from the germ of an idea, each area of human life is ripe for the cultivation of an array of fruit under human care. Each sphere, therefore, not only has its own differentiated power for its particular area of life but it has its own unique resources and contributions to make to the larger work of human stewardship of culture and society and for the shalom of all creation. There are academic treasures to be gleaned through education, justice treasures to be gleaned through political statecraft, and the treasures of greater knowledge of God in religion.[81] The riches of creation do not lie on the surface to be snatched up absent-mindedly but must be intentionally sought, pursued, and discovered in order for humanity to be faithful to its calling as the stewards of creation.

It is important to realize that for Kuyper these creational potentials are not limited to the resources of the physical natural world but extend to include the potentials of the human socio-cultural world as well. In fact, Kuyper is critical of those Christians who abandon their calling to steward the extra-ecclesial cultural world. He argues that "Christians, by refusing to participate in that development, were the reason why morally and religiously that development often took a wrong turn. Those who are in Christ must not oppose such development and progress, must not even distance themselves from it. Their calling also in this cultural realm is rather to be in the vanguard."[82] For Kuyper, Christian faithfulness in the church does not exempt one from this extra-ecclesial vocation in the whole of life. Rather, Christian faithfulness spurs one on to greater participation in the world.

This divine calling upon humanity to develop and steward the potentials of creation in every sphere is not something that can be done by a single

---

81. It is important to note that it is with ideas like this that Kuyper's successors developed the idea of *verzuilling* or pillarization, the socio-political theory that each confessional or ideological group in Holland was entitled to develop its own subculture of institutions rooted in their own worldview. Kuyper says that "considering that something begins from principle and that a distinct entity takes rise from a distinct principle, we shall maintain a distinct sovereignty for our own principle and for that of our opponents across the whole sphere of thought" (Kuyper, "Sphere Sovereignty" [*AKCR*, 484]).

82. Kuyper, "Common Grace," 175.

individual or even a single group of like-minded people but is a calling that humanity must engage in together as an organic unity.[83] And the way Kuyper envisions humanity engaging in this vocation together is through the organic emergence of distinct associations and institutions within the various spheres of human life that are uniquely tailored to the work of that particular sphere. More than that, due to the complexity of the world's fallenness, Kuyper anticipates that there will be a multiplicity of views for how to remedy the effects of the Fall in each realm of creation, meaning that within each sphere there will be multiple organizations, each with their own legitimate version of a Christian approach. Therefore, as a natural result of the nature of humanity as an organic unit, the mediating structures or institutions of civil society will emerge. These will be institutions that enable the unfolding of creation's potentials in their particular sphere of cultural activity.[84] Various political parties with their diverse views will seek to form or influence a government, for example.[85]

---

83. Chaplin, "Sphere Sovereignty," calls this the "forms of interconnectedness" people and spheres must create and maintain in order to fully develop the potentials of creation.

84. Wolterstorff captures both the ontological and the utilitarian nature of these mediating structures well: "In order to work together to achieve our shared goals we find it useful, and often necessary, to establish organizations and institutions. Scholarship could not flourish without an institutional base in such organizations as universities, research institutes, and publishing houses; the arts could not flourish without an institutional base in such organizations as conservatories, galleries, and opera houses; recreation could not flourish without such organizations as chess clubs and baseball teams" (Wolterstorff, *Mighty*, 161).

85. It is important to note here that Kuyper sees a distinction between institutions of civil society which emerge organically versus the mechanical or coercive nature of the state which is called to restrain injustice and police the boundaries and interrelationships of the spheres.

We mentioned Kuyper's preference for organic themes above and both Heslam[86] and Botha[87] have drawn attention to this motif in Kuyper.[88] Kuyper made the distinction between the organic nature of humanity and human society versus the mechanical nature of the state in his third Stone lecture by saying that "The idea is here fundamental therefore that the sovereignty of God, in its descent upon men, separates itself into two spheres. On the one hand the mechanical sphere of *State-authority*, and on the other hand the organic sphere of the authority of the *Social circles*. And in both these spheres the inherent authority is sovereign, that is to say, it has above itself nothing but God."[89] The organic view of human life and society rejects atomistic conceptions of human beings for "a living, human organism. Not a mechanism put together from separate parts; not a mosaic . . . inlaid with pieces like a floor; but a *body* with limbs, subject to the law of life. We are members of each other, and thus the eye cannot get along without the foot, nor the foot without the eye."[90] In addition to an organic view of human life and society, Kuyper holds to a *covenantal* view of humanity where each

---

86. Heslam notes that Kuyper viewed society organically because of the "innate power of [human] reproduction" which meant that all people were "naturally interrelated to each other. . . . The same kind of development was true for all the other spheres of society, through the exercise of powers which God had invested within nature: since these powers operated only in an organic way, the organic development of the social spheres was sustained" (*CCW*, 155–56). Heslam also remarks that the various differentiated spheres "derived their authority not from the State, which occupied a sphere of its own, but from God, to whom they were directly accountable. Each of the spheres developed spontaneously and organically, according to the powers God had given them in the first moments of creation . . . society should be understood as a moral organism" (Heslam, "Prophet," 17).

87. Botha, *Sosio-kulturele metavrae*, 143–46, analyzes the important topic of the organic motif in Kuyper and develops it philosophically and in dialogue with Dooyeweerd. Most recently, Eglinton, *Trinity and Organism*, has addressed this important topic. While his main focus is Bavinck, he does make note of Kuyper's work also.

88. In fact, Wolterstorff, *Mighty*, 160, says that "Kuyper typically employs organic metaphors." Chaplin, "Sphere Sovereignty," calls this "a complex social ecology."

89. *LC*, 121. Kuyper allows for the mechanical nature of the state due to the necessary coercive power of the state to restrain evil and lawlessness. This is also the view of Max Weber on the role of the state. He says that "the modern state can be defined only sociologically by the specific *means* that are peculiar to it, as to every political organization: namely, physical violence" or force. . . . Violence is, of course, not the normal or the only means available to the state. That is undeniable. But it is the means specific to the state. . . . We must say that the state is the form of human community that (successfully) lays claim to the *monopoly of legitimate physical violence* within a particular territory. . . . Hence, what 'politics' means for us is to strive for a share of power or to influence the distribution of power, whether between states or between the groups of people contained within a state" (Weber, *Vocation Lectures*, 33).

90. Kuyper, *Problem of Poverty*, 52.

person is related to the rest of humanity and the human race as a whole constitutes a single organically-united body.[91] As opposed to this, rival worldviews (like a modernist one) tend to view government as a mechanical force in society, an unnatural necessity for the pursuit of justice, and an imposition on human life to safeguard it from the tyranny of lawlessness.[92] Each sphere's resources must be sought out and developed by humanity covenantally working together to unfold the rich potentials of creation.

Each Sphere's Power Has a Unique Character Which Norms Its Action

As humanity works organically to discover, develop, unfold, and steward the potentials of creation in the various spheres, there will naturally and historically arise various associations and institutions within each sphere that are uniquely tailored to that sphere. Some examples of these associations and institutions are common sense: universities and teacher unions will emerge from within the educational sphere, churches and confessional service clubs will form within the religious sphere, legislative and judicial bodies will take shape within the state. But the development of sphere-specific institutions is not all that is to be expected. Kuyper also believed that each sphere would display a "principle characteristic" due to its divine createdness which norms the associations and institutions of that sphere, and the unique power operative within that sphere, in particular ways that distinguish each sphere, its institutions, and its power from other spheres and institutions and powers.[93] The emergence of a sphere's "principle characteristic" is the divine law which norms the activities of that sphere. For example, a soccer club might socialize together or clean up trash in a neighborhood or raise funds for one of their members to pay tuition costs but its "principle characteristic" is none of these but, rather, physical sport. Similar examples could be listed for each sphere.

Of particular significance, Kuyper argued that each sphere's principle characteristic would function normatively for the associations, institutions,

---

91. On Kuyper's use of the biblical theme of covenant, and its relationship with his ecclesiology, see *LC*, 80–83. See also Bartholomew, "Covenant and Creation," 11–33.

92. Wolterstorff, *Mighty*, 165, also recognizes this same distinction in Kuyper between the organic nature of human society and the mechanical nature of the state.

93. *LC*, 119. Chaplin, "Sphere Sovereignty," uses the language of "irreducible social purpose" for Kuyper's "principle characteristic." At other times, Chaplin calls this each sphere's "irreducible responsibility." See Chaplin, "God and Globalization," 497; "Concept of 'Civil Society.'"

activities, and power within that sphere in particular ways.[94] And each sphere's norm makes the power at work in each particular sphere unique to that sphere and different from the others. For example, the principle characteristic and power of a soccer club is of a different kind than the principle characteristic and power of a business corporation. While the principle characteristic of a soccer club is physical sport, the principle characteristic of a business is the production of capital through the distribution of needed services and products.[95] For the soccer club, the power at work in that sphere norms the club's activities so that its primary or leading function is and remains sport, even though it may engage in a range of other ancillary activities. And for a business, even though its employees might socialize together or organize fitness classes for personal health, the power at work in that sphere norms the business' activities so that its primary or leading function is the production of capital, products, and services.[96]

Clearly, the actualization of the power in each sphere is an area where the presence of human sin has a significant distorting influence on the proper, organic, and healthy functioning of the sphere, and the power within each sphere which norms its institutional activity. This was something about which Kuyper was especially perceptive. Kuyper's harshest critiques tend to be reserved for the many ways in which one sphere of human life abandons

---

94. Heslam, "Prophet," 19, observes that for Kuyper "the spheres existed in God's original creation and had been invested with divine laws [or norms] that governed their existence." Chaplin, "Sphere Sovereignty," notes that sphere sovereignty, for Kuyper, was "a deep biblical truth: that all sovereignty originates ultimately in God and is only delegated to human beings in their diverse social spheres for particular and limited purposes." And, connected with the organic motif noted above, "sphere sovereignty . . . went hand in hand with a parallel emphasis: an organic conception of society . . . [with] strong reciprocal ties of interdependency and mutual obligation."

95. There is significant debate about this. I am indebted to Chaplin's view in "Sphere Sovereignty" that "the structural purpose of a business corporation is 'the efficient production and delivery of socially needed goods and services by a producer community.'"

96. Mouw, "Church, Culture, and Civil Society," 57, makes the same argument: "Each mode of association has its own place in the divine ordering of human life. . . . Families are families, and churches are churches . . . families are different from churches. Each occupies an important place in the array of God-ordained spheres of interaction." Chaplin, "Concept of 'Civil Society,'" argues for the connection between sovereignty, authority, and power within the various realms of human cultural activity in this way: "The institution we call marriage is fitted to furnish a context of companionship and sexual bonding which meets human needs for intimacy and progeny, not merely to facilitate a certain arrangement of property-ownership. Or, educational institutions are fitted to serve as communities of whole-person formative learning and not merely as skills-training centers to prepare for adaptation to a world of global competition. Or, political parties are fitted to orchestrate communities of political conviction and not to serve as mere electoral machines facilitating an elite manipulation of a supine citizenry."

its unique principle characteristic and normative power and "copycats" or "lusts" for the power delegated to another sphere.[97] To use an example from Kuyper introduced in Chapter 1, this can be observed when the church functions toward its members as the state does toward its citizens. This same criticism could be made if the state were to exert its power toward its citizens as parents exert their power toward children in a family. As Kuyper says, "Scripture doesn't take exception to power but to the wrong kind of power."[98] Kuyper conceives of the world as being filled with a multiformity of powers which bump up against each other and which exert their influence on each other.[99] Thus, when an alien or unoriginal power begins to operate within a sphere that is antithetical to the normative nature of the power delegated to it by God, its principle characteristic, then abuses and injustices begin to happen and the social fabric of human life begins to disintegrate within and around that sphere. Each sphere's activities, in its associations and institutions and power, are normed internally by its principle characteristic which functions as a divine law for it. It is that force which characterises the activities of that sphere and maintain the integrity of that sphere.

Each Sphere Limits the Powers of the Other Spheres

Not only does the principle characteristic of a sphere function as a law which norms the internal life within that sphere, but the boundaries *between* the spheres is an important aspect for Kuyper as well. Each sphere's principle characteristic norms that sphere's internal activities and power. But each sphere's principle characteristic also regulates that sphere's external relationships with other spheres as the spheres bump up against each other in the marketplace of human society.[100] The principle characteristic of a sphere

97. Kuyper, "It Shall Not Be So among You," 136, 130.

98. For examples of Kuyper's criticisms along this line, see Kuyper, "It Shall Not Be So among You," 126–27, 130, 136.

99. Koyzis, *We Answer to Another*, 97, makes the same claim, saying that "Power is and always has been . . . manifested in a variety of ways in different settings."

100. Chaplin makes the important observation that the normativity of each sphere not only limits the other spheres but contributes to the organic whole of society: "Every community . . . can be seen to provide for others—perhaps every other—a distinctive kind of aid. Just by being themselves families aid the state, for example, in providing responsible and critical adults ready to assume the responsibilities of citizenship; businesses provide all manner of material necessities for families and other bodies; the state provides security and justice for all; and so on. Simply by being what it is, each social structure necessarily provides conditions in which other structures can be what they are. What each structure provides is unique to its type. Each offers a qualitatively distinct kind of aid to the others, corresponding to its irreducible qualification and the unique resources it possesses" (Chaplin, *Dooyeweerd*, 138).

also functions as a boundary marker for that sphere and governs that sphere externally by the unique power delegated to it by God.[101] This means that the power delegated to a particular sphere places limits on the over-extending tendencies of the powers of the other spheres which neighbor it. This is the way, in Kuyper's mind, that the concept of sphere sovereignty functions as a safe-guard against rampant state-power on the one hand or revolutionary popular-power on the other hand.[102] Each sphere's power, while designed for the flourishing of the internal life of that sphere, also serves to ensure that that sphere is not infringed upon by any other sphere.[103]

Kuyper sees this as the genius or

> the fundamental doctrine of Calvinism: its confession of the absolute sovereignty of God. For this confession implies that no authority or power[104] on earth is inherent but is imposed. Thus there is no natural authority to speak of either on the part of the ruler or of the people. Only God is sovereign; He regards all creatures, born in royal palace or beggar's hut, as nothing in comparison with Himself. One creature cannot have authority over another except as God gives it. And God does not relinquish that authority but allows it to be used to his glory. He is sovereign and gives that authority to whomever He will—sometimes to kings and princes, other times to nobles and patricians, but sometimes also to the people as a whole.[105]

---

101. Chaplin, "Full Weight of Our Convictions," summarizes this well: "Each social body [sphere] possess a distinctive nature and purpose, and a corresponding inherent authority to govern itself free from illicit intrusion by the state or any other body."

102. Chaplin also connects sphere sovereignty and differentiated power, saying: "We can expect to find 'radical' differences between church organization, business organization, and state organization. Organized power always appears as the power of a corporation, church, or state, and so on, and never simply as power as such. It assumes quite different characteristics according to the structural principle of the community in which it is present. Power is thus individualized in ways specific to each organized community . . . no community may attempt to exercise the kind of organized power uniquely characteristic of another type, since to do so entails a violation of the principle of sphere sovereignty" (Chaplin, *Dooyeweerd*, 168).

103. Kuyper does allow for the juridical function of the state which acts as an arbiter in disputes between competing spheres. Richard Mouw finds at least three roles for the state in Kuyper's thought: (1) patrolling the boundaries between the various spheres, (2) protecting the weak from the intrusion of the powerful, and (3) maintaining common infrastructure which equips the functioning of all the spheres (*AKASPI*, 30–37). As Wells, "Until the Trumpet Blows," 25, notes, this is "a rather active role for government."

104. Note here how Kuyper continues to use authority and power synonymously with each other and with sovereignty.

105. Kuyper, "Calvinism," 307.

Each sphere, as a unique realm where a unique power is active, functions as a limit on the over-reaching tendencies of other spheres. This can even, in Kuyper's worldview, extend to limits being placed on the state itself. Kuyper believes it is true that "an earthly sovereign possess[es] the power to compel obedience only in a limited sphere, a sphere bordered by other spheres in which another is sovereign and not he."[106] For example, Kuyper would vociferously argue that the state has no place in dictating dogma or confessions for the church. In fact, liberating the church from the oversight of the state was a key component of Kuyper's church reforms during his lifetime. In this way, the church might limit the power of the state.

By implication, not only does humanity have to work together as an organic entity to unfold and steward the potentials of creation but the various spheres which make up human life must interact with each other in a just manner and coordinate their unique contributions for the healthy and equitable functioning of human society while respecting the unique contributions from other spheres.[107] In addition, the limited role of the state must function properly to not only allow but also encourage the cooperation of the various spheres to work together to unfold the potentials of creation for the good of human society and without performing the functions of the spheres itself.[108] Kuyper insists that the spheres comprise an intermediate realm between the individual and the state so that people or groups of different gifts or capacities can serve each other out of their unique gifts and callings. Drawing on his democratic tendencies, Kuyper says that his worldview "cannot recognize any distinction among men, save such as has been imposed by God himself, in that He gave one authority over the other, or enriched one with more talents than the other, in order that the man of more talents should serve the man with less, and in him serve his God."[109] For Kuyper, differences in kinds of power or principle/characteristic function mean that those who have more power or authority are obliged to serve those with less power or authority in society, a point we will return to in greater detail below.

106. Kuyper, "Sphere Sovereignty" (*AKCR*, 466). Wolterstorff makes the same point: "There are also normative limited placed on the authority of the state by the presence in society of a wide range of social entities with authority structures, these including the church, business enterprises, educational institutions, and so forth" (Wolterstorff, *Mighty*, 158).

107. Heslam notes that this is Kuyper's Calvinistic emphasis on the sharing of power between the various realms of society (*CCW*, 145).

108. Chaplin, *Dooyeweerd*, 225, confirms that "not only is the state to refrain from violating the sphere sovereignty of other spheres, but it is to prevent any other structure from violating such sphere sovereignty."

109. *LC*, 27.

Summary

Having analyzed the worldview which shapes Kuyper's view of sovereignty, authority, and power, we can crystallize his worldview as it relates to power in the following way: God is the sovereign creator, the ultimate and original power that exists. And out of his plenitude of power, God has created a world filled with diversity, a multiform world at every level of analysis. As a component of this multiformity, God has divided the human socio-cultural world into various organic spheres or arenas of life, each with its own power delegated to it directly by God and not from any other source. God has mandated humanity to discover and develop and steward the rich potentials within his creation, potentials that exist in the natural world as well as in the socio-cultural world of human affairs. In order to accomplish this task, humanity must work together organically so that human life can unfold harmoniously and in line with its created telos. This means that human associations and institutions will naturally emerge over time in the various spheres of human life, associations and institutions which reflect the principle characteristic of each sphere and which characterize and norm their activity within their unique sphere. These corporate human acts of forming associations and institutions entail and reflect authority structures which not only norm and guide the activities within their sphere but also limit the encroachment or drift from other spheres, including the state. Thus, the world is filled with an abundance of various unique powers, forming a network of power-relations that humanity participates in at multiple levels. These multiform powers are for humanity's flourishing and comprise humanity's vocation to unfold and develop creation, in order to serve God, creation, and neighbor.

CONTRIBUTIONS FROM THE LATER KUYPERIAN TRADITION

For Kuyper, to approach power as a singular entity would be to engage in theoretical abstraction. In his worldview, there are a multitude of powers, each operative within a unique sphere of human culture and society. We could call these political power, educational power, social power, etc. As such, if we are to achieve our goal of understanding the power of the church within Kuyper's thought we must discern the unique power within the ecclesial sphere. This will be the task of the next chapter.

At this point, there are significant contributions which the later Kuyperian tradition has made that bring clarity to some of the contours of Kuyper's worldview. While the philosophical and theological survey of Chapter 2 is helpful in grappling with power, not only as an occasional coercive phenomenon but also as a persistent network of relations within a diverse social body, there are also explicitly non-dualistic biblical-theological attempts to understand the nature of creation which draw heavily upon Kuyper's worldview. By introducing these contributions to our analysis of Kuyper's worldview, we will be better prepared to analyze Kuyper's understanding of power as a creational structure and directional manifestation which participates in creation's biblical narrative arc, particularly related to the presence of sin and evil in Kuyper's worldview.

Creation-Fall-Redemption

Albert Wolters has sought to explicitly articulate the foundational worldview insights that too often remain implicit in Kuyper's work, particularly in terms of how sin distorts creation.[110] To accomplish this, he utilizes two helpful frameworks: the biblical narrative arc of creation-fall-redemption as well as the distinction between creation's structure and its actualized direction. Together, these contribute to making Kuyper's worldview even more clear. The first framework is Scripture's narrative trajectory (creation, fall, redemption).[111] This provides a normative and teleological way of understanding not only the world as a whole but also various elements within the world. When analyzing any given artifact in the human world, Wolters insists that we distinguish between (1) how that object evidences its God-created goodness, (2) its religious rebellion or fallenness from its original created goodness in actual existence, and (3) God's redemptive trajectory for it to be reformed or renewed to its original created goodness and purpose.[112]

We can offer a brief example of this framework using power itself. Reading Kuyper through Wolter's framework would result in there being something about power that evidences its creational goodness (what specifically that power or its creational goodness is depends upon the sphere of life we choose to examine). But, because of human rebellion and sin against God and one's neighbor, power has been subjected to an anti-creational deformation and no longer functions in its creational goodness but contributes to destruction and human misery (again, the specific form will depend

---

110. Wolters, *Creation Regained*.

111. This dramatic structure is developed in far more detail in Bartholomew and Goheen, *Drama of Scripture*.

112. After offering a summary of "worldview," Wolters's next three chapters present this narrative trajectory. See Wolters, *Creation Regained*, 13–86.

on the sphere and power in question[113]). And yet, through the redemptive mission of God, the rebellion of the creation is being turned back to its creational intention, power included, and one day every power will be fully renewed and will function within its sphere as intended at creation for human flourishing and not for destruction so that the whole world will be a place of flourishing, which is the eschatological kingdom of God. Therefore, each of the multiform powers within creation's spheres participates in both goodness and evil. This is opposed to a dualistic view that conceives of the various powers within creation being simplistically categorized according to the whims of ideology or preference (i.e., church is good, state is fallen). In this way, one avoids a dualistic understanding of power in which some forms of "hard power" are understood as evil and other forms of "soft power" are naively believed to be acceptable and good, untouched by and immune to human distortion. Rather, in every form of power, from "hard" forms of power such as coercion to "soft" forms of power such as influence, one can discern the ways in which each and every form of power participates in the creation-fall-redemption narrative framework of Scripture.

Structure-Direction

Additionally, Wolters further clarifies Kuyper's worldview by distinguishing between an object's creational *structure* (given to it by the creator God) as well as its actual or manifestational *direction* (the effects of sin upon each object within creation). This can assist one in being clear about the creational goodness of an object (its ontological creational *structure*) and either its good, flourishing, and holy manifestation or its perversion, fallenness, or rebellion against that creational goodness (its *direction*).[114] *Structure* refers to the creational or ontological nature of a created object before the effects of sin are reckoned with. And as Sykes observes, "nothing . . . [in] the classical Christian tradition would suggest the idea that power is inherently corrupt."[115] *Direction*, on the other hand, refers to the ways in which something has been corrupted, deformed, twisted, and rendered harmful—the ways in which it must be redeemed and reformed.[116]

---

113. At least we can say, from our analysis so far, that its principle characteristic which norms the sphere will drift or that one sphere will encroach upon another sphere.

114. This has come to be known as the "antithesis" in Kuyper's worldview: the particular ways in which fallenness is evident as a distortion of God's good creation. See Mouw, "Remember the Antithesis!," 9.

115. Sykes, *Power*, 152.

116. Kuyper, *Problem of Poverty*, 31, says that "misdirected actions [have] two

Direction is Wolters's way of grasping the distorting effects of human agency (Kuyper uses the term "art" for human agency) under the power of sin.[117] As Kuyper said,

> It has never been possible to speak of a wholly free and instinctive [organic] growth of society in any country with a high degree of national development. Everywhere, human art has shaped the development of natural powers and relationships. But while we must gratefully acknowledge that this intervention of human management has brought us, generally speaking, out of barbarism into an orderly society—indeed, although we must concede that such a continuous development of society strengthens belief in a higher providential rule—we cannot for a moment doubt that this intervention, often originating from false principles [idolatry], has in all ages created unhealthy conditions which could have been healthy. It has in many ways poisoned our mutual relationships and weighed us down with nameless misery.[118]

We can again use the concept of power to illustrate this framework. In terms of *structure*, the various powers given to the differentiated spheres of creation are the creational capacities and abilities given to human beings in the multiform spheres of culture and society to carry out the activities within that sphere. These powers are the human capacities to accomplish, do, achieve, implement, and make human cultural artifacts within the various spheres. The cultural mandate of Genesis 1:28 assumes human beings have real creational effectivity: in short, delegated creational power.[119] This is the *structure* of the powers within creation, embedded within the spheres of culture and emerging in history and society. *Direction* refers to the multitude ways in which these differentiated powers, through either faithful or

---

invariable causes: error and sin. *Error* insofar as there was ignorance. . . . *Sin* insofar as greed and lust for power" prevailed. "In time, both error and sin joined forces to enthrone false principles [i.e., Idolatry] that violated human nature [i.e., structure]."

117. In terms of directionality, Dooyeweerd helpfully says: "Insofar as power has been entrusted to man as a creature, it is always cultural. It implies a historical calling and task of formation for which the bearer of power is responsible and of which he must give account. Power may never be used for personal advantage, as if it were a private possession. Power is the great motor of cultural development. The decisive question concerns the direction in which power is applied" (Dooyeweerd, *Roots of Western Culture*, 67).

118. Kuyper, *Problem of Poverty*, 32–33.

119. "God blessed them [male and female] and said to them, 'Be fruitful and increase in number; fill the earth and subdue it. Rule over the fish in the sea and the birds in the sky and over every living creature that moves on the ground'" (Gen 1:28 NIV).

rebellious human agency, can be oriented either toward human good and the flourishing of creation or toward perversion and destruction when they are used to abuse, manipulate, harm, oppress or dominate contrary to their intended purpose. As Kearsley says, "power as a concept [can be] turned this way and that for different ends."[120] The powers are creational *structures* that exist in a fallen world and thus are able to be *directed* towards flourishing or destructive ends.

CONNECTING SOVEREIGNTY/AUTHORITY/ POWER TO STRUCTURE/DIRECTION

In the above analysis of Kuyper's worldview, as it relates to power, we mentioned a number of times but never took the opportunity to delve deeply into how Kuyper conceives of the unique powers given to particular spheres and how these lead to that particular sphere's leading or characteristic function which norms its activities and the power operative within that sphere according to divine law. This is further complicated by the dynamics inherent in a sphere's creational *structure* versus its implemented *direction*. In the remainder of this chapter, we address this and offer an example from Kuyper himself of how these elements of his worldview come together in actual theory-in-practice, aware that the *structural* power given to a certain sphere is susceptible to distortion and mis-*direction* due to human sin.

Kuyper wrote extensively on the normativity and flourishing of the spheres of the state, the academy, and the church (which we turn to in the next chapter). Kuyper also devoted much thought and attention to the emergence of unfettered capitalism in late-nineteenth-century Western Europe, to the role of business and economics in God's creation, and to the ways in which they could so easily be used for human domination, abuse, and destruction.[121] Using the example of the financial sphere and monetary power in Kuyper, we will bring our analysis of Kuyper's worldview to conclusion as well as set the stage for our analysis of the power of the church with the following illustration of his worldview in practice.[122]

---

120. Kearsley, *Church*, 11.

121. Economic concerns continued to be important for the ARP following Kuyper's leadership as well. See also Goudzwaard, *Capitalism and Progress*; *Idols of Our Time*; Goudzwaard and Lange, *Beyond Poverty and Affluence*; Goudzwaard et al., *Hope in Troubled Times*.

122. For a contemporary example of Kuyper's worldview and theory of Sphere Sovereignty being used in practice, see Goudzwaard, "Goals, Ways, and the Roots."

SOVEREIGNTY, AUTHORITY, AND POWER 139

Kuyper did not shy away from addressing the financial sphere during his lifetime.[123] For him, monetary power within the financial sphere of life directly addressed "the relationship between the rich and the poor."[124] Some "*do* and [others] do *not* have this [monetary] power at their disposal" and as a result everyone strives for "nothing other than acquiring more *financial power.*"[125] The reason for this striving after monetary power is that monetary power not only enables one to obtain the necessities and comforts of life but monetary power also produces social benefits which in turn lead to greater opportunities for civic participation and even further financial power.[126] As such, Kuyper affirms the creational goodness of the financial sphere that enables the exchange of goods and services between people nationally and internationally. But the radical dehumanization that was becoming more and more pronounced in the financial sphere is what caused Kuyper to consider the "social question . . . *the* question, the burning *life-question* of the late-nineteenth century."[127]

Kuyper's concern was not with the creational *structure* of the financial sphere in God's world. He believed in non-dualistic and non-reductionistic fashion that the financial sphere was a good creation of God's. Rather, Kuyper's concern was with the sinful *direction* of monetary power, how the financial sphere and its monetary power could (and actually did) so easily abandon its allegiance to Christ and become deformed and lead to the ruin

---

123. Besides a significant number of tangential remarks throughout his corpus, the two works in which Kuyper focuses directly on this sphere are Kuyper, *Problem of Poverty*; and *De Christus*, a portion of which was published in English translation as "Christ and the Needy." It should be noted that there is an on-going scholarly debate about how Kuyper's concern for the lower social class shifted with his political rise and his term as Prime Minister from 1901 to 1905. Some see an "early Kuyper," represented in the two sources cited above, who is concerned with power for the powerless (greater enfranchisement), versus a "late Kuyper," who tended to use power for the powerful (the example often cited is the brutal way in which Kuyper responded to the railroad labor strike of 1903). On this debate, see *AKMCCD*, 309–11. Mouw, "Learning from the Dutch," 152–53, also addresses this distinction within Kuyper's work as it relates to both Dutch and North American theological debates and ecclesiastical separations. Bratt connects this with the theological distinction Kuyper made between the antithesis (early Kuyper) and common grace (late Kuyper) (*DCMA*, 19).

124. Kuyper, "Christ and the Needy," 647. Kuyper spoke extensively of money as a power relative to the Eighth Commandment in his "Commentary on the Heidelberg Catechism," 728.

125. Kuyper, "Christ and the Needy," 650.

126. Not only social status, but in 1895 Holland, financial wealth also entitled one to vote. This is one reason why Kuyper's ARP was interested in electoral reform.

127. Kuyper, *Problem of Poverty*, 54. On the background to the late-nineteenth-century Dutch "social question," see Dyke, "Abraham Kuyper and the Continuing Social Question."

of people and communities. Monetary power is attended by a temptation to focus on and strive towards "nothing other than acquiring more *financial power*."[128] That is, misdirected monetary power reveals rebellious human desires that are fueled by and lead to idolatry.[129] "[Monetary] Power, prominence, wealth, honor, prosperity, and well-being seduce people much sooner to turning to themselves and putting their faith [not in God but] in the creature and thus to becoming proud and puffed up."[130] In this way, "*money on earth has become an unholy power opposed to God and . . . a curse therefore adheres to capital as such*."[131] Is Kuyper arguing that the financial sphere and monetary power are *structurally* sinful? No. Rather, when "it tries to act as a power that does not stand in the service of the Lord" that is when the inner-workings of the financial sphere become *misdirected, distorted, and sinful*.[132] It is in this way, as Kuyper argues with words that sound prophetic today, that the theological myopia of idolatry takes over:[133]

> Financial power, climbing higher, collecting treasures in stocks and precious metals, purchasing houses and landed properties, becoming the master of earthy goods—this, it may safely be said, is the main thought that exercises the heads and hearts and senses nowadays at the stock exchange and in the world of our young people. Everything talks money. Everything thirsts for money. Virtually all senses and thoughts are set on acquiring money. To gain control over money people will use cunning and guile; they will cheat and deceive each other; they will risk the goods of their wives and children, and sometimes even the goods of strangers that have been entrusted to them. Everything is measured by money. Whoever is rich is a celebrated and honored man. This is just what Jesus does *not* want. He sets himself diametrically *against* it. He proclaims that a world or a people who aim at it and pursue it corrupt themselves spiritually in the process . . . he regards [this] as cursed.[134]

Again, the question is important for the sake of clarity: is Kuyper condemning the financial aspect of human life or monetary power in general?

128. Kuyper, "Christ and the Needy," 650.

129. Kuyper, *Problem of Poverty*, 46, highlights that it is the love of money which is the root of all evil (cf. 1 Tim 6:10).

130. Kuyper, "Christ and the Needy," 664.

131. Kuyper, "Christ and the Needy," 665.

132. Kuyper, "Christ and the Needy," 666.

133. I derive the phrase "theological myopia" from Mouw, "Culture, Church, and Civil Society."

134. Kuyper, "Christ and the Needy," 666.

Is he cursing money in and of itself? No. On the contrary, Kuyper is drawing attention to the mis-*direction* that can (and often does) take over when the power of a particular sphere abandons its faithfulness to divine law and ruins the role which the power in that arena of human life ought to play, turning the financial sphere of human life into a dominating "aristocracy of money" with "its foot on our neck."[135] It is "the soul's longing and the heart's desire" that is turned away from allegiance to Christ to the aggrandizement of self that must be condemned.[136] "Your [mis-directed] *desire* dominates you," Kuyper says.[137] Clearly, he says, "we have all sorts of needs. . . . We must eat and drink; we must cover our nakedness; we need a place to live; and ever so much more. The desire to acquire provisions for our everyday needs is legitimate in itself, but it is precisely at this point that temptation slips in . . . and we are in the enemy's power."[138] Clearly, the financial sphere is an important and necessary structural sphere of human life. The same can be said for monetary power. But monetary power, like any form of power, causes significant suffering when it is misdirected and distorted.

This distortion is a foreign element, a *mis*-direction, because the powers within each sphere are meant to serve others rather than objectify and dominate them.[139] Kuyper thunders that "Every creature, our Confession says so beautifully, must serve man, so that man may serve his God. This rule also certainly applies in both the personal and social aspects of human life."[140]

The financial sphere and monetary power are structurally good components of creation. But, monetary power falls into misdirected abuse. Nevertheless, God seeks the redemption and renewal of monetary power specifically and the financial sphere generally. Therefore, to counter this distorting mis-direction of monetary power, Kuyper points to Jesus, who

> knew that such desperate needs grow from the malignant roots of error and sin, and so he placed the truth over against error and broke the power of sin by shedding his blood and pouring out his Holy Spirit on his own. Since rich and poor had become

---

135. Kuyper, *Problem of Poverty*, 48. Bratt, "Passionate About the Poor," 39, calls this the "Mammonization of life" following the Industrial Revolution, which Kuyper was opposing. Chaplin, "Full Weight of Our Convictions," calls this the "rampant marketization of society."

136. Kuyper, "Christ and the Needy," 666.

137. Kuyper, "Christ and the Needy," 667.

138. Kuyper, "Christ and the Needy," 667.

139. Kuyper, *Problem of Poverty*, 46. In a mis-directed financial system, "that is precisely what the workers are considered to be—instruments, tools."

140. Kuyper, *Problem of Poverty*, 30.

divided because they had lost their point of union in God, he called both together back to their Father who is in heaven. He saw how the idolizing of money had killed nobility in the human heart, so he held up the "service of Mammon" before his followers as an object for their deep contempt.[141]

With monetary power in the financial sphere, like every power in every sphere, "there is always one authority to which we [must be] prepared to surrender unconditionally from the outset: *the authority of our Lord and Savior*" Jesus Christ, he says. It is only when the differentiated powers in the various spheres of creation function in submission to the normative and absolute authority of Christ, rather than a foreign idolatry, that they can remain directed to their proper ends. Therefore, we can observe the Creation-Fall-Redemption trajectory of Kuyper's thought: The financial sphere is a part of God's creation that facilitates the exchange of goods and services to meet our human needs. But because of humanity's allegiance to false principles and desires instead of God, monetary power has been leveraged to benefit the wants of the wealthy at the expense of the poor, creating misery and injustice among the disempowered. But Christ comes to offer his teaching and his personal lived example to defeat the power of idolatry and show the way for humanity to live faithfully before God once again with their financial resources and monetary power in service of the kingdom of God.

CONCLUSION

In this chapter, we have examined Kuyper's understanding of power (which he refers to with the terms sovereignty and authority also) as it comes to us wrapped in his worldview. This is a unique contribution to the philosophical and theological debates about power for Kuyper represents a figure who transcends the typical approaches to power.[142] For Kuyper, the various powers within the creational spheres of human culture are part of the fabric of God's good creation.

---

141. Kuyper, *Problem of Poverty*, 37.

142. See Chapter 2. Heslam, "Prophet," 24–25, argues that the primary reason why Kuyper's worldview is unique or "distinctive" is that "he regards the norms that govern the life of the spheres as fundamental structural principles rather than as principles that provide the basis merely for individual morality or 'tagged-on' ethics." It is in this way, as I've argued in this chapter, that Kuyper's understanding of power is unique in its normative function within Kuyper's worldview.

And yet, power is not an abstract theoretical concept but a component of the authority structures in the differentiated spheres of human cultural life and activity. As such, there are different forms of power within the differentiated spheres of life. And within each sphere, the absolute sovereignty of Christ is mediated directly to characterize their associations and institutions and norm their activities. We have used the example of the financial sphere to illuminate how monetary power is a natural development of creation's potential, how it can be distorted and mis-directed by human sin, and how Kuyper envisions that the Christian gospel can address this rebellion and restore peace and allegiance to God once again. Returning to Clinton Stockwell from the beginning of this chapter, he observes that "Power is not necessarily a bad thing. Power is the ability to act. It is the ability to marshal the resources necessary for social restructuring. . . . We need to understand that power is actually a resource that can be used either for good or for evil. . . . Power represents the ability to effect meaningful change."[143]

The question that now remains for us to consider is this: If we can discern Kuyper's views on monetary power within the financial sphere of human society, can we do the same with the power of the institutional church within the ecclesiastical/confessional/religious sphere of creation? If we can, and Kuyper points us in a particular direction in this regard, then we will have discerned the power of the church in Kuyper's ecclesiology. It is this task that will occupy the next chapter.

---

143. Stockwell, "Cathedrals of Power," 86.

5

The Ecclesial Sphere and Kerygmatic Power

IN THE PREVIOUS CHAPTER we analyzed Abraham Kuyper's worldview and the place of power within it. We discovered that Kuyper's worldview discloses the world as God's creation, a realm of multiple, differentiated spheres of cultural human activity, each sphere having its own divinely delegated, unique, and independent power. This is because each sphere of creation has its own nature, its own primary characteristic, which norms its activity in the world, and therefore its own unique power. We concluded this worldview analysis with the example of the financial sphere and monetary power: its good creational structure and the multiple ways in which monetary power can be distorted and misdirected, causing either human grief and suffering or, through faithfulness to the divine law for a particular sphere, creational flourishing, faithfulness to God, and service of neighbor.

In this chapter, we now bring Kuyper's worldview to bear on the ecclesial sphere and the power of the institutional church. Our study in previous chapters gives us insight into the two foundational questions we must address here: what is the ecclesial sphere? That is, what is the unique function or characteristic of the ecclesial sphere? And, what is the unique power of the institutional church within its sphere? Both of these questions directly flow from Kuyper's worldview that each creational sphere and its institutions are unique and that each sphere has its own unique power.

Once we have analyzed these two questions, we will be in a position to more fully develop Kuyper's view of the source, telos, means, agents, and scope of ecclesial power. That is, where does the church's power originate? What is this power *for*? How is this power utilized? Who utilizes this power? And, to what field of human life does the church's power apply? By analyzing these aspects of ecclesial power we will be prepared to consider ecclesial power within the Kuyperian worldview frameworks of creation-fall-redemption and structure-direction. By this point, we will have spent considerable time analyzing ecclesial power's structure and so we will focus our concluding remarks on how the misdirection of the institutional church's power manifests itself.

By the conclusion of this chapter, we will have completed our presentation of Kuyper's view of the power of the institutional church. We will then transition to the final two critical chapters: one which challenges Kuyper's view of ecclesial power (Chapter 6) and one which counters a misunderstood and misguided interpretation of Kuyper's ecclesiology (Chapter 7). In order to set up those final chapters, the conclusion of this chapter will summarize our analysis thus far by presenting one important question that Kuyper's view of ecclesial power leaves us with. In so doing, we will be picking up some of the questions we briefly considered in earlier chapters related to Kuyper's legacy and the ways in which the Kuyperian tradition has been advanced in the twenty-first-century North American context.

WHAT IS THE ECCLESIAL SPHERE?

Kuyper, the Dutch Calvinist, was committed to the Reformed articulation of the Christian faith. In doing this, his Reformed worldview was the epistemological framework through which he perceived the world and discerned his active place in its unfolding history. From this worldview perspective, the church occupies a particular place in creation, like the family or the state also do in their own ways. But the intensity with which Kuyper addressed the legitimacy and abiding relevance of the ecclesial sphere is due to his historical-cultural context at the end of the nineteenth century in Holland.[1] In order to present Kuyper's understanding of what the ecclesial

1. For Herman Dooyeweerd's treatment of the church, see his *New Critique*, 216–561. Chaplin, *Herman Dooyeweerd*, 244–48, discusses Dooyeweerd's sphere-sovereignty-approach to the church by saying that (1) each institution in society functions within a particular sphere and that no sphere should operate as another sphere, (2) each sphere has its own unique structural principle which norms the institutions within that sphere, and (3) each sphere's distinctive structural principle is expressed through the unique character of its authority. Chaplin argues that regarding the church, Dooyeweerd views

sphere is, we must first consider the context out of which it emerged. After considering this historical-cultural context, we will examine the theological basis Kuyper articulates for his understanding of the ecclesial sphere, the place of the ecclesial sphere among the other spheres of civil society, the ecclesial sphere as distinct from a number of other closely-related spheres, and Kuyper's understanding of the ecclesial sphere as opposed to other Christian ways of viewing the place of the church in the world.

The Historical-Cultural Background to Kuyper's Articulation of the Ecclesial Sphere

Why was Kuyper such a strong advocate for a confessionally-grounded university (1880) or the Dutch Reformed church's full disestablishment from state control? The answer can be found in the historical-cultural context of the early-nineteenth century. In 1816, the Dutch king William I had centralized the administration of Christian worship throughout the Netherlands by bringing it under state control, both for Catholics and Protestants. Then, in March of 1853, the right of self-rule was returned to Dutch Roman Catholics. Only a month later and in response to this change, Rome reinstituted the archbishop of Utrecht and established five other bishoprics across Holland. The Dutch population, whom Bratt observes took Dutch Reformed "religion to be synonymous with political liberty and Dutch character,"[2] took to the streets in revolt. Nevertheless, the Dutch Reformed Church remained under state control. A government cabinet minister oversaw all the public activities of church property and clerical appointments. In hierarchical fashion, the king and a small band of advisors issued edicts for the church that were imposed upon local congregations.

The result of this centralization and near-legal establishment was that the Dutch Reformed church order, which granted autonomy to the local churches (and only to broader assemblies through voluntary confederation) was turned on its head. Now local congregations and ordained office-bearers were at the mercy of government bureaucrats who may or may not (and often did not) operate out of personal Christian convictions. In essence, the church had become an agent of the secular modern state.[3] Bratt observes that this arrange-

---

it as occupying the sphere of faith and that the church's authority is a faith-authority. The term "confessional" is taken from James K. A. Smith's characterization of Seerveld's gloss on Dooyeweerd in Smith, *Introducing Radical Orthodoxy*, 18.

2. *AKMCCD*, 12–14.

3. It was the events of 1816 which lead to the *Afcheiding*, the secession from the NHK in 1834 and a significant wave of immigration to the United States in the years

ment bore strong similarities to Enlightenment thought and values with the state growing in efficient power and centralizing control over more and more of the nation until the state reigned supreme over all of life.[4] Kuyper would have agreed with this assessment. He addressed this offensive arrangement that he deemed unfaithful to Reformed polity and Scripture by distinguishing between the independent and unique "spheres" of the state and church.

In addition to Kuyper's "Sphere Sovereignty" address, it is in his *Lectures on Calvinism* where we observe Kuyper's mature thought on the spheres, their differences, and their inter-relationships. The general contours of Kuyper's theory of sphere sovereignty were presented earlier. Here, it is important to note the contextual background that gave rise to Kuyper's formulation of this theory: it was in order to counterbalance the centralizing and dominating power of the secular liberal state. Kuyper distinguishes the independent and autonomous spheres of the state and the church so that the state is prevented from being "the supreme power on earth."[5] For Kuyper, this is a claim that only the world's creator God can make.[6]

The Theological Basis for the Ecclesial Sphere

Kuyper's articulation of sphere sovereignty was not only a politically expedient justification for the church's independence from the monopolizing power of the state. Rather, Kuyper was working from a distinctly *theological* foundation in his articulation of the world's nature as God's normed creation. As noted in previous chapters, Kuyper's worldview considered the world to be made up of various potentials that were to be developed through responsible human cultural activity over time. We can observe some of this human cultural development (as a sign of God's blessing of humanity even after the Fall) in Genesis 4 and following (agriculture, 4:3; animal husbandry, 4:4; urban development, 4:17; musical instruments, 4:21; metal-working, 4:22; etc.).[7] Likewise, Kuyper envisioned the emergence of the state to regulate human society, the family for procreation and the nurture of children to adulthood, business for the development and exchange of goods and

---

shortly thereafter to form the Reformed Church in America.

4. *AKMCCD*, 14.

5. *LC*, 99; "Sphere Sovereignty" (*AKCR*, 473).

6. It is worth noting that Kuyper was not attempting to return the institutional church to a position of supreme socio-cultural power either. It seems Kuyper was not interested in re-creating a Constantinian Christendom arrangement within society but rather of reforming the church to meet the secularizing forces of modernity.

7. Dooyeweerd, *Roots of Western Culture*, 66–70, calls this the historically developing "cultural power" of humanity in God's creation.

services, and the church for the official worship of God. These were stewardly and divine-norm-abiding human cultural developments. And each of these foundational spheres has a principle characteristic or divine law which norms the unique power within it and distinguishes the spheres from each other so that no single sphere becomes authoritative over all.

Kuyper argues that this is the cosmological structure of human society, for these spheres, he says, "we have not made but *find*. They exist outside of us."[8] And the powers within the various domains of creation are to be utilized by humans in order to unfold the potentials of creation, which is humanity's vocation. As such, human "dominion [over creation] cannot be acquired except by the exercise of the powers, which, by virtue of the ordinances of creation, are innate in nature itself. Accordingly all Science is only the application to the cosmos of the powers of investigation and thought, created within us; and Art is nothing but the natural productivity of the potencies of our imagination."[9] Likewise for the other spheres of creation and the institutions within those spheres: "The principle characteristic of government is the right of life and death"[10] and "The University exercises scientific dominion; the trades-union rules over labor."[11] And within "each of these spheres" there is "authoritative action" which is uniquely suited to that "proper sphere of operation."[12] This is Kuyper's general principle of sphere sovereignty and the powers of the spheres that we presented in the previous chapter in which the structure of creation entails multiple spheres with unique institutions and powers functioning within those spheres.

When we turn to specifically consider the ecclesial sphere, Kuyper comments that it is more than a social "circle of friends."[13] The reason for the church's uniqueness, Kuyper says, is that the church erupts as a unique institutional manifestation in creation like a certain kind of blossom emerging from its own unique root.[14] It is the unique root of faith, "a *unique* organism," he calls it, which produces the church as "a *unique* institution" in human society.[15] Kuyper consistently argues that it is by God's grace that faith is granted to humanity in light of sin and that this is the source of the church's existence in the world: organic faith coming to institutional

---

8. Kuyper, "Common Grace," 188.
9. *LC*, 92.
10. *LC*, 93.
11. *LC*, 96.
12. *LC*, 96.
13. Kuyper, "Conservatism and Orthodoxy," 75.
14. *R&G*, 17.
15. *R&G*, 19.

expression in history. As we saw earlier, Kuyper also recognized that human agency plays a part in the institutional manifestation and evolution of the church through various times and places as a historical institution.[16] Nevertheless, it is through Scripture as God's Word that the church maintains its vital connection to its root-source, an important aspect we will return to below. Therefore, within a multiform creation of multiple cultural spheres there is one sphere in which the church is the unique institutional manifestation of faith. As a shorthand reference to this sphere, we can call it the ecclesial sphere, though this exact terminology isn't used by Kuyper himself.

One misunderstanding that could be made here would be to understand Kuyper as an advocate for the ecclesial sphere as the only legitimate place for religious or confessional expression. This is where Kuyper's view of sphere sovereignty or autonomy needs to be balanced by his view of sphere universality. Faith is not limited to expression only within the church because Kuyper understands faith to be a universal human capacity. We see this in Kuyper's Stone lectures when he said that, there is "no sphere of human life [that] is conceivable in which religion does not maintain its demands that God shall be praised, that God's ordinances shall be observed, and that every *labora* shall be permeated with its *ora* in fervent and ceaseless prayer."[17] Whereas some might misunderstand the "ecclesial" sphere to be only for those so inclined to institutional Christian life, Kuyper believes that faith or religion permeates all of human life, all creational spheres, because the human religious impulse is universal. It is through faith that the "inner self" or "the very center of [one's] consciousness" is religiously oriented to that which is deemed ultimate and worthy of devotion and sacrifice.[18] For Kuyper, faith is expressed in the whole of life, not only within the ecclesial sphere where faith "qualifies" or characterizes the unique activity of the ecclesial sphere.[19] But Kuyper's point in demarcating the ecclesial sphere is that "Our intellectual, ethical, religious and aesthetic life each commands a sphere of its own"; yet this does not limit human capacities to be expressed only in their corresponding sphere.[20]

Neither is Kuyper to be interpreted as justifying the institutional pillarization (Dutch: *verzuilling*) of Dutch society along confessional lines. While Kuyper argues for "a *life-sphere*" or a "*life-view* of our own," Kuyper's original intention in this passage is to justify the unique sphere of the church in

16. Kuyper, *Tractaat van de Reformatie der Kerken* 1; 20.
17. *LC*, 53.
18. *LC*, 52.
19. On sphere universality, see Clouser, *Myth of Religious Neutrality*, 215–17.
20. *LC*, 150.

society rather than the unique confession of each particular church having its own sphere.[21] Kuyper is not arguing that each confessional group must have its own confessionally-based institutions (though there are those after him who have interpreted him in this way, as noted earlier). He is arguing, rather, that the *state* cannot take over the role of providing human society with a sense of ultimacy. This is the unique role of the institutional church.[22]

The Ecclesial Sphere among the Other Spheres

The diagrams below illustrate and distinguish between the modern state-centric, the medieval church-centric, and Kuyper's "Sphere Sovereignty" approaches to the ordering of human society. They are provided here for clarity's sake.

Table 1

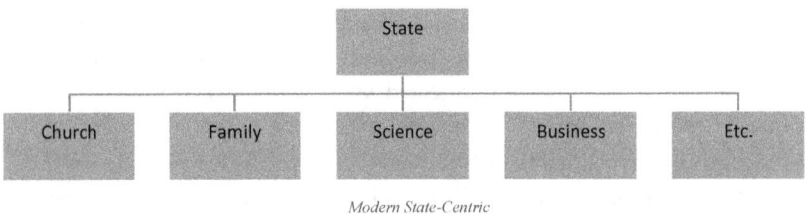

Modern State-Centric

Table 2

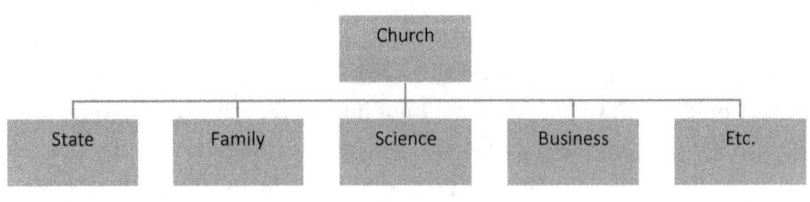

Medieval Church-Centric

---

21. Kuyper, "Blurring of the Boundaries," 400–401.

22. By arguing that the institutional church is called to provide a sense of ultimacy to society, I am not arguing that the institutional church is the only institution or sphere that has directionality. Following Clouser, *Myth of Religious Neutrality*; Goudzwaard, "Goals, Ways, and the Roots," all of life has a religious dimension and each institution/sphere is oriented towards certain ultimate goals.

Table 3

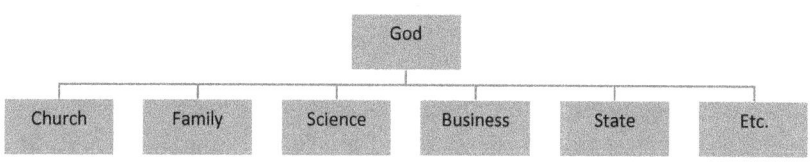

Kuyper's Sphere-Sovereignty

The Ecclesial Sphere Distinguished from the Spheres of the State, Individual Conscience, Science, and Art

In Kuyper's articulation of sphere sovereignty, he sought to clearly distinguish the ecclesial sphere from the other spheres which are closely related to it: the spheres of the state, individual conscience, science, and art, in particular. The reason why the ecclesial sphere is to be maintained as independent from the sphere of the state is *"because the government lacks the data of judgment,* and because every magisterial judgment here infringes the *sovereignty of the Church."*[23] As an organ of civic justice, the state is not qualified to make dogmatic determinations; that is the unique gift and calling of the church, which answers directly to God in confessional matters.

Likewise, the church (or the state) must not infringe upon the sphere of individual conscience. Each person "stands a king in his conscience," Kuyper said.[24] But he also said, "I do not point to this to over-estimate the importance of conscience . . . [but this is my way of] maintaining the sovereignty of conscience, as the palladium of all personal liberty, in this sense—that conscience is never subject to man but always and ever to God Almighty."[25] The sovereignty of the sphere of the individual conscience also must be respected by the ecclesial sphere: "this liberty of conscience [is] to be respected by the Church."[26] But this respect must go both ways: the church must respect the conscience of its individual members (Kuyper argues that the church "has no power over those who live outside of that sphere" of the institutional church[27]) but individual citizens may not intrude

23. *LC*, 136.
24. *LC*, 139.
25. *LC*, 139.
26. *LC*, 140.
27. *LC*, 140.

upon the sphere of the church, attempting to force it to change its beliefs or doctrines to suit the prevailing currents of cultural mood.

Kuyper likewise believed that the ecclesial sphere may not intrude upon or dictate to the spheres of science[28] or art. At issue here is whether science and art must be agents of the institutional church and whether the institutional church must directly supervise and approve all scientific inquiry and artistic expression. Kuyper argues in the negative. Science does not need to (in *a priori* fashion) confirm the church's doctrine. And art does not need to illuminate, through aesthetic beauty, the truths of ecclesial dogma. History has now reached a point of sufficient differentiation that science and art must be regarded as their own autonomous spheres of human cultural activity, liberated from the oversight and control of other spheres. The theological reason behind Kuyper's belief that science and art can be liberated from the supervision of the church is common grace: that God works his grace outside the institutional church to reveal truth and beauty. Science and art have inherent worth independent of the church's sanction.[29] Kuyper argues that "Our intellectual, ethical, religious, and aesthetic life each commands a sphere of its own. . . . Art also is no side-shoot on a principal branch, but an independent branch that grows from the trunk of our life itself."[30]

The Ecclesial Sphere as Opposed to Lutheran and Roman Understandings

To conclude our analysis of the ecclesial sphere in Kuyper's worldview, it is worth noting that Kuyper distinguishes his view of sphere sovereignty from the social ontologies of the Lutheran and Roman Catholic traditions. Kuyper observes a similarity between Lutheran and Roman Catholic churches in how they do not fully allow for the full independence or full universality of the various spheres as compared with his view that each sphere is sovereign, responsible directly to Christ alone, and animated by an aspect of human nature which transcends the spheres and is ultimately universal in scope. Lutherans, Kuyper argues, allowed for the civil magistrate to retain control over the church. This view blurs the distinction between the sphere of the state and the sphere of the church.[31] The Roman Catholic distinction between the earthly (secular) and heavenly (sacred) realms

---

28. By "science," Kuyper means the rational and empirical study of the world which is the purview of the academy. See *LC*, 146-47.
29. See *LC*, 164-65.
30. *LC*, 201-2.
31. *LC*, 137.

allows for the introduction of a "false dualism" which does not take seriously enough the distorting effects of human sin on all human capacities.[32] This results in privileging "spiritual" activities as opposed to more "natural" activities that need little guidance from the Word of God, a view which denies the universal applicability of the Word of God except as these activities are funnelled through the institutional church. Only the theory of sphere sovereignty, Kuyper argues, honors the distinctions created by God between the spheres while also liberating humanity to investigate the "masterpiece of the supreme Architect and Artificer" in all of life.[33]

It is worth pausing here and briefly summarizing this point: in Kuyper's socio-cultural worldview, the sphere of the institutional church is more limited than the human religious impulse which is universal. Neither the church nor the state can claim total sovereignty over the whole of human life. But the institutional church is not thereby relegated to optional or secondary status. But what does the institutional church give formal and official manifestation of, other than humanity's religious impulse? This would be to ask about the ecclesial sphere's primary characteristic or leading function. We turn to that question now.

THE LEADING FUNCTION OF THE ECCLESIAL SPHERE

Herman Dooyeweerd is the father of the modal scale, a multi-aspectival way in which any object can be studied comprehensively.[34] As a component of God's diverse creation, therefore, we can use this scale to consider the institutional church which, like other objects, has a range of aspects by which it can be described.[35] A church has multiple members so it has a numerical size. Those members gather in a specific building which occupies a particular geographic space in a particular place.[36] Sometimes that building is relocated and/or the members come and go (at least when they gather for and are dispersed after official worship services), giving the church a certain amount of motion. The physical health of the members and the organic health of the community gives a church biotic or communal vitality. As a

32. LC, 160–62.
33. LC, 164.
34. Dooyeweerd, *New Critique of Theoretical Thought*.
35. Chaplin, *Dooyeweerd*, 174, also notes that there are many ways to describe, for example, a church. These various ways may overlap with other institutions or other spheres, but the various ways of describing the church will be grounded in the church's "structural principle" or leading function. That is, "Every institution is multifunctional" (275).
36. On a Christian approach to place, see Bartholomew, *Where Mortals Dwell*.

community, the members individually and the group as a psychic collective has and manifests particular feelings or sensitivities. The community we call the church makes decisions and engages in deliberate logical actions that can characterize it. The church grows out of a tradition and lives in time so it could be characterized historically. A church uses words that are sung, read, and preached in particular places with a particular language or dialect, which means that a church could be described linguistically. How the members form and structure their community (rather than just being a random conglomeration of individuals) could describe the social nature of the church. The church collects the offerings of its members, pays its bills, and offers financial assistance to the poor which means that the church can be described economically. The types of songs, choices of ornamentation in the sanctuary, the dress of the minister, and the architectural style of the building gives an aesthetic aspect to the church. When complaints are voiced and decisions are made which affect the members, a juridical aspect begins to come into view that can characterize a church. And the quality of the individual members' lives and the quality of the community's life together means that the church has a moral aspect that can be described.[37] A church can be described in a diversity of ways.[38]

But what exactly makes the ecclesial sphere of the institutional church *unique*? What makes a church a church and not a family or a labor union? Or is it just like any other association of people gathered for a common task? Each of the aspects listed in the paragraph above could also describe other spheres or institutions. A school or a family or a business or a nation are each examples of people living together in groups but they are all clearly different from a church and from each other.[39] What makes the church a *unique* institution in a *unique* sphere?

---

37. This paragraph is based on the modal scale as presented by Dooyeweerd, *New Critique of Theoretical Thought*. A simplified presentation of this complex system can be found in Clouser, *Myth of Religious Neutrality*, esp. 196–227.

38. Mouw rightly notes the multiple aspects of a church's being as well as the caution this elicits, saying: "From a sphere sovereignty perspective, it is important to emphasize that churches are neither families nor businesses, even though there may be important links between churchly functions and things that happen in these other spheres. . . . When a clear focus on the unique patterns of ecclesial reality is not maintained, there is a constant danger that the church will borrow too heavily from other spheres for its understanding of its life and mission, thereby suffering from the distortions that these borrowings will inevitably effect" (Mouw, "Some Reflections on Sphere Sovereignty," 54). Herman Dooyeweerd gave a philosophical shape to Kuyper's notion of sphere sovereignty, which is summarized well by Witte Jr., "Introduction," 11–30.

39. Wolterstorff, *Hearing the Call*, 311, recognizes that "a state is strikingly different from the church." How this is so is not only the task of this project but many others studying the application of Kuyper's work to the various spheres of human life.

We have observed that for Kuyper it is an institution's primary characteristic or leading function that makes (or "qualifies"[40]) a sphere, or an institution within a particular sphere, unique. As Kuyper said, "If the church has a characteristic life principle, then—but only then—that life must manifest its independence in terms of essence and form."[41] That characteristic life principle of the church, Kuyper says, is "eternal election."[42] By "eternal election," Kuyper means "a confession that all honor, including that of spiritual greatness and courage of faith, belongs to God" as the ultimate orientation of life.[43] The only confession that leads to the honor and greatness of faith, according to Kuyper, is that God is always in gracious, immediate communion with humanity through his Word and Spirit.[44] This is what one assents to and orients one's life to through faith. In other words, the unique characteristic of the church, which can be stated a number of different ways, concerns *faith, religious ultimate allegiance, or life-orientation to that which is of highest value and deserving of greatest loyalty*. It is the religious, pistic, or confessional aspect of human life that marks the church as unique in the marketplace of civic institutions. No other institution is directly oriented to this aspect of human ultimacy, though as we've seen the confessional aspect of humanity universally relates to all of life trans-spherically. But it is this institution of the church which, for Kuyper, is that unique institution directly oriented to this faith-in-that-which-is-ultimate aspect of humanity.[45]

40. See Clouser, *Myth of Religious Neutrality*, 203, 216–31, for the qualifying aspect which distinguishes one sphere or institution from another.

41. *R&G*, xxiv.

42. *R&G*, xxiii.

43. Kuyper, "Common Grace," 309. Interestingly, while Kuyper places election within his ecclesiology, Barth places it within his doctrine of God. See Barth, *Church Dogmatics* 2/2.

44. *LC*, 59.

45. While Kuyper sought to discern the leading characteristic of the various social spheres, Herman Dooyeweerd gave a thorough philosophical rendering of social institutions along a modal scale. Each sphere or institution was not limited to one leading characteristic but could be analyzed in terms of its modal structure. The range of ontologically distinct and irreducible modal aspects that Dooyeweerd identified are: (1) numerical, (2) spatial, (3) physical, (4) biotic (organic life), (5) psychic (feeling), (6) logical (analytical), (7) historical, (8) lingual (symbolic meaning), (9) social, (10) economic, (11) aesthetic, (12) jural, (13) moral, and (14) faith. Simple objects (like non-organic physical objects) have a structure that is limited to the lower modal aspects while more complex objects (like a family, a natural institution, or a state, a social institution) extend farther up the range. The highest modal aspect of an object is what makes it normatively distinctive. In the neo-Calvinist tradition, this also explains the transformation in the meaning of "sphere sovereignty" from that of social institutions (Kuyper) to modal aspects (Dooyeweerd). While I have followed Kuyper's line of thought in this analysis, Chaplin summarizes Dooyeweerd's understanding of the institutional church's structural

Kuyper is explicit about his heavy dependence upon Calvin at this point.[46] For Kuyper, as for Calvin, the origin of religion is the "*semen religionis*" which God has implanted within humanity as part of the image of God. Rather than some human deficiency, fault, or need that requires humanity to search for missing ultimate meaning or provision through religion, Kuyper says that "God Himself makes man religious by means of the *sensus divinitatis*, i.e., the sense of the Divine, which He causes to strike the chords on the harp of his soul."[47] That is, "Religion is exclusively a sentiment of *admiration* and *adoration*" on the part of humanity through which we seek "to covet no other existence than for the sake of God, to long for nothing but for the will of God, and to be wholly absorbed in the glory of the name of the Lord, such is the pith and kernel of all true religion."[48] And this is what the sphere of the institutional church is uniquely oriented toward: "placing [one] in the presence of God Himself."[49] The life-principle of the church, namely election, functions to place humanity before the presence of God. This is the leading function of the institutional church, which its power is *for* and that we will turn to in a moment.

The other institutions of society (universities, art galleries, credit unions, etc.) have their own unique connection to the various aspects of human life (intellectual, aesthetic, economic, etc.). But, despite the many ways in which the institutional church is similar to other civic institutions, for Kuyper the church is the only institution that is uniquely oriented toward this ultimate aspect of human life, one's foundational commitment, ultimate loyalty, basic beliefs about the nature of reality, and the comprehensive glory of God. It is in this way that the church occupies that sphere in which humanity is explicitly brought before the face of God. How the church is equipped, enabled, and authorized to do this is what Kuyper means by the power of the church.

---

principle as "a pistically qualified and historically founded institutional community. The historically formative power on which the church is founded is that of Christ as Word of God. The church's leading function defines it as 'an institutionally organized community of Christian believers in the administration of the Word and the sacraments.' Everything that the church does must be directed by its character as a community of faith" (Chaplin, *Dooyeweerd*, 247). See also Dooyeweerd, *New Critique*; *Christian Theory*.

46. On Calvin's thoughts concerning the origin of humanity's natural religious impulse, see his *Institutes of the Christian Religion* 1.1–3. On the relationship between Kuyper and Calvin, especially related to the idea of "sphere sovereignty," see Spykman, "Sphere-Sovereignty."

47. *LC*, 46.

48. *LC*, 46.

49. *LC*, 72.

THE POWER OF THE CHURCH

Having addressed the unique and independent sphere of the institutional church and its principle characteristic of placing one face to face before God, we are now prepared to analyze the power at work within the institutional church. And as we observed in Chapter 1, Kuyper is sensitive to issues of power generally, not only within the church but in the other spheres and institutions of civic life as well, and not only when it comes to manifestations of power which are healthy but also to those distortions of power which cause personal suffering. We have seen, further, that Kuyper believes it is the primary characteristic of the institutional church to be that unique sphere of culture where humanity is before the face of God. This is what ecclesial power is *for* in Kuyper's view and it has its own particular source, telos, means, agents, and scope. Kuyper addressed each of these aspects of ecclesial power throughout his career and in his many publications such that we are able to compile and analyze them in turn. While Kuyper never names ecclesial power in the way we are naming it here, we will discover that he views the power of the institutional church as essentially kerygmatic in nature: the institutional church is for the proclamation of the good news or *kerygma* of the Word of God. This is the institutional church's primary characteristic and its unique role in society.

The Source of Ecclesial Power

What is the source of the institutional church's power? Where does it come from? Does it reside within the institutional church itself (in its polity, members, office-bearers, etc.) as a creational/civic institution or does the institutional church's power originate elsewhere (for example, in the state)? Kuyper is abundantly clear that the institutional church's power-source is Christ himself as the Head of his Body on earth. Through the incarnation of Christ, "*a historical phenomenon*,"[50] God "posits an all-embracing and absolute *principle* [Dutch: *beginsel*]: that is, from him [Christ] a whole new life derives its *beginning*."[51] As a result, the institutional church, which has received this Christocentric beginning/principle, "must hold on to the Christ not merely to maintain a distinct life, not only as the absolute principle of that life, but equally as the Eternal One in whom the fullness of that life is already present . . . in Christ we already *have* everything and need not first

---

50. Kuyper, "Conservatism," 78.
51. Kuyper, "Conservatism," 81.

acquire it . . . the only power that can heal the fatally sick world."[52] Christ, as creation's only true Sovereign and who has delegated his authority to the multiform spheres of life, is the direct and only source of the institutional church's power. This is the logical result of sphere sovereignty for the institutional church.

Kuyper's understanding of the Incarnation is conveyed through an agricultural metaphor which he develops in a sermon we analyzed previously, *Rooted and Grounded*. As we saw there, the Incarnation is God's *grounding* of his free, organic, and immediate work of grace in the midst of human life, and in its vital union with Christ the institutional church "bear[s] in its own core the power of life and in its own seed the law of its life."[53] This power of Christ, grounded in the institutional church, is "a power operating invisibly," bringing about "a natural growth," "a force that comes to outward expression from the inside."[54] But we should not view the institutional church as *passive* in this divine action; rather, it is better to understand it as *receptive* and cooperative, as soil receiving a seed. The institutional church receives this ecclesial power through its living union with Christ and together with "*the work of human hands*" it becomes an active agent in history (much like a house, temple, or city is *built*, Kuyper says).[55] This, as we saw before, is Kuyper's distinction of the church being both an organism (rooted) and an institution (grounded). But rather than Kuyper only distinguishing between the church as gathered institution versus sent organism, the distinction between God's power and human cooperation is also a description of how the power of Christ within the institutional church binds humanity to God who is "the Cause, the Source, the Fountainhead, and the Worker of whatever is built or is grown, of whatever is grounded or rooted. Everything is from and through and unto him!"[56] Christ is the vital source of the church's power that takes on institutional form through human agency in history. *How* this occurs is addressed below.

Therefore, the power of the institutional church originates in "the power of Jesus."[57] It is not human recommendation or admonishment, hard work, or the display of pathos, Kuyper says, but Christ alone is the root of the church's power.[58] In any account of ecclesial power, Kuyper reminds us,

52. Kuyper, "Conservatism," 81.
53. *R&G*, 4.
54. *R&G*, 5.
55. *R&G*, 5.
56. *R&G*, 9.
57. Kuyper, *Tractaat van de Reformatie der Kerken* 43.
58. The times Kuyper emphasizes this point is nearly countless. See, for example, Kuyper, *Tractaat van de Reformatie der Kerken* 7; 10; 12; 18; 28; 43; 46; 50; 52.

"*All* power in the church of Christ must forever be traced back to Christ. He and He alone is our King. To Him alone is given all power in heaven and on earth."[59] Yet, this Christocentric power-source of the church does not limit Christ's sovereignty to the church alone. Christ remains sovereign over all creation while simultaneously being the Lord of the institutional church. Christ is the source of both common grace in society and special grace in the church.[60] Some Calvinist ecclesiologies which attempt to discuss the role of the church *vis-à-vis* the kingdom of God result in truncating or calling into question the rule of God over all of creation.[61] Kuyper's theory of sphere sovereignty retains the lordship of Christ and Christ's kingdom over all creation while also understanding that Christ's ultimate and universal sovereignty is delegated to the multiform spheres of human activity. Ecclesial power is utterly Christocentric in its source.[62]

The *Telos* of Ecclesial Power

If Christ is the source and origin of ecclesial power, then what is this power *for*? What does it intend to accomplish? Where does it fit within the sweep of cosmic history? Kuyper argues that the source of ecclesial power is Christ alone. That is, it is not a power that emerges from the present fallen world. This is why Kuyper refers to it as "a new power" or a "new life" which is at work in the midst of the fallen world.[63] The institutional church is where, in the midst of fallen creation, "God will descend within it and within its sphere" with "the input of divine life in human life."[64] That is, the institutional church is where Christ by his Holy Spirit is present and active because "God is the light that shines in her."[65]

Therefore, ecclesial power, being a divine power from its source and operating in the midst of a *fallen* and *rebellious* creation, is necessarily a *redemptive* power.[66] Ecclesial power, flowing from Christ, meets creation in

59. Kuyper, "It Shall Not Be So among You," 131.

60. Bolt, "Church and World," 30, argues that "Calvin views the reign of Christ *extra ecclesiam* in the context of a Triune rule over all things."

61. For example, Heyns, *Church*, addresses the relationship between the kingdom of God and the church. It is unclear, though, whether his approach—primarily in the introductory diagram—limits the kingdom of God to only a portion of creation.

62. On the role of the Holy Spirit in Kuyper's ecclesiology, see Kuyper, *Work of the Holy Spirit*, 179–99.

63. Kuyper, *Menschwording*.

64. Kuyper, *Menschwording*.

65. Kuyper, *Menschwording*.

66. Chaplin, *Dooyeweerd*, 177, observes: "There are, it turns out, two societal

its sinful rebellion to reform and renew it in grace and love. The power of God, working in and through the institutional church, Kuyper says, is the "power to become children of God by believing in His name. And if you have already become one of His children, even then He gives you power, a power that comes from the Tree of Life called Immanuel, whose blossom is the merit of the cross and whose fruit is grace."[67] Ecclesial power addresses the fallen creation with redemption, a redemption that includes both justification and sanctification.

This means that through the Incarnation, God in Christ has planted his gracious power in a world which is rebellious against God. This gracious and redemptive power is active in the institutional church; it is a power that is oriented toward redeeming and renewing fallen life. This redemptive ecclesial power, therefore, has a distinctly redemptive *telos*. The purpose or goal of ecclesial power, for Kuyper, is the conversion and renewal of the entire creation to the glory of God.

This redeeming power of Christ, operating in and through the institutional church, is the power of divine grace for the renewing of fallen and sinful life. This renewing grace "penetrates into the world's joints, melts down whatever it finds [that is fallen], and transforms it into its own life."[68] As such, the power of God's grace in Christ intersects the forces and consequences of sin, producing a "double stream" in the world. In the present fallen world there are two powers: not only the power of sin but also "one that has trickled down from God's holy mountain . . . [which] carves out its own bed," a "new life," "a unique life" which results "in an independent institution . . . the church."[69] Thus, the power of the institutional church produces the emergence of an alternative community of people who are being converted and discipled out of their sinful rebellion against God and into Christian believers in God, who are being formed into a civic institution founded and empowered by grace in the midst of the fallen and rebellious creation. In light of sin, God's eternal *election*, the life-root and principle of the institutional church, results in a redemptive grace which produces a distinct and alternative institutional community in society, which is a sign and an agent of God's redemptive aim for the world.[70]

---

structures, which have been ordained after the fall: church and state. The former is an 'institution of special grace'; the latter, of 'common' or 'preserving' grace."

67. Kuyper, "It Shall Not Be So among You," 138.
68. *R&G*, 10.
69. *R&G*, 10–11.
70. This is Kuyper's argument in *R&G*, 11.

Kuyper emphasizes divine election as the root of the church's new life of grace because the "institution [of the church] alone never constitutes the church" for "A church cannot be manufactured; a polity, no matter how tidy, and a confession, no matter how spotless, are powerless to form a church if the living organism is absent."[71] Kuyper, the champion of nineteenth-century Dutch Calvinism, believed that God must be the origin of the power in the church that is for the renewing of sinful creation. And this power not only produces the appearance of renewal through the formation of a new institutional shell. Rather, God's redemptive power actually changes people's lives and the gathering together of these redeemed people forms the institution, organized in society. Ecclesial power, as redemptive, begins by redeeming sinful people to the glory of God. Ecclesial power is not human effort or human tendencies toward community. Rather, it is a converting work that only God can do by grace.

For Kuyper, therefore, an account of ecclesial power's telos must contain not only its redemptive emphasis but must also result in a God-glorifying emphasis. The renewing of creation through redemptive ecclesial power serves the glorification of God only when the witness of the church results in the conversion of life from its rebellion against God. In his Stone lectures, Kuyper argued that "the purpose that has been assigned to the Church in its pilgrimage through the world" is that

> the Church exists merely *for the sake of God*. . . . For the glory of our God it is necessary to have regeneration followed by conversion. . . . In the regenerate man glows the spark, but only in the converted man does the spark burst into a blaze, and that blaze radiates the light from the Church into the world, that, according to our Lord's commandment, our Father, which is in Heaven, may be glorified.[72]

Or, as Kuyper put it in an earlier sermon, the goal of the church is that instead of our sinful rebellion against God, "Christ will be formed and take effect in human life." The answer to the question "why God became man, [is] so that the man might possess the divine life." That is, "Transfiguration of Christ, that is the goal."[73] This means that through the church "a power of salvation" is at work in the world for "Christianity aims at a new creation. . . . It produces children of God not by calling them forth from the stones of the wilderness but by regenerating human beings" from their sinful rebellion

---

71. *R&G*, 12.
72. *LC*, 66.
73. Kuyper, *Menschwording*.

against God.[74] And this conversion of life from its rebellion against God glorifies God who is the source of this renewing power.

Unlike the French Revolution which sought to destroy all that was past and replace it with something entirely new, Kuyper argues that Christianity is a "real power" which, instead of revolution, works organically with the present circumstances of life to redeem, renew, and recreate that which is in rebellion against God.[75] So, rather than ecclesial power being magical or mechanical, it is organically and intimately connected with the historical and cultural processes of human life individually and collectively. As Kuyper explains,

> The Church on earth is not an institution for the dispensation of grace, as if it were a dispensary of spiritual medicines. There is no mystical, spiritual order gifted with mystical powers to operate with a magical influence upon laymen. There are only *regenerated and confessing individuals*, who, in accordance with the Scriptural command, and under the influence of the sociological element of all religion, have formed a society, and are endeavoring to live together in subordination to Christ as their King. This, alone, is the Church on earth—not the building—not the institution—not a spiritual order.[76]

Ecclesial power is a second stream, a stream of grace, an additional force, a force for redemption, introduced into the world which meets the world in its material factors and works organically for renewal and redemption, not its ahistorical revolution. The result is not only the renewal of rebellious creation but ultimately the glorification of God as the source and fountainhead of all grace. God is King; therefore, the power of his kingdom, which originates in him as grace, returns to him as glory.

The Means of Ecclesial Power

But how does ecclesial power accomplish this redemption? To say that ecclesial power has its source in Christ, that it is a divine, redemptive, and God-glorifying power that aims at the conversion and renewal of the entire creation, does not address how this power is mediated in and/or through the institutional church. This is an important question in light of Kuyper's many cultural roles. Is the power of the church mediated via the institutional

---

74. Kuyper, "Conservatism," 69.
75. Kuyper, "Conservatism," 70.
76. *LC*, 62.

church hierarchy's direct involvement in politics or education or journalism? Kuyper held key leadership roles in each of these cultural arenas with a distinct Christian identity and purpose. Is Kuyper advocating a strong role for the institutional church in civic matters? Does Kuyper envision a neo-Constantinian mode of cultural privilege and influence for the institutional church? And in light of Kuyper's emphasis on redemption, which could potentially be understood as coercive, this is a critical question. What are the *means* of redemptive ecclesial power?

Contrary to possible misinterpretations of Kuyper, Heslam argues that Kuyper was not interested in a "Christian hegemony" or an attempt to "re-Christianize society."[77] Kuyper himself strongly rejects any notion of the institutional church assuming the role of the state or of direct involvement in the affairs of government, academy, etc.[78] Rather, the institutional church must remain the institution it has been created and called to be and none other if it is to remain faithful to Christ. And yet, the institutional church is called to participate in the civic arena with authenticity and integrity *qua* institutional church, which means addressing all aspects of human life, politics and education and journalism included. As we uncover the means of ecclesial power in Kuyper it will become clear that this is an area in which Kuyper closely follows and rearticulates Calvin.

In Kuyper's 1870 sermon, "Conservatism and Orthodoxy," he addressed the means of ecclesial power by saying that the institutional church has "the power of the Word of God . . . the enormous task of bringing the power of the gospel to bear again" on society.[79] We find this same ecclesial concern with the Word of God in Kuyper's *Rooted and Grounded* sermon shortly thereafter as well. Rather than addressing the divide between conservatives and those of orthodox Reformed faith, Kuyper argues in this sermon against both arch-conservatives and modernists by saying that "Because the church is an organism, the church possesses her unique life and thus her unique principle of law [Dutch: *rechtsbeginsel*]."[80] What is this unique life and unique principle? Kuyper rallies the congregation to

---

77. *CCW*, 146. Luis E. Lugo also acknowledges that "Kuyper was very much aware of the deep, driving influence of competing religions in human society. He also understood that Christ's claims of authority extend to the entire world. That combination logically would seem to lead him straight to a declaration of cultural war against religious adversaries. Kuyper was of the view, however, that the Christian faith could speak meaningfully to this religious diversity, and do so in a noncrusading fashion" (Lugo, "Foreword," 8).

78. It is noteworthy that Kuyper's VU was free from the control of the state *as well as* the church.

79. Kuyper, "Conservatism," 84.

80. *R&G*, 27.

embrace a distinctly Reformed approach to the institutional church's role by saying that "God is her sovereign, eternal election is the heart blood of her life, and God's Word the foundation that cannot be dislodged, upon which she stands with both her feet."[81] This is a constant theme of Kuyper's: the means of ecclesial power is the contextual proclamation of the comprehensive Word of God to life.

Continuing to address himself to the role of the Word of God in the institutional church, Kuyper exhorts his listeners to "Let that Word hold sway with power in your own heart, let it hold sway with majesty around your hearth, let it govern life with its purifying influence in all of life."[82] That is, the Word of God must be proclaimed comprehensively and have its universal application to every aspect of human life, a goal which the institutional church is uniquely equipped to foster. As a Christian minister, an official agent of the institutional church, Kuyper speaks about the place of the Word of God in the institutional church with pathos:

> What moves my soul, what I beseech from my God, is that he may grant me to shine before your eye a single ray of light from that eternally rich, never exhaustively adored, mercy that is in Christ Jesus. What arouses my zeal is simply this, that I may dip the tips of my fingers in that Fountain of eternal Love, in order to lay a few drops of those cool waters of grace on the burning lips of your heart.[83]

How does Kuyper envision this ministry of consolation taking place? By "Building up the congregation spiritually, feeding her with the Word of the Lord, [this] remains our first calling in every battle."[84] Clearly, the Word of God is the key means of ecclesial power for Kuyper, but what are the means by which the church utilizes this Word addressed to her? In what form(s) is the Word of God proclaimed to the congregation?

Kuyper picks this up again in 1898 while delivering his Stone lectures, with distinctly Calvinist specificity. We would not be wrong to hear Calvin's threefold marks of the true Church in Kuyper's own tongue when he says that "the Church on earth consists only of those who have been incorporated into Christ, who bow before Him, live in His Word, and adhere to His ordinances; and for this reason the Church on earth has to preach the Word, to administer the sacraments, and to exercise discipline, and in everything

---

81. *R&G*, 33.
82. *R&G*, 36.
83. *R&G*, 36–37.
84. *R&G*, 38.

to stand before the face of God."[85] Kuyper is mining Calvin's *Institutes*, Book 4, quite deliberately here. What is unique is that Kuyper connects this to the important issue of *power*.

Kuyper is here arguing that the institutional church's power is for the "feeding and expanding" of the organic heart (faith in union with Christ) of the church through preaching, sacraments, and discipleship.[86] This is a work that can only ultimately be done by the Holy Spirit through the institutional church's faithful ministry of the contextually proclaimed Word of God, though clearly human agents are needed in this work (see below).[87] Kuyper then connects this distinction between the organic and institutional aspects of the church to Matthew 28:

> "Go, teach all nations and baptize them." "Teach and baptize," says the founding document of that institution. "Word and Sacrament"—behold the foundational parameters of the design according to which the institution is constructed. For neither the proclamation of that Word nor the administration of that sacrament is an organic operation. They presuppose human consciousness; they need human organization; they require a human act. They do not operate automatically, but through man as the instrument of the Lord.[88]

The means of ecclesial power are Calvin's marks of the true church: Word, sacrament, and discipline. This is *how* ecclesial power is transmitted in, by, and through the institutional church.

What we observe from Kuyper, then, is that once converted Christian believers are incorporated into the institutional church, the ecclesial power of the church is for nurturing and equipping them through the ministry of Word, sacrament, and discipleship.[89] As Kuyper himself says, "it is pre-

---

85. *LC*, 63. On Calvin's marks of the true church, see his *Institutes of the Christian Religion* 4.1–8.

86. *R&G*, 14. Chaplin, *Dooyeweerd*, 173, notes that Dooyeweerd follows Kuyper in maintaining that "the typically ecclesiastical power of the church, for instance, is 'the power of the Divine Word.'"

87. *R&G*, 15.

88. *R&G*, 15.

89. Mouw agrees and notes that, for Kuyper, "the institutional church is certainly an important part of Christ's Kingdom. It is where we as believers gather to worship—where we are shaped by the preaching of the Word, by participation in the sacraments, by instruction in the church's traditions and teachings, and by less formal patters of fellowship. In the life of the institutional church, believers regularly acknowledge the authority of Jesus Christ over their daily lives" (*AKASPI*, 57). It is important to note in this regard that there is significant controversy regarding Kuyper's view of "presumptive regeneration." On this matter, see Kuyper, "Heilsfeit en Heilswoord"; Pronk, *F. M. TenHoor*.

cisely this 'nurturing' that renders the institution [of the church] absolutely indispensable."[90] This is the indispensable means of the institutional church's power: proclamation of the Word, administration of the Sacraments, and Christian discipleship.[91] Kuyper uses two metaphors to communicate this: the institutional church is a 'nursery' for the nurturing of Christian believers[92] as well as an army tent in a battle where soldiers are strengthened before battle, where they treat their wounds after battle, and where one is a prisoner by the sword of the Word and is fed at the Lord's Table.[93]

Ecclesial power is exercised "by means of the preaching of the Word"[94] and "In the second place, the Church must fan this blaze [of faith], and make it brighten, by the communion of the saints and by the Sacraments."[95] Thus, Kuyper the pastor, professor, journalist, and politician-statesman has repackaged Calvin faithfully for a new generation: the institutional church must always seek to remain faithful as the unique sphere God has created, called, and gifted her to be and her institutional power is nothing less than placing humanity before the face of God through the preached Word and the symbolic action of the Sacraments which together achieve the discipling of Christian believers.[96]

The Agents of Ecclesial Power

If ecclesial power is mediated through the proclamation of the Word of God, the celebration of the sacraments, and Christian discipleship, who does

---

90. *R&G*, 16.

91. This is a key theme in Kuyper, *Tractaat van de Reformatie der Kerken*, esp. 13; 20; 22; 35; 54.

92. *R&G*, 16.

93. *R&G*, 22.

94. *LC*, 66.

95. *LC*, 66.

96. Mouw, "Some Reflections on Sphere Sovereignty," 47, rightly notes that by limiting the power of the church to Calvin's marks of the true church, Kuyper was "warning against the dangers of inflating any one of these mediating structures, political or otherwise. He was especially vocal about the dangers of an overextended church. For Kuyper, the mandate given to the institutional church—local congregations and the broader ecclesial assemblies—had to do primarily with such activities as worship, catechesis, and evangelism. Churches were not to take on functions that were appropriate to other spheres." By limiting the power of the institutional church in this way, it should be clear that direct Christian involvement in matters of government policy, educational administration, etc., is delegated to the church as an organism, the faithful lives of Christian believers in their various callings and occupations. This was a primary focus of both Kuyper's *Common Grace* and *Pro Rege* works.

Kuyper assume are the agents of this ecclesial power? This question takes one into the turbulent waters of Presbyterian-Reformed church polity.[97] For Kuyper, a biblical church polity insists upon a criticism of traditional hierarchical models. First, the local congregation is the ecclesial center of gravity.[98] The congregation then democratically selects elders and deacons from their midst (which make up the local church council) who lead the congregation and supervise the minister(s). The minister is ordained by the congregation and council to bring the Word of God to bear on their lives and to celebrate the sacraments with them.[99]

The "broader" assemblies of the church (the regional classis and national synod) are comprised of office-bearers delegated as representatives from local congregations. These broader assemblies provide a broader deliberative context in which mutual encouragement and ministry can take place as well as a "court of appeal" for unresolved matters of dispute in local congregations.

Kuyper conceives of ecclesial power working through these official channels in the following way: "Church power descend[s] directly from Christ Himself, into the congregation, concentrated from the congregation in the ministers, and by them being administered unto the brethren. So the sovereignty of Christ remains absolutely monarchial, but the government of the Church on earth becomes democratic to its bones and marrow."[100] That is, ecclesial power is monarchically directed from Christ to the local congregation, and then democratically through the local congregation to the local office-bearers so that the congregation can be served the Word of God, sacraments, and discipline/discipleship by them. These local office-bearers are then delegated to the broader ecclesial assemblies. Ecclesial power originates in Christ, is delegated to the congregation, then from the congregation to the office-bearers, and finally brought to bear by the ministers through the Word to the congregation again to the glory of God.

---

97. Mouw, "Learning From the Dutch," 145–58, seeks to place many post-Kuyper Reformed splits into the larger background of the various different understandings of Reformed church polity. He rightly notes that while many see the Presbyterian-Reformed polity as a hierarchical blend of "higher" and "lower" assemblies, Kuyper (and many Kuyperians) prefer to speak of "local" verses "broader" assemblies which do not relate to each other hierarchically. The Dutch Reformed church polity dates back to the Synod of Dordrecht, 1618–1619.

98. Kuyper's view that the ecclesial center of gravity is the local congregation is not intended to obstruct the local congregation's missional vocation to the world. Regarding Kuyper's view of the centripetal movement of the local congregation, see his *Encyclopedia of Sacred Theology*, 54, 320–21, 587–93.

99. See *Belgic Confession* 30–32; *Heidelberg Catechism* 83–84.

100. LC, 63.

Due to this emphasis on the priority of the local congregation, Kuyper has forceful words for the church's official institutional leadership in the broader assemblies, especially when those broader assemblies are controlled by agents of the state. Kuyper is well aware of "idle overseers and a lethargic church," of an institutional church that lacks its organic vitality and is reduced to a "church that could be only an institution." This state of affairs "is completely out of place in the church of the Lord that, as a living organism, is herself consecrated to the ministry of the altar. One who holds office must be rooted in the priesthood of the church. Apart from that intimate relationship, the office becomes domineering."[101] That is to say, the official leadership of the institutional church can never be a mechanical role, a function of an institution whose agents are cut off from vital union with Christ by a lack of faith. The agents of ecclesial power must be from among the priesthood of all believers. They must be in living and faithful union with Christ as well as officially delegated by the local congregation.[102]

Thus far, Kuyper's emphasis on the proclamation of the Word of God and the celebration of the sacraments in the life of the institutional church might lead one to believe that Kuyper retained little emphasis on the Reformed diaconate, which hasn't been mentioned yet. This would be a misunderstanding. Kuyper had a strong social impulse, observed in his tireless attention to "the social question" of his day (and his publications such as *The Problem of Poverty* reflect this) and a high view of the deacon in ministering ecclesial power within the congregation. For, Kuyper says, nobody "caught the real meaning of the Diaconate. Calvinism alone has restored the Diaconate to its place of honor, as an indispensable and constitutive element of ecclesiastical life."[103] The deacon, like the elder or minister, is a called and ordained office-bearer for ministering the Word of God to the congregation but in a uniquely justice- and compassion-oriented way. For "The Deacons are not *our* servants, but servants of Christ."[104] It is "in His name [that alms] must be distributed to His poor,—our brothers and sisters."[105] In fact, Kuyper warns, "The poor church-member, who thanks the Deacon and the giver, but not Christ, actually denies Him Who is the real and divine Giver."[106]

---

101. *R&G*, 29.

102. On Kuyper's localist tendencies, a constant point of tension within the Reformed tradition, see Mouw, "Learning from the Dutch," 145–58.

103. *LC*, 83.

104. *LC*, 83.

105. *LC*, 83–84.

106. *LC*, 84. Note that in this discussion Kuyper is addressing the role of the deacon in ministering to the institutional church member. For Kuyper's thoughts on the church's relationship to the poor of society, see Kuyper, *Problem of Poverty*.

To be true to Kuyper, then, we must adjust our understanding of ecclesial power to include the crucial role of the diaconate in ministering the Word of God in tangible form of compassion and justice. The agents of ecclesial power are the office-bearers of the local institutional church (minister, elder, and deacon) who, through the delegation of the congregation in democratic fashion, are called to minister the Word of God in its varied forms to the congregation. This Word is addressed through proclamation, sacraments, discipleship, and diaconal ministries of justice and compassion. But in all these ways, the source and origin of ecclesial power remains Christ at work among his people by his Word and Spirit.[107] We have discerned in Kuyper's ecclesiology, then, a *four*-fold nature to the kerygmatic or proclamational power of the institutional church.

The Scope of Ecclesial Power

By raising the question of the scope of ecclesial power, we are not interested in the question of how far the jurisdiction of the institutional church extends out beyond the boundaries of the church into the other institutions of society. We have already addressed this question via the notion of sphere sovereignty. The ministry of the institutional church does not invade the proper functioning of any other sphere but is directed to the contextual ministry of the Word through preaching, sacraments, discipleship, and diaconal ministries of justice and compassion in its own sphere. Rather, what is in view with this question is the scope of human life that occupies the institutional church's field of view as it seeks to contextualize the proclamation of the Word of God. Who or what does the institutional church have within its field of vision in its proclamational task? Only those members of its institution, all Christian believers more generally, those matters which pertain to the realm of faith, religion, or spirituality (values-ethics), or something other?

It is a characteristic of dualistic conceptions of Christianity that Christian faith and the institutional church only concern themselves with specifically Christian or ecclesial matters. And depending on whether one is of the theological Left (social justice) or Right (personal morality), the target shifts. Badcock claims that this is what North American evangelicalism, as well as the more liberal "mainline" churches in their own way, has done by prioritizing the individual conscience that must "choose" Christ

---

107. On the role of the Spirit in the congregation's official ministry, see Kuyper, *Tractaat van de Reformatie der Kerken* 16.

and the more "spiritual" aspects of human life.[108] Opposed to this, Kuyper's view is that the Christian faith and the institutional church must have a comprehensive, world-wide interest while operating within the ecclesial sphere. The institutional church must be concerned with all of creation for Christians are sent by the institutional church into the whole of creation. And this is where we begin to observe Kuyper's logic regarding the scope of ecclesial power.

The institutional church's scope is not limited to those people or matters that might typically be thought to lie immediately within its institutional purview. Rather, the scope of ecclesial power is universal. It has a comprehensive attention to all of life. This is not only a direct consequence of Scripture's attention to all of life but Kuyper's own understanding of humanity's universal religious nature. Just as humanity's religious impulse seeks the glory of God in all of life, so too the institutional church seeks to proclaim the Word of God as it addresses all of life, not only what current fashion deems to be "spiritual" or "religious." While this may seem initially to parallel Kuyper's distinction between the church as an institution and the church as an organism in the institution having an indirect relationship with the extra-ecclesial world and the organism having a direct relationship with the extra-ecclesial world, Kuyper's thought is more nuanced than this.[109]

Additionally, Kuyper's emphasis is on the comprehensive scope of ecclesial power because Christian believers, if they are to truly be discipled as followers of the cosmic Lord, must be equipped to live in and bear witness to him in the whole world for which they are gifted and to which they are called to serve God and neighbor. Because the institutional church equips the organic church (the church sent into the whole of life), the institutional church must contextualize its proclamation in order to adequately equip Christians for faithful life in the whole world, not just the "religious" part of life or the institutional church. If the institutional church's ministry were to limit itself to only what it deems "spiritual," then the institutional church would be limiting Christ's lordship and drawing a boundary line between those parts of the world which matter to God and those parts that do not.

We can see this comprehensive scope of ecclesial power equipping all Christian's various callings in Kuyper's work on *Common Grace*. He said

---

108. Badcock, *House Where God Lives*, 20.

109. The Christian Reformed Church in North America has recently engaged in a discussion of the nature of the relationship the institutional church has to the complex economic, legal, and political questions of the state. While one author attempts to root their argument in Kuyper, the simplistic reading of Kuyper does not do justice to the complexity of the matter. See, for example, Westerhof, "Church and the Exercise of Non-Ecclesiastical Power."

that "we cannot stop here" with the institutional church concerning itself with that which lies within its institutional boundaries. The institutional church, mediating the Word of God to Christians for their callings in the world, must address all of life.

> This [church] institution does not cover everything that is Christian. Though the lamp of the Christian religion burns within that institute's walls, its light shines out through its windows to areas far beyond, illuminating all the sectors and associations that appear across the wide range of human life and activity. Justice, law, the home and family, business, vocation, public opinion and literature, art and science, and so much more are all illuminated by that light, and that illumination will be stronger and more penetrating as the lamp of the gospel is allowed to shine more brightly and clearly in the church institute.[110]

Kuyper is not arguing for the institutional church to function like the state and directly legislate its religious convictions over everything. Rather, his argument is that the institutional church, as the bearer of the Word of God, must faithfully address that Word to every aspect of life because that Word is itself comprehensive and its light illumines every part of creation to which Christian believers are sent.[111]

This light of the institutional church that shines out into the whole world is "a sanctifying and purifying influence [which] must proceed from the church of the Lord to impact the whole society amid which it operates."[112] Kuyper specifically mentions the forms this influence takes:

> By arousing a certain admiration for the heroic courage with which it has borne persecution and oppression. Next it must inspire respect for the earnestness and purity of life lived in church circles. It must further excite feelings of sympathy by the warm glow of love and compassion in the community of faith. And finally, as a result of this, it must purify and ennoble the ideas in general circulation, elevate public opinion, introduce more solid principles, and so raise the view of life prevailing in state, society, and the family.[113]

---

110. Kuyper, "Common Grace," 194.

111. Bavinck, *Reformed Dogmatics*, 1:435–48, addresses the organic inspiration of Scripture in order to avoid a dualistic relationship between the Word in church and world.

112. Kuyper, "Common Grace," 197.

113. Kuyper, "Common Grace," 197.

This is a comprehensive view of the scope of ecclesial power, equipping Christian believers to be ambassadors for the kingdom of God in the whole of life without falling into a neo-Constantinian mode of engagement that tends towards cultural dominance.[114] It is a comprehensive view that does not depend on state or civic acknowledgement. And it does not attempt to achieve this in direct, theocratic, or direct fashion. Rather, it is accomplished as the institutional church addresses the whole of life and sends Christian believers into the whole of life. But the institutional church's proclamation is *indirect* as it is mediated through the organic church that is directly involved in the whole of life.

The institutional church's influence on society is always *indirect* for Kuyper. Rather than the institutional church exerting its kerygmatic power directly on state or academic policy, for example, Kuyper reminds us that "the church of Christ can never exert influence on civil society directly, only indirectly.... By its influence on the state and civil society the church of Christ aims only at a *moral triumph*, not at the imposition of confessional bonds nor at the exercise of authoritarian control."[115] These are insightful words and point us to the way in which Kuyper envisions this taking place: the institutional church exercises its power in a way that fosters a display of discipled human life that is beautiful, radiant, and desirable (one thinks of Irenaeus saying somewhere that the glory of God is the human being fully alive). These discipled Christian believers then are sent out from the institutional church into the whole of civil society as the organic church to not only display the radiance of being in communion with God but also to offer points of connection with the institutional church where this power is active.[116] This occurs both on the individual level as well as on the level of the mediating structures of Christian civic institutions which not only

---

114. Mouw also recognizes this comprehensive work of the institutional church in Kuyper's thought: "Kuyper's concept of the calling of the institutional church makes good sense.... What people need from the church is what is essential: the gospel and the way it sets forth the basic patterns for living the Christian life. Whether Christians happen to spend most of their time in our homes or in the marketplace, we need to know what is central to the biblical message and the Christian tradition, and we must be nurtured in our growth in the faith by Christian fellowship, spiritual formation, and the sacraments" (*AKASPI*, 59).

115. Kuyper, "Common Grace," 197.

116. Spykman, "Sphere-Sovereignty," 167, puts it very well: "God's Word lays its claim on our life as a whole. But obedience to that Word calls for a differentiated response in keeping with the nature of each sphere, since the various spheres bring with them varying sets of life-relationships." Goheen, "As the Father Has Sent Me," 258, refers to the "inner and outer life of the church" as it engages both in gathered worship and missional sending. These same issues are addressed in Goheen, "As the Father Has Sent Me," 354–69.

project the plausibility of the Word of God for life but which also display its attractiveness in light of human brokenness.[117] By serving to disciple Christian believers to make Christianity plausible, to invite those outside the church to a new faith, and to articulate the ways in which Christian faith makes a positive contribution to the world, the institutional church's power has a universal and comprehensive scope.

A topic that has become of ecclesiological interest in recent decades is the role of the laity within the functions of the institutional church. On this point, one may desire Kuyper to offer more insight than the little if any that he does provide. Rather, Kuyper approaches the role of the laity as receptive of ecclesial power's formative and discipling influence. The laity receive from the office-bearers of the church the Word proclaimed, the sacraments served, the discipleship provided, and the diaconal ministries of justice and compassion extended. In the institutional church, the responsibility falls to the ordained office-bearers. But when it comes to the organic church, the faithful witness of the discipled and equipped laity in their everyday lives, they bear responsibility for the direct witness of the Word to the world.

Leslie Newbigin's missiological concern would want to hear more from Kuyper on the role the institutional church plays in equipping Christians to verbally witness to Christ in all of life. He sees the institutional church's primary role being to prepare Christian believers to be witnesses in the non-Christian world, not merely maintaining Christian institutions.[118] On this point, Goheen writes that "The faithful calling of the laity required a fellowship within the congregation that nourishes the life of Christ through the means of grace, that supports believers in their callings through encouragement, financial support, prayer, and insight, and that develops congregational leadership structures that equip believers for their task."[119] Hall comments, in light of the cultural changes that have taken place in the twentieth century, that the institutional church's "ritual, pageantry, and the marking of highpoints of rites of passage in family life will not hold a laity which can no longer find even peripheral benefits in attendance upon such a cultus, and that, besides, finds itself increasingly skeptical about religious claims that, earlier, it could accept ('since everybody else does'!) without

---

117. Mouw rightly captures both elements as well as connects them: "The church has an important responsibility in *seeing to it* that Christians not only understand their daily lives as Kingdom activity, but also seek out other Christians for mutual discernment in the face of the significant challenges we face in our efforts to be faithful to the gospel in the larger cultural arena" (*AKASPI*, 102).

118. Cf. Goheen, "'As the Father Has Sent Me,'" 61.

119. Goheen, "'As the Father Has Sent Me,'" 431.

much thought."[120] At the same time, the contextual nature of the church's proclamation in Kuyper's vision and the emphasis on discipleship are helpful insights Kuyper provides for preparing Christians for their life outside the confines of the institutional church. In its own way, we could say that Kuyper's ecclesiology, which sees the institutional church as having a proclamatory power, is deeply missional at its heart because it is oriented to empowering the organic church to be the direct connection with the extra-ecclesial world.

ECCLESIAL POWER IS KERYGMATIC POWER

In the preceding analysis, we have allowed Kuyper to lay before us his understanding of the power of the institutional church. It is a unique power within its own unique sphere, unlike the powers at work within the other spheres of human society that may not (or, unfortunately, may) overlap with those of the church. It is a power that originates in Christ.[121] It is a power that is redemptive in nature, its goal being the conversion and renewal of the fallen creation to the glory of God. It is a power whose means are the four-fold proclamation of the Word of God through preaching, symbolic sacramental action, discipleship, and diaconal ministries of justice and compassion. And it is a power that is comprehensive in scope, contextually articulating the comprehensive Word of God to the entire creation so that the organic church can live faithfully in the whole world of God's creating.[122]

While Kuyper never names this as "ecclesial power" as such, what he is charting, and what we have analyzed up to this point, is what I will refer to as the kerygmatic (proclamational) power of the institutional church.[123]

---

120. Hall, *Waiting for Gospel*, 23.

121. Eglinton, *Trinity and Organism*, 185, argues that Herman Bavinck follows Kuyper's lead in this regard, saying that "the church's power is inherently related to the Holy Spirit. Its mission is not world domination through violence, political clout or slick marketing. Rather, the church has, through the Holy Spirit, an unparalleled spiritual power in which to communicate Christ's gospel. Through the church's possession of the means of grace, the Spirit uses the church to redeem the world."

122. Mouw notes that while this may at first appear to be "a fairly limited role" given to the institutional church, through focussed attention on proclamation of the Word of God, in all of its complex application, it actually is the means by which the church achieves its comprehensive influence in the world (*AKASPI*, 99).

123. Spykman, "Sphere-Sovereignty," 167, notes that God's "sovereignty comes into sharp focus and is given specific expression in the various differentiated spheres of our life relationships: parental authority in the home, kerygmatic authority in the church, pedagogical authority in the classroom, governing authority in the state's administration of public justice, and so on." First Corinthians 1:18–24 is an important passage for

This kerygmatic power of the institutional church is the (four-fold) proclamation of the Word of God which meets the fallen creation in its rebellion and, through the Holy Spirit, lovingly turns it, reshapes it, and restores it to its rightful, creational direction for human flourishing.[124] The power of the church is kerygmatic at its core for this captures both the proclamational and redemptive elements we've noted in Kuyper above. This kerygmatic ecclesial power takes the shape of verbal proclamation, symbolic sacramental action, whole-life discipleship, and compassionate diaconal acts of justice and mercy.

By naming ecclesial power as kerygmatic, we can also observe the way in which Kuyper understands the church's kerygmatic power as having both a structural and a directional component. Since Kuyper believes that each sphere has its own structurally unique power, this is why he can argue that "Scripture never takes exception to power, but only to the wrong *kind* of power."[125] For example, when the church copycats or lusts after the power of the state rather than employing its own kerygmatic power, it is mis-directed. Each sphere must utilize its own form of power within its own sphere in a structurally authentic manner or it becomes distorted. This is why, when it comes to the church, Kuyper says that "*God's Word* must rule" because it is the Christian *kerygma* which the church is called to proclaim.[126] In the institutional church, "her position . . . is not assigned her by the permission of the Government, but *jure divino*. She has her own organization. She possesses her own office-bearers. And in a similar way she has her own gifts to distinguish truth from the lie."[127] By gifts, Kuyper refers to what we're calling the kerygmatic power granted to the church within his sphere sovereignty framework. This is the institutional church's unique role in the world, an activity that no other sphere or institution is equipped or called by God to perform.

---

understanding the Christian kerygma, both the message and its act of proclamation, in relation to the power of God at work through the church. For, Paul says, it is this proclamation which is the redemptive power of God, mediated through the church to the world.

124. Bolt notes that a Calvinist and Kuyperian ecclesiology views the power of the church as "a specific, soteriologically defined task to proclaim in word and deed the gospel of reconciliation in Christ. Its integrity as church with respect to the world is maintained to the degree that it is faithful to this task . . . The church ministers to the world . . . by its faithful ministry of the Word which calls the world truly to be the creation which God fashioned through his Wisdom and destined for his sabbath glory" (Bolt, "Church and World," 31).

125. Kuyper, "It Shall Not Be So among You," 139.

126. *LC*, 104.

127. *LC*, 106.

In addition to kerygmatic power being structurally foundational to the church, Kuyper is also cognizant of the multiple ways in which this power can be misdirected and distorted due to human sin. The kerygmatic power of the church is, as we have seen above, Christocentric, gracious, comprehensive, and redemptive. And yet, one problem which the church can encounter is when "the true Christ is so little shown and preached" by the church.[128] That is, the proclamation of the church can become unhitched from its Christocentric moorings in the Word of God. Or, rather than being a gracious Word, it can be mis-presented as a manipulative, legalistic, or moralistic word. Rather than being a comprehensive Word, it can degenerate into a tribal, provincial, or dualistic word. And rather than being a redemptive Word, it can be emotional hype or sensational exhortation.

Another distortion Kuyper observes is the blurring of the boundaries between various spheres' forms of power, particularly problematic for the church and state.[129] This was Kuyper's criticism of the NHK following his deposition: that the NHK "having betrayed its holy calling . . . has been conformed to the world by lust for power."[130] This is the church engaging in "world-conformity" which, Kuyper wonders, might be "the whole sin of the church."[131] The way in which this world-conformity manifested itself was through the "hierarchy of power in both church and state" resembling each other, a kind of "alien" power in the church of Christ in the place of one "true authority," which is a lack of faithfulness.[132] "And of course where lordship [or a hierarchy of lordships] enters," Kuyper warns, "the desire to dominate comes along."[133] This desire to dominate others on the part of the church is "the sin of power lust." It is the lust for a power alien to the church which can result in a number of forms of oppression, as in the church engaging in "the sin of class prejudice" or granting the wealthy the privilege to sit "in the seats of power" in the church while the poor are related to the margins.[134]

---

128. Kuyper, *Menschwording*.

129. For Kuyper, the blurring of the boundaries between creational spheres was a quintessentially modern phenomenon. It introduces confusion to God's ordered creation. An institution operating out of an alien sphere's primary characteristic, like a church abandoning its unique leading function, is "like an association of teetotalers that eventually undertakes to run a distillery." Rather, Kuyper argues, a church must function within its boundaries which are not "determined arbitrarily but must flow from its very nature" (Kuyper, "Modernism," 47). On Kuyper's attack on modernist ecclesiology, see his "Modernism"; Molendijk, "Squeezed Out Lemon Peel."

130. Kuyper, "It Shall Not Be So among You," 126.

131. Kuyper, "It Shall Not Be So among You," 136.

132. Kuyper, "It Shall Not Be So among You," 127, 137.

133. Kuyper, "It Shall Not Be So among You," 130.

134. Kuyper, "It Shall Not Be So among You," 130.

When the church begins to imitate or resemble the forms of power within other institutions or adopt practices which distort the power of the church, the result is the misdirection and abuse of ecclesial *kerygmatic* power.

Again, Kuyper roots this criticism of the church and its misdirected power in the structurally differentiated powers that exist in the various spheres of civic life. "Religion and politics are two distinct spheres which touch at not a single point," Kuyper says.[135] He argues that "God has bestowed upon the state and nations a powerful sense of justice and a generous dose of legal talent. . . . But the Lord God did not bestow this talent on the church."[136] Rather, "If the people of the Lord in this city had consistently held high the power of the Lord, had honored all power and government only for the Lord's sake, had strictly maintained the power entrusted to them and not arrogated power that did not belong to them, there would everywhere have been a clear sense of the difference between a false invasive power and the powers instituted by God" in the church.[137] This, for Kuyper, is the "particular sin of the abuse of power" committed by distorted or misdirected ecclesial power.[138] As a result, Kuyper invites the church to "Give up all power you have wrongly assumed and again honor the divinely ordained influences and powers" that are given to the church and the church alone as a unique institution.[139]

IS KERYGMATIC ECCLESIAL POWER COERCIVE?

For Kuyper, the kerygmatic power of the institutional church is the contextual proclamation of the Word of God in preached Word, symbolic sacramental action, whole-life discipleship, and diaconal acts of justice and compassion. It is a comprehensive Word that originates in Christ, aims at the renewal of sinful creation, and is mediated by the democratically elected office-bearers of the local institutional church. And it is Kuyper's claim that through this kerygmatic power of the institutional church, faithfully carried out, "the victory of Christianity" in the midst of fallen human society will be realized.[140] As we conclude our analysis in this chapter, the question must be

---

135. Kuyper, "Wij, Calvinisten." I am drawing on a translation of a portion of this speech (149–52) done by Harry van Dyke and circulated electronically (Dyke, "Kuyper on Calvin," 5).

136. Kuyper, "It Shall Not Be So among You," 130.

137. Kuyper, "It Shall Not Be So among You," 137.

138. Kuyper, "It Shall Not Be So among You," 137.

139. Kuyper, "It Shall Not Be So among You," 137.

140. Kuyper, "Conservatism," 72.

raised whether Kuyper's view of the power of the church is guilty of triumphalism, an over-zealous attitude of hopeful expectation. Is ecclesial power a coercive power that destroys all resistance as it aims for the renewal of the world, no matter how many times "gracious" is used to qualify it?

These sorts of forceful references permeate Kuyper's writings. Wolterstorff admits that Kuyper's language can often be "rather too flamboyant and Romantic" for his taste, or possibly for anyone's.[141] Is Kuyper merely using "flamboyant" or rhetorical language relative to the "victory of Christianity" through the church's exercise of its kerygmatic power or does Kuyper honestly believe that through human faithfulness human actions can inaugurate the utopia of the Eschaton?

Kuyper prophesies that through Christian faithfulness, the church will regain its position of central importance and influence in society. As Kuyper preached in an early sermon:

> But it will also be up to the church to show that the spirit in which they live is indeed mightier than the spirit who works outside her. Our call will then be able to prove by deeds between us that in the sphere of Jesus' holy life is truly purer and more powerful than outside its borders. . . . [The church must live] more on a demonstration of power than on bravado, less feigned repentance and more true rebirth. So it will be in every way, my hearers, so will the Church of Christ again arise as the head with honor and He who died for us will heighten the flavors of joy as well as those who love him in the Netherlands.[142]

Language like this leads one to assume that the kingdom of God can be inaugurated through greater human attention to Christian faithfulness, personally and institutionally.

Then again, sentiments to the contrary can also be found in Kuyper. For example, when speaking about "the power of faith," Kuyper understands this to be a power unlike any other power, a power primarily to endure persecution and suffering. "A church under the cross is in fact always a persecuted church. If the magistrate of a land or city or village becomes hostile and misuses his power as magistrate to shut down the worship of the church, then the cross of persecution comes upon such a church."[143] Clearly, Kuyper has in mind a very different kind of power than the power of central dominance within the civic life of society.

---

141. Wolterstorff, *Mighty*, 159.
142. Kuyper, *Menschwording*.
143. Kuyper, *Tractaat van de Reformatie der Kerken* 36.

Likewise, when Kuyper discussed "that better, nobler, holier power" that "comes over the church," he says that it "does not seek its strength in force but finds its watchword in the apostolic saying: 'When I am weak, then am I strong.'"[144] Is the kerygmatic power of the church a mighty force like other forces but greater only by virtue of its origin in Christ? Or, is the kerygmatic power of the church something else entirely? This remains an open question. The further clarity we need relates to the similarity or dissimilarity of ecclesial power with other forms of power in other spheres. Is there any more to be said on the nature of power in the church versus other spheres?

In order to address this, we will bring Kuyper into critical dialogue with others in the remaining two chapters. In the next chapter, we will engage Kuyper in conversation with the French Reformed philosopher-theologian Jacques Ellul on the exact nature of ecclesial power as a *power*. And in the final chapter, we will return to the question of Kuyper's ecclesiology being a kind of sacramental ecclesiology by engaging the thought emerging from Vatican Council II and the idea of the church as a sacrament. In these two ways, we will not only conclude our analysis of the power of the church in the ecclesiology of Abraham Kuyper but also offer constructive avenues for moving his contributions forward.

CONCLUSION

Having concluded our analysis of Kuyper's views on the power of the institutional church, and before turning to the last two critical chapters, a summary is in order to bring this section to closure. We have positioned Kuyper in his historical and cultural context. He was a Dutch Reformed theologian, raised in a Christian environment deeply influenced by Enlightenment ideas and values. He was a citizen of a nation that had undergone recent political transformations that concentrated civic power in the state and had created a situation in which the state was dominant over nearly all of life, the church included. And, consequently, Kuyper was ordained as a minister in a church that was beholden to a secular liberal state, a church whose hierarchy mimicked the centralized power of the government, and a church whose theology had drifted from its Calvinist roots as the waves of Modernistic theologies made inroads to seminary, clergy, and laity alike. In response to this, Kuyper articulated the power of the institutional church that sought to address the perceived ills in church, state, society, and the character and flavour of the Dutch Reformed community at large.

144. Kuyper, "It Shall Not Be So among You," 138.

For Abraham Kuyper, the church is grounded in God's creation, taking root and growing over time as a unique institution of human society. It occupies an essential place in human society, an institution within its own unique sphere with its own direct accountability to Christ, independent from intrusion from the other spheres. But the church is unique in that it exists in two modes of being: both as an institution and as an organism. These are not two churches but a single entity which exists bi-modally as a gathered community (institution) and as a people or as organizations/associations actively participating in all of life with a unique identity and calling as Christians (organism). In both modes of being, the church exists to be the bearer of the salt and light of the Gospel to the world. But the institutional church does not accomplish its task with the same power as other cultural institutions. It has a unique form of power for its unique sphere of human life. This view of the unique power of the institutional church emerges from Kuyper's Calvinist worldview, a worldview that addresses the nature and structure of creation, humanity's calling within creation, the effects of sin on creation and humanity both, and the scripturally-disclosed narrative structure to human history.

Therefore, the power of the institutional church in Kuyper's ecclesiology is the unique ability and calling of this particular civic institution, in vital union with Christ, to proclaim the comprehensive Word of God (through proclaimed Word, celebrated sacraments, whole-life discipleship, and diaconal acts of justice and mercy), for the conversion of human beings to faith in Christ who are then equipped and discipled in order to be sent out into the whole of the world to bear witness to Christ in every realm of creation and to use their gifts for the service of God, creation, and neighbor, individually and in associations and organizations of like-minded others within civil society. The power of the institutional church does not lie in the dominance or coercion of its hierarchical offices over the consciences of members or over the other institutions of civil society, but rather the offices of the church graciously serve God and neighbor for the purpose of redemption and restoration. The power of the institutional church does not lie in its political, financial, or technological competence, but rather in contextually addressing the Word of God comprehensively to every aspect of life. This is a power that flows from Christ and his Word, through the agency of ordained ecclesial office-bearers in the local churches, toward the telos of God's new creation. The power of the institutional church is a kerygmatic power.

6

The Nature of Ecclesial Power

Further Philosophical, Theological, and Biblical Investigations

IN THESE LAST TWO chapters we turn to a critical and constructive engagement of Kuyper's understanding of ecclesial power. In this chapter, we address the exact nature of ecclesial power in further detail. In the next chapter, we will address the theological categorization of Kuyper's ecclesiology. The question that has propelled this project forward from the beginning has been: What is the power of the institutional church in the ecclesiology of Abraham Kuyper? As we noted in the conclusion of the previous chapter, Kuyper stands within the mainstream Calvinist tradition in understanding ecclesial power as essentially kerygmatic. As we have argued a number of times already, Kuyper's view of power generally is unique against the backdrop of other theories of power, primarily in his positive and pluralist view of power's ontology. We have already noted Kuyper's understanding of how the multiform powers that exist in the various spheres of creation are connected to the capacities of human nature and the institutions of human culture within God's creation.

In addition, Kuyper places the various powers within a biblical creation-fall-redemption epistemological framework or worldview. Kuyper accounts for not only the structural nature of the differentiated powers, the divine creational laws or norms for the powers within the spheres of human culture, but also their dynamic manifestation or directionality through human agency. Through his concept of sphere sovereignty, Kuyper argues for the proper integrity within and maintenance of the boundaries between the various spheres and powers within creation. It would seem, after this lengthy analysis, that there is little more to say about Kuyper's understanding of ecclesial power. But we turn now to consider a key unresolved question that arises from our analysis thus far.[1]

AN UNRESOLVED QUESTION

Against the backdrop of the previous five chapters, there remains a key unresolved question relative to Kuyper's view of power. That question concerns an as-yet unaddressed aspect of the nature of ecclesial power. In raising this question of the essential nature of ecclesial power we are asking how unique Kuyper's view of power truly is. Does Kuyper still view all the powers within creation's spheres as forces that inevitably overcome any possible resistance?[2] And of central concern theologically is to what extent Kuyper's view of ecclesial power arises from Scripture or from his historical-cultural context. It is possible that Kuyper's view of power is primarily shaped by his cultural or ideological frames of reference that are then superimposed on his reading of Scripture rather than his views arising from and being formed by Scripture.

This is an important question and worthy of investigation for at least three reasons. The first reason why subjecting Kuyper's view of the nature of ecclesial power to critical examination is because of the history since Constantine in which political and ecclesial power have often been welded together in a Christendom social arrangement. This is not only a historical question for the church but also a personal question for Kuyper who united these two spheres in his very person as church reformer and political leader. As Richard Mouw says, "The criticisms of the Constantinian arrangement are legitimate. When the church allies itself too closely with political power it loses the freedom to be the kind of church that God wants it to be."[3] Therefore, he says, "we must always do [our civic work as Christians] with

---

1. Heslam rightly notes that Kuyper's work is "a part of history and cannot be applied directly to today's circumstances" (*CCW*, 270). It is in that spirit that these two concluding critical chapters seek to bring Kuyper's insights into constructive engagement with the present realities of the early-twenty-first century. Mouw calls his own work of updating Kuyper a "Kuyperian *Aggiornamento*" (*AKASPI*, 75–79). These chapters proceed in the same spirit.

2. Bratt notes that Kuyper had a "penchant for militaristic imagery" (*DCMA*, 19). Militaries are forces that seek victory against opposition, a key insight into his view of power generally and ecclesial power specifically.

3. *AKASPI*, 114.

an awareness of the Constantinian danger of forming an unhealthy—and unfaithful—alliance between the church and political power."[4] In light of church history since Constantine and Kuyper's own personal roles in both the spheres of church and state, the question of whether Kuyper's view of ecclesial power has biblical and theological justification is crucial. Does the nature of ecclesial power, for Kuyper, arise out of his reading of Scripture, his historical context, his personal tendencies, or a combination of these?

The second reason for subjecting Kuyper's view of ecclesial power to further criticism is because of the Calvinist tradition in which Kuyper stands and which he seeks to apply to his own context. In the aftermath of the Calvinist Reformation, the medieval church-state relationship tended to break apart and more democratic developments were introduced in both civic and ecclesial life.[5] Yet, as Mouw observes, there are those instances, stemming from Calvin himself, in which church and state coordinated their powers in detrimentally coercive ways.[6] He says that "One of the reasons why Kuyper thought of himself as a 'neo-Calvinist' was because he wanted to distance himself from the way that earlier generations of Calvinists had used political power to further the church's cause."[7] Despite this history, Mouw observes that "Calvinists should be willing to live as a minority presence on the margins of the cultural status quo, consistently avoiding compromise with principles that are different from their own."[8] In light of the history of Calvinism, Mouw's suggestion that the church take up residence on the cultural margins would require a different view of ecclesial power than has historically been understood in the Calvinist tradition. Therefore, is Kuyper's view of the nature of ecclesial power reliant on or similar to state power or is it located more peripherally to culturally-accepted forms of power, functioning as a critique to state power?[9]

4. *AKASPI*, 118.

5. *CCW*, 142–47, contains a helpful analysis of Kuyper's interpretation and consequent application of Calvin's political principles. In general, Heslam argues that Kuyper overemphasized the democratic tendencies in Calvin.

6. While many point to Calvin's role in the execution of Servetus, Mouw is considering a far wider (and equally threatening) scope of church-state coordination. Lord Acton was particularly critical of Calvin on this point. Bolt notes: "In Acton's view, Calvin subordinated the political ends of the state to the religious. The protection of the Calvinist religion was the magistrate's chief task" (*FCHN*, 170).

7. *AKASPI*, 115.

8. Mouw, "Learning from the Dutch," 153.

9. Ecclesial marginality within culture does not necessitate the passivity of "presence" argued by Hunter, *To Change the World*. Proclamation, even from the cultural margins, retains an active mode for ecclesial power. On this point, Wolterstorff, *Hearing the Call*, 201, notes "the tragedy of humankind. We don't hear God when God speaks. Once again

Kuyper's "Oppressive Legacy"?

Finally, Kuyper's view of ecclesial power should be subjected to serious critique because of the history of the socio-political injustice of apartheid in South Africa, which has connections to the Kuyperian tradition. This is a significant and complex issue, worthy of extended examination, but we can only briefly summarize the problem here to highlight the need for further investigation into Kuyper's view of the nature of ecclesial power.[10] The South African theologian H. Russel Botman has named this the "oppressive legacy" of Kuyper in the South African context.[11]

Botman admits there is significant complexity to Kuyper's influence on apartheid.[12] Both Afrikaner Calvinism and the theology of apartheid had multiple aspects and influences to them. "Those who continue to seek an understanding, historical or theological, of the relationship between Afrikaner Calvinism and Kuyper will always find a selective use of Kuyper that strengthens their claims. The eclectic theology of apartheid leads to this dilemma."[13] Botman's argument is that Kuyper was used by some to construct "a theological foundation that undergirded the core value of the Afrikaner Calvinists."[14] That core value, Botman argues through a reliance on Martin Marty's work on the issue, is separateness. It is this value of separateness so as to maintain purity that, for Botman, "drives the church into an attitude of over-against-ness."[15] In turn, this value of separateness in addition to the attitude of superiority give rise to socio-cultural norms in which choices about

---

God's Word was spoken by outcasts. We expected it to be spoken by the respectable and the powerful." Ecclesial proclamation from the civic margins would require a rethinking of the means by which the church believes this Word to be plausible beyond the church.

10. On the connection between Kuyper and South African apartheid, see AK-MCCD, 294–96, 380–82; CCW, 262–64; AKASPI, 75, 80–85; Noll, *Adding Cross to Crown*, 43. On the history of apartheid, see Baskwell, "Kuyper and Apartheid"; Gruchy, "Church and the Struggle for South Africa"; "Church Always Reforming"; *Liberating Reformed Theology*; Boesak, *Black and Reformed*; Boesak, "Theological Reflections on Empire"; Hexham, "Dutch Calvinism."

11. Botman, "Is Blood Thicker Than Justice?," 342–61, argues that this oppressive legacy stems from Kuyper's belief in the superiority of whites, a belief reinforced by Kuyper's racial interpretation of the Tower of Babel story in Genesis 11. Those who translated Kuyper to the South African context, argues Botman, failed to distinguish correctly the state of humanity at the Tower of Babel from the state of humanity in Christ. Wolterstorff, *Hearing the Call*, 275, remarks, "In our century the Reformed tradition *has* often been oppressive in practice."

12. Botman, "Is Blood Thicker Than Justice?," 347.
13. Botman, "Is Blood Thicker Than Justice?," 348.
14. Botman, "Is Blood Thicker Than Justice?," 348.
15. Botman, "Is Blood Thicker Than Justice?," 349.

theological, ecclesial, and ministry partners are made. At bottom, Botman's argument is that "the value of separateness, which became the norm in the DRC [the Dutch Reformed Church of South Africa], was not initially based on [theological] truth but on a contextually experienced desirability."[16] Botman then points to the Dutch Reformed Church Synod of 1857, in which the desire for ethnic separateness in the midst of cross-cultural missions provided "the initial decision for church apartheid."[17] This ecclesial apartheid then shaped the historical-cultural development of social and political apartheid. Botman points to the reliance of the Dutch Reformed Church of South Africa on Kuyper's creation theology, a theology interpreted as "separate development,"[18] leading inevitably to apartheid's theological justification. This oppressive theological justification for racial separateness was finally implemented through the mechanical power of the state and the technological power of a globalized world resulting in the force of apartheid that spanned the various spheres of South African society.

Even in post-Apartheid South Africa today, this recent history has continued to exert its power of separation on society despite its legislative and institutional dismantling decades ago. As Botman has observed, our post-Apartheid world has been deeply affected by neo-liberal perspectives on power, especially economic power. "The forces of global exclusion have taken the place of apartheid, thereby replacing a racial problem with a dominant class issue."[19] A number of authors have pointed to the emergence of pillarization (Dutch: *verzuilling*) in the Netherlands as the theoretical foundation for the doctrine of separation along racial lines in South African apartheid.[20]

On the other hand, Botman argues that had a "full appropriation of Kuyper's theological system" taken place within the Dutch Reformed Church of South Africa, the theological justification of apartheid would have changed the course of history.[21] Rather, it was a *selective* appropriation of Kuyper, filtered through was what deemed to be contextually desirable, that took place. While there is clearly more to Kuyper's legacy than apartheid, and the pro- and anti-apartheid parties did not split neatly along either white/black or Kuyperian/non-Kuyperian lines, this oppressive legacy raises

---

16. Botman, "Is Blood Thicker Than Justice?," 349.
17. Botman, "Is Blood Thicker Than Justice?," 349.
18. Botman, "Is Blood Thicker Than Justice?," 353.
19. Botman, "Is Blood Thicker Than Justice?," 360.
20. In addition to Bratt, Mouw, and Heslam in previous footnotes, see Baskwell, "Kuyper and Apartheid," 1269–90.
21. Botman, "Is Blood Thicker than Justice?," 354.

the question of Kuyper's view of the nature of ecclesial power.[22] Whether Kuyper would have supported this rigidly segmented system of civil organization, either in the Netherlands or in South Africa, is debatable.[23] In either case, the ethnic, social, and confessional connections are suggestive enough to warrant further investigation. So, even if for no other reason, a close, critical examination of Kuyper's view of the nature of ecclesial power versus other forms of power (for example, state power) deserves deeper analysis.

Therefore, by raising the question of Kuyper's view of the nature of ecclesial power we are also raising the question of whether and/or to what extent Kuyper's view of ecclesial power retains the essential element of force within it, at least a version of force which is essential to state power. Does Kuyper view the kerygmatic power of the church as a force that accomplishes its intended effect through force, strength, and domination that overcomes all resistance?

From our previous analysis, it is clear that Kuyper went to great lengths to ontologically distinguish the various powers within creation. Yet Mouw observes that there are times when Kuyper unavoidably relies on conceptions of ecclesial power that perpetuate a hierarchical understanding of force that can introduce an air of arrogance. He counters this by using the example of Mother Teresa who accomplished her work through suffering service and the pain of spiritual crisis. Mouw even entitles the chapter in which this discussion takes place: "Kuyperianism Under the Cross" and he argues that "Christians must care deeply about culture, and they must recognize that true cultural obedience to their Lord has to take place under the cross."[24] This alone speaks to the tensions inherent within Kuyper's view of ecclesial power. Even "force" is an ambiguous term because the force of persuasion and the force of law, while different in degrees, are still forms of force. Therefore, the key unresolved question that we will address in this chapter is the exact nature of ecclesial power relative to conceptions of force versus resistance.

THE RELATIONSHIP BETWEEN SPHERE AND POWER

The relationship between sphere and power in Kuyper's theory of sphere sovereignty is crucial for addressing this question of ecclesial power's element

---

22. It is possible that there exists a tension within Kuyper on the issue of racial mixing. Kuyper praised the American mixing of blood whereas in his contact with the South African Boers during the Boer War he did not. See *LC*, 37–40; "South African Crisis" (*AKCR*, 232–360).

23. Botman's argument assumes Kuyper would not have approved. See "Is Blood Thicker Than Justice?," 354.

24. *AKASPI*, 136.

of force. As we noted in Chapters 3, 4, and 5, Kuyper's worldview conceived of God's power distributed directly to creation in the multiform spheres of created socio-cultural life. Each of creation's spheres is directly related to the multiple human capacities God wove into creation. And the kind of power within a sphere is related to the unique sphere where that power operates. We used the example of monetary power within the financial sphere earlier. The question now is: what is the exact nature of kerygmatic *power* within the ecclesial sphere? We began answering this question in the previous chapter by noting the source, telos, means, agents, and scope of ecclesial power in Kuyper's thought. It is one thing to describe ecclesial power as redemptive but is it a hegemonic redemption that overrides human will with divine force? This is the nature of our analysis in this chapter.

Roy Clouser has made a serious study of Kuyper's theory of sphere sovereignty as it relates to society and the power of the state in his work, *The Myth of Religious Neutrality*.[25] In order to develop his argument relative to the sphere of the state, he makes a number of helpful observations for determining the nature of the power operative within a particular sphere. First, he argues that within each sphere, the leading function of that sphere norms the nature of the power and activities of that sphere. This norm is purposeful and teleological. That is, it gives an intended direction to the contribution of that sphere and that sphere's power to the whole of life.[26]

Secondly, and flowing from the first, each sphere's normative leading function norms the power and activities of only that sphere and does not norm the other spheres. Otherwise, that sphere and its power would become totalitarian over the other spheres, something that Kuyper's theory disallows. Consequently, if power is treated as a conceptual abstraction and understood in a singular or generic fashion, without consideration of the particular sphere in which it operates and which gives power its essential nature, that understanding of power can be said to be reductionistic.[27] It leads to a hierarchical understanding of society, as in, for example, state power being normative for the whole of life and each sphere needing in some way to contribute to the actualization of state power. Clouser summarizes these two points in the following way: Power or

> authority in human life does not have any *one* nature at all. Within creation there is no one supreme kind of authority, because only God has that. Instead, the Scriptures speak of many

---

25. Clouser, *Myth of Religious Neutrality*.

26. Clouser, *Myth of Religious Neutrality*, 235.

27. See Clouser, *Myth of Religious Neutrality*, 252; "Blue Print for a Non-Reductionist Theory of Reality."

different kinds of earthly authorit*ies*. . . . No single kind of authority is the only kind or the source of all other kinds. . . . The only single overarching authority is God's, while within creation there is an irreducible plurality of kinds of authority, each delimited by its own social sphere.[28]

Finally, Clouser argues that there is an intimate connection between the leading function of each particular sphere and the essential nature of the power at work within that sphere. The power within each sphere exerts its "own sort of cultural-historical influence in society."[29] This means that within each sphere "the cultural influence or power that it wields is of a kind which corresponds to its leading function."[30] The implication of Clouser's argument is that just as the state has the authority to exercise its power with coercive force (not only to punish lawlessness but also to promote social justice and peace), so too the church has the authority to exercise its kerygmatic power in a manner which directly corresponds to the nature of its sphere and leading function. The nature of power within the ecclesial sphere will be kerygmatic, as opposed to, for example, coercive as it is for the state. We could say, therefore, that ecclesial power has its nature by its ecclesialness rather than its power-ness. The determining factor is not that ecclesial power is a kind of *power* but that it is *ecclesial*.

What Makes the Church's Power *Ecclesial*?

This is the important question of the nature of *ecclesial* power in Kuyper that we have not addressed thus far and about which Kuyper himself is silent. What is the essential nature of ecclesial power as a force that distinguishes it from, say, state power as a kind of force? This question of the difference in force must be more than the differences in source, telos, means, agents, or scope. Otherwise, the kerygmatic power of the church is open to interpretations which allow the church to exercise its power in a manner similar to or in cooperation with the state as both being forces that overcome resistance. Is it possible, in Kuyper's view, for the ecclesial power of discipleship to take the shape of coercive force? If there is nothing more to be said about ecclesial power, then a coercive attempt to advance its own interests (for example, the gospel or Christian morality) becomes possible even if it is understood as God's comprehensive redemptive power through

---

28. Clouser, *Myth of Religious Neutrality*, 253–54.
29. Clouser, *Myth of Religious Neutrality*, 266.
30. Clouser, *Myth of Religious Neutrality*, 266–67.

the proclamation, symbolic action, discipleship, and diaconal ministries of justice and compassion. It may still retain the element of coercive force. As we shall see in what follows, the nature of ecclesial power, to be true to Scripture, must be uniquely suited to the ecclesial sphere in which a different norm rules its leading function and shapes its essential nature. Rather than being a coercive force, it is something entirely different and unique because it flows from a different and unique sphere. Ecclesial power, for Kuyper, may not be Weberian force all the way down.

But this is precisely where Kuyper ceases to be explicit and where the Kuyperian tradition is open to what Botman calls its potentially *oppressive* influence. Therefore, in order to address this, we must chart the trajectory of Kuyper's worldview as it relates to addressing this question of the essential nature of ecclesial power as a force and determine the implications of Kuyper's view for the forcefulness of ecclesial power.

Three questions will guide our inquiry in this chapter. First, are there theologians who have addressed the nature of ecclesial power in this non-force sense and do they offer assistance to us in achieving clarity on this issue of force and the nature of ecclesial power? Then, second, does Scripture offer guidance to us in understanding the nature of the church's kerygmatic power as a kind of force? Finally, do any other Christian traditions, possibly contemporaneous with Kuyper's context, illuminate a way in which the nature of the church's kerygmatic power can exert its cultural-historical influence in a uniquely *ecclesial* manner without retaining the element of coercive force? This will conclude our analysis in this chapter and bring clarity to our understanding of kerygmatic power in Kuyper's ecclesiology before turning to the theological category of this ecclesiology and its potential for ecumenical dialogue.

AVOIDING THEOLOGICAL BIPOLARITY: JOHN CAPUTO AND NON-FORCE POWER

We begin with theorists who have contemplated alternative forms of power for the church. John Caputo has addressed this question of the nature of ecclesial power. While not working from the Kuyperian tradition, he does wrestle with how the church's power is different from the power at work in the other arenas of human cultural activity. The reason why he is an insightful place to start is because one of his interests is how to conceive of the nature of ecclesial power without immediately resorting to coercive force, which is the nature of the power of the state, the sphere that Clouser is focused on in his work examined above. In fact, as noted above, the Kuyperian tradition has reflected extensively on the power of the state. For this reason alone, it is important to be clear about how the nature of kerygmatic ecclesial power is essentially different from the nature of the coercive power of the state. One drawback that we will notice at the outset is that Caputo seeks to redefine or reinterpret power or force generally, which returns us to a reductionist view of power. While this reductionism is unhelpful, his insights remain illuminating for alternative frameworks for understanding the essential nature of ecclesial power.

Caputo does not think coercive force is an essential element of power. But he does recognize the challenge, especially for theology, of giving an alternative account of power without recourse to force. Theological talk of power runs the risk, he says, of becoming "intellectually bipolar, vacillating wildly between the heights of power and the depths of weakness."[31] In either the form of force or weakness, he says, power has been "a defining feature of theology right from the start."[32] According to Caputo, the problem is that theological accounts of power, even those which conceive of divine power as the weakness of God, are "too much in love with power, constantly selling its body to the interests of power, constantly sitting down to table with power in a discouraging contradiction of its own good news."[33] The result is that the more theology considers power, even power cloaked in the weakness of God,[34] "the more we can be sure it has power up its sleeve."[35] Thus, he concludes, "If theology were somebody, a person, the solution would be to find a good analyst to help him or her work through this conflict."[36]

The Divine Non-Force Power of Invitation

In giving his biblical and theological account of power, Caputo suggests we "stop thinking about God as a massive ontological power line that provides power to the world."[37] Rather, he suggests taking the concept of power as force and turning it on its head: thinking of power as "something that short-circuits such power and provides a provocation to the world that is

---

31. Caputo, *Weakness of God*, 8.
32. Caputo, *Weakness of God*, 7.
33. Caputo, *Weakness of God*, 8.
34. For example, "God's weakness is stronger than human strength" (1 Cor 1:25b NRSV).
35. Caputo, *Weakness of God*, 8.
36. Caputo, *Weakness of God*, 8.
37. Caputo, *Weakness of God*, 13.

otherwise than power."[38] Caputo calls such alternative conceptions of power a "weak force" and likens it to a call (Latin: *vocare*) or an invitation. A call in the sense of a weak power is

> not power pure and simple, but the powerless power of a provocation or a summons, a soliciting, seductive power—but it does not have an army to lend it support, and nothing stops us from turning a deaf ear to it. It lacks sheer brawn to coerce or to translate what it calls for into fact. It must make do with the power of powerlessness, not the power of pure strength.[39]

In some ways, Caputo speaks of an "invitation" or "invocation" in ways that parallel some of Kuyper's statements. Caputo even argues that, like Kuyper, the church's *raison d'être* is "the poetics of proclamation, of *kerygma*."[40] It is in this sense of a divine call or invitation to the world in which we see divine and/or ecclesial power as an active non-forceful form of power (what Caputo calls weakness) in the world. "Dead bodies rise, substances are transmuted, impermeable walls are permeated. But none of this is to be confused with a strong force, with the power of a super-being or a super-hero to bend natural forces to his almighty will with a display of awe-inspiring power."[41] What he dismisses as a deadeningly literalist view of divine power mediated through human beings reduces God to a determinist that no amount of human will can counter. Instead, Caputo re-envisions the "power of the kingdom [of God as] the powerless power to melt hearts that have hardened, to keep hope alive when life is hopeless, to revive the spirits of the dispirited and the despairing, to pray for something otherwise than the world that is closing in around us on every side, to pray for the possibility of something coming, in short, in a paradigmatically religious expression, the possibility of the impossible (Derrida), for with God all things are possible."[42]

This is not a hierarchical account of power in which God's power is at the top of the pyramid and, moving downward, we pass through divine weakness, then human strength, before finally ending with human

38. Caputo, *Weakness of God*, 13.
39. Caputo, *Weakness of God*, 13.
40. Caputo, *Weakness of God*, 16.
41. Caputo, *Weakness of God*, 16.
42. Caputo, *Weakness of God*, 16. To be clear, in speaking of the "weakness of God," Caputo is not employing a rhetorical device. He actually believes God is weak as opposed to powerful. The reason why God's weakness is victorious over human power is not because God's weakness is more powerful than human power but because God's weakness confounds, disturbs, evades, and unsettles human power and shows it to be truly anti-real and anti-creational. If God were truly powerful, Caputo observes, then with "such deadening literalism, God becomes the ultimate laser show at Disneyworld" (16).

weakness. Rather, God's weakness is in fact weak, not a variation or perfection of human force. And the reason why God's weakness is victorious over human force is not because God's weakness is more powerful or stronger than human force but because God's weakness confounds, disturbs, evades and unsettles human force, showing it to be truly anti-real, anti-creational.

This is an engaging critique of coercive forms of power despite the fact that, as noted above, Caputo's reductionist approach to power is open to serious critique.[43] But, his notion of God's weakness, which leads to ecclesial weakness, raises and clarifies the important question we have about Kuyper's understanding of the nature of ecclesial power: is ecclesial power the hierarchically strong force of medieval divine omnipotence working through the church which accomplishes divine purposes despite human objections, questions, or hesitation; the ultimate coercive force in the universe? Or might the nature of ecclesial power be something else, a non-forceful form of power, possibly even conceived as the weakness of divine invitation that subverts human cunning and calls humanity to a new reality? Caputo allows us to entertain alternatives, the primary alternative being the power of invitation rather than the power of coercive force.

Thus far, we have determined that Kuyper's view of ecclesial power is that it is kerygmatic in nature. It involves proclamation at its foundation. Caputo opens for us a way to conceive of this proclamation in a non-coercive manner, as non-coercive invitation. Yet, as proclamation it remains an act of communication. And communication, as an act in the contemporary West, is intimately connected to the question of technology in our globalized world of instant communication. Therefore, we turn next to a theorist who has reflected deeply on the nature of our technological society and how this has contributed to challenges of communication. If the nature of ecclesial power is kerygmatic (that is, a communicative act of proclamation), then we must be clear about the power-dynamics inherent in our own context, the context in which the Western church today must live.

JACQUES ELLUL: DIVINE AND ECCLESIAL NON-FORCEFUL POWER

In order to further analyze this critical question of the essential nature of ecclesial power, we turn to the twentieth-century French Reformed philosopher Jacques Ellul and his work on technology and power. Our introduction

---

43. It appears that Caputo's argument of divine weakness also runs into the problem of how to understand divine omnipotence. But this question of God's attributes is beyond the scope of our analysis.

of Ellul at this point opens further space for our critical analysis of Kuyper on the essential nature of ecclesial power, particularly as it is understood as a form of communication in a technological age. Following our analysis of Ellul's understanding of power and communication, we will turn to Scripture to discern the contours of divine power working in and through the church in its missionary encounter with the power of the state.

The Hiddenness of Divine Power

For Kuyper, Christ is the omnipotent and sovereign Lord of creation who brought all things into being from nothing, the One who has instituted his Law for his creation,[44] and the risen and glorified One who rules over all of creation as the Lord of lords and the King of kings. Based on this, his understanding of divine and ecclesial power relies on the force of both creation *ex nihilo* and of new creation in redemption that established and re-establishes, respectively, a normative "*order*."[45]

In contrast, Ellul views Christ as the presence of God hidden in human flesh, the suffering servant, the humiliated and executed rebel at the hands of the Roman Empire. As a consequence, his view of divine and ecclesial power is rooted in the divine humiliation of the Incarnation and the absurd weakness of poverty and placial marginality.[46] Rather than Jesus revealing and displaying the raw *power* of God, Jesus is the "hidden" power of God.[47] And as a "hidden" power, Ellul finds it more appropriate to refer to it as weakness, for "Just as [Jesus] remains hidden in the incarnation, so also his kingdom adopts the same kind of presence . . . and neither claims nor exercises any power whatsoever . . . it is a hidden power, thus implying a kind of weakness" which "is hidden and unknown to others."[48] Ellul is emphatic that while we might speak of God being "a power at work in secret" through the Incarnation, this is a misnomer for it is "the weakness and non-power of Jesus . . . who has no power, status, authority, or anything else of the kind."[49]

Ellul draws on the parables of Jesus to ground his argument of God's non-power. The parables of "the smallest grain of seed and the pinch of yeast" are insignificant potencies that "are hidden in something much larger

---

44. Bratt notes, "Kuyper's God was first of all a sovereign, a lawgiver" (*AKMCCD*, xix).
45. *AKMCCD*, xix.
46. See also Heuvel, *Humiliation of the Church*.
47. *FLP*, 149–50.
48. *FLP*, 154–55.
49. *FLP*, 166–67.

and work in secret"[50] and yet are able to transform creation and make all things new. Even the parable of the Wedding Feast, that seems at first glance to lead one to think of the power of the kingdom of God as a kind of "compulsion," is read in light of this non-power:

> It is one thing for angels to compel you to enter [the kingdom of God]; it is quite another for the state to use its armies to do so. The state has never been compared to an angel. Instead, it is a spiritual power, which is something entirely different . . . it has nothing whatsoever to do with converting people by force.[51]

This hidden and secret non-power of God and God's kingdom is then brought to bear on the church and the church's presence and activities in the world. The church is that community which bears the Word of God to the world like a humble lamp-holder who bears a light in a dark place.[52] But this light of the Word of God that the church proclaims to the world is unlike any other obvious light for the light of the Word of God requires that it be "recognized." It is "not obvious" but rather something that comes into the world "incognito." The metaphor Ellul utilizes may be questionable (why does light in a dark place require recognition?) but Ellul means that the proclamation of the church is something that requires "insight" in the midst of "a great uncertainty." Again, weakness is highlighted rather than the bald force of coercion or compulsion. God is hidden, even in the Word of God proclaimed by the church to the world. This is because we live, even in spite of God's Word being proclaimed to us, in "the silence of God . . . it is night. It is up to us to watch, to remain vigilant, and bear the light for the world."[53] Even the Word of God, for Ellul, is a form of weakness that doesn't force itself on humanity. In a world of fallen powers, God, the church, and the church's proclamation of the Word of God are all forms of weakness understood as the antithesis of coercive power.[54]

---

50. *FLP*, 168, 166. In this chapter, Ellul is focussing on the three parables found in Matthew 13:1–43. The references to "seed" and "yeast" are taken from Jesus' Parable of the Mustard Seed (Matt 13:31–32; 17:20–21; Mark 4:30–32; Luke 13:18–19; Luke 17:6) and the Parable of the Yeast (Matt 13:33; Luke 13:20–21).

51. *FLP*, 192. Ellul is addressing the element of force which is present in the version of the Parable of the Wedding Feast present in Luke 14:15–24 but absent in the version in Matthew 22:1–14.

52. *FLP*, 197.

53. *FLP*, 197–99.

54. Possibly owing to their common reliance on Barth, Dietrich Bonhoeffer writes in his letter of July 16, 1944, in ways that sound strikingly similar to Ellul: "God lets himself be pushed out of the world on to the cross. He is weak and powerless in the world, and that is precisely the way, the only way, in which he is with us and helps us."

Ecclesial Non-Power Elicits Persecution

This understanding of divine weakness is the basis of the church's non-power for Ellul. The church is the lamp-holder who proclaims the hidden kerygma, which is the light of the Word of God, in the midst of the silence and darkness of the world of sin. But because the fallen world prefers darkness rather than light, the result is that "persecution is a part of the Christian life."[55] Ellul eschews any notion of the church forcefully or triumphally bearing the Word of God to a ready and waiting or willing world. For, in fact,

> Christianity can only be that which calls into question what is most fundamental and central to the world. When [the church] challenge[s] this world in a manner that does not threaten it, there will be no persecution. The world is threatened only when the prince of this world or its spirit is called into question, not by a process of conquest and domination but by a presence of what is opposite to the world.[56]

As a non-power, the Christian kerygma primarily calls the world's fallen understanding and activity of power (understood as force) into question. And this provokes the world's persecution of the church.

By saying that the church is animated in ways alternative to those of the world, Ellul is thinking primarily of power-as-force. For the world caught in sin, power means the strong force of conquest and domination. The life of the church that operates out of a provocative non-forceful power and elicits persecution involves

> humility, poverty, freely giving, and so on. It cannot be authority, spectacular conversions, breakthrough works, a strong organization of the church, miracles, or anything of this kind. The

---

Matt 8:17 makes it quite clear that Christ helps us, not by virtue of his omnipotence, but by virtue of his weakness and suffering. Here is the decisive difference between Christianity and all religions. Man's religiosity makes him look in his distress to the power of God in the world: God is the *deus ex machina*. The Bible directs man to God's powerlessness and suffering; only the suffering God can help. To that extent we may say that the development towards the world's coming of age outlined above, which has done away with a false conception of God, opens up a way of seeing the God of the Bible, who wins power and space in the world by his weakness" (Bonhoeffer, *Letters and Papers from Prison*, 360–61).

55. *FLP*, 205.

56. *FLP*, 205. Elsewhere Ellul argues that in addition to the external persecution by the world another form of this persecution is internal to the church's very faithfulness to God: "The opposition between this world and the Kingdom of God is a total one . . . an intolerable situation," which produces "acute suffering" because the "Christian can never regard himself as being on the winning side" (*PK*, 35).

> kingdom of heaven [at work in and through the church] knows no efficient means. . . . This kingdom grows differently from any power in the world, and certainly not by the way of efficiency.[57]

The church, therefore, presents to the world a provocatively rival worldview relative to power-as-force.

This is why the church, for Ellul, is marked by the humility, weakness, and non-forceful power of the child,[58] the excluded,[59] the humble and powerless, poor and destitute disciple.[60] In short, the Word of God that the church bears to the world "does not come through power"[61] because what is "at stake [in the church] is obedience [to Jesus] instead of seeking to do exemplary works. This obedience includes following the way of non-power and non-domination" for if one is "possessed by a spirit of domination, power, or the spectacular, you are not participating in the work of the Lord and the kingdom of heaven. You are doing something else."[62]

The church must be willing to endure (at least) the scorn of the fallen world of power if it is to be faithful to the alternative of non-forceful power revealed and necessitated by the gospel. These are strong and revolutionary words and present the church with a temptation: will the church faithfully embrace weakness, suffering, and even persecution as it seeks to bear witness to the invitation of the gospel or will it unfaithfully embrace and incorporate forms of power which are alien to its being but which are more "effective" and "efficient" and "understood" by the world?

Power: The Church's Temptation

Stanley Hauerwas has commented that "Christians have been forever tempted to derive our status from those forms of power valued by the wider culture."[63] For Ellul, the church has only one legitimate choice between either the fallen power-as-force of the world or the weak non-forceful power of God. The only legitimate choice is clearly the latter. The purposes of God and the church only come about through the apparent weakness of non-forceful power. God and the church can only bear faithful witness to the

---

57. *FLP*, 205–6.
58. *FLP*, 206.
59. *FLP*, 206.
60. *FLP*, 209.
61. *FLP*, 208.
62. *FLP*, 208.
63. Hauerwas, *In Good Company*, 56.

world of the kingdom of God through non-conquest and non-domination. Faithfulness, for Ellul, "is to take the direction of imitating Jesus Christ. He is the servant who is entirely obedient, without violence, without power, and full of grace."[64] And this reveals the vocation of the church: to proclaim the hidden, secret, incognito Word of God all the while rejecting the efficient and effective means of the world's reliance upon the particular form of power as coercive force. The means which the church of Jesus Christ has are non-forceful forms of power: the non-domination of weakness, marginalization, poverty, and persecution. This is what it means that the church is the community of God's elect. Election is "not an election to salvation or damnation but to carry out a particular mission . . . election is a point of departure. . . . A Christian is simply someone who is charged by God to perform a particular function and role" which does not include privilege or advantage.[65] This means that the way of the faithful church will not include the conquest or dominating imaginations that "our actions and interventions [can] possibly hope to bring about a Christian order that entirely conforms with the gospel, or create an ideal society."[66] The church's role is not "progress" or "effectiveness." Rather, for Ellul, it is about being a sign that another world, and another power, is possible.

Because the world in its rebellion against God is fixated on forms of coercive power, conquest, and domination and the church for Ellul is a community of non-forceful power, non-conquest, and non-domination, this presents the church with a critical temptation. Will the church attempt to "Christianize" society through the establishment of a Christian state and the fostering of Christian institutions through force and coercion? If so, Ellul says, the church glosses over "the actual situation of the present world" and accommodates itself to the very fallenness and rebellion against God to which the church is to be the alternative.[67] When the church succumbs to this temptation, it allows the world to remain unchanged because the church has abandoned its unique calling and role and accommodated itself to the fallen world. It does this through a tangible exchange of its own form of ecclesial power for other forms of power operative in other spheres, like the state. In fact, this is Ellul's diagnosis of the contemporary church: the church has become the world.

> The world of the present day is reaping what Christians have sown: confronted by a spiritual danger Christians called men to

64. *FLP*, 210.
65. *FLP*, 156.
66. *FLP*, 163.
67. *PK*, 7–8.

> arms and fought with material weapons. We have conquered on the material level, but we have been spiritually defeated. Christians alone could wage the spiritual conflict; they did not do so. They did not play their part in the preservation of the world.[68]

This is not an argument for the church's resignation or withdrawal from the world of culture, though. Just the opposite. Ellul argues that the church, in its engagement with the world, must remain faithful to its own identity and calling in its own sphere in such a way that its proclamation of the Word of God becomes "incarnated in a real world, and our action, as well as our message, ought to be guided by the present situation of the world, without allowing this to modify either the content or the unity of this will of God."[69] There is no point at which the church can adopt the ways of the world, even to proclaim the kerygma of God's Word to the world. The church can only pursue authentic engagement with the world if it is entirely separate from the fallen ways and means of the world, including power. The church cannot engage the world on the world's terms of coercive force for then, in doing so, it would cease to be the church.

This points to the central role the kerygmatic power of the church plays for Ellul. The church proclaims the Word of God, "not in order to 'bring in' the Kingdom of God, but in order that the gospel may be proclaimed, that all men may *really* hear the good news of salvation, through the death and resurrection of Christ."[70] But in order to do this, the church "must plunge into social and political problems" so that its proclamation takes into account the world as it actually exists in its rebellion and brokenness.[71] This is not, for Ellul, an argument that the institutional church should try and directly fix the brokenness of the world with its dogmatic solutions in the various domains of culture, for "all solutions—all economic, political, and other achievements—are temporary. . . . Thus the Christian is constantly obliged to reiterate the claims of God, to reestablish this God-willed order, in the presence of an order that constantly tends toward disorder."[72]

For Ellul, the twentieth-century church is in a state of crisis because it has deeply compromised itself by aligning with the ways of the world rather than remaining faithful to the alternative ways of the kingdom of God. The church has given in to the temptation to embrace the world's coercive power instead of remaining faithful to the alternative nature of its kerygmatic

68. *PK*, 17.
69. *PK*, 19.
70. *PK*, 35.
71. *PK*, 35.
72. *PK*, 36.

power of invitation. Because of the church's immersion in a politics that is synonymous with the world, it has failed to exist "as a ferment or a leaven in society," having "lost touch with ordinary life," with the result that "churches have proved to be lamentable ambassadors" for Christ.[73] While this compromise has rendered the church less than "fully alive" and its spiritual vitality "seems to have faded away," it has come about through the deep cultural changes witnessed during a century of radical social evolution.[74] What does this mean for the church's proclamation, an act of communication with the world? It means that the institutional church today exists in a state of crisis and this crisis especially concerns its communication.

Ecclesial Non-Power and the Crisis of Communication

Kuyper and Ellul would agree that ecclesial power is proclamational. But Ellul argues that ecclesial power properly understood is the non-forceful power of weakness, along the lines of Caputo's weak force of invitation. This introduces a crisis of communication: what language can the church adopt in order to proclaim its message to the world so that the world will actually, but still freely, hear it? Ellul is keenly aware of this crisis. Ellul is critical of social changes that have had a profoundly negative impact on the church, many of which are related to the development of a technological society and the consequential widespread crisis of communication it has introduced.[75] It is the nature of a technological society, argues Ellul, that ends and means are split from each other, that means have become the sole focus of attention and that ends have been discarded from consideration. The result is that the technical focus on means has made the coercive forms of efficiency, control, and progress the highest values of Western culture. The church, too, has become caught up in this network of technical powers, resulting in the church often adopting the same technical attitude and orientation as the surrounding culture, what Ellul calls the church's "miserable imitation of the world."[76] That is, "Christians are so deeply imbued with the fundamental doctrines of this world that they no longer have any liberty of thought or life."[77] Christians merely "accept the fundamental outlook of the world, to

---

73. *PK*, 44–45.
74. *PK*, 45.
75. Ellul, *Technological Society*.
76. *PK*, 75.
77. *PK*, 75–76.

share its prejudices and its reactions."[78] In short, Ellul says, the church has become the world in its patterns of coercive communication.

The result is that the church's historic or theologically understood ways of being are seen more and more as ineffective and inefficient and "this is the main reason . . . why the church and Christianity have lost so much ground. If the church no longer plays a great part in the world it is because of this new position of the problem of means."[79] In order to address this, Ellul says, the church must recover the importance of *ends* once again. The church must turn its focus away from the mechanical administration of institutions and instruments (means) and foster the presence of the kingdom of God and its King, Jesus Christ, in the actual lives of people who have been formed as citizens of that rival kingdom (ends). This is not Ellul's argument against the "institutional" or "collective" in favour of the "individual." But, rather, this is his attempt to regain a proper perspective in order "to manifest the gift which has been given us, the gift of grace and peace, of love and of the Holy Spirit: that is, the very end pursued by God and miraculously present within us."[80]

What Ellul is arguing for is a more intimate and a more theologically sound relationship between the kingdom of God, the church, and the Christian institutions of a culture. The world's forceful means must be purged from the church. "Institutional reforms," he says, "ought to spring out of the faith of the church, and not from the technical competence of a few experts" in the world.[81] For the only role the church is able or called to play, Ellul reminds us, is that which it is uniquely empowered to do by God: proclaim the Word of God, Jesus Christ, the King who transforms us so that we might truly and freely *live* in a world enslaved by ideologies that run counter to life. "To be alive means the total situation of man as he is confronted by God," Ellul says, and this is what the church is empowered to bear witness to: the proclamation of Christian liberty from the forces of a sinful and dehumanizing world so that one might freely stand before God. But the church that is unfaithful to Christ will adopt methods of communication which turn its power of proclamation into the opposite of non-forceful invitation: propaganda.

Propaganda Is Non-Communication

Ellul perceives a crisis of communication today. This crisis affects everyone but is particularly applicable to the church whose very purpose involves

78. *PK*, 76.
79. *PK*, 60.
80. *PK*, 67.
81. *PK*, 69.

proclamation, an act of communication. Within a technological society, concerned primarily with the means that guarantee efficiency and effectiveness, instead of communication all we are left with is propaganda. Propaganda is the form of force applied to communication, turning it into non-communication. At the heart of propaganda is the desire to overpower freedom with control, manipulation, and domination. That is, propaganda contains within itself the mechanical and technical force or leverage to achieve its intended effect despite resistance. It is a self-empowering means of communication. It is communication that seeks to manipulate the listener, force the listener, to a predetermined outcome. Propaganda, Ellul explains, aims toward "the adhesion of the crowd"—it is a power that attempts to control so as to achieve "distraction" from reality or the truth or liberty.[82] So, not only is the church tempted to adopt forms of power alien to itself, like the state's coercive power, but the technological world the church inhabits has transformed communication itself into the forceful power of propaganda and thereby plunged the institutional church's kerygmatic power of proclamation-as-invitation into crisis. The Western church today, therefore, faces a double crisis.

Ellul contrasts the forceful power of propaganda with the non-forceful power of church proclamation in this way: whereas propaganda carries within itself the force to control, ecclesial proclamation is a non-force which is carried out in freedom because ecclesial proclamation is empty on its own and is "only effective if it is filled with the fullness that God gives it—that it only accomplishes anything if God gives it the power to do so . . . and if God does not give this, let there be no illusion . . . nothing remains. . . . It is dead; it fades into nothingness."[83] The ecclesial non-forceful power of proclama-

82. *PK*, 87. Vincent J. Donovan offers the following thoughts on the difference between propaganda and evangelization: "Evangelization is not a call to restore Christendom, a kind of solid, well-integrated, cultural complex, directed and dominated by the church. It is not an activity set in motion because the church is endangered, a nervous activity to save the remnants of a time now irrevocably past. It is not a winning back of those people who have become a prey to sin in such a way that the organized church no longer reaches them. Evangelization is not propaganda. Propaganda leaves nothing to the Spirit, but predetermines the outcome down to the last detail. Its essential character is a lack of expectant hope and an absence of due humility. Propaganda seeks to make exact copies. It attempts to make man in the image and likeness of the propagandist. Quite the opposite of propaganda is evangelization, filled with hope, which means moving forward in a world with unlimited possibilities, in which we won't be surprised if something unforeseen happens" (Donovan, *Christianity Rediscovered*, 190).

83. *PK*, 97. It is worth noting that Ellul was heavily influenced by the theology of Karl Barth. Greenman et al., *Understanding Jacques Ellul*, 10, note that Ellul's "favorite Christian thinker was the Swiss Reformed theologian Karl Barth (1886–1968), whom he preferred to John Calvin (1509–1564) the fountainhead of Reformed theology." In fact, they argue that "Ellul saw his chief intellectual project as arising from Barth's work" (10). They quote Ellul as saying that he "was not satisfied with his [Barth's] volume of

tion honors the freedom and dignity of people made in the image of God, even if that allows for their rejection of the invitation of the Word of God. Unlike propaganda, ecclesial proclamation is non-forceful, non-controlling, non-dominating. It is not based on mechanical or technical control of the hearer. It is a non-forceful form of power.

The result of widespread propaganda within a technological society, which has become normative for "communication" within a mechanical and technical culture, is that the church will come to realize "the fundamental weakness of our evangelization . . . [for the] world as a whole no longer listens to the gospel. The Word of God no longer penetrates into the reality of human life."[84] In light of this situation, the church is tempted to abuse its theological doctrines concerning "'the efficacy of the Word of God'" which in the hands of anxious ecclesial technicians "betrays a lack of charity towards men, and an indifference to their actual situation."[85] The church's doctrines cannot be used as excuses for a lack of interest in penetrating the current obstacles between the world and the Word of God. As Ellul cautions:

> We cannot give everything into the hands of God . . . until we have wrestled with God till the break of day, like Jacob; that is, until we have struggled to the utmost limits of our strength, and have known the despair of defeat. If we do not do this, our so-called confidence in God and our "orthodoxy" are nothing less than hypocrisy, cowardice, and laziness . . . in the heart of this conflict, the Word can be proclaimed, but nowhere else. When we have really understood the actual plight of our contemporaries, when we have heard their cry of anguish, and when we have understood why they won't have anything to do with our disembodied gospel, when we have shared their sufferings, both physical and spiritual, in their despair and their desolation, when we have become one with the people of our own nation and of the universal church . . . *then* we will be able to proclaim the Word of God—but not till then![86]

---

ethics and politics, which seemed to be based on an insufficient knowledge of the world and of politics" (10). The result is that "Ellul's position on the role of Christian action in the world is very closely patterned after that of Karl Barth" (159n43).

84. *PK*, 114.
85. *PK*, 115.
86. *PK*, 116.

The Abuse of Kerygmatic Power

Ellul's argument means that the church is unfaithful not only when it errs in the content of its proclamation but also when it adopts forms or methods of proclamation that are at odds with the nature of ecclesial power as the non-force of invitation. It is an abuse of the nature of the church's power when it "proclaim[s] the word of God to men in the abstract, to people who are in a situation which prevents them from understanding it" for this is what it "means that we are tempting God" by tossing the "pearls of the gospel" to the world "with pious indifference."[87] The church cannot abandon its responsibility to the history and concrete reality of the world. But neither can the church adopt what is culturally "fashionable" in terms of efficient and effective means for then it

> has ceased to be a "leaven" in the life of the world. . . . [And] when the church is in this position, it is no longer the salt of the earth, or the light of the world. It is no more than one of the forms in which the will of the world is expressed, and actually it is helping the world to realize its own ends. It no longer represents the power of the action of God in the world.[88]

At that point, the church has become the ambassador of the *world*, not the world's true Sovereign. The church cannot resort to coercive forms of power and control in its proclamation to the world. That is not its power. It can only bear witness in historical and material responsibility, through its non-controlling proclamation, the scandal of its apparent weakness, of an alternative reality which is where true liberty and true life are to be found. For Ellul, this is the crisis of ecclesial power, which involves communication since the church's power is proclamational: the church cannot avoid the pitfall of coercive force by choosing to proclaim the Word of God indifferently. This would make the church guilty of being unconcerned about the actual factors which make the world disinterested in hearing this message. But, on the other hand, neither can the church resort to the propagandistic means of the world through controlling and managing its message to achieve a desired outcome. This would result in resorting to forceful forms of coercive communication and thereby negate its identity as the bearer of God's invitational message. The unbearable tension of this crisis is the weakness of ecclesial non-forceful power combined with the simultaneous inability of the church to ignore the inherent tension. Simply

---

87. *PK*, 117.
88. *PK*, 125.

put, the church has no escape from this place of suffering tension without abandoning either its identity or its calling.

Summary

To summarize, Ellul's view of power is deeply rooted in the Incarnation: God set aside his power, privilege, and authority to enter into and subject himself to human history, human misery, human rebellion, and human defeat. Ellul represents a deeply kenotic view of divine power that not only speaks of *apparent* weakness but *essential* weakness in suffering as opposed to force. Human attempts at mechanical or technical force, control, and domination are the results of human fallenness. And only through the church (in Barthian fashion) disassociating itself from these fallen forms of human agency can it participate in the ways of the kingdom of God which is not only eschatological but present in human life *hic et nunc*. Rooted in the Incarnation, Ellul's view of power is Christocentric which then informs his ecclesiology: the church is authentically the body of Christ only as it lives in ways which are resonant with the kingdom of this powerless God (what Ellul calls "non-power") which respects human freedom and dignity. This inevitably leads the church to a place of suffering. And it is only when the church, in solidarity with suffering humanity, suffers along with the world that it is able to discern the form that the invitational proclamation of the Word of God ought to take in any given time and place that is both responsible to the world and faithful to God.

ACTS 10: ECCLESIAL POWER OR NON-FORCEFUL POWER

For both Ellul and Kuyper, the church's unique vocation is proclamational. The content of this proclamation is the Word of God.[89] For Kuyper, this Word of God is proclaimed through preaching, sacraments, discipleship, and diaconal ministries of justice and compassion. Thus, for both Ellul and Kuyper, the church's proclamation is kerygmatic at its core. But is the church's kerygmatic proclamation a power of coercive force like the state's power? As we've seen in the preceding sections of this chapter, Ellul outlines a number of significant reasons to understand the nature of ecclesial power

---

89. For a fuller treatment of the theological interpretation of Scripture, see Billings, *Word of God for the People of God*.

as a form of love and service that is accomplished through weakness and self-abasement. It is a non-forceful form of power.

Having presented, then, both Kuyper's and Ellul's views on ecclesial power, we now turn our attention to analyze the Christian Scriptures in order to discern in them the nature of the church's proclamation as presented to us in its narratives. Due to the constraints of space and not to take us too far afield of this project's aim, we must limit our inquiry to a representative selection rather than an exhaustive treatment of the New Testament. In order to accomplish this, we need to select a passage that contains clear elements of power, both divine and ecclesial if possible. Since we are interested in the power of the institutional church, a passage that featured not only Christian individuals but also official agents of the church would be ideal. And, if possible, we would look to a passage in which the church is coming into contact with the world in a kerygmatic or proclamational encounter. A passage that meets these three criteria would offer clarity on the nature of ecclesial kerygmatic power and be highly illustrative of the form of the church's power within the New Testament itself.

Such criteria are met with Acts 10. In Acts 10, we have the church, represented by the apostle Peter, engaged in a missionary encounter with the Gentile world, represented by the Roman centurion Cornelius. Peter, as an apostle, is an official ambassador of the church, sent from Jerusalem to proclaim the news about Jesus. And Cornelius, as a Roman centurion, represents not only the non-Christian world but also the Roman empire of coercive power, force, control, and domination. We also have Luke's narrative connection of this Roman encounter with the power of Jesus, a key element of this passage we will examine more closely below.

Acts 10: The Context

Acts 10 occupies a central place in Luke's narrative of the early church.[90] In fact, Willimon calls this chapter and its narrative of Peter and Cornelius "a pivot for the entire book, a turning point in the long drama of redemption."[91] Justo Gonzalez says that this chapter represents "one of the critical points in the entire narrative"[92] of the book of Acts. Martin Debelius

---

90. Literary analyses of Acts are rare. Literary analyses of Acts 10 are even rarer. In this section, I am relying on Johnson, *Prophetic Jesus, Prophetic Church*; Handy, "Gentile Pentecost"; Malas, "Literary Structure of Acts." For further references to Acts consulted, see the bibliography.

91. Willimon, *Acts*, 95.

92. González, *Acts*, 130.

says this passage has "special importance."[93] Together with Chapter 9, Luke is narrating the conversion of Saul/Paul and the opening of the Christian missionary movement from the community of Israel to the wider world of the Gentiles within the first-century Roman empire. These chapters are an account of the conversion of Saul/Paul the Jew so that the conversion of the Gentile world can follow, beginning in Chapter 10 with Cornelius, a symbolic representative of the world beyond Israel. But is this all that Acts 10 depicts: the expansion of the missionary movement of the early church? I contend that there is much more going on in Luke's narrative in Acts 10 and that commentators have (curiously) neglected to engage this passage at its depths.

Our specific focus will be on Peter's sermon as recorded in Acts 10:34–43, but a brief outline of the chapter will orient us to its narrative structure. Acts 10 presents us with two key figures: the Apostle Peter who is recorded as staying in Joppa and the Roman centurion Cornelius described by Luke as "devout and God-fearing; [who] gave generously to those in need and prayed to God regularly" along with the rest of his family (Acts 10:2). The rest of the chapter is an intentionally crafted and intriguing narrative of how these two persons, radically different and living in marked tension with each other, are brought together and experience reconciliation through the power of God at work through the institutional church's kerygmatic power.

Little detailed work on the literary structure of Acts 10:1–48 has been done. My own literary analysis of this section, while not central to the overall argument on the power of the institutional church in Kuyper's ecclesiology, nonetheless serves as a background to it and will be presented briefly.[94] Acts 10 is comprised of two parts, each with three sections that stand in parallel to each other. The chapter begins with a first set of three sections: an initial focus on Cornelius, then a shift to Peter, followed by bringing Peter and Cornelius together. Then, there is a parallel set of three sections: a focus on Cornelius, then on Peter, and then on the two of them being brought together in a new relationship. The first set of three sections displays Cornelius and Peter in a state lacking reconciliation. The parallel second set of three sections displays Cornelius and Peter in a state of reconciliation in Christ. Even within each section there is a parallelism between Cornelius's and Peter's actions, a narrative device that Luke utilizes to highlight the relationship between these two figures under the guidance of the Holy Spirit. A brief outline of the chapter can be sketched as follows:

---

93. Dibelius, *Studies in the Acts of the Apostles*, 109.

94. I am unaware of any literary analysis of Acts 10 that goes to (or beyond) the level of detail that will be presented here.

A—Cornelius	
a—Introduction of Cornelius	Acts 10:1–2
b—The Lord appears to Cornelius	Acts 10:3–4
c—The Lord instructs Cornelius to send for Peter	Acts 10:5–6
d—Cornelius responds to the Lord's instructions	Acts 10:7–8
B—Peter	
a1—Introduction of Peter	Acts 10:9–10
b1—The Lord appears to Peter	Acts 10:11–18
c1—The Lord instructs Peter to go to Cornelius	Acts 10:19–20
d1—Peter responds to the Lord's instructions	Acts 10:21–22
C—Peter + Cornelius	
e—Peter welcomes Cornelius's men into his home	Acts 10:23
e1—Cornelius welcomes Peter and his men into his home	Acts 10:24–26
f—Peter voices the lack of reconciliation between he and Cornelius	Acts 10:27–29
A1—Cornelius	
Cornelius recounts the Lord's appearance to him	Acts 10:30–33
B1—Peter	
Peter proclaims the gospel to Cornelius and his household	Acts 10:34–43
Peter witnesses the conversion of Cornelius	Acts 10:44–48a
C1—Peter + Cornelius	
f1—Peter and Cornelius are reconciled in Christ	Acts 10:48b

Acts 10:34–43: The Sermon in Focus

If we turn our attention to the sermon Peter preaches in Cornelius's house (Acts 10:34–43), we discover that within the literary structure we have outlined above, the sermon occurs in the central place of the second set of sections (B1) with its own parallel structure, as charted below. It is worth noting that it is this proclamation that is immediately followed by the ecstatic evidence of Cornelius's conversion, which follows from Cornelius's and Peter's faithful responses to the Lord's appearance to each of them.

A1—Cornelius	
Cornelius recounts the Lord's appearance to him	Acts 10:30–33
(This is parallel to the Lord appearing to Cornelius in Acts 10:3–6.)	
B1—Peter	
Peter proclaims the gospel to Cornelius and his household	Acts 10:34–43
(This is parallel to the Lord appearing to Peter in Acts 10:11–20.)	Acts 10:44–48a
Peter witnesses the conversion of Cornelius	
C1—Peter + Cornelius	
Peter and Cornelius are reconciled in Christ	Acts 10:48b

If we expand the sermon and outline this particular sub-section of the chapter, we find evidence of an intentional structure here also. Luke appears to have organised the recounting of Peter's sermon in a chiastic fashion, with the central element highlighting Peter's apostolic mission (E). And, just one level removed from the center, we find the crucial details of the apostolic kerygma proclaimed (D and D1): the anointing of Jesus by God with the Holy Spirit and power, in parallel with God exercising his Spirit and power in Jesus' resurrection. It is this, then, that constitutes the apostolic witness to the gospel: Jesus' anointed mission confirmed by God through his resurrection that is carried into the entire world through the proclamation of eye-witness apostles.

A—God does not show favoritism—"every nation"	Acts 10:34–35
B—The message, the "good news," of Jesus the Lord over all	Acts 10:36
C—Jesus' public ministry known	Acts 10:37
D—God anointed Jesus [with Spirit and power]	Acts 10:38
E—Apostles are the witnesses of these things	Acts 10:39
D1—God raised Jesus [assumed: in Spirit and power]	Acts 10:40
C1—Jesus' post-resurrection ministry seen by eye-witnesses	Acts 10:41
B1—Apostles commanded to preach about God who is judge over all	Acts 10:42
A1—The prophets' confirmation that God does not show favoritism—"everyone"	Acts 10:43

If we turn specifically to verse 38, a passage of "intolerable syntactical structure,"[95] we see that it represents the heart of the kerygmatic proclamation concerning Jesus: that he was anointed with the Spirit and with power. This is echoed in parallel later in verse 40 with the resurrection, clearly a reference to the Spirit and power at work on Jesus' behalf following his death and in confirmation and vindication of his ministry by God. Therefore, we want to explore verse 38 in greater detail at this point.

The Greek text of verse 38 is as follows, with my literal translation beside it:

Ἰησοῦν	Jesus
τὸν ἀπὸ Ναζαρέθ,	the one from Nazareth—
ὡς ἔχρισεν αὐτὸν ὁ θεὸς	as God anointed him
πνεύματι ἁγίῳ καὶ δυνάμει,	with/in the Holy Spirit and power,
ὃς διῆλθεν εὐεργετῶν	he went through/around doing good (things)
καὶ ἰώμενος πάντας τοὺς καταδυναστευομένους ὑπὸ τοῦ διαβόλου,	and healing/curing all those being oppressed by the devil,
ὅτι ὁ θεὸς ἦν μετ' αὐτοῦ.[96]	because/for God was with him.

There are a number of important linguistic and stylistic elements in this one key verse, elements that will be significant for our theological interpretation below. The first is that there are two occurrences within this single verse of verbs from the δύνα-stem. The first occurrence is used relative to Jesus' anointing: "ὡς ἔχρισεν αὐτὸν ὁ θεὸς πνεύματι ἁγίῳ καὶ δυνάμει" (Jesus was anointed in the Holy Spirit and in [the straight-forward meaning of the word] power). The second occurrence is used relative to the "διάβολος": Jesus went around doing good, which is followed by this apposition: "καὶ ἰώμενος πάντας τοὺς καταδυναστευομένους ὑπὸ τοῦ διαβόλου." Here, the present passive participle of the compound verb κατα + δυνάμει (καταδυναστευομένους) has the meaning of being oppressed, exploited, or dominated. The δυναστ-verb has the sense of "dominion" in the sense of one under a ruler or one who exercises authority or power over another.

---

95. Barrett, *Critical and Exegetical Commentary*, 497.
96. *Novum Testamentum Graece*.

Luke is tapping into the long-developed sense of hope and anticipation from the Old Testament into Second Temple Judaism for God's Anointed One to exercise divine authority and power to remove the occupying forces from Israel's shame. But this is done with a distinctly new, Christological understanding.[97] First, by combining the third person singular aorist indicative of χρίω with δύναμις, Luke is pointing to Jesus as that foretold figure who would liberate God's people by nullifying the oppressive forces around them. *The Theological Dictionary of the New Testament* (*TDNT*) captures this well, saying that Luke is working within "the hope and longing [in the Old Testament] that God will demonstrate his power in a last great conflict, destroying His opponents and saving those who belong to him."[98] But Luke is also incorporating an extra-biblical, Hellenistic idea that the world has been subjected to demonic powers (represented in Judaism by the διάβολος), necessitating divine intervention to return the creation to its good and shalomic state. The resulting idea, therefore, is that at a certain point in the unfolding of history, God would exercise his redemptive power through "an overthrow of demonic powers" symbolized in the defeat of the διάβολος.[99]

Further, Luke is also intentionally contrasting two kinds of power: the healing power of the Spirit of God (embodied in Jesus) and the dominating or enslaving power of the διάβολος (embodied in the Roman empire). In addition to the contrast between the διάβολος/Rome and Jesus, Luke intentionally leaves the δύναμις of Jesus ambiguous. I take this to be a rhetorical move on Luke's part. This alternative δύναμις that Jesus has is a different kind, so different in fact that it escapes clear demarcation. And Luke's narration of this passage makes this abundantly clear without resorting to literal definition. The kerygma does not come through soldiers, military means, or imperial force, the form of Rome's and the διάβολος' power—aspects which are highlighted in Luke's narrative. Jesus' power is altogether different. According to Luke, it is intimately connected with "εὐεργετῶν" and "ἰώμενος"—doing good and healing, an implicit subversion of Rome and simultaneously deeply Jewish in character.

According to Luke, therefore, Jesus' anointing consists in his bearing a healing power to do good. If we take this to be an example of a Greek hendiadys, then Luke is saying that Jesus is anointed with the power *of* the Holy Spirit—resulting in an even greater emphasis on the power-aspect of

---

97. On Second Temple Judaism as background to the New Testament, see Wright, *New Testament and the People of God*, 145–338; Ferguson, *Backgrounds of Early Christianity*.

98. Grundmann, "dunamai," 295.

99. Grundmann, "dunamai," 295.

Jesus' anointing, giving content to the kind of power with which Jesus is anointed for his work. It is the Spirit-given power of goodness and healing to accomplish the kingdom of God's re-creation. There are echoes here of Genesis 1 and the Spirit of God hovering over the waters of chaos, bringing an ordered creation forth.[100] The result of this logic is that in this passage Luke reveals Jesus as the bearer of divine power and the exercise of his power results in the particular good of liberating and healing those under the oppressive domination of the διάβολος. It is interesting to note here that, for Luke, power and Spirit are linked.[101] So also are διάβολος and power. But their power is strikingly different. In fact, it appears that, for Luke, Jesus' ministry of εὐεργετῶν is rooted in his ἔχρισεν with the power of the Holy Spirit. This is the kind of power with which Jesus exercises his ministry. It is a power of liberating, life-giving fullness that restores and renews creation. The δυνάμει of Jesus is not for his own sake but for the sake of subverting the oppressive rule of the διάβολος, setting free from the oppressive and exploitative domination of the διάβολος those on whom Jesus has compassion to heal and do good.

To push Luke's logic even further, we could say that Jesus is not only "anointed" with the power of the Holy Spirit but that a deep identification exists between Jesus and this liberating power. Jesus not only *has* the power of God, but *is* the power of God.[102] In the proclamation of this Jesus, he is invoked whereby his power is made present to do its healing and good work.

A Theological Interpretation of Power in Acts 10

One cannot help but notice the pervasiveness of power in Luke's comparison between Jesus and the διάβολος. Johnson connects this with Luke's prophetic vision.[103] This prophetic vision is "inspired by the Holy Spirit, speaking God's word, embodying God's vision for humans, enacting that vision through signs and wonders, and bearing witness to God in the world."[104] This is carried through in Luke-Acts by the church engaged in "a prophetic manner of life—being led by the spirit, sharing possessions, engaging in

---

100. On the relationship between power, force, and being, see Tillich, *Love, Power, and Justice*, 35–48.

101. Grundmann, "dunamai," 301.

102. Grundmann, "dunamai," 306, notes that "the power of Christ is always the power of God.... In the Christ event the power of God which shapes history and leads it to its goal is active as an eschatological event."

103. Johnson, *Prophetic Jesus, Prophetic Church*, vii.

104. Johnson, *Prophetic Jesus, Prophetic Church*, 4.

an itinerant mission, exercising servant leadership, [and] bearing powerful witness before religious and state authorities."[105] Johnson has a forceful interpretation of Luke's prophetic vision as it relates to contemporary life:

> In sharp contrast, Luke portrays the prophetic vision in terms of the reversal of human norms, above all with respect to wealth and power: the poor are blessed and the hungry are filled; the rich receive woes and the full will be hungry; the powerful will be cast down from their thrones. Whether in the mouth of Mary, of John, of Jesus, or of the apostles . . . the kinds of oppression and sin that God most opposes have to do with the abuse of possessions and power . . . churches today should be moved to ask certain questions.
>
> Why, for example, are Christians' conceptions of sin so concentrated on the weaknesses of the flesh rather than on the willful and predatory practices of economic and political oppression of the weak? Does the church have a prophetic vision with respect to power and possessions that can challenge a world in which both economics and politics are so disordered? Or is the church too often coopted by the world's vision rather than the prophet's in these areas? How can the church challenge the world's use of power when its own structures of authority exhibit the same patterns of self-seeking and exclusion? How can churches today profess to be Christian when their 'prosperity gospel' has no connection with the prophetic vision and so obviously mimics the worst of an acquisitive society that measures worth by wealth?[106]

Returning to Acts 10, the διάβολος exerts καταδυνάμει over people. But Jesus has a different δύναμις, that of the Holy Spirit, which operates for good and healing, undoing the power of the διάβολος. Thus, we have come to the point of discerning why this verse is of such significance in Peter's sermon. The heart of the Christian kerygma that Peter proclaims is that the power of Jesus is a liberating and healing δύναμις for the world which undoes the enslaving and destructive δύναμις of the διάβολος. But this δύναμις does not operate in the ways of the world, only stronger (Rome, for example—the contrast in posture and approach is intentional and striking). The δύναμις of Jesus subverts, confuses, and liberates "πάντας τοὺς καταδυναστευομένους ὑπὸ τοῦ διαβόλου." This is the content of the apostolic kerygma: the δύναμις of Christ that subverts and sets free from sin, darkness, and διάβολος. And, this is why verse 38 is in parallel with verse

---

105. Johnson, *Prophetic Jesus, Prophetic Church*, 4.
106. Johnson, *Prophetic Jesus, Prophetic Church*, 94–95.

40: because the δύναμις of Christ is a δύναμις that, though it appears weak and defeated in the crucifixion, is vindicated in the resurrection, the parallel δύναμις to Jesus' pre-crucifixion life.

Thus, verses 38 and 40 supply the content of the apostolic witness (in verse 39) that Peter proclaims to Cornelius. Jesus' good, liberating δύναμις is the heart of the Christian kerygma which appears weak in comparison to that of the διάβολος or Rome but which actually is life-giving as it is the power of the kingdom of God for the renewal of creation. It is oriented towards life rather than death. When this message is proclaimed, it does not come in imperial force or domination (like Rome) but as a simple invitation spoken by a humble preacher witnessing to life and liberty in the Holy Spirit who is renewing the creation. Therefore, speaking of Jesus, Grundmann says that "He is the power of God. As such He is the theme and content of the Christian kerygma."[107] Through this kerygma, a new age dawns: in the human person (in Acts 10, it is Cornelius), in the church (in Acts 10, it is the church's Gentile mission), and in the world (Rome is put on notice that its days are limited). Johnson summarizes that "It cannot be by accident, either, that in Peter's speech to Cornelius's household he gives such attention to the prophetic ministry of Jesus—a feature lacking in the other speeches of Acts—and above all, Jesus' liberating and healing outreach. . . . By so highlighting Jesus' ministry of healing, Peter (and Luke) draws an implicit connection between Jesus' embrace of the marginal and the church's inclusion of the Gentiles."[108]

Luke is reinterpreting the Old Testament and Second Temple Jewish eschatological hope and expectation.[109] Not only will God's decisive action in the future remove Israel's foreign (Gentile/Roman) oppressors, but this future comes proleptically into the present (through the proclamation of this Christian kerygma) and addresses the διάβολος' powers of darkness and oppression with healing and goodness. In fact,

> These [demonic] powers will be deprived of their strength with the cosmic catastrophe [in the present rather than the future]. Indeed, this has already taken place with the resurrection and exaltation of Jesus Christ. They will be publicly deprived of their strength when Christ publicly takes power at His return. The

---

107. Grundmann, "dunamai," 304.

108. Johnson, *Prophetic Jesus, Prophetic Church*, 155–56.

109. On the eschatological hope of Israel leading up to the first Christian century, see Wright, *New Testament and the People of God*, 280–338.

statements reflect this fact in its duality and tension, which are distinctive of the NT and which give rise to its kerygma.¹¹⁰

The distinctiveness of the Christian kerygma is that it takes the purely future-oriented eschatological hope of a comprehensively renewed creation and brings it forward into the present through the healing goodness of Christ verbally proclaimed and symbolically performed. "The disciples who looked to Jesus knew that He brought the saving power of God and that they could attain it in Him. This is the NT and early Christian kerygma."¹¹¹

The result of this proclamation in verse 38 is the outpouring of the δύναμις of Christ's Holy Spirit on Cornelius and his household which Peter and his companions witness in verses 44–48a and which results in social restoration and reconciliation across ethnic, religious, and political lines. Therefore, Luke is saying, the Christian kerygma is the proclamation of the liberating, healing, and life-giving power of Christ and the very working of that subversive, liberating, and eschatological power in the present. The Christian gospel which Peter proclaimed to Cornelius is the healing and liberation in Christ's Spirit which is far different from the oppressive and coercive power of the διάβολος and alternative to Rome's way of being in the world.

In Peter's sermon to Cornelius, the gospel was not a proclamation of the juridical substitutionary atonement of Christ on behalf of sinful humanity.¹¹² Rather, it was the highly and personally contextualized proclamation of an alternative to the power of Rome's oppression and subjugation, a power Cornelius knew intimately and a power that presented itself to Cornelius's face in the person of the Apostle Peter. The non-force of the church's proclaimed kerygma is an alternative to the fallen world's coercive power. And when that kerygma is faithfully proclaimed by the church to the world, it is active for healing and restoration wherever this invitation is received in faith. The Christian kerygma is a proclamation of the life of Christ, which is the power of God and God's coming kingdom, for the world's renewal. And

---

110. Grundmann, "dunamai," 307.

111. Grundmann, "dunamai," 309.

112. On the debate over Paul's doctrine of justification, see Wright, *Justification*; Piper, *Future of Justification*. Harink, *Paul among the Postliberals*, 44–65, brings the debate about justification into dialogue with both New Testament biblical scholarship and a post-Christendom mindset. See also Aulén, *Christus Victor*. In this regard, the observation of life-long missionary Vincent Donovan is apt: "If you study the apostolic approach very closely, you will see that something is missing. Sin is missing. There is no mention of original sin or any other kind of sin. Sin will come in later, after Christ, after getting to know Christ, in relation to Christ, but the sin portrayed by the first preachers of the Christian gospel is forgiven sin, something entirely different" (Donovan, *Christianity Rediscovered*, 61).

this proclamation is the actual working of this liberation in the face of all other rebellious and dehumanizing powers. Where the gospel is proclaimed in Christ to liberate and restore, God's cosmic renewal of all things is present and active (Col 1:15–20).

Thus, we discover the logic of Luke's recording of Peter's sermon, a logic recognized by Grundmann:

> In the message of Christ we thus have the power of God which is the power of salvation. The power of God in the gospel consists in the fact that it mediates salvation, that by the gospel God delivers man from the power of darkness and translates him into the kingdom of His dear Son. The δύναμις θεοῦ, which is the gospel, is not an empty word. It is grounded in the divine act of deliverance in the Christ event, which overcomes the rule of Satan and which works itself out in the continued, factual deliverance accomplished by the preaching of the gospel.[113]

The preaching of the gospel of Christ is the revelation of God's salvation and liberation, which in turn forms the reconciled Christian community in its wake. This was Peter's experience in Cornelius's household. As he proclaimed the universal Lordship and liberating and healing goodness of Christ, God was at work creating the church there and then, even if that time and place were outside the boundaries of Israel and before the final judgment at the end of history. "[The] δύναμις θεοῦ as the saving power of God is the basis of the faith and existence of the community, delivering from the bondage of guilt, demons and Satan, and from the power of death, and translating into the divine kingdom of light and life."[114] This is the reason why the true preaching of the Word is a mark of the true church: because it is only through this proclamation of the liberating Christ for life, salvation, and re-creation that the saving δύναμις θεοῦ continues this apostolic mission which Peter participated in as recorded in Acts 10. This is the kerygmatic vocation of the church: to contextually proclaim as witnesses the ongoing restoration of God for deliverance and freedom for life in the midst of oppression and death.

---

113. Grundmann, "dunamai," 309.

114. Grundmann, "dunamai," 313. Grundmann does not consistently render δύναμις as a subversive, non-forceful kind of power. He is inconsistent, as can be seen in this example where δύναμις clearly has the nature of force: "In all His words He speaks 'from the mouth of omnipotence,' and thus overcomes the kingdom of demonic powers ruling in sickness, sin and death. This brings us to the heart of the NT view. The miracles of Jesus are part of the invading dominion of God which Jesus brings with His own person in proclamation and act. They are the dominion of God overcoming and expelling the sway of demons and Satan" (302).

Acts 10 and the Ecclesial Power of Proclamation

What we discover in Acts 10 is not the church asking "Will the Gentiles be saved?" but instead *"How* will the Gentiles be saved?" The answer we find is that the Gentiles will be saved as Israel has been saved: through the liberating and healing goodness of God's Anointed which subverts the oppressive dominion of the διάβολος and re-establishes the peace and justice intended for creation.[115] This kerygma-in-apparent-weakness was Jesus' anointing, a commission which we see has now passed on to Peter as an official representative of Jesus' early ecclesial mission directed beyond Israel into the whole of the world.[116]

We have observed how the gospel of Christ's healing and liberation in Acts 10:38 is the heart (or "climax," as Robert W. Wall calls it[117]) of the Christian kerygma.[118] It is both the announcement/proclamation and actual working of Jesus' victorious liberation over the oppressing, dominating power of the διάβολος. It is when the Apostle Peter proclaims this Word to the gentile and Roman Cornelius, confirming Peter's commission as apostolic witness (verse 39), that the healing and reconciliation of God bursts into Cornelius's life (verses 44–48), into the church's life, and into the mission of the church throughout the world. This conversion wasn't merely the end of the story but its beginning. For, as we see in Acts 10, the church discerned how it was to follow its Lord through the proclamation of the kerygma.

Acts 10:38 juxtaposes Jesus' ministry of healing, liberation, and reconciliation in the Holy Spirit (evidenced by Cornelius's entire life being transformed by the proclaimed kerygma) with the dehumanizing power (for bondage and oppression) of the διάβολος. Luke's point is clear: if Jesus heals

---

115. It is unclear whether, though plausible that, Luke intended readers of Acts 10 to remember the Exodus and the other historic mighty acts of God's deliverance, mighty acts which were mighty because of their subversiveness. The narrative of the Exodus flight reveals that the armies of Egypt are anti-creational as they are engulfed in the Red Sea's waters of chaos, a return to the primordial chaos of Genesis 1:1.

116. Many commentators have noted the similarities in Acts 10 with the Old Testament book of Jonah. There are many allusions, in fact: Jonah and Peter both sent from Joppa, both initially object to God's call, three nights in the fish/three visions of Peter, Peter's name is Simon bar *Jonah*, both Jonah and Peter are sent by God to proclaim his word of salvation to those considered "outside" and "beyond redemption" by Israel, and both result in the surprising conversion of these who formerly were considered enemies. This is an example of what Luke has recorded in his first volume, where Jesus exhorts his followers to forgive their enemies; and the Roman military force—of which Cornelius was an officer and thus official representative—was certainly an enemy of the Jewish people.

117. Wall, *Acts of the Apostles*, 166.

118. It is surprising to note that there is only one peer-reviewed journal article that addresses verse 38 in Peter's sermon recorded in Acts 10.

THE NATURE OF ECCLESIAL POWER   217

and liberates those under the power of the διάβολος, then Jesus and his power are radically different than the διάβολος or Rome and their power. As Rome was a force of death, Jesus is a force of new life for the world's renewal. And since all this takes place squarely within Gentile territory, this shows the cosmic lordship of Jesus. Jesus is not a mere geographically-limited minor deity (like Caesar who must constantly reinforce the boundaries of his empire with an oppressive and deadly force that Luke would encourage us to equate with the διάβολος).

Not only is this, then, the first Gentile convert but this is Luke's way of suggesting that this is the pattern for the creation and extension of the church. Whether Luke intends for this to have allusions to Genesis 1 or the Exodus narratives is debatable; but it is worth noting that here in Acts 10 we have an example from Luke of the proclaimed *Word* about Jesus bringing about deliverance and conversion, nothing less than a new creation, in fact. That is, the kerygmatic proclamation of Jesus by the institutional church liberates and creates new life where beforehand there was darkness, ignorance, rebellion, and the chaos of oppression and domination. And as Peter and we see in verses 44 and following, Jesus as the alternative to Rome is confirmed by the surprising display of the Spirit's presence within the members of the Gentile household of Cornelius, a display of renewed life manifested in reconciliation, hospitality, and mutual sharing across previous lines of exclusion.

This is the "witness" element which occupies a central place in Peter's sermon and which is a significant theme of the entire tenth chapter of Acts (particularly verse 39). Cornelius sent for Peter, the messenger he came to expect would reveal to him the meaning and significance of his encounter with the Lord through his vision. In this way, Cornelius functions within Acts 10 as a type of waiting humanity to which the church must intentionally offer an alternative way of life. In light of Rome's dominating power, the church proclaims a message of deliverance, liberation, and salvation, the opposite of coercive imperial or state power. It is only through this unique means that a new creative act will take place for the life of the world. And Peter, being sent as an apostle by Jesus, bearing the very message of deliverance, liberation, and salvation that Cornelius is waiting for, continues the ministry of Jesus in his own ministry. Moltmann writes of

> the messianic messenger of good tidings who will speak "the word" which, in the power of God's Spirit, will open up the new era and the new creation. It will be the word in which God reveals his coming and makes his victory and final lordship over

his creation known. It will be the word which frees captives and brings the nations to peace."[119]

The surprise of Acts 10 is not so much that Peter the Jew crosses into Gentile territory or that he is the apostolic messenger who proclaims the Word of the Lord to Cornelius. Rather, the surprise we encounter in Acts 10 is that this kerygmatic proclamation is not only the revelation of an alternative way of goodness and healing to Rome's coercive power but that the act of proclamation actually produces the eschatological liberation and reconciliation of Cornelius and his family under the shadow of Rome's power, the oppressive power of the διάβολος, and sets them free. Acts 10 is, therefore, the narration of the strikingly different, non-forceful power of Jesus which comes in disguise, working through the church, to liberate and make new once again the creation he is busy redeeming and renewing now through the apostolic ambassadors of his church. The proclamation not only points to the Word but it is the presentation of that very Word *hic et nunc*.

THE NATURE OF ECCLESIAL KERYGMATIC POWER

In conclusion, let us summarize the contributions of this chapter for understanding the essential nature of ecclesial power. Acts 10 depicts an ecclesial encounter that ends with the surprising conversion of Cornelius and his entire household apart from the coercion or domination typical of Rome. This is clearly described as the result of Jesus' goodness, the fruit of his anointing by the Holy Spirit, which is mediated through the apostle Peter, an official ambassador of the first-century institutional church. So, Acts 10 contains the element we are interested in: the essential nature of ecclesial kerygmatic power. And the contrast is clear between that of Jesus and the church on the one hand and that of the διάβολος and Rome on the other. In the case of the former, it is the hidden and subversive goodness that leads to healed and restored life through the apparent weakness of ecclesial proclamation that bears its own kind of power distinct from that of Rome.[120] In the case of the latter, all the διάβολος can perform is a coercive and domineering

---

119. Moltmann, *Church*, 217. It would have been preferable for Moltmann to be more clear about the nature of Jesus' "power" and "victory," for, as we've seen, these can either be cast in the form of force and domination or as weakness and invitation.

120. Luke must intend the humorous (at least, ironic) juxtaposition between powerful Roman Centurion Cornelius and lowly Jewish Peter. Also, Ellul's non-power does not fall prey to Caputo's critique of theological accounts of power as weakness (which is really just another form of power) because Ellul's non-power is, in reality and not just in appearance, non-power, the antithesis of power. The Incarnation ended in an actual and not just a seemingly real death.

force that takes the shape of armies and empires that lead to dehumanizing subjugation and death.

What is the essential nature of this ecclesial power we find in Acts 10? Somewhere Barth famously quipped to his liberal theologian counterparts that God is not 'man' said in a loud voice. For our purposes here, we might rephrase this by saying that the power of the church is not the power of the 'empire' deployed or proclaimed by the church. Rather than the kerygmatic power of the church being the coercive power of a greater force that overcomes all opposing dominations in the fallen culture, ecclesial power is rooted in and emerges from a different sphere than the state and therefore its power is essentially distinct and different.[121] Ecclesial power is normed by the leading function of the ecclesial sphere which means that ecclesial power is altogether different in essence from that of the state (or any other sphere). The essentially unique power of the church is the contextual proclamation of the Word of God that thwarts and subverts the fallen powers of the world through an invitation and a call to an alternative to the oppression of the διάβολος.[122] Our analysis in this chapter has revealed that while Ellul does not work out of Kuyper's sphere sovereignty framework (a framework which acknowledges different forms of power in different creational spheres) his insights into the alternative power of God mediated through the church's proclamation is insightful. Additionally, we observed in Acts 10 that ecclesial kerygmatic power critiques views of power that still retain an essential element of force. We can therefore conclude by noting three aspects of the nature of the church's kerygmatic power that flow directly from its location within the ecclesial sphere and set it apart as essentially unique compared with the powers at work in the other spheres of creation.

---

121. On the difference between the power of the state and the power of the church, see Dooyeweerd, *Roots of Western Culture*, 67, 80; Chaplin, *Herman Dooyeweerd*, 244–48. On the nature of coercive state power, see Wolterstorff, *Hearing the Call*, 311.

122. Even though Brunner, *Church in the New Social Order*, 23, has a rather anti-institutional understanding of the church and describes the church in very personal/subjective ways (10–11), he agrees with this interpretation of the power of the institutional church being the proclamation of the Word of God: "It is not the primary, not the essential task of the Church to create, to change, to improve the social order. The task of the Church lies beyond any social order, because its task is to preach the Gospel of Jesus Christ, the Kingdom of God which transcends all social orders, the good and bad alike. The immediate, primary task of the Church is not to preach and to fight for a social programme, but to preach the message of redemption and eternal life" (7). On Brunner's anti-institutional view of the church, see also his *Misunderstanding of the Church*, 10–11.

Kerygmatic Power Is Kenotic

The first aspect of ecclesial kerygmatic power is that it is kenotic: self-emptying, self-oblating. We can see this not only in the above analysis of Ellul or Acts 10 but this also sheds light on the relatively few comments Kuyper makes in which he acknowledges the inherent weakness and powerlessness of Christian faith, weak and powerless from the perspective of those who operate out of a mindset of force and coercion. In Kuyper's sermon, "It Shall Not Be So among You," Kuyper goes to great lengths to encourage his hearers to adopt "the power of spirited resistance to the false domination that would force your submission" to the rulers of the present fallen age.[123] Against these rulers is the "better, nobler, holier power [of the church] which does not seek its strength in force but finds its watchword in the apostolic saying: 'When I am weak, then am I strong.'"[124] This faithful power of the orthodox church is "a power against which violence is powerless."[125] In fact, this power "comes from the Tree of Life called Immanuel" (Christ).[126] And as Skillen rightly observes, this Immanuel wears a *cross* as well as a crown: "Christ really is ruling now as servant."[127] True spiritual and ecclesial power, Jesus taught, is embracing and serving those who are weak, even if it means divesting one's self of power and embracing the shame of sacrifice. These comments from Kuyper shed light on his perspective of ecclesial power and should function as the interpretive lens through which Kuyper's other comments about power as strength and force should be interpreted and heard. In fact, as Hall argues, "the cross is at the center of our faith where it ought to condition the whole of our ecclesiology."[128]

While Acts 10 depicts the "successful" conversion of Cornelius, this text by no means offers a guarantee that Christian witness or proclamation will always result in desirable Christian outcomes. The arrest, trial, and execution of Jesus serve as clear signals that this message is not welcome to the fallen world. Ellul reminds us that ecclesial kerygmatic power is an invitation extended without the mechanical or technical means of force, control, or domination which cancel out human freedom, the type of coercive power the state has been given. Faithful ecclesial proclamation is never propaganda. As such, Christian witness to the world is open-ended. The

---

123. Kuyper, "It Shall Not Be So among You," 138.

124. Kuyper, "It Shall Not Be So among You," 138.

125. Kuyper, "It Shall Not Be So among You," 138.

126. Kuyper, "It Shall Not Be So among You," 138.

127. Skillen, "Where Kingdom Politics Should Lead Us," in Noll, *Adding Cross to Crown*, 86.

128. Hall, "Metamorphosis," 74.

future is unknown and indeterminable, and the world is still free to kill the messenger. Ecclesial power subverts attempts at control and manipulation in order to honor human dignity. The institutional church is marked by the posture of witness and sign rather than as a center of cultural power or hegemony. The results and the future, from the human vantage point, remain hidden because they are subject to God's will and the circumstances of an unfolding history. The future, even actions in the present, are ambiguous and require painstaking discernment.

In this regard, Mark Noll is insightful. Regarding Kuyper's statement, at the founding of the VU, that there is not one square inch over which Jesus does not cry, "Mine!," Noll writes that while "no truer words could ever be spoken," "this picture is not quite complete." For this Jesus who points to his entire creation and claims it as his own, his "footprints are spattered blood. And the hand that points is marked with a wound." For, Christ's sovereign lordship over all creation was evidenced by following "the road to Calvary that the Lord Jesus took to win his place of command."[129] Therefore, the entire Christ is normative for theology, not in a selective fashion, but in the full range of his person, revelation, and Word. This brings us to the second aspect of ecclesial power: it is incarnational.

Kerygmatic Power Is Incarnational

Second, ecclesial power is incarnational. That is, while there is not less, there is more to Christ than his ascended power and glory. For the Ascended One is also the Incarnate and Crucified One. In the Incarnation, the sovereign God took on weakness to meet rebellious humanity in the concrete realities of the human condition, realities abounding in brokenness, alienation, suffering, and death.[130] Taking the Incarnation seriously means that we must attend to Ellul's caution that we not "accept the essential basis of this civilization"[131] and, instead, we must continue to engage Kuyper's "architechtonic critique" of our culture.

In this regard, Gertrude Himmelfarb's study of the British Enlightenment is noteworthy as the church's incarnational response to nineteenth-century cultural shifts. Whereas Kuyper responded to the cultural shifts in

---

129. Noll, *Adding Cross to Crown*, 46.

130. *PK*, 80.

131. *PK*, 25. Hauerwas and Willimon, *Resident Aliens*, 31, capture the sense in which the church is tempted to subject only the surface of its surrounding culture to critique with their question, "After all, what other way was there to achieve justice [for the church and Christianity] than through politics?"

the Netherlands with reforms addressed at the elite level of society (media, academy, the state, etc.), Himmelfarb points to John Wesley in England who focused on "the working classes" and tirelessly worked to instil in them "a sense of purpose and power."[132] She writes of Methodism's deep contextual nature, in how it "shared the social ethos of the British Enlightenment . . . Methodist preachers were giving practical effect to that idea by spreading a religious gospel of good works, engaging in a variety of humanitarian causes, and welcoming the poor into their fold."[133] In fact, Wesley made *the poor*

> his special mission. When the Anglican churches were closed to him, he made a virtue out of necessity by preaching in the open fields, thus reaching multitudes who were not welcome in churches or did not feel comfortable there. He assured the clergy that they need fear no competition from him. "The rich, the honorable, the great, we are thoroughly willing . . . to leave to you. Only let us alone among the poor." . . . It was an article of his faith that no one was beyond salvation, no one too poor, benighted, or uncivilized to attain the spiritual and moral level deserving of the name Christian.[134]

The Methodists, under John Wesley's leadership, distributed "food, clothing, and money to the needy, paid visits to the sick and to prisoners in jail, and set up loan funds and work projects for the unemployed. . . . Methodists helped establish and support philanthropic enterprises and institutions of every kind: hospitals, dispensaries, orphanages, friendly societies [i.e., SPCK], schools, and libraries. They also played a prominent part in the movement for the abolition of the slave trade."[135] In fact, Wesley's itinerant preachers also "doubled as amateur doctors and pharmacists."[136]

Wesley is an historical illustration of the kerygmatic power of the church that was deeply incarnational by taking its historical-cultural context seriously through proclamation, symbolic action, discipleship, and diaconal ministry to the *needy*. Ecclesial power, therefore (to some extent *contra* Ellul), is still a form of power but ecclesial power is a power *for* the powerless not the power *of* powerlessness. As a kenotic, incarnational form of power it is a non-forceful form of power, the power of invitation and service.

The incarnational nature of the church's kerygmatic power means that the church will be kenotic, self-emptying for others who have been

---

132. Himmelfarb, *Roads to Modernity*, 118.
133. Himmelfarb, *Roads to Modernity*, 120.
134. Himmelfarb, *Roads to Modernity*, 120–21.
135. Himmelfarb, *Roads to Modernity*, 123.
136. Himmelfarb, *Roads to Modernity*, 125.

marginalized, oppressed, or drawn into dehumanizing visions of life. Paul Avis writes about the alternative of the church's power for the powerless: "In a world where power is measured by armed might, financial muscle, and in the ability to appeal to people's baser instincts through the mass media, it is all too easy for Christians to hanker after a form of power that produces empirically measurable results—instantaneous healings, overpowering spiritual conviction with emotional manifestations, apparently inexplicable gifts of knowledge, and other forms of knock-down evidence for a spiritual reality from beyond this world yet impinging manifestly upon it. This understandable thirst for signs and wonders savours, however, of the temptation Jesus rejected in the desert when he turned his back on bread and circuses and embraced the way of obscurity, humility, suffering, rejection and death."[137] In fact, Avis writes that instead of the more glamorized forms of cultural influence,

> The distinctive charisma of the Christian life is found in identification with Christ's way of self-emptying, self-sacrifice, suffering in solidarity with all victims of human hurt of natural affliction, and self-oblation to the will of the Father. For out of that will come the self-evidencing authority of justice, truth and love. Ultimately, the power that the Spirit gives is the power of love.[138]

The contemporary plight of the world's multitudes, locked into conditions of powerlessness, means that the institutional church has ample opportunity to utilize its cultural-historical influence for their service. But like the Incarnation, it will be a costly service for it is not a cheap form of grace.[139]

Kerygmatic Power Is Sacramental

Finally, ecclesial kerygmatic power is sacramental in nature. For Kuyper, the *telos* of ecclesial power is the ultimate renewal of all creation. Ellul, while not disagreeing, places the church's *telos* in a penultimate position, reminding us that as a distinct, alternative community in the world, the institutional church is, first of all, a sign to the world of God's presence and eschatological promises. This is a helpful insight for without it, in both the church's internal

---

137. Avis, *Authority, Leadership, and Conflict*, 82.

138. Avis, *Authority, Leadership, and Conflict*, 83.

139. Bonhoeffer, *Cost of Discipleship*, 43–44. For a comparison between Bonhoeffer and Kuyper on the institutional church, see Dekker and Harinck, "Position of the Church."

and external life, the presence of the church in the world can degenerate into merely a utilitarian function for conversions. By understanding ecclesial power as sacramental, ecclesial proclamation aims not only for conversion and renewal but also serves as a mysterious or eschatological presence through the nature of its life together displayed to the world. Ellul writes of the churches "that are completely without direction at this time," that they "are tempted to speak [proclaim] in the ways of the world, to assimilate ourselves into the world" which means that the church will "cease being a sign of who God is."[140] As Ellul put it in *The Presence of the Kingdom*, "in the sight of men and in the reality of this world, the Christian is a visible sign of the new covenant which God has made with this world in Jesus Christ."[141] And this "is why it is essential that Christians should be very careful not to be wolves in the spiritual sense—that is, people who try to dominate others."[142] In fact, a sacramental interpretation of Kuyper's ecclesiology has been made recently.[143] It deserves an extended analysis. This is the matter we turn to in the next chapter.

CONCLUSION

Abraham Kuyper understands the power of the institutional church to be kerygmatic in nature. The institutional church's unique role in the world is to be the herald of the Word of God through proclamation, sacraments, discipleship, and diaconal acts of justice and mercy. While this may be so, we observed that some of those who followed Kuyper historically sought to apply his theology in oppressive ways within their different contexts. While the problem of the joining of state and ecclesial power has persisted since the fourth and sixteenth centuries (to a variety of degrees), the unresolved issue in Kuyper's theology that we observed at the outset of this chapter is the degree to which he successfully distinguished ecclesial power from the other forms of power operative within other spheres. To that end, Caputo and Ellul functioned as foils for highlighting and clarifying Kuyper's view of ecclesial power and Acts 10 functioned as a normative Christian standard of depicting ecclesial power in action (particularly in relationship with the state power of the Roman empire).

While Caputo and Ellul tend toward understanding divine and ecclesial power in terms of ontological weakness, as a stark antithesis to or negation of power, they do not share Kuyper's understanding of sphere sovereignty

---

140. *FLP*, 199.
141. *PK*, 3.
142. *PK*, 4–5.
143. Wood, "Introduction" (*R&G*, xviii).

and the differentiated powers within differentiated institutions of society. As such, while their work initially may seem promising for clarifying ecclesial power, they actually engage in another kind of reductionism that sheds little light on the heart of the matter. For example, neither Caputo nor Ellul would have any vocational counselling for Cornelius besides encouraging him to quit his Centurion post in order to divest himself of coercive power. Peter offers no such command to him. Rather, there seems to be inherent within Acts 10 an understanding that the role of apostle and the role of state military officer comprise two different callings, within two different institutions, with two essentially different forms of power. State power is clearly coercive by nature. But ecclesial power, as displayed by Peter, is Word-oriented and redemptive in nature. It seeks the renewal of the world rather than its revolution or overthrow. Ecclesial proclamational power is still a power but it does not contain within it the element of coercive force that is constitutive of state power.

For Kuyper, therefore, ecclesial power is a unique power operative within a unique institution for a unique purpose. And that purpose is to renew, disciple, and equip Christian believers to live faithfully before God in the whole of life and to discharge their responsibilities, in their various roles in life, faithfully. While a minister of the state is not called to discharge his duties in an incarnational or self-emptying manner, this is the nature of the institutional church's power. And as the institutional church participates in the civic life of the world, incarnationally and kenotically, it thereby functions as a sacramental sign to the world of the kingdom of God. We now turn to this important element of Kuyper's ecclesiology in the next chapter.

7

The Sacramental Nature of Ecclesial Power

Abraham Kuyper's Ecclesiology and Vatican Council II

On Maunday Thursday, April 14, 2001, Dr. John Webster preached a sermon on the sacrament of the Eucharist in Christ Church Cathedral, Oxford. Wading into the theological debates concerning the sacraments, Webster argued that sacraments are inherently "*backward*"-looking.[1] But the backward-looking action of sacraments is not purely memorial, only oriented to the past. Sacraments function as the exclusive action of God, through our looking back in faith, to make real and present to us in the here and now the reality and significance of the past for today.[2] Sacraments are the actions of God in which his Word is addressed to us and we receive that Word in all of its power through faith. And in this sacramental action, God's mighty redemptive acts of the past are brought to bear and achieve their intended effect of grace in the present.

We observed in the previous chapter that the nature of ecclesial power, in addition to being incarnational and kenotic, is sacramental. The purpose of this chapter is to analyze this sacramental aspect of ecclesial power in Kuyper's theology. This final step is important for two reasons: first, because

1. Webster, *Grace of Truth*, 96.
2. Webster, *Grace of Truth*, 98–99.

one recent interpreter of Kuyper's ecclesiology has classified it as sacramental; and second, because while Kuyper never explicitly named ecclesial power as sacramental we will show in this chapter that this term captures a significant insight that needs to be excavated and highlighted in Kuyper's ecclesiology.

WOOD'S SACRAMENTAL INTERPRETATION OF KUYPER'S ECCLESIOLOGY

Kuyper has "a sacramental vision of the church," that is, a "sacramental ecclesiology."[3] Such is the argument advanced by one recent scholar who has taken up the task of interpreting Kuyper's ecclesiology from a historical perspective. While there have been those who see in Calvin himself or Calvinism more generally a sacramental version of the Christian faith, the Reformed tradition is not often considered a sacramental tradition within Christianity.[4] Sacramental is a description more often attributed to the Anglican, Roman, or Orthodox churches. Rather, the Reformed tradition's ecclesiology has more often conceived of the church, to utilize Dulles's categories, as the *herald* of God's verbal announcement of the truth revealed in Jesus Christ.[5] Having analyzed Kuyper's view of the *kerygmatic* power of the institutional church, despite the challenges posed by our contemporary crisis of communication noted in the previous chapter, Wood's assertion that Kuyper's ecclesiology is a sacramental one should catch one's attention, for it is at least initially a curious and possibly even a questionable interpretation. In light of our previous analysis, which shows Kuyper's ecclesiology to be kerygmatic, or proclamational, how can Kuyper's ecclesiology be *sacramental*? And in light of the Second Vatican Council, which argued that the church is primarily a sacrament, what parallels are there between Wood's sacramental understanding of Kuyper's ecclesiology and that of other more traditional sacramental ecclesiologies?

In order to respond to these important questions about the supposed sacramental nature of Kuyper's ecclesiology, this chapter will begin by presenting Wood's argument in detail. Having understood the shape of Wood's argument, we will then turn to Vatican II and those twentieth-century

---

3. Wood, "Introduction" (*R&G*, xviii); *GD*, 56–58.

4. See, for example, Smit, "Developing a Calvinist Sacramental Theology." The classic text on the sacramental model of ecclesial classification by Dulles, *Models*, makes no mention of Calvin or the Calvinist tradition in his chapter on sacramental ecclesiologies.

5. Dulles, *Models*, 71–82.

theologians who have presented the sacramental ecclesiology model. Having this material before us, we will be prepared to evaluate Wood's claim and also discern in what ways Kuyper's ecclesiology is or is not sacramental in nature. Not only will this respond to Wood's argument as either sound or flawed but it will clarify the nature of ecclesial kerygmatic power with which we concluded the previous chapter. This will have brought our analysis of the power of the church in the ecclesiology of Abraham Kuyper to its conclusion.

WOOD'S ARGUMENT IN DETAIL

There are three primary places where Wood makes the claim that Kuyper's ecclesiology is sacramental. First, in his introduction to the English translation of Kuyper's sermon, *Rooted and Grounded*; second, in an article considering Kuyper's developing baptismal theology during the early phase of his pastoral career; and, third, in a chapter in his major work, *Going Dutch in the Modern Age*. We will analyze all three in an attempt to understand the shape of Wood's argument.

Rooted and Grounded: Inner/Mystical vs. Outer/Institutional

In his introduction to Kuyper's *Rooted and Grounded* sermon, Wood makes the brief observation that Kuyper's advocacy for a free Dutch church, liberated from its national establishment and centralized state administration, was based on a critical theological distinction: that being between the outer, institutional form of the church and the inner, mystical life of believers' spiritual union with Christ. We noted Kuyper's distinction between the church as an organism and the church as an institution previously. The organic mode of the church's "rootedness" is its union with Christ in the heart of each believing Christian. Wood points to the same terrain we covered previously in Kuyper's metaphors to explain this distinction. But the church also has an institutional mode of being, Wood rightly notes. That institutional mode of being requires that the church be "built" or "grounded" in the historical and cultural context of its time and place. Again, Wood cites the same sources we did in Chapter 3. Wood correctly notes that for Kuyper these two modes of being do not constitute two churches but a single entity, such that "the hidden mystical life and the outward form, were not to be separated but existed in a reciprocal dependence."[6] But then, without any

---

6. Wood, "Introduction" (*R&G*, xviii).

further explanation or argumentation after this point, Wood summarizes this ecclesial distinction of Kuyper's with the claim that "This was a sacramental vision of the church."[7]

To support his claim that Kuyper's ecclesiology is sacramental, Wood immediately turns to and quotes the classic ecclesiological work of the Roman Catholic theologian, Avery Cardinal Dulles, who wrote that "The corporal expression gives the spiritual act the material support it needs in order to achieve itself; and the spiritual act gives shape and meaning to the corporal expression."[8] Wood relates Dulles to Kuyper by saying that this "neatly fits the way Kuyper had described the church a century before."[9]

From this point, Wood moves on to address the religious pluralism of Kuyper's day but returns to the sacramental ecclesiology theme a paragraph later by saying that "Kuyper's sacramental ecclesiology also included a social ethic."[10] Wood then points to Kuyper's sphere distinctions (state and church, for example) which provided the groundwork for Kuyper's free church model: a church free from state control, free from dependence on state financial support, free from the congregation's lethargy because they had no reason to work for the church's well-being since it was being cared for by the state. The two most curious elements in Wood's argument are that (1) with the vast amount of primary source material on Kuyper's social ethic,[11] Wood makes no mention of this to support his claim that "Kuyper's sacramental ecclesiology also included a social ethic," and (2) Wood does not explain the connection between Kuyper's "sacramental ecclesiology" (his categorization) and Kuyper's "social ethic." The distinction is presented but neither argued nor explained. This, then, is the first place Wood makes the claim (with little to no argument) that Kuyper's ecclesiology is a sacramental one.

The Church Question and Kuyper's Early Baptismal Theology

We now turn to Wood's article on Kuyper's early baptismal theology.[12] Here, we observe Wood's repeated claim again that Kuyper's ecclesiology is sacramental. He begins this article by placing Kuyper's church reform efforts within their nineteenth-century European context. Wood notes, "The

7. Wood, "Introduction" (R&G, xviii); GD, 56–58.
8. Dulles, Models, 60, quoted in Wood, "Introduction" (R&G, xviii–xix).
9. Wood, "Introduction" (R&G, xix).
10. Wood, "Introduction" (R&G, xix).
11. For example, a prime candidate for studying the connection between Kuyper's ecclesiology and his social ethic, which Wood ignores, would be *Problem of Poverty*.
12. Wood, "Church, Sacrament, and Society."

modern era presented a crisis for theology in several respects, sacramental theology not least of all."[13] In light of this context, Wood notes that while "the renowned, Dutch, public theologian, Abraham Kuyper, is not often recognized as a sacramental reformer . . . the sacraments [baptism in particular] were essential to his plans to reform the church."[14]

Wood sets up "the church problem" faced by Kuyper by pointing to the increasingly differentiated nineteenth-century Dutch society in which the previous place and role of the national Dutch church (Dutch: *volkskerk*) was subjected to serious question in the wake of the centralizing power of the Dutch state. As more and more of civil Dutch society came under the centralizing influence of the Enlightenment's ideology, the Dutch Reformed Church was no longer able to continue giving the Dutch population a sense of collective identity, though it had for centuries in the past. Now, as the church became independent from the state (under Kuyper's leadership, no less), the result was that the identity-conferring function that the church had been providing to Dutch society was being taken up by the state instead. Wood nicely summarizes this "church question" by saying that "The identity of the church, which claimed to be the *church* [Dutch: *kerk*] of the Dutch *volk*, was in fact gradually becoming separated from the identity of the Dutch nation."[15] This summary of the historical-cultural situation is perceptive and correct.

How would Kuyper continue to advocate for church independence from the state while also maintaining the church's objective place in Dutch society? Or would Kuyper's efforts for the church's independence from the state result in a culturally self-marginalized church? To address this potential problem, Wood looks to "Kuyper's early baptismal theology" and argues that it was "part of his attempt at constructing a free church in which church membership and admission to the sacrament were not taken for granted and which was an objective divine institution in its own right."[16] That is, in the midst of the differentiation of Dutch society, Kuyper worked to ensure that the institutional church didn't become marginalized or relegated to the subjective status of a voluntary organization. He did this by requiring a profession of orthodox Christian faith before being admitted to participation

---

13. Wood, "Church, Sacrament, and Society," 275.
14. Wood, "Church, Sacrament, and Society," 275–76.
15. Wood, "Church, Sacrament, and Society," 276.
16. Wood, "Church, Sacrament, and Society," 276. Alexander, *Dark Side of Modernity*, 16, notes the larger European context of this, saying: "By the 1880s one could observe on the continent, in France and in Southern and Central Europe, a growing reaction against progressive forces. . . . In Germany, a mystical and backward-looking *Volk* ideology fermented . . . spreading throughout the intellectual classes."

in the church's sacramental life. This would give the institutional church objective authority and status because membership in the church was not voluntary and thus the church was not a voluntary organization. That is, it was not through personal, individual decision that one joined the church but, rather, the church as an objective institution made that decision about the individual. So, Wood argues, through Kuyper's bolstering of the church's doctrine and practice of baptism, he responded to this increasingly differentiated (and state-centralized) society with an institutional church that was not only free from the state but also remained an objective, authoritative institution.

The majority of Wood's article traces the historical development of Kuyper's views on the church and the church's sacraments as they related to this cultural and societal shift. In the end, Wood argues that "For Kuyper . . . the sacraments played an essential role in the work of salvation, and the church could no more do without the sacraments than humanity could do without the church."[17] Therefore, Wood claims that because Kuyper's ecclesiology focused on the importance of the sacraments in maintaining the institutional church as an objective and authoritative civic institution, his ecclesiology is a sacramental one. For Wood, then, a sacramental ecclesiology is an ecclesiology that gives the church's sacraments importance because the church is an objective authority in society.

The French Revolution as Ecclesiological Crisis

Finally, we turn to the third chapter of Wood's major work on Kuyper's ecclesiology, "The French Revolution as an Ecclesiological Crisis: Abraham Kuyper's Sacramental Ecclesiology."[18] In this chapter, Wood deepens and develops the same argument made in the two sources we have already considered. First, Kuyper's context meant that his distinction between the church as an organism and the church as an institution responded to the cultural shifts he perceived at the middle of the nineteenth century. Wood again notes here that in light of the French Revolution, which plunged not only the church but the whole culture into crisis, the church needed to find a way to remain objective and authoritative (for individuals as well as society

---

17. Wood, "Church, Sacrament, and Society," 296.

18. GD, 56–81. Two notes: (1) This is the published version of Wood's PhD thesis, and (2) this chapter follows the previous one in which Wood argues that Kuyper's ecclesiology is a "free church" one. Granted that Wood's methodology is historical, it does raise the possibility of a lack of theological clarity in Wood's understanding of Kuyper's ecclesiology.

as a whole) while simultaneously breaking free from state control (should the state become ideologically-possessed and discriminatory).

Second, Wood makes the same argument as above that Kuyper discovered the path through this problem by emphasizing the critical importance of the church's sacraments within the life of the church and the life of the church member. Wood's argument once again is that prior to the emergence of the "church question" in the nineteenth century, the Dutch nation and the Dutch church were coterminous. To be born Dutch was to be born into membership in the Dutch church in which baptism was assumed to be automatic and entitled based upon national citizenship. With the differentiation of Dutch society, these identities (national Dutch and ecclesial Dutch Reformed) were split apart institutionally. This raised the important question of how the Dutch church would continue to function within Dutch society to contribute to Dutch national identity since the state fulfilled this function now.

Wood's claim is that because Kuyper's reform efforts assumed the freedom of the church from the state while still retaining an objective and divinely sanctioned authority for baptism following profession of faith for membership in a voluntary church, this makes Kuyper's ecclesiology sacramental. Thus, according to Wood in these three sources, Kuyper's ecclesiology is a sacramental one because the sacraments of the institutional church received significant theological attention as Kuyper sought to respond to the challenges posed by the differentiation of Dutch society and the growth of the Dutch state in the nineteenth century.

RESPONSE TO WOOD'S ARGUMENT

Wood's work is excellent in the detailed way it traces the historical development of Kuyper's ecclesiology. His attention to historical detail and his appreciation of nuance are extremely helpful for understanding Kuyper's context and how his theology developed in dynamic response to that context. But when Wood turns to *theological* interpretation of Kuyper, particularly when the theological category of sacrament is used as an interpretive filter for Kuyper's ecclesiology, serious problems result. There are three ways in which this can be seen: in Wood's use of Dulles's ecclesial models, the category of sacramental ecclesiology, and the larger theological background to sacramental ecclesiology within twentieth-century (especially, Roman Catholic) theology.

Wood's Reliance on Dulles

As noted above, in Wood's introduction to Kuyper's *Rooted and Grounded* sermon, Wood quotes Dulles to support his interpretation of Kuyper's ecclesiology as sacramental. The crucial problem with this is that Wood has misinterpreted Dulles. While Wood argues that his quotation from Dulles summarizes "sacramental ecclesiology in the twentieth century," a closer examination of the larger context of Dulles at this point from where the quotation is taken reveals that Dulles was not addressing sacramental ecclesiology but rather "The structure of human life" in general, which, Dulles argues, is "symbolic" or sacramental.[19]

Therefore, in the passage Wood has quoted, Dulles was not offering a summary of how to understand sacramental ecclesiology per se but rather how to conceive of the symbolic nature of human life which the Second Vatican Council also observed and which served as background to the Council's statements regarding the sacramental nature of the church. This means that while there may be parallels between Kuyper's organic versus institutional modes of the church's being on the one hand and the Roman Catholic distinction between the corporal and symbolic/mystical aspects of human life on the other hand, the application Wood makes to Kuyper's ecclesiology is not possible using Dulles at this point. It is not what Dulles was addressing. The quote from Dulles is not about ecclesiology and, therefore, Wood's exclusive use of Dulles to support his argument that Kuyper has a sacramental ecclesiology is inherently flawed. But no further support is offered by Wood for his claim that Kuyper's ecclesiology is sacramental.

Sacraments and Sacramental Ecclesiology

The second important response to Wood's claim is brief and functions to set up the third response below. Yet, it is worth highlighting as a separate response. It concerns the move Wood makes from observing the importance Kuyper places on the institutional church's sacraments to classifying Kuyper's ecclesiology as sacramental. Simply put, focusing on sacraments or insisting on their importance, either in the objective life of the institutional church or in the subjective life of the Christian believer, does not make one's ecclesiology sacramental. I do not necessarily have a sacramental ecclesiology if I believe baptism is important for a Christian believer's discipleship.

The same logical error could be made if an interpreter were studying the ecclesiology of the Roman Catholic Church. Dulles notes that the Roman

---

19. Dulles, *Models*, 60.

Catholic Church falls cleanly within the institutional model.[20] But there are ample sources one could turn to for support in constructing the critical importance of the proclamation of the Word in Roman Catholic worship and theology. But even if a list of sources could be cited about the importance of proclamation, this does not make the Roman Catholic Church "fit" Dulles's model of the church as herald (which Dulles even himself connects to the classical and Barthian Protestant traditions).[21]

Wood's argument is a non-starter because he has misunderstood how the ecclesial models function in Dulles's work from the outset.[22] It is true that as a Christian theologian and church reformer, Kuyper devoted much energy to the sacraments but this does not necessarily equate to him having or advocating a sacramental ecclesiology. It may be the case but not because he addresses the sacraments in his theology generally or ecclesiology specifically.

Sacramental Ecclesiology

These two objections above raise the most basic question we need to consider: what is meant by describing an ecclesiology as "sacramental"? For example, does bolstering one's view of the importance of the sacraments in order to address a growing ecclesial or cultural problem make one's ecclesiology sacramental? This is the most critical response to Wood's argument about Kuyper's ecclesiology: Wood's argument reveals a theological ignorance about what makes an ecclesiology sacramental. On this point there is a robust body of literature to draw upon but which is not evident in Wood's treatment of the topic. In order to demonstrate this, we will show below the theological roots of sacramental ecclesiology as they are presented in the Second Vatican Council. It is this ecclesiological formulation, as well as the interpreters who work in the wake of Vatican II, that are definitive for any sacramental ecclesiology to be considered properly. As we will see, in light of our analysis of what is entailed by a sacramental ecclesiology, Wood's argument is deeply misguided. This analysis will conclude by presenting the truly sacramental nature of Kuyper's ecclesiology, particularly as it relates to the nature of the church's kerygmatic power.

---

20. Dulles, *Models*, 31–32.
21. Dulles, *Models*, 71–72.
22. On how the models function for Dulles, see his *Models*, 13–30.

VATICAN COUNCIL II AND SACRAMENTAL ECCLESIOLOGY

The field of sacramental ecclesiology is too broad to analyze comprehensively here and engaging in a detailed theological or historical analysis would take us too far afield from our project's aim. But in order to respond to Wood's misunderstanding of this important concept and his claim that Kuyper's ecclesiology is sacramental, we will present the contours of this concept as they reached adoption at the Second Vatican Council and have been reflected upon in the Roman Catholic theological tradition since then. Like Kuyper for the Dutch Reformed tradition, Vatican II sought to engage the Roman Catholic church in a theological response to the pressing questions and issues of the modern world. To do this, Vatican II could be envisioned as asking, "What is the most basic ecclesiological claim one can make about the nature of the church in the modern era?" Its answer was that the church is a sign, the primal sacrament from which the other sacraments of the church originate. The church is the sign and instrument of the (present and coming) reign of God.

Background to Vatican II

Vatican II lies at the recent end of a series of major councils addressing Roman Catholic life and dogma. The first thirteen canons of the seventh session of the Council of Trent (1545–1563) are directed to the proper understanding of the sacraments in general.[23] Dulles summarizes these canons by saying that the council defined a sacrament as "the visible form of an invisible grace."[24] Then, in the nineteenth century, Vatican Council I (1869–1870) hinted at a sacramental ecclesiology when it affirmed that the church "is a divine sign."[25] Between the first and second Vatican councils, a number of theologians sought to give clarity and substance to this emerging sacramental ecclesiology. In this regard, the work of Henri de Lubac, Yves Congar, and others associated with the *nouvelle theologie* served as significant theological precursors to Vatican Council II's articulation of a

---

23. Council of Trent, "Seventh Session," 53–56.
24. Dulles, *Models*, 61.
25. Dulles, "Church, Sacrament, and Ground of Faith," 259. Since the active years of Kuyper's career overlap with Vatican I, an important area for further research would be whether—and to what extent—Kuyper's work reveals influence from the documents of this council, especially in terms of sacramental ecclesiology. To date, I have not found any evidence of direct influence.

sacramental ecclesiology.[26] In the period just before Vatican II, a renewed interest in the Patristic period,[27] the theology and liturgy of the Church Fathers, and a desire to open up the Roman Catholic church to the intellectual currents and ideas beyond the bounds of the church all marked the theological explorations of a number of theologians. A desire to escape the limiting and even mechanical understandings of a number of doctrines that had developed during the Scholastic period created a new space for reframing key components of the church's self-understanding. It was in this period that conceiving of the church as the primal sacrament became of particular interest. Working during this period, Cardinal Ratzinger, before becoming Pope Benedict XVI, said that the sacramental nature of the church was "foundational" to Roman Catholic theology.[28]

Vatican II

The foundational importance of a *sacramental* ecclesiology can be seen in the opening words of the documents of Vatican II. The first article of the first chapter of the first document of Vatican II says that "the church, in Christ, is in the nature of sacrament—a sign and instrument, that is, of communion with God and of the unity of the entire human race."[29] This union with God occurred through the Incarnation of Jesus Christ and the church now continues the work of Christ in the world. Christ was historically present as "the light of the nations" and he was the one through whom God gathered his people to himself by proclaiming the saving message of the gospel.[30] In turn, the church is now the on-going sacramental presence of Christ as sign and instrument. The church is the sign of the saving reconciliation with God that the gospel announces and it is also the instrument by which the alienation between God and humanity and even within humanity is overcome. The church embodies and proclaims both the promise and the reality of reconciliation between God and humanity.

26. Dulles, "Half a Century of Ecclesiology," offers an extensive background and bibliography for the pre-Vatican II development of a sacramental ecclesiology. Küng, *Church*, also offers a good background with helpful biblical references.

27. One important area of future research that this project highlights is finding the patristic sources common to both the Roman Catholic and Kuyperian theologians during the first half of the twentieth century, which moved both toward interest in the idea of the church as a sacrament.

28. Ratzinger, *Principles of Catholic Theology*, 44–55, contains a concise but surprisingly thorough summary of the background to Vatican II's adoption of this article of faith.

29. Flannery, *Vatican Council II*, 1.

30. *Lumen Gentium* 1 (Flannery, *Vatican Council II*, 1).

Vatican II develops this by arguing that the sacramental (in the sense of sign and instrument) aspects of the church's nature relate both to the internal and external aspects of the church. Internally, the church is a visible sign for its members of the spiritual reality of the saving unity that has been achieved between God and humanity in Jesus Christ. For "all those, who in faith look towards Jesus . . . God has gathered together and established as the church, that it may be for each and every one the visible sacrament of this saving unity."[31] As a member of the church looks upon and contemplates the church of which they have become a member, the image that the church proclaims to them is that by the grace of God they personally enjoy reconciliation and unity with God and are part of the corporate redemption God has worked with the rest of redeemed humanity and creation. The church is made up of those whom "Christ mystically constitutes as his body [to be] his brothers and sisters who are called together from every nation."[32] And just as a soul indwells the body to make it a living being, so too the Spirit of Christ indwells the church, giving life and animating the church to be the sacrament of unity and reconciliation by grace.[33] And as a community in which Christ continues his work, the church is the instrument and means by which this reconciliation continues between God and humanity. That is, the sacramental nature of the church issues forth in a missional engagement of the gospel with the world for its further redemption and renewal.

Extra-ecclesially, Vatican II taught that the church has a special sacramental nature in terms of its relationship with the world that is not yet (part of) the church. The church is "on earth, the seed and the beginning of that kingdom [of God]."[34] That is, the church is a sign to the nations and peoples of the earth, which are not members of the church presently, of a reality's small beginning that one day, when the seed reaches mature growth and bears its fruit, will be true for the entire scope of creation. On this point, Dulles notes that "the church is the place where the Kingdom of God and of Christ is present in mystery and is initially budding forth. It is thus a sign and anticipation of God's definitive eschatological reign."[35] The church is not one entity and the world a separate, different entity. Rather, the church is a part of the world, a part that has been set aside as a sign to the rest of the world, that points to and symbolizes the future when the kingdom of God

---

31. *Lumen Gentium* 9 (Flannery, *Vatican Council II*, 13–14).
32. *Lumen Gentium* 7 (Flannery, *Vatican Council II*, 7).
33. *Lumen Gentium* 8 (Flannery, *Vatican Council II*, 9).
34. *Lumen Gentium* 5 (Flannery, *Vatican Council II*, 4).
35. Dulles, *Church to Believe In*, 20.

will have spread across the entire creation. At present this future reality only appears in isolated, limited, and ambiguous form in the church.

The way in which the reign of God in the church will extend to become the reign of God over all of creation, though, is not through force or domination, not through armies or imperialism. Rather, this eschatological promise is achieved through the instrumentality of the church as a sacramental witness that proclaims the promises of God to God's beloved creation. "Rising from the dead (cf. Rom 6:9) he [Jesus] sent his life-giving Spirit upon his disciples and through him [the Spirit] set up his body which is the church as the universal sacrament of salvation."[36] Through the church, Christ is sacramentally and mystically present to his whole creation, a presence which is instrumental and redemptive for the world. Thus, that same Christ who sought to redeem the world through love (cf. John 3:16) now continues his redemptive mission with his apostles and all those who follow them up to today. What began with the apostles' missionary activity continues in the always-growing community of the redeemed, the church on earth. The institutional church is Christ's perpetual Body on earth which "is driven by the holy Spirit to play its part in bringing to completion the plan of God, who has constituted Christ as the source of salvation for the whole world."[37]

Pope John Paul II summarized Vatican II's sacramental ecclesiology well:

> The church, inasmuch as it is the Body of Christ, is simply an instrument of this salvation.... As the people of God the church is thus, at the same time, the Body of Christ.... This life, which is life from God and in God, is the actualization of salvation. *Man is saved in the church by being brought into the Mystery of the Divine Trinity*, into the mystery of the intimate life of God. This cannot be understood by looking exclusively at the visible aspect of the church. The church is a *living body*.[38]

KARL RAHNER AND AVERY DULLES INTERPRET VATICAN II

In light of Vatican II's formulation of the church as the primal or foundational sacrament, sign and instrument, from which the other sacraments

---

36. *Lumen Gentium* 48 (Flannery, *Vatican Council II*, 72).
37. *Lumen Gentium* 17 (Flannery, *Vatican Council II*, 23).
38. John Paul II, *Crossing the Threshold of Hope*, 136–37.

of the church originate, Karl Rahner and Avery Dulles have been two key Roman Catholic theologians who have worked to interpret, develop, and apply this sacramental ecclesiology. Their interpretations have highlighted, in particular, the Christocentrism and placial dynamism of sacramental ecclesiology. We will highlight each of these additional contributions below as they not only help to explain the sacramental ecclesiology of Vatican II and the post-Vatican II interpreters, but they will also function to highlight the pathways that will lead to our re-interpretation of sacramentality in Kuyper's ecclesiology.

Sacramental Ecclesiology Is Christocentric

Discourse about the church (the body) must include Christ himself (the head) if it is to be authentically Christian ecclesiology. In fact, for both Rahner and Dulles, this means that saying the institutional church is the primal or foundational sacrament misses an even more foundational fact: Christ is of such primacy that *he* is the foundational sacrament, sign and instrument, of salvation for the world. Only through the sacramental nature of Christ can the institutional church, his body on earth presently, be viewed in a sacramental way. As such, it is only as the church remains in union with Christ and faithfully bound to him as the head that the church is able to be the on-going presence of *Christ* in the world and that the church can be said to be a sacrament. In Christ, the institutional church is sacramental in nature as the primary historical sign and instrument of God's grace that is temporally manifest in visible institutional form. That is, the church is the vanguard of God's world-oriented and missional grace. The church is the visible and observable fact and event of God's grace. The church is the way in which grace is made sacramentally visible in and to and for the world.

Karl Rahner has sought to interpret and explain the Christocentrism inherent within a sacramental ecclesiology. Since Avery Dulles's views are also of interest, we will comment by way of footnotes where he also contributes on this point.

There are two primary works in which Rahner explores the Christocentrism of sacramental ecclesiology. First, he writes in his second volume of *Theological Investigations* that the church is the "incarnational presence of God" after Christ and is "the real, permanent and ever valid presence of God in the world."[39] But, second, Rahner also writes his primary thesis on this subject in *The Church and the Sacraments*.[40] Here, Rahner develops

---

39. Rahner, *Theological Investigations*, 2:76.
40. Rahner, *Church and the Sacraments*.

the sacramental ecclesiology that is eventually codified in Vatican II: that the church is the incarnate presence of the grace of God, ever-present and ever-valid for the world's redemption.

In *The Church and the Sacraments*, Rahner argues that the institutional church is a sacrament only through its vital union with Christ.[41] "Christ," he writes, "is the historically real and actual presence of the eschatologically victorious mercy of God"[42] and through Christ, who unites in his very person the divine and the human, God has taken "the world fundamentally and once and for all into his mercy."[43] This is the foundational grace of God at work in redemption: Christ, through his Incarnation, life, death, and resurrection, revealed God's mercy and redemption for the world which is irrevocable. As through Adam all of humanity was stained with sin, so through Christ all of humanity is accepted into God's forgiving mercy (cf. 1 Cor 15:22). That is, Christ was not only the historically visible *sign* of this spiritual reality of redemption in the world, but Christ was also the *instrument* through which this redemption was actively taking place in the world through his ministry. It is only through Christ, as sign and instrument of God's grace, that humanity is accepted into God's mercy. In fact, Rahner argues, Christ has made real that of which he is the sign. Christ is the foundational *sign* that God's grace has been victorious over human rebellion and Christ is also the one who *instrumentally* makes this a present reality for the world. Rahner concisely states that "Christ in his historical existence is both reality and sign, *sacramentum* and *res sacramenti*, of the redemptive grace of God."[44]

Consequently, the nature of the church flows from the role, function, and nature of Christ, the first sacrament. The church, as the historically continuous presence of Christ in the world, is therefore the continuing sacrament, sign and instrument, of God's redemptive work in the world's history. Rahner explains that

> Christ is the primal sacramental word of God, uttered in the one history of mankind, in which God made known his irrevocable mercy that cannot be annulled by God or man, and did this by effecting it in Christ, and effected it by making it known.
>
> Now the church is the continuance, the contemporary presence, of that real, eschatologically triumphant and irrevocably

---

41. Dulles argues this in his *Models*, 60; *Dimensions of the Church*, 51, 73; *Church to Believe In*, 30, 46.
42. Rahner, *Church*, 14.
43. Rahner, *Church*, 14.
44. Rahner, *Church*, 15.

established presence in the world, in Christ, of God's salvific will. The church is the abiding presence of that primal sacramental word of definitive grace, which Christ is in the world, effecting what is uttered by uttering it in sign.[45]

In Christ, God spoke the message of grace and mercy to the world. He spoke this message in the historically incarnate person of Jesus Christ who instrumentally secured the redemption of which he was the sign: God's victorious grace over sin and human rebellion. Now, in like manner, Christ's on-going sacramental presence of victorious mercy continues to be evident to the world through the church. As the abiding sacrament of God's redemption, the church not only is a *sign* of salvation but it also *instrumentally* makes salvation manifest for the human community to behold, receive, and experience.

Christology Shapes Ecclesiology

This Christocentrism has important implications for Vatican II's sacramental ecclesiology. Rahner continually connects his sacramental ecclesiology back to Christ, fundamentally grounding the church's being and mission in the nature and work of Christ. Thus, following Jesus' historical ministry on earth, the salvation of God in Christ is proclaimed to the human community through the ministry of the institutional church that lives moment by moment in union with Christ. The historical Jesus called to himself a community of faithful followers who obtained grace and mercy from his word and deeds throughout his ministry. For Rahner, this continues to take place through the church as Christ's on-going presence on earth. Now, as Jesus himself did, the institutional church continually calls to herself a faithful community. This faithful community obtains redemption through the church's ministry of instrumentally making Christ present and effective by means of the proclamation of the gospel. Yet, this proclamation on the part of the institutional church is also performed symbolically (as a sacrament). That is, the church as a civic institution (the body of Christ within the body politic) proclaims the gospel verbally as well as nonverbally by symbolically making present the redemption which is available in God through Christ by her very life as an alternative community in the world. The church manifests and makes present to the human community this redemptive grace that has brought about her presence in the world in the first place. The church is the

---

45. Rahner, *Church*, 18.

tangible form of the continued presence of God's grace in the world, the same grace to which the church points by her very existence in the world.

The church is a cultural organism of human persons that takes on organized, institutional form in human society through the operation of God's grace in Christ. And those who come to receive this grace and are reconciled to God through the church are also built up and incorporated into this body of the church that manifests God's grace in visible social and institutional form to the world as a distinct people. Rahner summarizes:

> If it is true to say that the church is the continuance of Christ's presence in the world, is the fundamental sacrament of the eschatologically triumphant mercy of God, then salvation is offered and promised to the individual by his entering into positive relation to the church. . . . God's life is offered to men plainly and once and for all in Christ, through whose incarnation the people of God exists. This has socially organized form in the church, which is consequently the abiding and historically manifest presence of this saving grace in Christ, the fundamental sacred sign or sacrament of this grace.[46]

A sacramental ecclesiology, therefore, is deeply Christocentric, flowing from the historical and bodily presence of Christ in the world, a real presence which continues post-Ascension by his Spirit. As Christ revealed and proclaimed God's grace and mercy for humanity in his suffering on the cross, so also the institutional church functions, as Christ's continuing presence in the world, as a sacrament of God's salvation, symbolically pointing humanity to the grace of God that is triumphant over human sin and unbelief and also instrumentally makes present humanity's reconciliation with God through her ministry of grace. But it is only as the church is "the presence of [Christ's] saving grace in the world" that she is the "fundamental" or "primal" sacrament.[47] By this, Rahner means that Christ, and now by extension the church, is "the one abiding symbolic presence, similar in structure to the incarnation, of the eschatologically redemptive grace of Christ; a presence in which sign and what is signified are united inseparably but without confusion, the grace of God in the 'flesh' of an historical and tangible ecclesiastical embodiment."[48]

---

46. Rahner, *Church*, 21.
47. Rahner, *Church*, 39.
48. Rahner, *Church*, 23–24. Dulles, *Church to Believe In*, 28, summarizes Rahner's interpretation by commenting that "the institutional forms of the church [liturgy, sacraments, etc.] express and mediate the life of grace."

Thus, the church is "the presence of redemptive grace for men, historically visible and manifest as the sign of the eschatologically victorious grace of God in the world."[49] As the church remains in union with Christ, only then does "Christ [continue to act] through the church in regard to an individual human being, by giving his action spatio-temporal embodiment" in the world.[50] A sacramental ecclesiology, therefore, is fundamentally Christocentric in orientation: Christ working through the church, making the church his on-going presence in and to the world, and continuing the proclamation of the gospel to the world for its redemption. It is an ecclesiology in which the church is "the definitive sign, impossible to deprive of meaning, of God's grace in the world, which is rendered present by being manifested in this way in the church."[51]

The church is, therefore, more than a social organism of like-minded people but the "visible outward expression of [God's] grace."[52] And as Christocentric, it is an ongoing component of the *missio Dei* because "in the church God's grace is given expression and embodiment and symbolized, and by being so embodied, is present."[53] The institutional church that the world beholds, then, "in her visible historical form is herself an intrinsic symbol of the eschatologically triumphant grace of God" and "in that spatio-temporal visible form, this grace is made present" to the world.[54] This means that the church is missionally engaged with the world not due to the church's actions but, rather, due to the actions of God in and through the church as an effective sacrament, sign and instrument, in union with Christ. As the church remains in vital union with Christ, then the church's ministry of proclamation becomes sacramental in nature.

Sacramental Ecclesiology Is Placially Dynamic

Not only is a sacramental ecclesiology Christocentric but it is also, as I will call it, placially dynamic. By "placially dynamic" I mean to highlight (1) the importance of the institutional church's physical presence and place in

---

49. Rahner, *Church*, 22.

50. Rahner, *Church*, 39. On the importance of the church abiding in union with Christ for the church to be and remain a sacramental presence, see Dulles, "Half a Century of Ecclesiology," 432; "Church and Salvation," 75–76; *Dimensions of the Church*, 27, 52–53; *Church to Believe In*, 20, 41, 94; "Church as 'One,'" 14; Rahner, *Theological Investigations*, 6:163–177; *Lumen Gentium* 1 (Flannery, *Vatican Council II*, 1).

51. Rahner, *Church*, 24.

52. Rahner, *Church*, 34.

53. Rahner, *Church*, 34.

54. Rahner, *Church*, 39.

the world, and (2) the distinction between the institutional church as the location of salvation's event versus the church as the revelation and manifestation of salvation's agent. In this section, we will turn and primarily follow Dulles as he argues how the church functions in these two different ways, placing Rahner's additional contributions to this discussion in the footnotes for extended analysis.

Dulles argues that within a sacramental ecclesiology framework, the institutional church is not the focus of attention but, rather, the focus of attention moves through the church to the world. By viewing the church as pointing beyond itself, Dulles does not thereby jettison the necessity of the institutional form of the church in his sacramental ecclesiology. On the contrary, he still claims it is necessary for one's salvation but the institutional church is not the goal but, instead, the means by which God's grace is related to the world. Dulles articulates this by pointing to the priority of grace over the institutional church in the priorities of God's redemptive economy. For Dulles, a sacramental ecclesiology insists upon the necessity of the institutional church but primarily as a vehicle for God's grace for the redemption of the world. He writes that

> The notion of the church as sacrament preserves the priority of God's action. A sacrament is not an arbitrarily constructed sign, but one that comes into being because of the spiritual reality that is contained in it. The church, therefore, is present where, and only where, God's irrevocable self-gift in his incarnate Son continues to come to expression in symbolic form.[55]

Dulles is distinguishing between two different senses in which the church can be said to be a sign. On the one hand, as noted above, Rahner conceives of the church as a marking sign, pointing from somewhere else to the here-and-now of the church's place, a marker that the event of God's grace is actively taking place and temporal shape here.[56] On the other hand, Dulles wants to also retain a more dynamic notion: that the church is also a directional sign, pointing away from itself to the grace of God in Christ *for the world*. Dulles calls the combination of these two directional senses the "full sign" sense of a sacrament.[57] In fact, all sacraments function in this double way: drawing attention to themselves so that they can point that attention

---

55. Dulles, *Church to Believe In*, 49.

56. This can be seen in how Karl Rahner conceives of the church as a "down-payment" (Rahner, "What Is a Sacrament?," 280). See also Rahner, *Theological Investigations*, 10:10, 16–17, 23.

57. Dulles, *Models*, 61.

beyond themselves. For Dulles, the emphasis falls on this latter movement: away from the church to the world.

If the church primarily points beyond itself to the freedom of the grace of God in Christ for the world, this means that the institutional church does not have a privileged position as the sole locus of salvation's activity in the world. The institutional church cannot monopolize God's grace for itself for who or what can limit God's activity? Dulles argues that the institutional church is not primarily "a means by which salvation is effected" or "the locus in which salvation occurs." Rather, the church is "the sign or sacrament of God's saving action in Christ."[58] That is, the church is not the sole destination for the dispensing of divine grace. The church is, first of all, where grace has erupted in the world, "an objectification of the communal life of grace" at work.[59] In this way, the church functions in the same way that Jesus functioned in his historical earthly ministry: "Just as Christ [was] . . . so the church is the sacrament in which God's redemptive action in Christ manifests itself as a sign of his powerful mercy toward all men of all times and places. The church as a visible institution is necessary not because God's grace has to be channeled through a human organization (it does not!), but because grace has an inherent exigency to achieve its proper sacramental expression."[60]

The institutional structure of the church is not necessary for God to funnel his grace into the world. Rather, the institutional church is necessary for salvation because the presence of the institutional church means that God's grace has achieved its appropriate incarnational expression in human reality. And the institutional church, having reached its appropriate incarnational expression, is, in turn, the sign of God's on-going graciousness to the world. Like Jesus' teaching about knowing a tree by its fruit, one can know that the grace of God is present and active in the world because it has become manifest in the fruit of the institutional church. And this fruit of the institutional church means that God and God's grace in Christ are still active *for the world*. Or, as Dulles concisely puts it, "Wherever the grace of Christ reaches an appropriate self-expression, something of the church is present, and wherever the church is authentically present, the life of grace is achieving a symbolic embodiment."[61] The corporate language Dulles uses is important, for sacraments are communal symbols.[62] And as communal

58. Dulles, "Church and Salvation," 74–75.
59. Dulles, "Church and Salvation," 75.
60. Dulles, "Church and Salvation," 75.
61. Dulles, "Church and Salvation," 75.
62. See Dulles, *Models*, 62.

symbols, they orient the church in an on-going relationship to the world as the object of God's redemptive purposes.

Distinguishing the Inner and Outer Aspects of a Sacramental Ecclesiology

Dulles's missional understanding of the church as a sacrament is based on his distinction between the inner and outer aspects of the sacraments (a distinction we noted above in our early analysis of Wood's argument). Dulles contends that there is no direct or automatic correspondence between the physical sacramental sign and the spiritual sacramental reality. The reason for this is God's freedom in bestowing grace. But this means that there is no direct or automatic correspondence between the institutional church and the grace, mercy, and love of Christ at work in a particular place. Just because we observe a church in the societal marketplace of civic institutions does not automatically mean God's grace is active in that location. These realities (sacramental sign and active instrument of grace) are in a placially dynamic relationship. As Dulles teaches,

> As a sacrament the church has both an outer and an inner aspect. The institutional or structural aspect of the church—its external reality—is essential, since without it the church would not be visible. . . . On the other hand, the institutional or structural aspect is never sufficient to constitute the church. The offices and rituals of the church must palpably appear as the actual expressions of the faith, hope, and love of living men. Otherwise the church would be a dead body rather than a living Christian community.[63]

Thus, rather than viewing a sacramental ecclesiology as issuing forth in a static relationship between sacramental sign and active instrument of grace, these components have a placially-dynamic character.[64] The institutional church can be a faulty sign, less than a "full sign" in Dulles's sense. It is possible for the institutional church to be present within society but for God's grace in Christ to be absent, not manifesting itself to the world, possibly concealed from view, if the church is unfaithful to Christ. But when the church properly and faithfully functions as a sacrament, as "a sign of grace realizing itself" actively, then it takes on "an event character; it is dynamic.

---

63. Dulles, *Models*, 64.

64. Caputo, *Weakness of God*, consistently calls this the "event" character of God's grace active in the world.

The church becomes church insofar as the grace of Christ, operative within it, achieves historical tangibility through the actions of the church as such."[65] The institutional church is a dynamic sacrament. It is dependent upon the grace of God in Christ being operative within and through it. It is not an automatic or mechanical relationship that can be treated casually. When the church is faithful and grace is active, the church is not only a place where grace has "happened" but also a place where grace may still "happen" and become tangibly manifest in human history and society as the grace within the church continues to reach out into the world redemptively. We will return to the place-aspect of the sacramental nature of ecclesial power below.

Conclusion

Having analyzed Vatican II's sacramental ecclesiology, in the documents of Vatican II itself and in the theologies of both Karl Rahner and Avery Dulles, now we can appreciate that Wood's understanding of sacramental ecclesiology in general or as applied to Kuyper specifically contains a crucial misunderstanding. In no substantive way does Wood develop a distinctly *theological* account of Kuyper's ecclesiology as *sacramental* in the sense of Vatican II, Rahner, or Dulles. Wood does not engage or reference the wider sacramental ecclesiological tradition. And while Wood mentions the importance of sacraments for Kuyper, ecclesial *sacramentality* does not function in his account of Kuyper's ecclesiology except to highlight the place sacraments have in Kuyper's reform efforts. Wood does not delve into the theological relationship between Christ and the church or how the church sacramentally presents Christ to either the church's members or the extra-ecclesial world as sign or instrument.[66] We must conclude, therefore, by saying that Wood's use of the category of sacrament to describe Kuyper's ecclesiology is misunderstood and/or misguided at worst, incomplete at best. It is an argument that, on the grounds he provides, needs to be rejected.

But this does not necessarily mean that the category of sacrament is entirely out of place relative to Kuyper's ecclesiology. As we observed in the conclusion of the previous chapter, the concept of sacrament serves to describe one of the aspects of the nature of the institutional church's kerygmatic power. Therefore, in the remainder of this chapter, we return to

65. Dulles, *Models*, 64.

66. It is important to note the important difference(s) between the Roman Catholic understanding of the institutional church and that of Kuyper, as a Reformed/Calvinist theologian. For Rome, the institutional church is far more central to faith and the institutional church functions as a quasi-state, two aspects which are lacking in Reformed ecclesiology.

Kuyper's understanding of the kerygmatic power of the institutional church within its sphere and revisit our presentation of the sacramental aspect of that power's nature. It is for the purpose of developing an alternative sacramental argument, one which takes into account the sacramental ecclesiology we have just analyzed, to which we will now devote our attention in the remainder of this chapter.

THE SACRAMENTAL NATURE OF ECCLESIAL KERYGMATIC POWER

In the previous chapter, we observed that while Kuyper views the institutional church as essential for God's kingdom-renewal of the world, Ellul places the institutional church's evangelistic mandate in a penultimate position. Ultimately, the purpose of the church is to be a sign of the kingdom of God. For Ellul, this ensures that the institutional church does not get co-opted by the technological dreams of the fallen world that could reduce the institutional church to merely a tool in the hands of anxious ecclesial technicians.[67] The institutional church's proclamation, therefore, functions sacramentally, as a sign to and an instrument within the world of a true and gracious alternative, an alternative for the redemption, healing, and flourishing of the fallen world.[68]

Therefore, our task now is to develop this idea and to discern the implications of Kuyper's ecclesiology regarding the sacramental nature of the institutional church's kerygmatic power within its sphere. As stated earlier, this is an area about which Kuyper is silent and that we must therefore formulate in light of Kuyper's larger ecclesial worldview and project. Can we develop a Kuyperian view of ecclesial kerygmatic power as being, in part, sacramental in nature, as suggested by Ellul and developed most fully by Vatican II? Is there a way to connect the apparent "spirituality" of sacrament with the apparent "physicality" of the institutional church? Indeed there is and a number of authors working within the Reformed and/or Kuyperian tradition have taken an interest in a sacramental view of the institutional

---

67. Milbank, "Stale Expressions," is a prime example of what results when the church is managed by anxious technicians.

68. Hendrikus Berkhof cautions some interpretations of the church as sacrament: "In saying that the church is the instrument of the mission, we speak a half-truth.... The church is ... the provisional result of the mission. The movement of the Spirit has an end—it [the church] is not an end in itself. That end is beyond the church; it is that 'the earth shall be full of the knowledge of the Lord as the waters cover the sea' (Isa 11:9).... [The church] is a little bit of realized Kingdom" (Berkhof, *Doctrine of the Holy Spirit*, 39).

church. Even though these thoughts have not yet been integrated ecclesiologically, they will assist us in fleshing out the contours of the institutional church's kerygmatic power along sacramental lines. In fact, to be sacramental is not to be "spiritual" at all. A sacrament is deeply material, physical, even worldly. Sacraments take *place*. So does the institutional church.

Connecting Proclamation and Sacrament

Let us begin by recalling the conclusion of the previous chapter: in addition to ecclesial kerygmatic power (in preaching, sacrament, discipleship, and diaconal ministries of justice and compassion) being kenotic and incarnational, a third aspect was its sacramentality. This means that proclamation and sacrament are not necessarily two separate categories. As we have seen earlier in this chapter, primarily in the formulations of Vatican II, there is solid theological ground to stand on when making the claim that the kerygmatic power of the church's proclamation is sacramental in nature.[69] Yet, viewing the church sacramentally is not only a Roman Catholic perspective. The work of the International Roman Catholic-Reformed Dialogue reveals that this idea is an ecumenical one.[70] The work of this dialogue leads us to see that the sacramental is not hermetically sealed off from the proclamatory. In this ecumenical dialogue between Rome and the world Reformed churches, the theological connection between the proclamatory (as we have seen, Kuyper's view of the power of the institutional church) and the sacramental (a common Roman Catholic view of the institutional church) aspects of the church is discovered. In fact, their report says that both the proclamational and the sacramental are necessary for a complete account of the doctrine of the church.

The authors of this report write that the proclamatory and sacramental aspects of the church are "as complementary to each other as two sides of the same coin."[71] On the one hand, the church is the creation of Jesus, the Word of God enfleshed, which is called and gifted to be a sign through its proclamation of that same Word to the world. On the other hand, through the church's faithful participation in its kingdom-announcing activity, it is a divine instrument (i.e., a sacrament) for the further introduction of the grace of God into the world.[72] Thus, while initially appearing to be divergent, proclamation and sacrament are actually intimately linked to each

---

69. Bosch, *Transforming Mission*, 374, also addresses this.
70. "Church as Community of Common Witness."
71. "Church as Community of Common Witness," 189.
72. "Church as Community of Common Witness," 190–91.

other. Sacraments are proclamational in nature; proclamation has a sacramental nature as sign and instrument. It is through the institutional church's proclamation that the church is a sacrament of God's kingdom. Or, put the other way around, it is by being a faithful and effective sacrament, sign and instrument, that the institutional church proclaims the grace of God to the world as a living and faithful partner in the *missio Dei*.[73]

The *Missio Dei* (Kingdom of God) and the Church-in-Mission

To speak of proclamation and sacrament is to speak about the mission of the church. But how does the mission of the church relate to the *missio Dei* and can this further assist us in discerning the relationship between ecclesial proclamation and sacramentality? Actually, the idea of the church as a sacrament has been utilized by mid- to late-twentieth-century (Protestant) missiologists who have sought a way to combine the proclamational and sacramental aspects of the institutional church as they relate to holistic mission. David Bosch wrote that "The church-in-mission . . . may be described in terms of sacrament and sign. It is a *sign* in the sense of a pointer, symbol, example or model; it is a *sacrament* in the sense of mediation, representation, or anticipation."[74] Bosch remarks, in ways parallel to that of Rahner and Dulles noted above, that the utilization of the theological category of sacrament has allowed for the clear distinction between the institutional church and the kingdom of God. The church, he says, "is not identical with God's reign yet not unrelated to it either."[75] Bosch observes that, while sacramental ecclesiology was originally and predominately a Roman Catholic concept, since 1968 sacrament has become a more and more prominent theological category for Protestants as well.

It should be noted that this is more than the Protestant idea that the church exists for others.[76] Rather, as sacrament, the church is also a sign and instrument of the kingdom and mission of God in the world. This places the church's primary relationship to that of Christ and Christ's kingdom rather than to a technical or utilitarian program for the church's numerical growth or geographical expansion. While Bosch notes that there can be a patronizing attitude that creeps into the view that the church is for others, in the sense that the church assumes from the outset what the other really needs,

---

73. See also the commentary on "Church as Community of Common Witness" in Brinkman, "Church as Sacrament of the Kingdom."

74. Bosch, *Transforming Mission*, 11.

75. Bosch, *Transforming Mission*, 11.

76. See Bonhoeffer, *Letters and Papers*, 382; Temple, *Christianity and Social Order*.

this is avoided when the sacramental idea of the church is anchored in the *missio Dei* in and through Jesus Christ who is the primordial sign of God's grace.[77] Sacrament can therefore function as a way of relating while also carefully distinguishing the kingdom of God and the institutional church.[78]

Newbigin's Sacramental Ecclesiology: Sign of the Kingdom

Leslie Newbigin was a practical Protestant missiologist who devoted an entire book to the church as a *Sign of the Kingdom*.[79] We find in him the same Roman Catholic concern that the sacramental aspect of the church must find its foundation in Jesus Christ. He writes that "In the New Testament it is clear that the only sign of the Kingdom is Jesus himself. The central task of the Church, as it prays 'Your Kingdom Come!' is to bear witness to him in whom the kingdom *has* come, to call all men to that U-turn in the mind which we call conversion so that they may acknowledge him as King and join his whole Church in prayer: 'Come, Lord Jesus!'"[80] Therefore, as the church remains faithfully united to Jesus, partnering in Jesus' redemptive mission, the church and its proclamation to the world have a sacramental nature through the way in which the church points to Jesus Christ who is the ultimate sacrament, sign and instrument, of God's kingdom which has come and which is renewing the entire creation by grace.

Goheen has devoted significant attention to interpreting Lesslie Newbigin's missionary ecclesiology, an ecclesiology in which sacrament is an enduring and important concept. Goheen notes that Newbigin utilized the concept of sacrament in his ecclesiology right through his career. Beginning with Newbigin's Kerr lectures in 1953, he expounded on the church as the sign (in the sense of the first-fruits), foretaste, and instrument of the kingdom of God.[81] This is deeply sacramental language. As such, the church's

77. Bosch, *Transforming Mission*, 375–76.

78. Berkhof, *Christian Faith*, 415, comments on the mediating function of the institutional church: "As the [church as] institute mediates Christ to the congregation, so the congregation in turn mediates him to the world. In this chain the world comes last, yet it is the goal that gives meaning and purpose to the preceding links. . . . The fact of being church is thus not something static; it is a perpetual movement, a bridge-event." Yet in this bridge event, Berkhof notes that it is important that the church not sacrifice her "being-herself . . . rather it is precisely her being-herself that is to work in the world in an epistolary way. That can only be done if her being-in-the-world is a being-different-from-the-world. For precisely possessing that character she is a witness to the world" (419).

79. Newbigin, *Sign of the Kingdom*.

80. Newbigin, *Sign of the Kingdom*, 69–70.

81. Goheen, "'As the Father Has Sent Me,'" 50.

sacramental nature cannot be divorced from its proclamational nature. In fact, the institutional church's proclamation is sacramental in nature. Since the church is the emergence of the kingdom of God in the world, the sign that God is at work in the midst of the world, then the church is an integral component of the mission of God while also not being a complete identification of that mission. Thus, Goheen argues that "when the church is separated from [its proclamational] mission, the church is reduced to a repository for converts and mission is reduced to the management of large institutions, which paralyzes the missionary calling of believers."[82] But Goheen recognizes that by saying this he does not interpret Newbigin as having an exclusively instrumentalist view of the church's proclamation. Rather, he argues that

> Newbigin emphasizes the church as a foretaste and first fruits [sign] of the reign of God, even while maintaining that the church is an instrument of the kingdom. The church cannot be reduced to its functional role as instrument; it is more than an action group within culture. It is the provisional result of the entry of the reign of God into history. Nevertheless, the church is also an agent of the reign of God.[83]

Thus, ecclesial sacramentality captures a two-dimensional aspect of the institutional church's proclamation. First, united to Jesus Christ and in partnership with him in God's cosmic redemptive mission, the church is the instrument called by God to proclaim the gospel to the world. But, second, as that part of the world which has heard the Good News and responded to it in faith, the church is the sign or first-fruits of God's redemptive mission, a sacrament in the world through its life as a sign of renewed community in the kingdom of God.

Padilla's Sacramental Ecclesiology of Word and Deed

Latin American evangelical theologian René Padilla also captures this sacramental idea well. He bases the unity of ecclesial proclamation and sacramentality specifically in the unity of word and deed in Jesus' earthly ministry. Jesus not only proclaimed the arrival of God's kingdom, he also demonstrated that claim with his miraculous healings. Padilla summarizes the Gospel accounts, and their patterning after *inter alia* Isaiah 35, by saying that "His [Jesus'] miracles as well as his proclamation of good news to the poor are

---

82. Goheen, "'As the Father Has Sent Me,'" 52.
83. Goheen, "'As the Father Has Sent Me,'" 429.

unmistakable *signs* that the Coming One has come."[84] Padilla immediately notes the ways in which Jesus' words and deeds did not conform to the expectations of his audience, thereby necessitating their careful discernment, a theme we noticed in the last chapter concerning God's apparent weakness in the Incarnation. But the key for us here is that Padilla connects the sacramental aspect or sign-function of the proclamation of the Christian gospel with the emergence of the church: "The proclamation of the good news . . . brings about a community that embodies the blessings of the new age—the church."[85] What this means, therefore, is that sacrament, sign and instrument, appropriately connects as well as distinguishes the redemptive move of the kingdom of God into the world with/from the institutional church. At the same time, sacramentality shows how the verbal (word) proclamation of the church is related to the actions (deed) of the institutional church, both of which are integral to a proper understanding of the *missio Dei*.

Distinguishing and Connecting Spiritual and Physical

There is a caution, though, in the conjoining of proclamation and sacramentality. Protestant theology's incorporation of sacramental theology, especially in the Zwinglian tradition, can too easily reduce sacrament to the spiritually symbolic in a non-material sense. Padilla highlights an important connection for us in this regard: the sacramental nature of the church's proclamation takes on a necessary materiality. Padilla conceives of a trajectory from the words and deeds of Jesus, to the formation of an actual, observable community who follows him (disciples, Apostles, and church), and finally to the material transformation of the fallen creation into the kingdom of God. These are what we might call "spiritual" effects that nevertheless take on significant *physical* or *material* form.

This process of the spiritual becoming material has been observed from a variety of religious or even non-religious perspectives. This is not even a uniquely Christian concept. For example, the Roman Catholic philosopher Phillip Bess has written insightfully about how the materiality of space and time become spiritually sacred under the rubric of sacrament. He analyses, specifically, how secular architecture and even cities and suburbs take "holy" shape.[86] The process of the spiritually holy taking material shape, Bess explains, was charted by Rudolf Otto: the pre- or non-rational

---

84. Padilla, *Mission Between the Times*, 89.
85. Padilla, *Mission Between the Times*, 95.
86. Bess, *Till We Have Built Jerusalem*, 65–66.

numinous is experienced as a "fascinating power"[87] that when rationally reflected upon exerts an imperative to the recipient that it must be shared with others. In the process of sharing it, the holy takes on material and, eventually, institutional form. A sacrament, therefore, is not an other-worldly or escapist mode of being. It is not spiritual as opposed to material. Rather, it "is an action or object in which the sacred is present" within the material world.[88] As opposed to being a means by which world-bound mystics seek a connection with the divine beyond the world as a form of escape, sacraments are the physical and material manifestations of the divine in the midst of the material world. Sacraments are how the spiritual becomes material.

Bess describes how this encounter between the divine and the human takes on a certain "structure." It is a structure that resembles a "sacred call and human response."[89] Remarkably, this returns us to the previous chapter and Caputo's view of divine power as the power to call or to invite. And if divine invitation manifests itself in the midst of the material world, by eventually taking on institutional shape, then the institutional church's proclamatory power, being by nature sacramental, comes into focus. The materiality of the institutional church is the result of divine invitation and, in turn, the institutional church is that place within creation from which the divine invitation continues to be extended to the world. As Bess observes,

> Historically, the most obvious human response to the sacred has been to worship it; and human worship typically entails ritual actions in which the presence of the sacred is invoked. But the experience of the sacred as call and response is not limited to the religious ritual . . . human culture itself is, in its origins, the human response to the sacred.[90]

This does not mean that we can manufacture sacraments through sheer human effort. Bess rejects any kind of merely human or mechanical operation. Rather, the only human means by which the material becomes sacred is through worship and dedication through "*sacrifice.*"[91] But, again, this is

---

87. Bess, *Till We Have Built Jerusalem*, 66.
88. Bess, *Till We Have Built Jerusalem*, 68.
89. Bess, *Till We Have Built Jerusalem*, 70.
90. Bess, *Till We Have Built Jerusalem*, 70. Bess goes on to explain how the architectural similarities between major religious buildings all have certain themes in common because they are all seeking to offer a faithful human response to the divine which is envisioned as vertically lofty, suffused with light, delightful attention to detail, mathematically complex, compositionally unified, and hierarchical.
91. Bess, *Till We Have Built Jerusalem*, 69. In this regard, see also Bartholomew, *Where Mortals Dwell*, 246–47, 264–61, and his engagement of Bess as it relates to the place-making activities of Christians and the institutional church.

where the concept of sacrament is helpful for it is through sacrament that human beings proclaim and sacrifice as well as, in the other direction, receive. Even on the level of proclamation, sacraments are the means of the proclamation and the proclamation itself: thing and thing signified. Proclamation and sacramentality are intimately linked.

Conclusion

At the conclusion of the previous chapter we noted that the institutional church's kerygmatic power, in addition to being kenotic and incarnational in nature, also had a sacramental nature. That is, while the institutional church's proclamation is *instrumentally* for redemption, it is for redemption by first being a *sign* to the world of God's ongoing presence and eschatological promises. Only by being a *sign* can it also be an *instrument*. The institutional church is a sacrament, sign and instrument, to the world of the covenant promises of God in and through Jesus Christ. Through the sacramental nature of the institutional church's kerygmatic power, the church is (sign) and proclaims (instrument) an alternative to the fallen world of God's grace for redemption and renewal. At first glance, proclamation and sacrament appear to be far more "spiritual" than the institutional church's physical presence in the world. But the sacramental nature of the church's kerygmatic power is a deeply material affair. As sign and instrument, the sacramental nature of the church's kerygmatic power takes on physical and material shape in a particular place, the societal place of the church as a public civic institution.

This apparent spiritual/physical disjunction is reconciled by pointing to the official Roman Catholic-Reformed dialogue in which proclamation and the institutional church are joined through the notion of sacrament. The institutional church emerges in the world through the Word of God, Jesus Christ, which the institutional church has received and is called to proclaim to the world. The institutional church is the *sign* of God's Word as well as the *instrument* of that Word's ongoing proclamation. Further, through the *missio Dei* God sends the Incarnate Word into the world which, in turn, produces the mission of the church to continue to proclaim that Word to the world. In the sense of mediation, the institutional church's kerygmatic power has a sacramental nature in the way that the church mediates the Word: the church receives the Word and the church proclaims that same Word, both a sign and instrument of the kingdom of God in the world. It is in this way that the institutional church's proclamation, as a sign of the kingdom of God, is a fore-taste and first-fruits of that kingdom. The institutional church is not the kingdom of God but it is its vanguard as sign and instrument. In its sacramental nature, therefore, the institutional church's kerygmatic power is the sign and instrument of the kingdom's coming. As the institutional church faithfully proclaims the Word of God, the kingdom comes. Without the proclamation, the institutional church becomes divorced from the *missio Dei*. This parallels Jesus' own ministry of word and deed in which his symbolic actions pointed to and verified his proclamation.

Bess reminded us that in using the category of sacrament to describe the kerygmatic power of the institutional church, an escapist or other-worldly vision is clearly avoided. The church's kerygmatic power, sacramental in nature, can not tend toward world-flight for the sign and instrument function require the church to have a missionally-engaged posture to the material world. Sacrament points to the material emergence of the sacred or divine in the midst of the physical world. Worship, sacrifice, and sacrament are the ways in which humans receive from and discern the movement of the holy in the world. Sacraments, then, are the means by which the proclamation is received as well as the means of the message being proclaimed. And as this takes place within and through the institutional church it is a very worldly affair. In light of these observations about the sacramental nature of the institutional church's kerygmatic power before us, we now return to Kuyper to highlight the relevant elements of his ecclesiology to draw out the implications for the sacramental nature of the institutional church's kerygmatic power.

ABRAHAM KUYPER AND SACRAMENTAL ECCLESIOLOGY, REVISITED

We are now prepared to return to Kuyper's ecclesiology and apply to our analysis these reflections on sacramental ecclesiology. Having considered at length a sacramental analysis of the church, we can readily observe that Wood's use of the category in regard to Kuyper is mistaken. Simply put: a sacramental ecclesiology is not an ecclesiology which emphasizes the place or the role of the sacraments in the life of the church. Rather, a sacramental ecclesiology views the nature and being of the church sacramentally, as a sacrament, as having a symbolic nature and instrumental function given to it by God both in relationship to its having received the Word of God and in it being an instrument of the further proclamation of the Word of God to the world. Clearly, in light of this, Kuyper cannot be said to have formally or explicitly articulated a sacramental ecclesiology as Wood suggests.[92]

92. In addition, the exhaustive annotated bibliography of Kuipers, *Abraham*

But, on the other hand, based on our analysis of his ecclesiology in the previous chapters and Vatican II's sacramental ecclesiology in this chapter, we can perceive how Kuyper's ecclesiology nonetheless moves at points in the direction of sacramentality, but for very different reasons than Wood suggests.[93] It is worth listing here the relevant findings from our previous analysis to show the lines the argument would include. First, we should recall that for Kuyper the church is grounded in creation. It has emerged historically in the midst of God's creation to be that sphere in which humanity's deepest beliefs are expressed, where humanity ultimately comes face to face with God. And while, in Kuyper's theory of sphere sovereignty, the church is accountable directly to Christ (in vertical fashion), it is also interconnected with the rest of the world (horizontally). For Kuyper, there is no dualistic split between the church and the world. While the church is not *of* the fallen world, it is indeed *in* the world so that it can be *for* the world. This means that even within Kuyper's ecclesiological framework itself, the institutional church has a missional *instrumentality*.

Further, we observed how Kuyper metaphorically compared the church to the Incarnation of the Word, Jesus Christ, through which a hidden, inner redemptive power of the kingdom of God was at work through external means. But this power was not only oriented inwardly for the church's own benefit (for example, holiness through world-withdrawal) but it also manifested itself externally for the benefit of the entire world (what we referred to as an open-posture, world-oriented church). The institutional church, by nature, is a signpost pointing to the present and active grace of God. Additionally, in Kuyper's second Stone lecture, we noted him speaking of the "concentration of religious light and life in the Church" and how "in the walls of this church, there are wide open windows, and through these spacious windows the light of the Eternal has to radiate over the whole world" which makes the institutional church "a city, set upon a hill, which every man can see afar of. Here is a holy salt that penetrates in every direction, checking all corruption."[94] Kuyper speaks of this "light" and "salt" influence of the church in synonymous terms as God's "common grace" which

---

Kuyper, does not contain a single reference in all of Kuyper's known works to anything resembling a sacramental ecclesiology. In fact, the term sacrament only occurs twice in the entire bibliography and these are related to Kuyper's dogmatic lectures in which he teaches the Reformed view of the sacraments alongside Reformed preaching, polity, etc.

93. The third session of the International Roman Catholic-Reformed Dialogue advanced the idea of the church as a sacrament of the kingdom of God for fruitful ecumenical discussions. For commentary on this, see Brinkman, "Church as Sacrament of the Kingdom"; Eijk, "Sacrament of the Kingdom of God."

94. *LC*, 63.

works in the world through the organic church for the well-being, preservation, and redemption of society. God's grace is spread into the world by the institutional church indirectly and the organic church directly; but it is the same spreading of the "salt" and "light" that is taking place. Here we have in Kuyper the institutional church's sign-function which is exerted instrumentally through the organic church in the whole of life. Thus, we have the same sacramental understanding of the church within Kuyper's thought as well.

Finally, we noted in Chapter 3 that Kuyper re-presented Calvin's threefold marks of the true church as the power of the institutional church in his ecclesiology (adding the diaconal ministries of justice and compassion to Calvin's threefold list of preaching, sacraments, and discipleship). In Chapter 1, we discussed how Kuyper, in his *Common Grace* articles, wrote about the church as a means of grace: a direct means of grace to Christian believers gathered as the institutional mode of the church and an indirect means of grace to the whole world through the organic mode of the church. As a means of grace, the institutional church has been given its kerygmatic power to proclaim in Word, sacrament, discipleship, and diaconal actions of justice and compassion. The institutional church receives the grace of God and in turn, after the pattern of Christ, is called to orient its institutional ministry toward the rest of the world, in the whole of life, through Christian believers in their everyday lives as the organic church in the world. This is the institutional church's mediational nature between God and the world, the very sign and instrument function of sacramentality engaged in mission.

As such, the contours of Kuyper's thought display the essential elements of a sacramental ecclesiology in which the institutional church, as sign and instrument of the kingdom of God, receives the Word of God and then proclaims that Word to the world (in its four-fold manner). There is little reason to see Kuyper's ecclesiology as antithetical to a sacramental view. In fact, one can even see how these core aspects of Kuyper's ecclesiology place it on a trajectory that would, in time, have become explicitly picked up and noted to be sacramental in nature similar to that which we have observed in Vatican II and other Protestant theologians who have resorted to this image to understand the church's nature and calling. This raises an intriguing question: if one were to follow this sacramental trajectory in Kuyper's ecclesiology, especially as it relates to the power of the institutional church, how might one articulate this? The following three headings summarize the implications of this line of reasoning and round out our presentation of the sacramental nature of ecclesial kerygmatic power as it emerges in Kuyper's world-oriented ecclesiology.

Kuyper and the Nature of the Institutional Church's Kerygmatic Power

In Kuyper's sermon, "Conservatism and Orthodoxy," he argued for a church that would be orthodox in theology in order that the gospel might be presented with dynamism and persuasive influence, bearing the Christian faith into all areas of life through the church sent as an organism. The institutional church's primary role (and unique power) is proclamational. In his later speech, "It Shall Not Be So among You," Kuyper railed against the NHK hierarchy for their abuse of power, a betrayal of the church's calling because the church is intimately and immediately connected to Christ and not to or through the state.[95] The proclamation of the church is Christocentric. The kerygmatic power of the institutional church having a sacramental nature means that the Christocentric proclamation of the church functions as both sign and instrument of the reign of Christ. This means that when the institutional church, through its faith or its practices, severs its vital connection to Christ, it abuses its kerygmatic power. Being vitally connected to Christ, the nature of the institutional church's kerygmatic non-force power is uniquely different than the power within the other spheres of creation. Kerygmatic power is oriented to proclaimed Word, sacrament, discipleship, and diaconal acts of compassion and justice which equip God's people to be agents of historical-cultural influence through their worldly vocations as the organic church. Even a small and powerless church, Kuyper argued, can be used by God to influence a culture in this way.[96]

This raises an important question: how does a church abuse its kerygmatic power? We have observed that for Kuyper a primary way in which the church abuses its power is by taking into itself forms of power from other spheres of life. By adopting forms of power that are alien to the ecclesial sphere, which operate in the other spheres of creation, the institutional church exchanges its unique calling for the calling of the institutions in the other spheres. In doing so, the institutional church ceases to be an authentic church. This unfaithfulness of the institutional church can take a variety of forms, depending on the way in which kerygmatic power is abused. It can refuse the possibility (or actuality) of sacrifice, of kenotic self-emptying for the sake of others, in order to appear "successful" in the eyes of the world, particularly the financial sphere where faithfulness is measured in terms of the accumulation of monetary power. It can opt for holiness through

---

95. Kuyper, "It Shall Not Be So among You," 131.
96. Kuyper, "Common Grace," 190, is explicit that even "the comparatively small circle of the church will radiate influence upon civil life outside the church."

world-withdrawal and the formation of a highly nurturing power as in a family instead of faithfully seeking the ways in which it can be incarnated in its own time and place as a church serving others.[97] Or, in terms of the sacramental nature of the institutional church's kerygmatic power, it can forfeit its proclamational power, reject the non-force power of speaking the gospel and equipping the organic church in exchange for the purely justice-oriented coercive power of the state which seeks to control, judge, and enforce strict legislative codes of conduct for those within its membership as well as imposing those on the extra-ecclesial community. The details of how this may look or the means by which it is done can take a variety of forms. But the aspect of unfaithfulness here on the part of the institutional church is its abandonment of the uniquely sacramental nature of its kerygmatic non-force power, the symbolic and instrumental means of Christocentric proclamation.

Direct Ecclesial Power and Indirect Cultural Power

In Kuyper's Stone lectures, he argued that the power of the church was christocentrically world-engaging, not in the sense of being "a dispensary of spiritual medicines" but the only institution which is called and empowered "to preach the Word, to administer the sacraments, and to exercise discipline, and in everything to stand before the face of God."[98] By this Kuyper means that the church is a means by which God is present to his creation by his Word.[99] If this is not clearly enough a sacramental ecclesiology, his work on *Common Grace* gives us a clear sign of where Kuyper's thought was headed as he neared the end of his career and life. For, he said, "Christ's church and its means of grace cover a broader field than that of special grace alone."[100] Kuyper explains that the church's kerygmatic power "works *directly* for the well-being of the elect . . . [and] it works *indirectly* for the well-being of the whole of civil society, constraining it to civic virtue." The church's indirect means of God's common grace, Kuyper says, is achieved through "the

---

97. As Wolterstorff, *Hearing the Call*, 213, correctly observes, "Over and over the church, when confronted by social realities that are unjust but that it prefers not to change, retreats into spirituality."

98. LC, 76.

99. Koyzis, *We Answer to Another*, 195, remarks in light of the importance of church discipline that the "voluntaristic conception of the church [today] has probably gone furthest in the United States, where denominationalism has made a mockery of any effort by the church to act authoritatively. This has likely been exacerbated by the rise of congregations independent of any larger ecclesial fellowship."

100. Kuyper, "Common Grace," 189.

church [being] as a city on a hill amid civil society."[101] It is the organic rather than the institutional church which has a direct engagement with society.

In fact, Kuyper repeatedly makes this claim that the institutional church's cultural influence is indirect.[102] The institutional church is called to disciple Christian believers through Word, sacrament, discipleship, and diaconal acts of justice and compassion so that they are equipped to live out their callings faithfully in the world as the sent organic church, directly involved in all the spheres of civil society. Viewed sacramentally, therefore, the church is the Christological sign of a suffering, sacrificial kind of divine love which empties itself for the other. The church as a sacrament must be not only an *effective* but also a *complete* sacrament, complete in the sense of sign *and instrument* of the love of God for the world. To put it in the simplest terms possible: ecclesial power is sacramental in nature because the church is *for the world* as sign and instrument of the mission and kingdom of God.

In Kuyper's worldview, the institutional church proclaims the Word so as to convert, disciple, and equip the organic church to be the means of the direct influence of the Gospel on culture. The institutional church only has an indirect relationship with culture and society and this is how its proclamational power is non-forceful. Countless examples abound of churches that turn this exactly around: the institutional church saps the resources of its membership so that it, as an institution, can engage in the "culture wars" directly. As Lesslie Newbigin puts it correctly, "the Church as a corporate society cannot identify itself with particular political programs, it must be the responsibility of the Church to equip its members for active and informed participation in public life in such a way that the Christian faith shapes that participation. Public life is the area where the principalities and powers operate."[103] This is not a case for the church resigning itself from responsibility for the broken realities of a fallen world. As Newbigin goes on to explain, the institutional church disciples and equips Christians so that "a Christian neither accepts them [the elemental powers which structure human life] as some sort of eternal order which cannot be changed, nor seeks to destroy them because of the evil they do, but seeks to subvert them from within and thereby to bring them back under the allegiance of their true Lord."[104] The sacramental nature of ecclesial kerygmatic power distinguishes the institutional church from the kingdom of God by placing the church

---

101. Kuyper, "Common Grace," 190.

102. Lugo, "Foreword," 11, agrees that "the church's engagement in politics is indirect rather than through an immediate seizing of political power."

103. Newbigin, *Truth to Tell*, 81.

104. Newbigin, *Truth to Tell*, 82.

in a mediating position between the world and the grace of God in such a way that the institutional church is the effective sign and instrument of the redemptive grace of God.

Seen in this light, we can return to an issue raised earlier about whether the institutional church should have a direct or an indirect relationship with matters of state policy.[105] This question assumes that either the institutional church gives policy advice and advocates for particular governmental actions or the institutional church preaches the gospel to Christian believers and leaves the Christian influence in the civic realm up to individual Christian believers' subjective convictions and assumptions. This binary way in which Kuyper's ecclesiology is often framed is not only unhelpful but grossly over-simplifies Kuyper's view. True, as we have seen, Kuyper would advocate for the institutional church having an *indirect* relationship with the state and its matters of governmental policy. But this does not absolve the institutional church from addressing or discussing important civil matters within the context of the proclamation of the comprehensive gospel. The institutional church's kerygmatic power is for receiving the Word of God as it relates to *all of life* and for articulating this comprehensive Word through preaching, sacraments, discipleship, and diaconal ministries of justice and compassion with equal comprehensiveness. This will mean that the institutional church will proclaim the Word in a contextual way that will equip Christian believers as the organic church to articulate the Word of God in appropriate and faithful public ways directly. The institutional church will not abandon Christian believers to themselves or to their uncritical opinions formed through worldviews in competition to the Christian faith. The power of the institutional church being oriented to the ecclesial sphere does not mean that it becomes provincial or introverted or unconcerned about the broad (or even specific) movements of the culture around it. Indirect influence does not mean the institutional church doesn't have a Word that contextually relates to the practical matters in the whole of life. But the institutional church will seek to make the Gospel relevant to its context by faithfully and fully forming Christians as the organic church in the mind and heart of Christ so as to carry out their direct influence of culture and society.

Ecclesial Identity

Finally, to speak of the church sacramentally, as sign and instrument, we must be clear about the church's identity: what the church is a sign and instrument *of*. That is, in the cultural context of the twenty-first-century West,

---

105. Westerhof, "Church and the Exercise of Non-Ecclesiastical Power."

a context deeply influenced by political, social, and economic liberalism and its attendant values of inclusiveness and individualism,[106] the church is not a screen upon which our culturally-derived values can be projected. The church is not a symbol of our culturally-given good intentions or ideologically-fueled political desires. Rather, even though it may sound overly simplistic, possibly even naive, the church is a sacrament *of the God revealed in Jesus Christ*. The hermeneutical starting point for a sacramental ecclesiology must always be God and not God's creation. The church belongs to God, and God alone. As such, the church, as the community of the new creation, bears the image of God and not the image of the culture in which it happens to find itself at any given moment. The church is not a sign of the world but of the world's creator, redeemer, and sustainer. It is only by being a sacrament of this God that the church can ever possibly be *for the world* in a sacramentally redemptive sense.

This raises all kinds of practical questions for the church today in the West. These questions are not only limited to whether the institutional church can directly advocate to government but places the entire life of the church under the critical power of the gospel. Every aspect of the church's life is open to analysis: the church's polity, its worship, its use of technology, its ways of relating socially, its building usage, its means of interacting with persons and agencies in society, etc. If the church is going to function in its complete sacramentality, as sign and instrument, of the God who has created and is re-creating the world, then the institutional church must seriously consider the ways in which it is and is not at present a sign and instrument of the grace of God. It is entirely possible that due to syncretism with the host culture the institutional church has lost its prophetic edge and is effectively functioning as a sign and instrument of a range of other realities contrary to or alongside of Jesus Christ. The institutional church is called to ask itself over and over again: what is it proclaiming, as sign and instrument, today?

As Kuyper would remind us, the Reformed confessions argue that a sacrament, despite human appearances to the contrary, is a sign and seal of God's grace in Christ.[107] Sacraments are the promises of God made visible to creation that, by being made visible, signify, seal, and pledge his renewing grace to fallen (and redeemed) humanity. As we have seen, the sacramental aspect of the institutional church's kerygmatic power has a distinctly proclamational nature to it and that proclamation has a specific and normative content. The institutional church exercises its kerygmatic power

---

106. Cf. Badcock, *House Where God Lives*, x–xii.

107. Cf. *Belgic Confession* 33: "We believe that our good God, mindful of our crudeness and weakness, has ordained sacraments for us to seal his promises in us, to pledge his good will and grace toward us, and also to nourish and sustain our faith."

by proclaiming the Word of God in Scripture, sacraments, discipleship, and diaconal ministries of justice and compassion to its members without force but through invitation. And this is a task that cannot be short-circuited. This four-fold proclamational task is constitutive of the church's identity and calling in the world. Without it the church is not the church. As the institutional church should not allow itself to be marginalized in society but ever seek to continue to faithfully play its part alongside the other divinely ordained institutions, so too the church cannot marginalize or downplay the significance of its kerygmatic power even though it lacks the element of force that other powers in other spheres may have. The Word must be proclaimed to the people of God. The sacraments must be celebrated to feed them. All Christians must be brought into the formative discipleship of Jesus Christ. And the justice and compassion of God must be ministered to them diaconally in a fallen and challenging world context. Apart from these activities, the institutional church is not the church but some other community. And when the church fails to be the church, the church fails to be the primordial sacrament, sign and instrument, of God's comprehensive and redemptive grace in Jesus Christ for the world. When the church fails to be sacramental in the sense of the *sign* of God's grace received, then the church also fails to be sacramental in the sense of the *instrument* of God's grace extended. These are some of the contours of Kuyper's sacramental understanding of the nature of the institutional church's kerygmatic power, sign and instrument, of invitation.

CONCLUSION

Ellul spoke of the need for insight in order to recognize or discern Jesus amidst a great uncertainty because he comes incognito rather than as obvious to our human senses. This is due to the fact of God's hiddenness from us. We live in the silence and night in which God's overwhelming presence is concealed from us. Because of this, the church is constantly tempted to bear the light of Christ, to act and speak in the obvious and forceful ways of the world, to assimilate itself to the world rather than Christ. Therefore, Ellul said, the church is, and must always remain, "a sign of who God is."[108]

This is the same for every Christian living in a fallen world. They are, as a member of the organic church directly engaged with the world, "a visible sign of the new covenant which God has made with this world in Jesus Christ."[109] And what is true of the individual Christian is even more true of

---

108. *FLP*, 199.
109. *PK*, 3.

Christians gathered together as the institutional church. The institutional church's kerygmatic power is sacramental, the sign and instrument of God's gracious promise to his creation. The power of the institutional church is the non-forceful power of a gracious invitation.

The sacramental nature of the kerygmatic power of the institutional church is its ability to be the true *sign* and invitational *instrument* of the presence and grace of God in Jesus Christ *in and for the world*. The church is the reminder, the pledge, the invitation to remember and believe that the world is God's loving creation, his patient work of redemption, and his promised realm of sustained and renewed life and joy. The church not only proclaims this instrumentally through its institutional words, sacraments, ministries of discipleship, and symbolic actions of justice and compassion, but the church also is the visible sign that the promises of God are still valid and will be fulfilled until the world is completely re-created and God's kingdom comes in all its fullness. This kerygmatic power of the institutional church has a kenotic, incarnational, and sacramental nature. When fully and faithfully employed, the institutional church receives and proclaims the Word of God and therefore is the instrument of the comprehensive and redemptive mission of God to restore his creation and usher in the kingdom of God.

8

Conclusion

THE PLACE OF THE church in the imaginative and societal landscapes of the West in the early-twenty-first century has shifted significantly.[1] Whereas the church in previous generations occupied a central place of importance and a significantly influential role in the formation of the individual, culture, and of society, many other forces have replaced it. This is one of the provocative interpretations of "Reading Between the Lines," the art installation of a transparent church near Brussels introduced in Chapter 1.

But the factors that have led to a rising crisis for the church in contemporary Western culture and society are not only external to the church. There are also internal reasons why the church needs a renewed theological vision for itself today. We have examined one reason for this need already: a crisis of ecclesial power highlighted by recent claims that the church has abused its power. Even churches that have not experienced formal abuses of power appear to be unsure of their place in or contribution to the marketplace of civic institutions. Thus, for many living in the societies formerly or historically part of Christendom, the ecclesial crisis being faced is fundamentally a crisis of faith.[2]

---

1. Badcock argues that "there has come about a fundamental change in the cultural, social, and political contexts in which the church is located. . . . In fact, the situation has changed more radically than most of us realize" (Badcock, *House Where God Lives*, 12).

2. Badcock notes that many aspects of the church have been thrust into a critical

What is the power of the institutional church in the ecclesiology of Abraham Kuyper? We have answered this question by analyzing the concepts of both power and church. Kuyper's theory of sphere sovereignty understands each creational sphere as having its own kind of power, delegated to it by God, and normed for that unique sphere. The institutional church's power is a uniquely *kerygmatic* non-forceful form of power, the power to proclaim God's Word (in the four-fold manner of Scripture, sacraments, discipleship, and diaconal acts of justice and compassion) which is oriented to humanity's universal religious impulse in order to invite humanity into a face to face encounter with the creating, redeeming, and sustaining Triune God in all of life.[3]

But this ecclesial power is an ontologically different kind of power from other forms of power in the various spheres of the (created or fallen) world. As Gorman has written, the church's power is not the same as the coercive power of the state but rather is "the slaughtered Lamb [which] is the revelation of God's power" and the church is the "peaceful, nonviolent . . . community of the Lamb" that is animated by this alternative power.[4] As an alternative to the coercive power of the state, or the monetary power of the financial sphere, or the formative power of a family, or the educational power of the academy, ecclesial kerygmatic power has a kenotic, incarnational,

---

juncture: the church's "worship, its values, its order, and its claims. Once the point of its life has been abandoned, its prayer, ministry, and proclamation (which in a sense constitute the forms of its existence) no longer have any coherent purpose. Having lost their anchor in God and in the revelation of God, they appear as a kind of flotsam drifting on the wide ocean of human experience, and they become expressions not of the worship and service of God, but of the experience, worship, and service of humanity itself" (Badcock, *House Where God Lives*, 22).

3. Donovan clarifies what is meant by "Word of God" or "Gospel" which the church proclaims: "The gospel is not progress or development. It is not nation building. It is not adult education. It is not a school system. It is not a health campaign. It is not a five-year plan. It is not an economic program. It is not a ranching scheme or water development. It is not an independence movement. It is not the freedom fighters. It is not the liberation movement. It is not the black power movement. It is not the civil rights movement. It is not violent revolution. It seems that never has the temptation been stronger than it is now to identify the gospel with these very worthwhile things. To see the gospel as adaptable and applicable to real life in all its dimensions is good. No one would deny the connection between the gospel and development. But what has to be denied is the identification of the two things. As Ivan Illich pointed out long ago, in reference to South America, we must get out of this business, this business of identifying the gospel with system, any system, or we leave to a future generation the agony of separating once again the two realities. Our business, as Christians, is the establishment of the kingdom [of God]. It is a kingdom that takes its beginnings here in this real world, and aims at the fulfilling of this world, of bringing this world to its destiny" (Donovan, *Christianity Rediscovered*, 165).

4. Gorman, *Reading Revelation Responsibly*, 115n52.

and sacramental (sign and instrument) nature for participating in God's ultimate redemption of the world. The institutional church is the means of this grace being displayed (sign) and spread (instrument) through the world by the proclamation of the Word in a four-fold manner. Its spread takes the form of a non-forceful and gracious invitation: a free summons to join the redeemed community of the slaughtered Lamb, to become the means of God's grace in and for the world.

James Skillen writes that out of the nations of the world, God's grace has produced the church, a "new nation in Christ; the multigenerational, worldwide church of Christ . . . God's new nation in Christ, the bride of Christ, will be satisfied with nothing less than the final revelation of God's kingdom, which cannot be achieved by human political means."[5] The reign of God's grace takes shape in the world through the institutional church living a life of grace and love as a light shining in the world. As such, the institutional church participates in the grace of God by being the grace of God for the world through the proclamation of God's Word. In the end, Kuyper's ecclesiology is sacramentally *for the world.*

KUYPERIAN ECCLESIOLOGY *FOR THE WORLD*

Throughout these chapters we have encountered a number of unresolved questions related to power generally, ecclesial power specifically, and the place of the institutional church in the midst of the world. Now, having the totality of Kuyper's worldview and ecclesiology before us, we are able to respond to these critical questions by showing the rich insights of Kuyper's ecclesiology and how Kuyper illuminates positive theological pathways forward for reflection on power, ecclesial power, and the church's relationship to the rest of the world.

A Non-Reductionistic View of Ecclesial Power

We have seen how Kuyper's worldview epistemology intersects the long history of reflection on power's ontology with a unique contribution. Kuyper's view of power is a non-reductionistic understanding in which power is rooted in the multiform nature of God's creation; but, in addition, also subject to the disastrous effects of sin through human agency. Each of the multiform powers has a creational (i.e., law-normed) structure that under

---

5. Skillen, "Where Kingdom Politics Should Lead Us," in Noll, *Adding Cross to Crown*, 85.

human agency can be oriented in various directions, either for flourishing or destruction. This ontologically multiform view of differentiated powers within creation grounds the different forms of power in the different spheres of human cultural life where they are operative in unique ways, all directly accountable to Christ. We used a number of examples throughout this project to illustrate this, including the difference between monetary power in the financial sphere versus formative power in the family sphere and coercive power in the sphere of the state. The institutional church's power is yet another form of power operative and normed within its own sphere.

Distinguishing Spheres and Roles

When we introduced Kuyper's social philosophy of sphere sovereignty, we recognized that a component of power's ontology within creation is that there are structural boundaries between the different spheres and, thus, between the operations of the different unique powers within those spheres. Mouw utilizes an excellent example to illustrate this.[6] "Imagine," he writes, "a woman and a man who are related in three different ways. She is the young man's mother. She is also an elder in the church where their family worships. And she is the academic dean at the university where her son serves on the faculty."[7] In this illustration, three spheres are in view: the family, the institutional church, and the academy. In each sphere a different power is at work, which means that in the various ways in which this woman and this man relate there are different relationships, each normed by the power of the sphere in which they are related. In Mouw's thought experiment, the young man does something immoral and worthy of discipline in his job. As the man's academic dean and employer, she will fire him. As his elder, she may engage him in pastoral care and discipleship to restore him to faith. But as his mother, she will continue to support, encourage, and love him no matter what. These are the diverse implications of Kuyper's theory of sphere sovereignty.

This illustration serves to highlight the structural ways in which power is at work in different ways in the different spheres. Kuyper's notion of sphere sovereignty assists one in being clear about the relationships and roles in the various ways that elements of culture relate to each other, and how the power relations are different in each of those roles. The power of the employer (academy) is different than the power of the mother (family), which is different yet from the power of the elder (institutional church).

6. *AKASPI*, 24–26.
7. *AKASPI*, 25.

Clear Sphere Boundaries

In addition, when we recall Kuyper's distinction between the organic and the institutional modes of the church's being, we find the means by which to understand the various roles that Kuyper himself played as well as the way in which the church relates to the world. Ellul would criticize Kuyper for leaving his role within the institutional church and taking up a political and therefore coercive role in society. Viewed from this angle, Kuyper is abusing the power of the church by seeking to deploy his Christian faith in a public and state-like way. Yet, as we observed earlier, Ellul does not work from a sphere sovereignty framework. While his insights into power are perceptive, his view is too reductionistic when it comes to the multiform arenas of human activity. This is where Ellul's work discloses its limits and drawbacks. Through Kuyper's distinction of these two modes of the church, we observe the way in which the power of the institutional church within the midst of the world is different from the cultural activities of ordinary Christians in the whole of life. True, the institutional church can not operate according to the coercive power of the state. That would blur the boundaries of the spheres and various spheres' different powers. But a Christian seeking to be faithful to God in the whole of life, through employment in the state, seeks to be faithful to Christ within the sphere of the state which is not only a public and therefore pluralist setting but also rightly operates with a coercive form of power to enforce the rule of law and justice in society. Within this framework, there is nothing unfaithful about a Christian, who is a member of the institutional church, being employed by the state that, Paul writes in Romans 13, has been divinely given the power of the sword. But the Christian employed by the state is not exerting the power of the institutional church in their work; they are exerting the power of the state. Sphere clarity is required. Each sphere of creation is a field ripe for humanity's work of unfolding the potentials of creation for the benefit of the world and to the glory of God. Kuyper's view is thoroughly non-dualistic and non-reductionistic in this matter.

The Uniqueness of Ecclesial Power

Returning then to the sphere of the institutional church and its unique form of proclamational power, we observed that as opposed to state power which is coercive in nature, the power of the institutional church is kerygmatic, that is invitational in nature. Since the leading (norming) function of the ecclesial sphere is faith, humanity is elected by God in Christ to live, in the totality of one's being, before the face of God. As such, ecclesial power is redemptive in our post-lapsarian world. And because this redemption functions as grace restoring nature, it is a redemptive Word that is comprehensive in scope. It is a redemptive Word that addresses the world "far as the curse is found."[8]

While we may be tempted, through our Western cultural conditioning, to continue to think of this ecclesial power *qua* power as coercive, Scripture assisted us earlier in analyzing Kuyper's views in this matter. Our analysis revealed an understanding of ecclesial power, in addition to being invitational, as having a *kenotic* and *incarnational* nature in a way deeply analogous to the life, ministry, death, and resurrection of Jesus Christ. As such, as an alternative to the assumed negative views of power, ecclesial proclamational power at work in the midst of creation is operative in its own unique non-forceful manner through preaching, sacraments, discipleship, and diaconal ministries of justice and compassion.

In this way, we observed that ecclesial power is essentially *sacramental* in nature as well. By sacramental, we meant the way in which the institutional church is a sign of and instrument for divine action in the world, bringing God's historic gracious acts into the present. The institutional church and its kerygmatic power are God's means for inviting a fallen creation into the converting and renewing work of Christ through the four-fold ministry of the Christocentric Word. Through the four-fold proclamation of the Word by the institutional church, humanity is invited, in the present, before the crucified, resurrected, and ascended Christ who is Lord over all and is redeeming all things. This is how the kingdom of God advances graciously in a fallen world.

The Church's Mission *for the World*

In conclusion, an important point that deserves highlighting and further attention, not only as it applies to the new field of practical theology but also for ecclesiology itself, is Kuyper's ecclesial vision that the institutional church *qua* church is *for the world*. We have repeatedly raised the question of Kuyper's legacy. This is not only a question for today's highly secular Dutch culture or the diaspora Dutch communities in North America in the early twenty-first century who have maintained Kuyper's vision and built numerous Christian institutions in a surprisingly brief period of time. But this is also a deeply *ecclesiological* matter. In contrast to ecclesial practices which place the institutional church in the center of the centrifugal forces of

---

8. Watts, "Joy to the World."

faith and life, where the activities of the institutional church monopolize the life of the Christian believer, Kuyper's ecclesiology is deeply missional. The activities of the institutional church are oriented toward the world. This is not achieved directly as an institution but through the organic mode of the church, through the faithful lives of Christians and Christian organizations in the whole of life.

For example, rather than ecclesiologies which see the institutional church's proclamation solely in terms of evangelism and conversion, Kuyper's ecclesiology adds to this the sanctifying, discipling, and equipping ministries through which the institutional church equips Christian believers for faithful living in their vocations, not in the church but *in the world*. This is because the kingdom of God, which is related to but much broader than the institutional church, is the actual center of the faith and life of Christians who stand before the face of God in all of life.

In fact, we can now see how an improperly misplaced emphasis on the institutional church's centrality contributes to the church's cultural marginalization. If Christians are solely occupied with institutional church activities rather than the institutional church equipping Christians for and sending them out into active faithfulness and service *in the world*, the church becomes introspective to the point that it no longer has genuine and organic connections with the wider world and, thus, becomes obsolete to the world through lack of Christian engagement with the world. And, unfortunately, once the church has capitulated to its own cultural marginalization, if it seeks to re-engage the culture, often the most problematic options are chosen: the attempt to cultivate a civil religion or opting for state-like or mechanical means of controlling the world directly which reduce the proclamation of the Gospel to moralism or legalism because of the deep cultural chasm that is perceived to exist between the church and the world.

Therefore, because of Kuyper's contributions to a robust ecclesiology which eschews dualism and reductionism by introducing critical distinctions at the level of culture and at the level of the church's bi-modal existence, Kuyper's ecclesiology is able to foster an institutional church which is able to participate fully in the differentiated and pluralistic life of contemporary society. And in these ways, it is probably true that Kuyper's ecclesiological vision, even a century after his own work in Holland, has failed to become fully integrated into Reformed ecclesial practice or theology. To echo G. K. Chesterton, it is not that Kuyper's ideal has been tried and found wanting; it has been found difficult and left untried.[9] Kuyper's ecclesiological vision

---

9. Chesterton, *What's Wrong with the World*.

still retains significant insight and application for the church's life in today's pluralistic, diversified world.

POWER AND THE ABUSE OF POWER

Any account of ecclesial power must at least suggest ways of moving forward in light of the numerous claims of ecclesial abuse of power. This project's sustained attention on the power of the institutional church ought to be followed-up by an examination of the theological issues involved in abuses of ecclesial power since here we have tried to keep the focus on the positive, creational, and normative nature of ecclesial power. There are numerous ecclesial communities worldwide that struggle with a theologically robust examination of power and often, when abuses of ecclesial power are alleged to have happened, the resources with which to think about and respond to such accusations are difficult to find. The Reformed tradition is not immune to this struggle. And those communities with ethnic, historic, cultural, or theological ties to Abraham Kuyper have significant reasons to address this question directly, even if pressing issues of ecclesial abuse are not presenting themselves in the moment. The work and the influence of Kuyper are not limited to the past or to northern Europe.

In light of the potential abuses of ecclesial power, it is important to note what Botman calls Kuyper's "liberative legacy" for nonviolence, justice, and ecclesial equality. As he writes

> Kuyper's world is no longer ours. We no longer see the opposition of an organic society to a mechanical government, but instead the adversarial power of a technological, global society that has left the nation-state superfluous. We can no longer affirm the concept of the sovereignty of God without an equal emphasis on God's freedom and historical vulnerability. The strict differentiation of the church as organism on the one hand, and the church as institution on the other, has become counterproductive, perhaps even meaningless to people in the church today.[10]

As a result, Botman argues, we are "facing the . . . question of how to live with the golden calf."[11] The golden calf that flirts around Botman's writing and that lurks around the edges of this project at times is the golden calf of liberalized forms of economic, political, religious, and cultural power

---

10. Botman, "Is Blood Thicker Than Justice?," 359–60.
11. Botman, "Is Blood Thicker Than Justice?," 361.

that are exercised through force, domination, coercion, manipulation, and control. These forms of power have become not only normalized but also entrenched in the extra-ecclesial spheres of contemporary culture (the state, business, etc.) and have become the only forms of power that are commonly understood to exist. Power, in any area of culture or society, is simply assumed to be effective, efficient, normal, and desirable in its coerciveness and forcefulness. At times, as we have noted, the institutional church is also tempted toward these other forms of power in exchange for its kerygmatic form of power. And there are real instances where the trade-off has been made.

Therefore, it is all the more crucial that the power of the institutional church in the ecclesiology of Abraham Kuyper, while not jettisoning the proclamational and kerygmatic nature we have identified in this project, clearly retain its grounding in the eschatological kingdom of God which is antithetical to the fallen forms of creational life. This is not a move toward an anabaptist withdrawal or separation from the world. Rather, it is to argue that one must always remember that the church is the church and no other cultural institution. It is unique. Its power is unique. The church is a creature of the Word and does not arise from the fallen world (cf. John 18:36, not "ἐκ τοῦ κόσμου"). The church is the presence of Christ in and for the world rather than any other ruler or ideology. The church is the channel of the power of grace rather than the ubiquitous economic or technological forces that subject multitudes to the desperation of grinding poverty and other forms of indignity while the privileged few bask in superlative comforts.

Koyzis remarks that the holding of office and the exercise of authority within that office are for manifesting love. In a classroom of students, the professor shows love "by preparing well for lectures and seminars, informing students of expectations," etc. Likewise, students show love "by fulfilling the assignments, contributing to discussion," etc.[12] In an analogous manner, we could say that the exercise of the invitational power of the institutional church shows love: love to God by bearing faithful witness through proclamation, sacraments, discipleship, and diaconal actions of justice and compassion. And the institutional church shows love to the world by being the sacrament, sign and instrument, of grace in the world, receiving from God and bearing to the world the proclamation that the world's true Sovereign is Jesus Christ, the one who laid down his life for his friends without retaliation in any form other than forgiveness. This, then, is what forms converted Christians who are equipped to engage the whole world with the practical application of the Gospel to each sphere of culture. The retrieval

---

12. Koyzis, *We Answer to Another*, 224–25.

of this fundamental theological vision would assist the institutional church in responding to claims and actual instances of abuse of ecclesial power as well as assisting the church in more fully being a community of servant love and inviting grace.

BETWEEN THE LINES, REVISITED

We began by reflecting on the public art installation *Between the Lines* in Belgium. That "see-through" church building, we said, spoke of the disappearing place of the church in contemporary Western society (in actual societal fact as well as in the imaginative mindset of Western culture). The "disappearing church" is juxtaposed to the actual church buildings on the horizon which were built during a time when the institutional church functioned closer to (or even, at) the center of civic life. Today, the disappearing church sits closer to the extreme margins of society, nearly invisible from view for many.

In the ecclesiology of Abraham Kuyper, we find an alternative to either the church attempting to re-assert its central cultural location through a kind of neo-Constantinian force or to its reluctant but quiet acquiescence to the marginalizing forces of modern secular culture. The power of the church in Kuyper's ecclesiology is neither civic institutional dominance nor holiness-through-separation spirituality. Rather, ecclesial power is fully engaged and active as the proclamation of a gracious invitation. The institutional church has received the Word of God and its very purpose is for the further proclamation of the Word through sanctified Christian lives to the world.

Proclamational ecclesial power is kenotic, incarnational, and sacramental in nature. As kenotic, the proclamation of the church is less concerned about its central social position or effective influence than whether it is God-honoring and other-serving. Abraham Kuyper envisioned a church that was willing to be small if it was able to faithfully proclaim God's grace and disciple Christian believers for their callings *in the world*. In particular, the kenotic nature of ecclesial kerygmatic power will take special note of those persons in our globalized world who are marginalized or stigmatized due to political, economic, or ideological forces. The church will pay careful attention to serve and equip them to reassert their dignity as fellow image-bearers of God and contribute to society (possibly even as a prophetic critique of and communal alternative to society).

Ecclesial power that is incarnational in nature means that the proclamation of the church must be aware of the context in which it finds itself.

The history, culture, and challenges of each age must be deeply ("architechtonically") attended to and studied if the proclamation of the Gospel through Word, sacrament, discipleship, and diaconal ministries of justice and compassion are to retain their proclamational faithfulness. The institutional church is meant to serve Christian believers so that they, in turn, might be the contextualized hands and feet of Jesus *for the world*.

And as sacramental in nature, the proclamational power of the church discloses the church as a sign and instrument of the world's ultimate renewal through the grace of God. The institutional church is the evidence and the first-fruits that God is making all things new through the historical coming of his kingdom. The institutional church is the divinely-ordained instrument by which the kingdom of God makes its way in the world, missionally and in love.

In these ways, we observe the place that the institutional church has in the overall worldview of Abraham Kuyper. The institutional church is meant to serve the organic church.[13] The institutional church, empowered with the Christian kerygma through Word, sacrament, discipleship, and diaconal acts of justice and compassion, is to build up Christian believers to be the organic church *for the world*. The kerygmatic power of the institutional church in the ecclesiology of Abraham Kuyper is for the invitational equipping of Christian believers to be the organic church that will faithfully exert cultural-historical influence *in the world* for Christ.

---

13. We can see this in Acts 10 and the conversion of Cornelius. Acts 10 does not contain any judgment on the fact that Cornelius is a Roman Centurion, a position of significant state power. One could engage in a thought experiment regarding what kind of vocational counselling Peter would give Cornelius after his conversion. Would Peter encourage Cornelius to quit his job because he was to eschew forms of coercive power? It seems that since coercive power is natural for the sphere of the state that would not be necessary. In fact, there are countless biblical examples of persons who are faithful to God and who still retain positions of significant power (Moses, Esther, David, Daniel, etc.). Rather, it seems likely that Peter would have encouraged Cornelius to discern where he is called to follow Christ as a Roman Centurion. Indeed, there would be times when he would find himself in a place of conflict between the call of the Emperor and the call of Christ. But the role of the institutional church (in this case, the Apostle Peter) would be to serve Cornelius with the Word of God (through preaching, sacraments, discipleship, and diaconal acts of justice and compassion) to equip him to fulfill his calling in the world faithfully to Christ and the coming of God's kingdom on earth. As Wolterstorff, *Hearing the Call*, 348, argues, "Nowhere are Christians urged to go off by themselves to set up their own social institutions. With the exception, of course, of religious institutions, they are to participate side by side with non-Christians in the institutions of their society: marriage, family, economy, and polity. They are to do so with a difference, however, a difference both in how they understand the significance of those institutions and in how they conduct themselves within them."

In conclusion, the following extended quotation from David Wells captures Kuyper's vision of the kerygmatic power of the institutional church, a power which is grounded in the received Word of God and for the gifting and sending of the church (as organism) into the world:

> The Word of God, read or preached, has the power to enter the innermost crevices of a person's being, to shine light in unwanted places, to explode the myths and deceits by which fallen life sustains itself, and to bring that person face to face with the eternal God.
>
> It is [the] biblical Word which God uses to bring repentance, to excite faith, to give new life, to sustain that life once given, to correct, nurture, and guide the Church. The biblical Word is self-authenticating under the power of the Holy Spirit.
>
> This Word of God is the means by which God accomplishes his saving work in his people, and this is a work that no evangelist and no preacher can do. This is why the dearth of serious, sustained biblical preaching in the Church today is a serious matter. When the Church loses the Word of God it loses the very means by which God does his work. In its absence, therefore, a script is being written, however unwittingly, for the Church's undoing, not in one cataclysmic moment, but in a slow, inexorable slide made up of piece by tiny piece of daily dereliction.[14]

---

14. Wells, *Above All Earthly Pow'rs*, 9.

Appendix 1

A Chronology of Abraham Kuyper[1]

1837   October 29: Born in Maassluis, Holland, to Henriett Huber (1802–1881) and Jan Fredrik Kuyper (1801–1881), a minister in the NHK (who served parishes in Hoogmade, Maassluis, Middelburg, and Leiden). Kuyper is their third child and oldest son.

1841   Moves with family to Middelburg in the province of Zeeland.

1849   Begins studies at the Gymnasium in Leiden.

1855–1862   STUDENT AT THE UNIVERSITY OF LEIDEN

1855   Graduates from the Gymnasium and enrols at the University of Leiden to study literature.

Works on a Calvin-á Lasco treatise, which later becomes part of his doctoral dissertation.

The "miracle of the Lascania."

1857   Receives his *propaedeuse* in literature, *summa cum laude*.

1858   April 29: Takes qualifying exam in classical languages and letters.

November 24: Enrolls in theology at the University of Leiden to train for church ministry.

---

1. Primary sources are Kuipers, *Abraham Kuyper*, and the excellent website maintained by Steve Bishop, "All of Life Redeemed."

1860	October 11: Receives the gold medal in an essay contest sponsored by the University of Groningen for *Commentatio*—Kuyper describes Calvin's and á Lasco's concepts of the church.
	Niet de Vrijheidsboom maar het kruis [Not the Liberty Tree but the Cross].
1861	February–July: Interrupts study due to exhaustion from overwork. Reads *The Heir of Redclyffe* by Charlotte M. Yonge during a nervous breakdown which leads to conversion experience.
	December 6: Takes qualifying exam for theology (*summa cum laude*).
1862	September 20: Defends doctoral thesis—"Disquisitio historico-theologica: exhibens Joannis Calvini et Joannis à Lasco de ecclesia sententiarum inter se compositionem [Theological-Historical Dissertation Showing the Differences in the Rules of the Church, between John Calvin and John Łaski]."
	Promoted to Doctor in Theology.
	Admitted to the candidacy for the NHK ordained ministry.

1863–1874 PASTOR IN THREE NHK CONGREGATIONS, SUCCESSIVELY

1863	July 1: Marries Johanna Hendrika Schaay (1842–1899) in Rotterdam. They have five sons and three daughters between 1864 and 1882.
	August 9: Takes up role as minister in NHK in Beesd. His inaugural sermon was on 1 John 1:7.
	Meets Pietronella Baltus one of the Reformed "pious malcontents" at Beesd.
1864	Begins corresponding with Guillame Groen van Prinsterer (1810–76).
	Article 23—Kuper's response is published.
1866	Publishes a two-volume work on à Lasco in Latin with a 121-page introduction.
1867	November 10: Moves to Utrecht to become pastor at the Domkerk.

Active in church government reform.

De menschwording Gods het levensbeginsel der kerk [*The Incarnation of God—the Life-Principle of the Church.*]

Wat moeten wij doen: het stemrecht aan ons zelven houden of den kerkeraad machtigen? [*What Must We Do?*—addresses the question of democracy in the church].

1868 March 20 (April 1, according to Kuyper): Founding of the Marnix Society, of which Kuyper serves as director until 1874.

Kuyper writes brochure on Church Visiting: *Kerkvisitatie te Utrecht.*

Toelichting der memorie ingediend door den algemeenen kerkeraad van Utrecht ann het classicaal bestuur van Utrecht den 21 September 1868.

1869 June 17: Becomes member of the Maatschappij der Nederlandsche Letterkunde (Leiden).

Kuyper meets Groen Van Prinsterer. They become friends and co-workers.

Starts writing articles for *De Heraut.*

De Nuts Beweging.

Het beroep op het volksgewetern—speech to Christelijk Nationaal-Schoolonderwijs at Utrecht.

De kerkelijke goederen [*The Church Property*].

De werking van artikel 23 [*The Effect of Article 23*].

Eenvormigheid, de vloek van het moderne leven [*Uniformity: the Curse of Modern Life*] *Vrijmaking der kerk* [*Liberalization of the Church*].

Zestal leerredenen [*Six Sermons*].

Kuyper publishes his works with H. de Hoogh in Amsterdam[2] (continues until 1873).

---

2. They are also the publishers of *De Heraut* and *De Standaard*.

1870–1872   EDITOR IN CHIEF OF THE WEEKLY *DE HERAUT*

1870   January 6: Becomes editor in chief of *De Heraut* after Dr. C. Schwartz's death.

Conservatisme en orthodoxie—farewell speech at Utrecht [*AKCR*, 65–85].

August 10: Moves to Amsterdam to be the pastor at Nieuwe Kerk. First sermon is *Rooted and Grounded: The Church as Organism and as Institution*.

Struggles with the liberals in the NHK.

Van Prinster breaks with the Conservatives to work with Kuyper.

De Schrift: het woord Gods [*Scripture: The Word of God*].

De strijd over het Vrije Beheer te Sneek [*The Battle Over Free Management in Sneek*].

De leer der onsterfelijkheid en de staatsschool [*The Doctrine of Immortality and the State School*].

De Hollandsche gemeente te London in 1570–1571 [*The Dutch Church in London 1570–1571*].

1871   Delivers lecture "Modernism, a Fata Morgana in the Christian World" [*AKCR*, 87–124].

Een perel in verkeerde schelp.

O, God! wees mij zondaar genadig!

Tweede zestal leerredenen.

1872–1920   EDITOR IN CHIEF OF THE DAILY *DE STANDAARD*

1872   April 1: ARP produces daily newspaper *De Standaard* with Kuyper as editor in chief—with "For a free church and a free school in a free land" in its masthead.

Given a house at 183 De Prins Hendrikkade as a birthday gift.

Catechism classes for orphans in his home.

De Bartholomeusnacht [St. Bartholomew].

Het vergrijp der zeventien ouderlingen [The Offense of the Seventeen Elders].

1873   Kuyper stands for election for the constituency of Gouda.

Publishes "Confidentially" [*AKCR*, 45–61].

Lecture at Utrecht, "Calvinism, the Origin and Guarantee of our Constitutional Liberties: A Netherlands Reflection"—in print 1894.

Eenheid rede, ter bevestiging van Ds. P. van Son, gehouden 31 Augustus 1873 in de Nieuwe Kerk te Amsterdam.

Vrijheid. Rede. Ter bevestigin van Dr. Ph. S. van Ronkel, gehouden den 23 Maart 1873, in de nieuwe kerk.

Ons huis—sermon in the Nieuwe Kerk, Amsterdam.

Uit het Woord—Bible studies/meditations.

1874–1877 MEMBER OF THE SECOND CHAMBER OF THE STATES GENERAL

1874   Kuyper is elected to the Second Chamber of the States General.

March 16: Kuyper leaves pastorate (as emeritus or inactive pastor) to enter politics.

March 20: Assumes duties as member of the ARP, wins an interim election in Gouda district.

April: J. H. Kruyt in Amsterdam begins publishing *De Standaard* and Kuyper also beings publishing with Kruyt.

Het Calvinisme: oorsprong en waarborg onzer constitutineele vrijheden. Een nederlandsche gedachte [*AKCR*, 279–322].

Grieven tegen de schoolwet en het geheim verraden.

Serves as elder in the Amsterdam NHK church until 1886.

1875   Dr. Gunning proposes the idea for a Christian university.

May 29–June 5: Travels to Brighton, England, to hear D. L. Moody, invited by Robert Pearsall Smith.

Series of articles on fasting.

De Scherpe Resolutie en het decretum horribile.

Het redmiddel.

De schoolkwestie [The School Issue].

De schoolwet voor de vierschaar van Europa [Education for the Tribunal of Europe].

1876   Complete nervous exhaustion.

February 3–April 14, 1877: Travels to convalesce in southern Europe.

Enjoys Alpine mountain climbing.

G. G. Van Prinsterer dies.

1877–1920   EDITOR IN CHIEF OF THE WEEKLY *DE HERAUT*

1877   Begins writing "Our Program," outlining the political ideals of the ARP as a series of articles in *De Standaard*.

July 1: Honorary discharge from duties as member of the Second Chamber.

December 7: *De Heraut* relaunched.

Begins series of articles on perfectionism (contra Brighton experience).

1878   January 1: programmatic platform for the ARP is released.

August 3: Petition to king not to sign Kappeyne's education bill.

December 5: Association for Higher Education on the Basis of Reformed Principles founded.

Liberalisten en Joden

1879–1918 CHAIRMAN OF THE CENTRAL COMMITTEE OF THE ANTI-REVOLUTIONARY ELECTORAL ASSOCIATIONS (BRIEF INTERRUPTION FROM 1904–1907)

1879   January 23: Founding of The Union: "A School with the Bible," on the executive committee of which Kuyper serves (1879–1884, 1885–1891).

April 3: ARP is founded and becomes first national party under Kuyper's leadership as chairman of the Central Committee.

"Our Program" for the ARP is published.

Revisie der revisie-legende

De leidsche Professoren en de Executeurs der Dordtsche Nalatenschap.

Twaalftal leerredenen (eerste en tweede zestal) [*Dozen Sermons*].

"Perfectionism" [*AKCR*, 141–63].

September 6: Appointed professor in the theological faculty of the yet-to-be-opened VU.

1880–1908 PROFESSOR AT THE VRIJE UNIVERSITEIT, AMSTERDAM

1880   October 20: VU opening ceremony, Kuyper delivers the inaugural address, "Sphere Sovereignty" [*AKCR*, 461–90], in the Nieuwe Kerk.

Family moves back to Amsterdam from The Hague.

Princess Wilhelmina reaches majority age and becomes queen.

"*Strikt genomen*" [*Strictly Speaking*].

Bede om een dubbel Corrigendum, aan A.W. Bronsveld [*Petition for Double Corrigendum to Bronsveld*].

"The Antithesis between Symbolism and Meaning."

Kuyper writes *Antirevolutionair óók in uw huisgezin* [*Anti-Revolutionary in Your Family Too*].

Publishes the first of ten collections of weekly meditations.

	November 26: Receives honorary membership in the Dutch Workingmen's Union "Patrimonium."
1881	VU has 5 professors and 5 students.
	Serves as the first Rector of the VU.
	Appointed professor of language and literature at the VU.
	Kuyper's mother and father die.
1882	Appointed as an elder by the Electoral Commission of the State Church.
1883	Starts writing a series on the Holy Spirit for *De Heraut*.
	March-May: Lectures in the Circle of Brothers (like-minded members of the Amsterdam consistory) on the reformation of the church.
	November 1–15: Serves as advisor in London to the three-member delegation from the Transvaal.
	November: Publishes *Tractaat van de Reformatie der Kerken* and *De drie formulieren van eenigheid*.
1885	Writes brochure "The Threatening Conflict."

1886–1888   LEADING FIGURE IN THE *DOLEANTIE*

1886	January 4: Church conflict in Amsterdam. Kuyper breaks into the Amsterdam consistory room with a locksmith, carpenter, and guards. Begins sit-in protest.
	J. A. Wormser founds publishing house and becomes Kuyper's publisher of choice.
	July 1: Kuyper is deposed from the NHK and removed from office of elder in Amsterdam council.
	December 1: General Synod of the NHK confirms Kuyper's sentence.
	December 16: Forms *Doleantie* (grieving ones) in the Reformed Congregation of Amsterdam.
	"It Shall Not Be So among You" [*AKCR*, 125–40].
	"The Conflict Has Come"—three pamphlets.

1887–1892 CHAIRMAN OF THE REFORMED CHURCH CONGRESS, THE SYNODICAL CONVENTION, AND THE FINAL THREE OF THE FOUR PROVISIONAL SYNODS OF THE NHK

1887 Serves as Rector to VU for the second time preached on "Calvinism and Art."

July 1: Wormser becomes publisher of *De Standaard* and *De Heraut*.

1889 May 10: Named knight in the Order of the Dutch Lion during the fortieth anniversary of the rule of King Willem III.

600 ARP delegates meet in 10th convention—Kuyper delivers "Not the Liberty Tree but the Cross."

"Manual Labor" [*AKCR*, 231–54].

1890 King William III dies.

1891 November 9–12: Serves as chairman at the Social Congress and delivers opening address which becomes *The Problem of Poverty*.

Writes "Calvinism and Confessional Revision" in response to a proposal to revise the Westminster Standards.

At ARP convention delivers speech on "Maranatha" [*AKCR*, 205–29].

Presides over a provisional Synod for the *Doleantie* in The Hague.

Voor een distel een mirt.

Student notes of Kuyper's lectures in dogmatics become available.

Kuyper writes *Het sociale vraagstuk en de Christelijke Religie* [*The Social Question and the Christian Religion*]

1892 LEADING FIGURE IN THE FORMATION OF THE GKN

1892 Kuyper's nine-year-old son Willie dies.

June 7–16: Serves as chairman of the Fourth Provisional Synod of the Dutch Reformed Churches which on June 16 unites with the Christian Reformed Church (*Afscheiding*—the 1834 secession group) to become the GKN.

Delivers lecture on panthesism, "The Destruction of the Boundaries," at VU [*AKCR*, 363–402].

1893   *Encyclopedia of Sacred Theology* published.

E Voto Dordraceno, a series of articles from *De Heraut* on the Heidelberg Catechism is published.

In de Schaduwe des Doods.

1894–1901   MEMBER OF THE SECOND CHAMBER OF THE STATES GENERAL

1894   May 16: Re-elected to Second Chamber for Sliedrect constituency and begins duties, serving as chairman of the parliamentary caucus of the ARP.

Concentrates on suffrage, labor and foreign affairs.

Begins series on "The Angels of God" in *De Heraut*.
Breach with A. F. de Savornin Lohman.

July-December: Travels to Brussels and southern France to recover from a serious illness.

1895   Publication of the new and revised edition of the Dutch Authorized Version (1637).

September 1: Publishes the first article in the series *De Gemeene Gratie* in *De Heraut*—completed in 1901.

De Christus en de sociale nooden en democratische klippen.

Proeve van pensioenregeling voor werklieden en huns gelijken.

1896   September 3: The *Rapport inzake de zending* is accepted by the Synod of Middelburg.

1897   Serves as chairman of the Federation of Anti-Revolutionary Electoral Associations in Amsterdam (until 1901).

De Drie Formulieren van Eenigheid.

Openingswoord ter deputatenvergadering.

April 1: Celebrates 25th anniversary of *De Standaard*.

May 27: Receives honorary membership in the Dutch Federation of Young Men's Associations on Reformed Principles.

June 27: Re-elected to the Second Chamber.

Serves as chairman of the committee of the Dutch Association of Journalists for the reception of foreign journalists visiting the Netherlands for the 1898 coronation of Princess Wilhelmina.

Kuyper writes "Vrouwen uit de Heilige schrift" ["Women from the Holy Scripture"].

1898　Serves as rector to the VU for the fourth time.

Invited by B. B. Warfield to USA to give the Stone Lectures at Princeton Seminary: *Calvinism*. Departs on August 11. Returns home on December 31. The full itinerary is given in Appendix B of *FCHN*.

October 22: Receives Honorary Doctorate in Law from Princeton.

Serves as chairman (1898–1901) of the Dutch Association of Journalists.

Van het kerkelijk ambt.

1899　Publishes *Calvinism: Six Stone Lectures*.

March 29: Named commander in the *Ordre Royal Hospitalier et Humanitaire de Sainte-Catherine du Mont-Sinaï* by Guy de Lusignan the grandmaster of the order and crown prince of Jerusalem, Cyprus, and Armenia.

August 25: Kuyper's wife dies in Meiringen, Switzerland.

September: Serves as chairman of a parliamentary commission investigating a draft bill on statutory assurance for laborers against the financial consequences of accidents.

Moves from Prins Hendrikkade house to 164 De Keizersgracht next to VU.

First peace conference.

Start of the Boer War, South Africa.

Evolutie—lecture delivered at VU [*AKCR*, 403–40].

Band aan het woord.

Amendement-Kuyper op de Ongevallenwet.

Varia Americana.

Als gij in uw huis zit.

1900   *The South-African Crisis*—published by Stop the War Committee in London [*AKCR*, 323–60].

The Work of the Holy Spirit published in English, translated by B. B. Warfield.

To Be Nearer unto God—a series of devotions published.

De Englen Gods [*The Angels of God*] published.

Gave lectures at Yale.

1901–1905   PRIME MINISTER OF THE NETHERLANDS AND MINISTER OF INTERNAL/HOME AFFAIRS

1901   July 11–25: Charged by the queen to form a cabinet.

July 31: Named Minister for Internal/Home Affairs.

Moves to The Hague (5 De Kanaalstraat).

October 7: Named honorary chairman of the Dutch Association of Journalists.

October 23: As a result of a change in the cabinet's rules of order, Kuyper is named permanent chairman of the council of ministers, thus becoming the first prime minister in the parliamentary history of the Netherlands.

At ARP national convention keynote speech on "Perseverance in the Pursuit of Our Ideal."

Queen Wilhelmina marries the Duke Heinrich of Mecklenburg-Schwerin.

Drie kleine vossen [*Three Little Foxes*]—the three are: intellectualism, mysticism, and practicalism.

Evolutionismus: das Dogma moderner Wissenschaft [German translation].

Volharden bij het ideaal [*Insisting on the Ideal*]—remarks at a meeting of the deputies.

1902 Queen Wilhemina becomes gravely ill.

Common Grace [AKCR, 165–201].

In Jezus ontslapen: meditatien [Asleep in Jesus: A Meditation].

1903 Country plagued by rail strikes.

February 25: proposes laws to counteract the railway strikes.

July 16: Becomes foreign honorary member of the Vlaamsche Academie voor Taal—en Letterkunde (Ghent, Belgium).

Vier uwe vierdagen: meditatiën.

Albert Hahn produces "Abraham de Geweldige" cartoon.

1904 September 5: Resigns his chairmanship of the Central Committee of the Anti-Revolutionary Electoral Associations and of the Association for Higher Education on Reformed Principles.

Russian-Japanese war begins.

"Common Grace in Science" [AKCR, 441–60].

German translation of *Lectures on Calvinism* published translated by Martin Jaeger.

"The Biblical Criticism of the Present Day" in *Biblica Sacra*.

1905 January 6: Awarded the Great Cross of the Order of Leopold by the king of Belgium.

May 20: Higher Education Law revised.

June 28: Suffers electoral defeat and becomes part of the opposition.

Sociale hervormingen [*Social Reform*]—bills devised by Kuyper's party.

Herman Bavinck delivers keynote speech to ARP convention.

August 5: Departs for Bad Kissingen in Germany and then for a trip around the Mediterranian Sea (until June 1906).

August 16: Kuyper cabinet resigns.

November 13: Awarded the Great Cross of the Order of Medjedjé by the sultan of Turkey.

1906 *Verplichte verzekering.*

Awarded the Great Cross of the Royal Military Order of Christ by the king of Portugal.

150th anniversary of poet Bilderdyk—interrupts tour to give speech, *Bilderdijk in zijne nationale beteekenis*, in Amsterdam.

1907   January 8: Receives honorary doctorate in applied sciences from the Technische Hoogeschool (Delft).

October 17: Re-elected Chair of the Central Committee of the Anti-Revolutionary Electoral Associations and of the Association for Higher Education on Reformed Principles.

Resumes editorship of *De Heraut*—begins series on *Pro Rege*.

Om de oude wereldzee [*Around the Ancient World Sea*]—contains "Mystery of Islam" [translated by Jan Boer].

December 12: J. H. Kok buys nearly all the unsold stock of Kuyper's works published by Wormser and proceeds to purchase the unsold stock of titles published by other publishers as well.

1908–1912   MEMBER OF THE SECOND CHAMBER OF THE STATES GENERAL

1908   January 1: Becomes emeritus professor of VU.

June 17: Receives honorary doctorate of philology from Hope College (Holland, Michigan).

August 27: Honorary title of Minister of State bestowed on Queen Wilhelmena's birthday.

November 13: Returns to the Second Chamber for Ommen district (until September 18, 1912).

"Our Instinctive Life" [*AKCR*, 255–77].

Nabij God te zijn.

Zelfstandig gemeentewezen.

Parlementaire redevoeringen [*Parliamentary Speeches*] (1908–1910).

Verjaardag-album met motto's uit de werken van Dr. A. Kuyper. A retrospective of his career to mark the end of his work at the VU.

1909   June 27: Controversy erupts over the so-called "decorations affair" (Kuyper's name is cleared in 1910).

Wij, Calvinisten—opening remarks to ARP national convention (400th anniversary of birth of Calvin).

October 4: Serves as chairman of the state commission reviewing proposed changes in Dutch spelling.

Brings Hendrik Colyn into politics.

Receives honorary doctorate from the Katholieke Universiteit van Leuven (Belgium).

Book of cartoons of Kuyper published.

Nadere verklaring.

De leer der Verbonden.

Voor den slag.

Practijk der Godzaligheid [*Practice of Godliness*].

Heils termen

Honig uit den rotssteen

Dat de genade particulier is

Het heil ons toekomende

Het heil in ons

1911   Begins a series on the consummation in *De Heraut*—completed in 1918.

Pro Rege: of Het Koningschap van Christus—[contains "You Can Do Greater Things Than Christ," translated by Jan Boer].

Onze Eeredienst [*Our Worship*]—began as a series of articles in 1897.

1912   September 18: Resigns as member of the Second Chamber due to increasing hardness of hearing.

Fortieth anniversary of *De Standaard*.

Een geloofsstuk—address to VU society in Haarlem.

Uit het diensthuis uitgeleid [*Brought Out of the House of Bondage*]—speech in Leeuwarden, Groningen, and Rotterdam.

Zijn uitgang te Jerusalem—meditations on the suffering of our Lord.

In Jezus ontslapen [*Asleep in Jesus*].

Afgeperst.

1913–1920 MEMBER OF THE FIRST CHAMBER OF THE STATES GENERAL

1913   March 29: Promoted to commander in the Order of the Dutch Lion.

September 16: Elected to the First Chamber (until September 21, 1920).

De meiborn in de kap—delivered to the meeting of the ARP delegates/deputies.

Der Jongelingen sieraad is hun kracht—address given at the Jubilee of the Confederation of Reformed Young Men.

Heilige orde—speech to ARP in Amsterdam.

1914–18   Sided with the Germans in WWI—an anti-British rather than a pro-German stance; he opposed the British ever since the Boer War.

1914   March 26: Death of Mrs. P. Baltus, whose influence on Kuyper's spiritual development is memorialized in *De Standaard* on March 30.

De eereposite der vrouw [*Women in the Bible*—articles first appeared in the Amsterdam Church Messenger].

A kálvinizmus lényege—in Hungarian translated by Czeglédi Sándor with introduction by Sebestyén Jenö.

1915   *Starrentritsen: Editio castigata.*

Eudokia—speech delivered to the Eudokia Institute in Rotterdam.

J. H. Kok compiles bibliography of Kuyper works.

1916   2000th issue of *De Heraut* published (Kuyper wrote about 2000 meditations for it).

De wortel in de dorre aarde—delivered to a meeting of the Deputies.

First volume of the two-volume *Antirevolutionaire staatkunde: met nadere toelichting op ons program* is published—this was the last book he wrote.

"The Evolution of the Use of the Bible in Europe." In *Centennial Pamphlets 2*. New York: American Bible Society, 1916

1917 *Luther herdacht*

De positie van Nederland.

November 23: Delivers the speech *De 'kleyne luyden'*—at meeting opening of the Deputies of the ARP. Kuyper's last speech to this body.

1918 November 5: Resigns as chairman of the Central Committee of the Anti-Revolutionary Electoral Associations.

To Be Nearer Unto God published in English translated by J. H. De Vries.

Wat nu?—at opening of the Deputies.

1919 December 18: On medical advice, Kuyper ceases writing for *De Standaard*.

Deaths of Jan Woltjer and F. L. Rutgers.

Rev'd W. F. A. Winckel's *Leven Arbeid van Dr. Kuyper* [*Life and Work of Dr A. Kuyper*] is published.

1920 September 21: Resigns as member of the First Chamber.

November 8: Kuyper dies in The Hague.

November 12: Buried in the cemetery Oud Eik en Duinen, The Hague.

Appendix 2

The Church in the Reformed Confessions

THERE ARE FOUR DOCUMENTS surveyed in this appendix: the Belgic Confession (1561), the Second Helvetic Confession (1562), the Heidelberg Catechism (1563), and the Canons of the [NHK] Synod of Dordrecht (1618–1619).[1] Some of these historical confessional documents provided (and still do provide today in Reformed churches around the world) the "forms of unity" for the various Reformed churches in the Netherlands, including Kuyper's own GKN. As a champion of the Calvinist Reformation in the Netherlands, Kuyper stood within the theological tradition marked out by these documents and therefore they provide an important piece of the theological background to Kuyper's ecclesiological worldview and reformist approach.

The Calvinist/Reformed confessions of this period are marked by their consistent application of Reformed theology to the on-going disputes with the Roman Catholic church, the various regional civil authorities, and other ecclesial splinter groups. McNeill claims that there are "no great fundamental variations of thought" during this period. Rather, these documents and theologians "differ in phraseology, in the order of treatment, in the structure of their argument; but they can hardly be said to contradict one another."[2] On the other hand, Muller has shown that this assessment is not entirely accurate.[3]

---

1. While these documents are readily available in English translation in a number of online and published forms, I am relying on the translations in CRC, *Ecumenical Creeds and Reformed Confessions*. Only the Second Helvetic Confession is not included in this collection. For this document, I rely on Schaff, *History of Creeds*, 395.

2. McNeill, "Church in Post-Reformation Reformed Theology," 98.

3. For example, see Muller, *Calvin and the Reformed Tradition*.

THE BELGIC CONFESSION

The Belgic Confession was composed by Guido de Brès for Reformed churches facing persecution in "Belgica" which comprises modern day Belgium and Holland. de Brès was a preacher in the Reformed churches of the Netherlands and sought to convince the Spanish and Roman Catholic government of the time that those belonging to the Reformed movement and who were being persecuted were not rebels but law-abiding citizens who professed true Christian doctrine. In 1561, de Brès drafted the Belgic Confession and sent it to King Philip II along with a petition declaring that they were ready to obey the government in all things lawful but that they were loyal adherents to the Reformed faith and would not waver. Rather than accomplishing the purpose of reducing or eliminating the persecution, de Brès died as a martyr in 1567 and the persecution of Reformed Christians in the Netherlands continued.

Of the Belgic Confession's thirty-seven articles, about a third address the church. The majority of these instances occur in articles 27–36 which specifically address the doctrine of the church. In articles 4, 5, and 6 the church is mentioned in regards to which texts constitute Scripture. Article 4 indicates that the church is that authoritative body which receives the Scriptures from God while article 5 subordinates the authority of the church to the subjective authority of Christian conscience perceiving the attestation of the Holy Spirit regarding which texts are Christian Scripture and which are not. In article 6, regarding the apocryphal books, the church is regarded as a society "which may certainly read these [non-canonical] books and learn from them" but they do not function authoritatively in either the church or the life of a Christian. In articles 9 and 12, "the true church" is referred to as being that entity which rightly maintains true doctrine and that body which, united to God through Christ, the forces of evil "lie in wait for," respectively.

These ad hoc early references to the church become more clear, focused, and doctrinal once the Belgic Confession arrives at articles 27 through 35, a section dealing specifically with the church. Here, the "one single catholic or universal church" is defined as "a holy congregation and gathering of true Christian believers, awaiting their entire salvation in Jesus Christ, being washed in his blood, and sanctified and sealed by the Holy Spirit."[4] Here we perceive Calvin's emphasis on the church as the congregation of the Christian faithful, participating in a gracious union with Christ, and kept secure through the Holy Spirit.

---

4. *Belgic Confession* 27.

The ambiguity of the Belgic Confession, in the language used to define the church, allows for the double meaning of the church in Calvin and the post-Reformation period. On the one hand, the church is organic: "A holy . . . gathering of true Christian believers" united to Jesus Christ as his mystical Body. On the other hand, the church—according to this definition—is also an institution: "A congregation . . . awaiting their entire salvation in Jesus Christ" within history and the temporal congregations of particular places. This represents a common Reformed understanding of the church as the *ekklesia*: "A society of men [sic] called out . . . and assembled . . . to signify especially the people of God, the assembly of men [sic] called from the mass of humankind by the preaching of the gospel." It is this assembly which is in "communion with Christ." Or, this assembly may refer to "those who profess the faith of Christ and participate in the same means of grace" in local congregations.[5] The ambiguous language is intentionally crafted to refer to either the church as the mystical body of Christ or as its temporal and institutional manifestation in time and place.

The subtlety of definitions in the Belgic Confession is not limited to the church but also of the "catholicity" of the church addressed in article 27, also representative of the post-Reformation Reformed tradition. Here, the catholicity of the church is referred to as the church "exist[ing] from the beginning of the world and [which] will last until the end," being "preserved by God against the rage of the whole world" and "not confined, bound, or limited to a certain place or certain persons. But it is spread and dispersed throughout the entire world, though still joined and united in heart and will, in one and the same Spirit, by the power of faith."

As McNeill notes, the standard understanding of the catholicity of the church following the Reformation is the church's temporal perpetuity, its spiritual preservation, and its perseverance in orthodoxy. McNeill quotes a number of interpreters: Bucanus says that the church is catholic "because it is of all estates and periods of time; and is the same and enduring, it was and is and shall be." According to Wolleb, the church is catholic "in respect to time, because she hath not utterly failed since the beginning of the world, but still there hath been some visible church" and the church "is catholic because she is not tied to place or persons." Turretin, says McNeill, expounds catholicity "in terms of the church's freedom from limitation with respect to places, persons, and times." The church is catholic because God is always faithfully maintaining at least a remnant of true Christian believers for

---

5. McNeill, "Church," 99. On the multiple ways in which Paul uses the Greek term "ekklesia," see Ridderbos, *Paul*, 327–95. His conclusion is that "from the beginning Paul in his epistles ascribes more than one meaning to the title *ekklesia*" (330).

himself.[6] Catholicity is not tied to a geographic, temporal perpetuity (as in apostolic succession, for example) but secured in God's divine will that there always be a people marked as his very own and kept safe in Jesus Christ.

We can observe in the Belgic Confession the seeds of a typical, though minor, Reformed strain of thought which equates the church with the kingdom of God. The roots of this idea come from the Belgic Confession's article 27 where the temporal perpetuity of the church is guaranteed because "Christ is eternal King who cannot be without subjects." Here, in these words, the kingdom of Christ or God is equated conterminously with the temporal church. For the author(s) of the Belgic Confession, the cessation of the church's temporal existence would mean the cessation of Christ's reign as King. Whether this is the intended teaching of the Belgic Confession on this point is another question. A related question is what degree of indebtedness the Confession has to Calvin for at one point Calvin also equates the church with the kingdom of God when he writes that "the church is Christ's Kingdom."[7]

Article 28 refines the initial definition of the church offered in article 27 by adding that the church is "the gathering of those who are saved," which "no one ought to withdraw from," and which is marked by unity through mutually "submitting to its [the church's] instruction and discipline . . . and serving to build up one another, according to the gifts God has given them as members of each other in the same body." In this expanded definition of the church, the temporal church is more in view than the supra-temporal mystical Body of Christ. It is the institutional church that Christian believers are exhorted to join which is now in focus; and this church is one in which instruction (the first mark of the church: proper preaching of the Word of God), discipline, and the dynamic and servant social community takes shape. It is this concrete, historical dimension of the church which will occupy the remaining articles of the Belgic Confession, as the Confession addresses ecclesial polity (articles 30–32) and the sacraments (articles 33–35).

Article 29 clarifies the "true church" as opposed to not only "false" churches but also fellowships which claim to be the church but which, according to the Reformers, are not. It is of note that the Belgic Confession lists three marks of the church ("pure preaching of the gospel," "pure administration of the sacraments," and "church discipline for correcting faults"), following the lead of Calvin prior to his 1559 *Institutes* in which he lists only two marks. These three marks delineate the "true church" which "governs

---

6. McNeill, "Church," 103.

7. Calvin, *Institutes of the Christian Religion* 4.2.4.

itself according to the pure Word of God"—thereby creating a hierarchy within the marks of the true church with the Word of God occupying the place of preeminence among the others.

It would take us too far afield to delve deeply into a detailed analysis of the ecclesiology of the Belgic Confession in this appendix. But it is worth noting that not only does article 29 outline the marks of the true church but it also outlines the marks of the true Christian in addition to the marks of the false church. True Christians, those and only those who are called to join the true church, are those who have faith, flee from sin and pursue righteousness, love God and neighbor, and crucify their flesh and its works. It is these persons, who recognize these marks within themselves, who are members of the true church. In contrast, the false church is known by its own or human authority (rather than Scripture), does not subject itself to Christ, does not administer the sacraments according to Christ's command, and persecutes those who live according to God's Word. "These two churches," the Confession concludes, "are easy to recognize."[8]

The Belgic Confession, composed within a few short years after Calvin's completion of his final edition of the *Institutes,* follows Calvin's ecclesiological emphases and highlights many of the same themes as Calvin: the church is the elect mystical Body of Christ, a human society of instruction and encouragement, governed by Scripture, celebrating the sacraments, and ruled by true biblical polity. It is this church which true Christians are called to join, a community which (this author would want to nuance) is an integral *part* of Christ's kingdom on earth.

THE SECOND HELVETIC CONFESSION

The Second Helvetic Confession is the most widely accepted confession among the world's Reformed churches today. It originates in the Swiss Reformed movement of Zwingli and was penned by Ulrich Bullinger at the request of Frederick III, Elector of the Palatinate, who sought to dispel tensions with the Lutherans over his allegiance to the Reformed faith. Completed in 1562, it was finally accepted by the Swiss Reformed churches in 1566. It is only surpassed by the Heidelberg Catechism in widespread liturgical use and authority in the Reformed family of churches. Armed with the Second Helvetic Confession, Frederick III inspired awe and devotion among his Lutheran detractors at the Diet of Augsburg (March 1566) for his piety, knowledge, and faith. Philip Schaff writes that "Upon the whole, the Second Helvetic Confession, as to theological merit, occupies the first

---

8. *Belgic Confession* 29.

rank among the Reformed Confessions, while in practical usefulness it is surpassed by the Heidelberg and Westminster Shorter Catechisms, and in logical clearness and precision by the Westminster Confession, which is the product of a later age, and of the combined learning and wisdom of English and Scotch Calvinism."[9]

In many ways, the Second Helvetic Confession parallels the Belgic (and other Reformed confessions), though it is far more detailed and thorough. Chapter 17 addresses "The Catholic and Holy Church of God and the One Only Head of the Church." After beginning with an assertion about the temporal perpetuity of the church, the Second Helvetic Confession defines the church in far more temporal ways than the Belgic Confession, which began with Christ's mystical Body as God's elect. Rather than beginning with the mystical Body of Christ and then working toward the temporal realm, the Second Helvetic Confession says straightaway that "the Church is an assembly of the faithful called or gathered out of the world; a communion, I say, of all saints, namely, of those who truly know and rightly worship and serve the true God in Christ the Savior, by the Word and holy Spirit, and who by faith are partakers of all benefits which are freely offered through Christ." The Second Helvetic Confession has an institutional rather than mystical ecclesial focus.

We can observe in this definition that union with Christ continues to play a foundational part. Yet, it very quickly moves from union with Christ to union with other Christian believers as "citizens of one commonwealth" in which the church lives together as a society "under the same Lord, under the same laws, and in the same fellowship of all good things" in the midst of the world. It is this temporal church which is catholic, that is, geographically "scattered through all parts of the world, and [temporally] extended until all times, and is not limited to any times or places." The emphasis here is on manifestational geographic and temporal extension rather than God's faithful preservation of the church through time. There are distinctions to be reckoned with in the church (militant vs. triumphant or Old Testament vs. New Testament saints, for example) but this does not destroy the unity of the church as a single people of God called to assemble together in the world. The church remains the single "temple of the living God," the "bride of Christ," the "flock of sheep under the one shepherd, Christ," the "body of Christ" its Head and only true pastor.

In the Second Helvetic Confession, the marks of the church are again listed but only the "lawful and sincere preaching of the Word of God" is expounded. The proper preaching of the Word is amplified to include the

9. Schaff, *History of Creeds*, 395.

"worship [of God] in spirit and in truth," loving God, praying unto God through Christ the only Mediator, daily renewal through repentance and bearing of each one's cross, "unfeigned love" for fellow Christians, and participation in the sacraments. And yet, all of these various elements are included in the Confession's understanding of what occurs when the Word of God is rightly preached. Chapters 18 (ministers of the church), 19 (the sacraments in general), 20 (baptism), 21 (Eucharist), 22 (ecclesial assemblies), 23 (liturgy), 24 (holy feast days), 25 (catechism and pastoral care for the sick), 26 (Christian burial), 27 (rites and other ceremonies), 28 (church property), 29 (celibacy, marriage, and domestic affairs), and 30 (civil magistrates, the relationship of the church to the state) round out the conclusion of the Confession.

THE HEIDELBERG CATECHISM

Elector Frederick III of the Palatinate, who ruled from 1559 to 1576, requested that a catechism be composed for his region, a task that was taken up by the polish Reformed theologian at the University of Heidelberg, Zacharius Ursinus (Caspar Olevianus may have also played a secondary role in its composition). The catechism was approved by the Heidelberg synod in January 1563. It is composed of fifty-two "Lord's Days," meaning that during each Sunday's worship throughout the year one Lord's Day could be preached in a congregation, a practice that has continued in Reformed churches up to the present day (we should note that the Catechism is clear that preaching is the primary means of Christ's rule in the church as Q/A 98, in its argument against images in sanctuaries, explicitly says that God "wants his people instructed by the living preaching of his Word"). After an introductory first Lord's Day, the catechism is organized thematically, beginning with human guilt and misery in sin, followed by a reflection on God's gracious salvation in Jesus Christ (primarily organized around the Apostle's Creed), and then a very lengthy final section on how salvation naturally leads to grateful service of God and neighbor (primarily through teachings on the Ten Commandments and the Lord's Prayer).

It is within the context of salvation from sin and reflection on the Apostle's Creed, that the catechism begins its teachings on the church. Occurring first in Q/A 23 (Lord's Day 7) where the Creed is presented for the first time, it is not until Q/A's 50 and 51 where the ecclesial lines of the creed are expounded upon.

50 Q. Why the next words: "And is seated at the right hand of God?"
A. Christ has ascended to heaven, there to show that he is head of his church, and that the Father rules all things through him.

51 Q. How does this glory of Christ our head benefit us?
A. First, through his Holy Spirit he pours out his gifts from heaven upon us his members. Second, by his power he defends us and keeps us safe from all enemies.

Here we begin to see the numerous Calvinist ecclesial themes being woven together, with the distinctly noted purpose of the Heidelberg Catechism: how the truths of the Christian faith benefit or "comfort" (Q/A 1) the Christian believer. The ascended Christ is Head of his body, the church, and through this organic union, mediated by the Holy Spirit, the gifts of God are bestowed on the church, Christ's Body on earth, with the added emphasis on the protection and preservation of the church by the powerful rule of God. The church is that temporal community which is united to the risen and ruling Christ through the Holy Spirit who gifts and guards his people on earth. And according to Q/A 74, baptism is the outward ecclesial sign of membership in the church as this covenantal community (which is both for converted adults and the children of believing parents).

These themes are then brought together in Q/A 54 and 55.

54 Q. What do you believe concerning "the holy catholic church"?
A. I believe that the Son of God through his Spirit and Word, out of the entire human race, from the beginning of the world to its end, gathers, protects, and preserves for himself a community chosen for eternal life and united in true faith. And of this community I am and always will be a living member.

55 Q. What do you understand by "the communion of saints"?
A. First, that believers one and all, as members of this community, share in Christ and in all his treasures and gifts. Second, that each member should consider it a duty to use these gifts readily and cheerfully for the service and enrichment of the other members.

We can see at this point quite readily that the twin themes of union with Christ salvifically and union with each other socially within the Christian community are clearly in focus. Not only is the church a "gathering" of God's electing grace, but it is also a "community" in which the members share with each other as they also share in Christ—what Hendrikus Berkhof refers to as a "fortunate combination" of two meanings of this line of the creed.[10] In fact, Q/A 55 ends on a clear note that to be united to Christ in the church means that there is a "duty" upon the members to serve each other for their mutual enrichment. The Heidelberg Catechism highlights both the theological and sociological aspects of the church.

By the time the Heidelberg Catechism reaches its discussion on the sacraments, these two aspects of the church are brought together in a lengthy discussion on the "keys of the kingdom"—in this case, the true preaching of the Word and proper church discipline. Q/A's 82 to 85 all address this concern that the unrepentant must be kept from the Lord's Supper so that God's covenant is not "dishonor[ed]" and the congregation is not defiled and "God's anger [brought] upon the entire congregation" (Q/A 82). Thus, the marks of the church in Reformed ecclesiology are not only for identifying the true church in the midst of a highly polemical extra-ecclesial context but also so that, within the church, true Christian believers can be identified in the mist of many who may profane their Christian profession of faith through doctrinal errors or impure living.

Finally, as was noted above, there is a tendency within some branches of the Reformed tradition to equate the kingdom of God with the church. We saw above how an ambiguous section of the Belgic Confession could lead to this interpretation. We also observe this in Heidelberg Catechism Q/A 123 (Lord's Day 48). Here, the catechism is teaching what the line of the Apostle's Creed, "your kingdom come," means. In response, the answer amplifies the request to mean: "Rule us by your Word and Spirit in such a way that more and more we submit to you. Keep your church strong, and add to it. Destroy the devil's work; destroy every force which revolts against you and every conspiracy against your Word. Do this until your kingdom is so complete and perfect that in it you are all in all." Again, the church is equated with the kingdom of God.

It is important to note that the catechism interprets this request (that God cause his kingdom to come) in two primary ways: (1) in the faithful proclamation of God's Word and (2) in the preservation of the church. Again, one wonders whether the drafter(s) of the Catechism intended to communicate the idea that the kingdom of God and the church are virtually synonymous. The way this catechism answer is worded, it leaves the reader with the impression that the church is the sole arena of the kingdom of God's rule. The reader is left wondering if there is any part of the world, outside the church, in which the coming of God's kingdom is being prayed for or being actualized. It seems that this ambiguity leaves a rather large swath

---

10. Berkhof, *Christian Faith*, 404.

of created life unaddressed by the Heidelberg Catechism's interpretation of this line of the Lord's Prayer. It will not be until Herman Bavinck completes his *Reformed Dogmatics* in the late nineteenth and early twentieth centuries that this issue will be clarified theologically in anything approaching a clear or final way. As Bavinck writes in that work, "'Church,' as the people of God, must not be confused or identified with the eschatological notion of the kingdom of God. The kingdom is not organized on earth, the church is . . . and remains an object of faith . . . the church is in the process of becoming. The true and full measure of the church's identity is not achieved until the consummation."[11]

THE CANONS OF DORT

We conclude with a brief consideration of the controversial judicial ruling in 1618–1619 at the Dutch Reformed church's national synod meeting in the city of Dordrecht between the Calvinist position and that of Jacob Arminius and his followers following his death in 1610. Arminius, a theology professor at the University of Leiden, and his followers had questioned some of the Calvinist teachings related to election, the scope of Christ's atoning work, the extent of human depravity after the Fall, the efficacy of God's grace, and whether Christian believers could fall from God's electing grace. Each of these five points were addressed and a judicial ruling was made on each one. The Canons of Dort not only present the official Reformed teaching on each point of this controversy, but also counter the Arminian teachings at each step of the way. In the end, Arminius was ruled a heretic to the true Reformed faith.

We can observe the intimate connection in Reformed ecclesiology between election and membership in the church when the Canons state:

> This plan [of salvation], arising out of God's eternal love for his chosen ones [election], from the beginning of the world to the present time has been powerfully carried out and will also be carried out in the future, the gates of hell seeking vainly to prevail against it. As a result the chosen are gathered into one, all in their own time, and there is always a church of believers founded on Christ's blood, a church which steadfastly loves, persistently worships, and—here and in all eternity—praises him as her Savior who laid down his life for her on the cross, as a bridegroom for his bride. (2.9)

---

11. Bavinck, *Reformed Dogmatics*, 4:274.

Again, the themes are clearly present even sixty years after the drafting of the Belgic Confession: the church arises from God's electing grace which produces a Body united to Christ, a community which responds to God in praise and worship and mutual love, an institution which has always existed and will continue to exist until God's purposes are completed, thanks to God's faithful grace and love.

Bibliography

PRIMARY SOURCES BY ABRAHAM KUYPER

Kuyper, Abraham. *Asleep in Jesus*. Grand Rapids: Eerdmans, 1929.
———. "The Blurring of the Boundaries." In *Abraham Kuyper: A Centennial Reader*, edited by James D. Bratt, 363–402. Grand Rapids: Eerdmans, 1998.
———. "Calvinism: Source and Stronghold of our Constitutional Liberties." In *Abraham Kuyper: A Centennial Reader*, edited by James D. Bratt, 279–322. Grand Rapids: Eerdmans, 1998.
———. "Christ and the Needy." *Journal of Markets and Morality* 14.2 (2011) 647–83.
———. "Commentary on the Heidelberg Catechism Lord's Day 42." *Journal of Markets and Morality* 16.2 (2013) 713–57.
———. "Common Grace." In *Abraham Kuyper: A Centennial Reader*, edited by James D. Bratt, 165–201. Grand Rapids: Eerdmans, 1998.
———. "Confidentially." In *Abraham Kuyper: A Centennial Reader*, edited by James D. Bratt, 45–61. Grand Rapids: Eerdmans, 1998.
———. "Conservatism and Orthodoxy: False and True Preservation." In *Abraham Kuyper: A Centennial Reader*, edited by James D. Bratt, 65–85. Grand Rapids: Eerdmans, 1998.
———. *De Christus En De Sociale Nooden En Democratische Kippen*. Amsterdam: Wormser, 1895.
———. *De Gemeene Gratie*. Amsterdam: Höveker & Wormser, 1903.
———. *De Menschwording Gods Het Levensbeginsel Der Kerk*. 1867. Neo-Calvinism Research Institute. Online. https://sources.neocalvinism.org/kuyper/?ka_num=1867.06.
———. *Encyclopedia of Sacred Theology*. Translated by Hendrik de Vries. New York: Scribner's Sons, 1898.
———. "Heilsfeit En Heilswoord." In *Uit Het Woord: Stichtelijke Bijbelstudien*, 69–160. Amsterdam: H. De Hoogh & Co., 1873.
———. "It Shall Not Be So among You." In *Abraham Kuyper: A Centennial Reader*, edited by James D. Bratt, 125–40. Grand Rapids: Eerdmans, 1998.
———. *Lectures on Calvinism*. Grand Rapids: Eerdmans, 1943.

———. "Modernism: A Fata Morgana in the Christian Domain." In *Abraham Kuyper: A Centennial Reader*, edited by James D. Bratt, 87–124. Grand Rapids: Eerdmans, 1998.

———. *Nabij God Te Zijn: Meditatiën*. Kampen: J. H. Kok, 1908.

———. *Noah–Adam*. Translated by Nelson D. Kloosterman and Ed M. van der Maas. Edited by Jordan Ballor and Stephen Grabill. Vol. 1.1 of *Common Grace*. Grand Rapids: Christian's Library, 2013.

———. "Perfectionism." In *Abraham Kuyper: A Centennial Reader*, edited by James D. Bratt, 141–63. Grand Rapids: Eerdmans, 1998.

———. *The Problem of Poverty*. Edited by James W. Skillen. Translated by James W. Skillen. Grand Rapids: Baker, 1991.

———. *Rooted and Grounded: The Church as Organism and Institution*. Edited by Nelson D. Kloosterman. Translated by Nelson D. Kloosterman. Grand Rapids: Christian's Library, 2013.

———. *Sphere Sovereignty: A Public Address Delivered at the Inauguration of the Free University of Amsterdam*. Translated by George Kamps. Amsterdam: Free University of Amsterdam, 1880.

———. *Tractaat Van De Reformatie Der Kerken*. 1884. Neo-Calvinism Research Institute. Online. https://sources.neocalvinism.org/kuyper/?ka_num=1884.06.

———. "Uniformity: The Curse of Modern Life." In *Abraham Kuyper: A Centennial Reader*, edited by James D. Bratt, 19–44. Grand Rapids: Eerdmans, 1998.

———. "Wij, Calvinisten." In *Geen Vergeefs Woord; Verzamelde Deputaten-Redevoeringen*, translated by Harry Van Dyke, 139–53. Kampen: Kok, 1951.

———. *Wisdom and Wonder: Common Grace in Science and Art*. Edited by Jordan J. Ballor and Stephen J. Grabill. Translated by Nelson D. Kloosterman. Grand Rapids: Christian's Library, 2011.

———. *The Work of the Holy Spirit*. Translated by Henri De Vries. New York: Funk & Wagnalls, 1900.

SECONDARY SOURCES ON ABRAHAM KUYPER AND THE KUYPERIAN TRADITION

"Abraham Kuyper Bibliography." *Princeton Theological Seminary*. Online. https://kuyperbib.ptsem.edu.

Bacote, Vincent. "Abraham Kuyper's Rhetorical Public Theology with Implications for Faith and Learning." *Christian Scholar's Review* 37.4 (2008) 407–25.

———. "Beyond 'Faithful Presence': Abraham Kuyper's Legacy for Common Grace and Cultural Development." *Journal of Markets and Morality* 16.1 (2013) 195–205.

Bartholomew, Craig G. "Covenant and Creation: Covenant Overload Or Covenantal Deconstruction." *Calvin Theological Journal* 30 (1995) 11–33.

———. *Where Mortals Dwell: A Christian View of Place for Today*. Grand Rapids: Baker Academic, 2011.

Bartholomew, Craig G., and Michael W. Goheen. *The Drama of Scripture: Finding our Place in the Biblical Story*. Grand Rapids: Baker Academic, 2004.

Baskwell, Patrick. "Kuyper and Apartheid: A Revisiting." *HTS Teologiese Studies/ Theological Studies* 62.4 (2009) 1269–90.

Bavinck, Herman. *Reformed Dogmatics*. Grand Rapids: Baker Academic, 2003.

Beeke, Joel R. *Living for God's Glory: An Introduction to Calvinism.* Orlando: Reformation Trust, 2008.
Begbie, Jeremy. "Creation, Christ, and Culture in Dutch Neo-Calvinism." In *Christ in Our Place: The Humanity of God in Christ for the Reconciliation of the World: Essays Presented to Professor James Torrance,* edited by Trevor A. Hart and Daniel P. Thimell, 113–32. Exeter: Paternoster, 1989.
Berkhof, Hendrikus. *Christ and the Powers.* Translated by John Howard Yoder. Kitchener: Herald, 1977.
———. *Christ, the Meaning of History.* Richmond: John Knox, 1966.
———. *Christian Faith: An Introduction to the Study of the Faith.* Translated by Sierd Woudstra. Grand Rapids: Eerdmans, 1986.
———. *The Doctrine of the Holy Spirit: The Annie Kinkead Warfield Lectures, 1963–1964.* Richmond: John Knox, 1964.
———. *Two Hundred Years of Theology: Report of a Personal Journey.* Grand Rapids: Eerdmans, 1989.
Berkhof, Louis. *Systematic Theology.* Grand Rapids: Eerdmans, 1996.
Berkouwer, G. C. *The Church.* Translated by James E. Davison. Studies in Dogmatics. Grand Rapids: Eerdmans, 1976.
Biema, David van. "#3 the New Calvinism." *Time International* 173.11 (2009) 25.
Billings, J. Todd. "Calvin's Comeback?" *The Christian Century* 126.4 (2009) 22–25.
———. *The Word of God for the People of God: An Entryway to the Theological Interpretation of Scripture.* Grand Rapids: Eerdmans, 2010.
Bishop, Steve. "All of Life Redeemed." Online. www.allofliferedeemed.co.uk.
Bishop, Steve, and John H. Kok, eds. *On Kuyper: A Collection of Readings on the Life, Work & Legacy of Abraham Kuyper.* Sioux Center: Dordt College Press, 2013.
Boesak, Allan A. *Black and Reformed: Apartheid, Liberation, and the Calvinist Tradition.* Edited by Leonard Sweetman. Maryknoll, NY: Orbis, 1984.
———. "Theological Reflections on Empire." *HTS Tiologiese Studies/Theological Studies* 65.1 (2009) 645–51.
Bolt, John. "Church and World: A Trinitarian Perspective." *Calvin Theological Journal* 18.1 (1983) 5–31.
———. *A Free Church, A Holy Nation: Abraham Kuyper's American Public Theology.* Grand Rapids: Eerdmans, 2001.
———. "From Princeton to Wheaton: The Course of Neo-Calvinism in North America." *Calvin Theological Journal* 42 (2007) 65–89.
Boonstra, Harry. *Our School: Calvin College and the Christian Reformed Church.* Grand Rapids: Eerdmans, 2001.
Botha, Elaine M. *Socio-Kulturele Metavrae.* Amsterdam: Buijten en Schipperheijn, 1971.
Botman, H. Russell. "Is Blood Thicker Than Justice?" In *Religion, Pluralism, and Public Life: Abraham Kuyper's Legacy for the Twenty-First Century,* edited by Luis E. Lugo, 342–61. Grand Rapids: William B. Eerdmans, 2000.
Bratt, James D., ed. *Abraham Kuyper: A Centennial Reader.* Grand Rapids: Eerdmans, 1998.
———. "Abraham Kuyper, J. Gresham Machen, and the Dynamics of Reformed Anti-Modernism." *The Journal of Presbyterian History* 75.4 (1997) 247–58.
———. *Abraham Kuyper: Modern Calvinist, Christian Democrat.* Grand Rapids: Eerdmans, 2013.

———. *Dutch Calvinism in Modern America: A History of a Conservative Subculture*. Grand Rapids: Eerdmans, 1984.

———. "In the Shadow of Mt. Kuyper: A Survey of the Field." *Calvin Theological Journal* 31 (1996) 51–66.

———. "Kuyper's Legacy." *Twelve* (blog), January 18, 2014. Online. https://blog.reformedjournal.com/2014/01/18/kuypers-legacy.

———. "Passionate About the Poor: The Social Attitudes of Abraham Kuyper." *Journal of Markets and Morality* 5.1 (2002) 35–44.

———. "Raging Tumults of Soul: The Private Life of Abraham Kuyper." In *On Kuyper: A Collection of Readings on the Life, Work & Legacy of Abraham Kuyper*, edited by Steve Bishop and John H. Kok, 33–38. Sioux Center: Dordt College Press, 2013.

Brinkman, Martien E. "The Church as Sacrament of the Kingdom: A Reformed Commentary." *Exchange* 37 (2008) 497–507.

Calvin, John. *Institutes of the Christian Religion*. Edited by John T. McNeill. Translated by Ford Lewis Battles. Philadelphia: Westminster, 1960.

———. *Institutes of the Christian Religion*. 1541. French ed. Translated by Elsie Anne McKee. Grand Rapids: Eerdmans, 2009.

Chaplin, Jonathan. "The Concept of 'Civil Society' and Christian Social Pluralism." In *Politics, Religion, and Sphere Sovereignty*, edited by Gordon Graham, 14–33. Vol. 1 of *The Kuyper Center Review*. Grand Rapids: Eerdmans, 2010.

———. "'The Full Weight of Our Convictions': The Point of Kuyperian Pluralism." *Comment*, November 1, 2013. Online. http://www.cardus.ca/comment/article/4069.

———. "God and Globalization: I. Religion and the Powers of the Common Life." *Political Theology* 5.4 (2004) 493–500.

———. *Herman Dooyeweerd: Christian Philosopher of State and Civil Society*. Notre Dame: University of Notre Dame Press, 2011.

———. "Sphere Sovereignty and Canadian Public Life." *Cardus* (blog), December 22, 2010. Online. http://www.cardus.ca/policy/archives/2370.

———. "Subsidiarity: The Concept and the Connections." *Ethical Perspectives* 4.2 (1997) 117–30.

———. "Subsidiarity and Sphere Sovereignty: Catholic and Reformed Conceptions of the Role of the State." In *Things Old and New: Catholic Social Teaching Revisited*, edited by Francis P. McHugh and Samuel M. Natale, 175–202. New York: University Press of America, 1993.

Christian Reformed Church (CRC). *Belgic Confession*. 1561. Reformed Confessions Translation. 2011. Online. https://www.crcna.org/welcome/beliefs/confessions/belgic-confession.

———. *Ecumenical Creeds and Reformed Confessions*. Grand Rapids: CRC, 1987.

———. "History." Online. http://www.crcna.org/welcome/history#Abraham_Kuyper.

Clouser, Roy A. "A Blue Print for a Non-Reductionist Theory of Reality." Unpublished essay.

———. "A Critique of Historicism." *Critica* 21.85 (1997) 41–63.

———. *The Myth of Religious Neutrality: An Essay on the Hidden Role of Religious Beliefs in Theories*. Notre Dame: Notre Dame University Press, 1991.

———. "Puritanism on Authority." *Anakainosis: A Journal for Reformational Thought* 1.4 (1979) 18–19.

Dekker, Gerard, and George Harinck. "The Position of the Church as Institute in Society: A Comparison between Bonhoeffer and Kuyper." *The Princeton Seminary Bulletin* 28.1 (2007) 86–98.

Dennison, William D. "Dutch Neo-Calvinism and the Roots for Transformation: An Introductory Essay." *Journal of the Evangelical Theological Society* 42.2 (1999) 271–91.

DeYoung, Kevin, and Ted Kluck. *Why We Love the Church: In Praise of Institutions and Organized Religion*. Chicago: Moody, 2009.

Dooyeweerd, Herman. *A Christian Theory of Social Institutions* [Grondproblemen der wijsgerige sociologie]. Edited by John Witte Jr. Translated by Magnus Verbrugge. La Jolla: Herman Dooyeweerd Foundation, 1986.

———. *A New Critique of Theoretical Thought*. Translated by David H. Freeman and H. De Jongste. Philadelphia: Presbyterian and Reformed, 1957.

———. *Roots of Western Culture: Pagan, Secular, and Christian Options*. Edited by Mark Vander Vennen and Bernard Zylstra. Translated by John Kraay. Toronto: Wedge, 1979.

Dyke, Harry van. "Abraham Kuyper and the Continuing Social Question." *Journal of Markets and Morality* 14.2 (2011) 641–46.

———. "Abraham Kuyper: Heir of an Anti-Revolutionary Tradition." In *On Kuyper: A Collection of Readings on the Life, Work & Legacy of Abraham Kuyper*, edited by Steve Bishop and John H. Kok, 7–26. Sioux Center: Dordt College Press, 2013.

Eglinton, James. *Trinity and Organism: Towards a New Reading of Herman Bavinck's Organic Motif*. London: T&T Clark, 2012.

Garber, Steven. *The Fabric of Faithfulness: Weaving Together Belief and Behavior*. Downers Grove, IL: InterVarsity, 1996.

Garcia-Alonso, Marta. "Calvin and the Ecclesiastical Power of Jurisdiction." *Reformation and Renaissance Review* 10.2 (2008) 137–55.

Gelder, Craig van, ed. *Confident Witness—Changing World: Rediscovering the Gospel in North America*. Grand Rapids: Eerdmans, 1999.

———. *The Missional Church in Context: Helping Congregations Develop Contextual Ministry*. Grand Rapids: William B. Eerdmans, 2007.

Goheen, Michael W. "'As the Father Has Sent Me, I Am Sending You': J. E. Lesslie Newbigin's Missionary Ecclesiology." PhD diss., Universiteit Utrecht, 2000.

———. "'As the Father Has Sent Me, I Am Sending You': Lesslie Newbigin's Missionary Ecclesiology." *International Review of Mission* 91.362 (2002) 354–69.

———. *A Light to the Nations: The Missional Church and the Biblical Story*. Grand Rapids: Baker Academic, 2011.

Goheen, Michael W., and Craig G. Bartholomew. *Living at the Crossroads: An Introduction to Christian Worldview*. Grand Rapids: Baker Academic, 2008.

Goudzwaard, Bob. *Capitalism and Progress: A Diagnosis of Western Society*. Edited and Translated by Josina Van Nuis Zylstra. Grand Rapids: Eerdmans, 1979.

———. "Goals, Ways, and the Roots of Our Economic Crisis." *Koers—Bulletin for Christian Scholarship* 79.1 (2014). Online. http://dx.doi.org/10.4102/koers.v79i1.2158.

———. *Idols of our Time*. Sioux Center: Dordt College Press, 1984.

Goudzwaard, Bob, et al. *Beyond Poverty and Affluence: Toward an Economy of Care with a Twelve-Step Program for Economic Recovery*. Grand Rapids: Eerdmans, 1995.

———. *Hope in Troubled Times: A New Vision for Confronting Global Crises.* Grand Rapids: Baker Academic, 2007.

Gruchy, John W. de. "The Church Always Reforming." *The Princeton Seminary Bulletin* (1991) 154–85.

———. "The Church and the Struggle for South Africa." *Theology Today* 43.2 (1986) 229–43.

———. *Liberating Reformed Theology: A South African Contribution to an Ecumenical Debate.* Cape Town: David Philip, 1991.

Haas, Guenther. "Reformational Theology: A New Paradigm for Doing Dogmatics." *Calvin Theological Journal* 30.2 (1995) 501–6.

Hansen, Collin. "Young, Restless, Reformed." *Christianity Today* 50.9 (2006) 32–38.

Harinck, George. "Abraham Kuyper's Historical Understanding and Reformed Historiography." *Fides Et Historia* 37.1 (2005) 71–82.

———. "A Historian's Comment on the Use of Abraham Kuyper's Idea of Sphere Sovereignty." *Journal of Markets and Morality* 5.1 (2002) 277–84.

Harink, Douglas Karel. *Paul among the Postliberals: Pauline Theology Beyond Christendom and Modernity.* Grand Rapids: Brazos, 2003.

Heslam, Peter. *Creating a Christian Worldview: Abraham Kuyper's Lectures on Calvinism.* Grand Rapids: Eerdmans, 1998.

———. "Prophet of a Third Way: The Shape of Kuyper's Socio-Political Vision." *Journal of Markets and Morality* 5.1 (2002) 11–33.

Heuvel, Albert H. van den. *The Humiliation of the Church.* Philadelphia: Westminster, 1966.

———. *These Rebellious Powers.* New York: Friendship, 1965.

Hexham, Irving. "Dutch Calvinism and the Development of Afrikaner Nationalism." *African Affairs* 79.315 (1980) 195–208.

Heyns, Johan Adam. *The Church.* Translated by B. Roy Briggs. Pretoria, South Africa: N. G. Kerkboekhandel Transvaal, 1980.

Hofman, Tyman E. *The Canadian Story of the CRC: Its First Century.* Belleville: Guardian, 2004.

Holder, R. Ward. "Ecclesia, Legenda Atque Intelligenda Scriptura: The Church as Discerning Community in Calvin's Hermeneutic." *Calvin Theological Journal* 36 (2001) 270–89.

Holwerda, David E., ed. *Exploring the Heritage of John Calvin.* Grand Rapids: Baker, 1976.

Horton, Michael. *Christless Christianity: The Alternative Gospel of the American Church.* Grand Rapids: Baker, 2008.

———. *The Gospel-Driven Life: Being Good News People in a Bad News World.* Grand Rapids: Baker, 2009.

Keller, Timothy. *The Reason for God: Belief in an Age of Skepticism.* New York: Riverhead, 2008.

Kennedy, James C. "The Problem of Kuyper's Legacy: The Crisis of the Anti-Revolutionary Party in Post-War Holland." *Journal of Markets and Morality* 5.1 (2002) 45–56.

Koyzis, David T. "A Neocalvinist Ecclesiology." *Comment*, September 1, 2011. Online. https://www.cardus.ca/comment/article/a-neocalvinist-ecclesiology.

———. *We Answer to Another: Authority, Office, and the Image of God.* Eugene, OR: Pickwick, 2014.

Kromminga, John. *The Christian Reformed Church: A Study in Orthodoxy*. Grand Rapids: Baker, 1949.

Kuipers, Tjitze. *Abraham Kuyper: An Annotated Bibliography, 1857-2010*. Brill's Series in Church History 55. Boston: Brill, 2011.

Kuyper in De Caricatuur: 100 Uitgezochte Caricaturen: Met Een Brief van Dr. A. Kuyper. Baarn: Bosch & Keuning, 1920. Online. https://archive.org/details/kuyperindecaricaoobaar.

Lonkhuyzen, Jan van. "Abraham Kuyper—A Modern Calvinist." *Princeton Theological Review* (1921): 131-147.

Lugo, Luis E. "Foreword." In *Adding Cross to Crown: The Political Significance of Christ's Passion*, by Mark Noll, 7-12. Grand Rapids: Baker, 1996.

———, ed. *Religion, Pluralism, and Public Life: Abraham Kuyper's Legacy for the Twenty-First Century*. Grand Rapids: Eerdmans, 2000.

Machen, J. Gresham. *Christianity and Liberalism*. Grand Rapids: Eerdmans, 2009.

Marsden, George. "The State of Evangelical Christian Scholarship." *The Reformed Journal* 37.9 (1987) 12-16.

McGoldrick, James Edward. "Claiming Every Inch: The Worldview of Abraham Kuyper." In *On Kuyper: A Collection of Readings on the Life, Work & Legacy of Abraham Kuyper*, edited by Steve Bishop and John H. Kok, 97-106. Sioux Center: Dordt College Press, 2013.

McKim, Donald K., ed. *Encyclopedia of the Reformed Faith*. Louisville: Westminster John Knox, 1992.

McNeill, John T. "The Church in Post-Reformation Reformed Theology." *The Journal of Religion* 24.2 (1944) 96-107.

Middleton, J. Richard, and Brian J. Walsh. *Truth Is Stranger Than It Used To Be: Biblical Faith in a Postmodern Age*. London: Society for Promoting Christian Knowledge, 1995.

Molendijk, Arie L. "'A Squeezed Out Lemon Peel': Abraham Kuyper on Modernism." *Church History and Religious Culture* 91.3-4 (2011) 397-412.

———. "'Mine': The Rhetoric of Abraham Kuyper." *Journal for the History of Modern Theology* 15.2 (2008) 248-62.

———. "Neo-Calvinist Culture Protestantism: Abraham Kuyper's Stone Lectures." *Church History and Religious Culture* 88.2 (2008) 235-50.

Monsma, Steven. *Healing for a Broken World: Christian Perspectives on Public Policy*. Wheaton: Crossway, 2008.

Mouw, Richard J. *Abraham Kuyper: A Short and Personal Introduction*. Grand Rapids: Eerdmans, 2011.

———. *Calvinism in the Las Vegas Airport: Making Connections in Today's World*. Grand Rapids: Zondervan, 2004.

———. *The Challenges of Cultural Discipleship: Essays in the Line of Abraham Kuyper*. Grand Rapids: Eerdmans, 2012.

———. "Culture, Church, and Civil Society: Kuyper for a New Century." *The Princeton Seminary Bulletin* 28.1 (2007) 48-63.

———. "Learning from the Dutch Calvinist 'Splits.'" In *The Challenges of Cultural Discipleship: Essays in the Line of Abraham Kuyper*, 145-58. Grand Rapids: Eerdmans, 2012.

———. *Praying at Burger King*. Grand Rapids: Eerdmans, 2007.

———. "Remember the Antithesis!" *Books & Culture: A Christian Review*, March 6, 2009. Online. https://www.booksandculture.com/articles/2009/marapr/4.9.html.

———. "Some Reflections on Sphere Sovereignty." In *The Challenges of Cultural Discipleship: Essays in the Line of Abraham Kuyper*, by Richard J. Mouw, 33–57 Grand Rapids: Eerdmans, 2012.

———. *Uncommon Decency: Christian Civility in an Uncivilized World*. Downers Grove, IL: InterVarsity, 1992.

Muller, Richard. *Calvin and the Reformed Tradition: On the Work of Christ and the Order of Salvation*. Grand Rapids: Baker Academic, 2012.

Naugle, David K. *Worldview: The History of a Concept*. Grand Rapids: Eerdmans, 2002.

Noll, Mark A. *Adding Cross to Crown: The Political Significance of Christ's Passion*. Edited by Luis E. Lugo. Grand Rapids: Baker, 1996.

———. *Jesus Christ and the Life of the Mind*. Grand Rapids: Eerdmans, 2011.

Pennings, Ray. "The Whole and Heart of the Gospel." *Comment*, September 18, 2009. Online. http://www.cardus.ca/comment/article/1191/the-whole-and-heart-of-the-gospel.

Perry, John. "The Weight of Community: Alasdair MacIntyre, Abraham Kuyper, and the Problem of Public Theology in a Liberal Society." *Calvin Theological Journal* 39 (2004) 303–31.

Petry, Ray C. "Calvin's Conception of the 'Communio Sanctorum.'" *Church History* 5.3 (1936) 227–38.

Plantinga, Cornelius. *Engaging God's World: A Christian Vision of Faith, Learning, and Living*. Grand Rapids: Eerdmans, 2002.

Pronk, Cornelis. "F. M. Ten Hoor: Defender of Secession Principles Against Abraham Kuyper's Doleantie Views." ThM thesis, Calvin Theological Seminary, 1987.

Ridderbos, Herman N., and Richard B. Gaffin. *Redemptive History and the New Testament Scriptures. Biblical & Theological Studies*. 2nd rev. ed. Phillipsburg, NJ: Presbyterian and Reformed, 1988.

Riggs, John W. "Emerging Ecclesiology in Calvin's Baptismal Thought, 1536–1543." *Church History* 64.1 (1995) 29–43.

Schaap, James C. *Our Family Album: The Unfinished Story of the Christian Reformed Church*. Grand Rapids: CRC, 1998.

Schaeffer, Francis A. *How Should We Then Live? The Rise and Decline of Western Thought and Culture*. Old Tappan, NJ: Fleming H. Revell, 1976.

Skillen, James W. "The Development of Calvinistic Political Theory in the Netherlands, With Special Reference to the Thought of Herman Dooyeweerd." PhD diss., Duke University, 1993.

Skillen, James W., and Rockne McCarthy, eds. *Political Order and the Plural Structure of Society*. Emory University Studies in Law and Religion 2. Atlanta: Scholars, 1991.

Smit, Dirkie. "Trends and Directions in Reformed Theology." *The Expository Times* 122.7 (2011) 313–26.

Smit, Laura. "Developing a Calvinist Sacramental Theology." Unpublished essay.

Smith, James K. A. *After Modernity? Secularity, Globalization & the Re-Enchantment of the World*. Waco, TX: Baylor University Press, 2008.

———. *Desiring the Kingdom: Worship, Worldview, and Cultural Formation*. Grand Rapids: Baker Academic, 2009.

———. "The 'Ecclesial' Critique of Globalization: Rethinking the Questions." *Faith & Economics* 56 (2010) 5–19.

———. *Introducing Radical Orthodoxy: Mapping a Post-Secular Theology*. Grand Rapids: Baker Academic, 2004.

———. *Letters to a Young Calvinist: An Invitation to the Reformed Tradition*. Grand Rapids: Brazos, 2010.

———. *Who's Afraid of Postmodernism?: Taking Derrida, Lyotard, and Foucault to Church*. Grand Rapids: Baker Academic, 2006.

Spykman, Gordon. *Reformational Theology: A New Paradigm for Doing Dogmatics*. Grand Rapids: Eerdmans, 1992.

———. "Sphere-Sovereignty in Calvin and the Calvinist Tradition." In *Exploring the Heritage of John Calvin*, edited by David E. Holwerda, 163–208. Grand Rapids: Baker, 1976.

Synod of Dordrecht. "Church Order." 1618–1619. Online. https://www.sacred-texts.com/chr/nethord.htm.

Van Til, Kent A. "Subsidiarity and Sphere-Sovereignty: A Match Made in . . . ?" *Theological Studies* 69 (2008) 610–36.

Venema, Cornelis P. "Abraham Kuyper—Answering Criticisms of His Worldview." In *On Kuyper: A Collection of Readings on the Life, Work & Legacy of Abraham Kuyper*, edited by Steve Bishop and John H. Kok, 81–95. Sioux Center: Dordt College Press, 2013.

Vos, Geerhardus. *Biblical Theology: Old and New Testaments*. Edinburgh: Banner of Truth Trust, 1975.

Wagenman, Michael R. "Abraham Kuyper and the Church: From Calvin to the Neo-Calvinists." In *On Kuyper: A Collection of Readings on the Life, Work & Legacy of Abraham Kuyper*, edited by Steve Bishop and John H. Kok, 125–39. Sioux Center: Dordt College Press, 2013.

———. *Engaging the World with Abraham Kuyper*. Bellingham: Lexham, 2019.

Walsh, Brian J., and J. Richard Middleton. *The Transforming Vision: Shaping a Christian Worldview*. Downers Grove, IL: InterVarsity, 1984.

Warfield, B. B. "Calvinism." In *Basilica—Chambers*, edited by Samuel Macauley Jackson, 359–63. Vol. 2 of *The New Schaff-Herzog Encyclopedia of Religious Knowledge*. Grand Rapids: Baker, 1953.

Wells, Ronald A. "Until the Trumpet Blows: Getting Personal with Kuyper Under the Cross." *Books and Culture* 19.2 (2013) 25.

Westerhof, Karl. "The Church and the Exercise of Non-Ecclesiastical Power." *Network* (blog), November 19, 2013. Online. http://network.crcna.org/elders/church-and-exercise-non-ecclesiastical-power.

Witte, John, Jr. "Introduction." In *A Christian Theory of Social Institutions*, by Herman Dooyeweerd, 11–30. La Jolla: Herman Dooyeweerd Foundation, 1986.

Wolters, Albert M. "Creation and 'The Powers': A Dialogue with Leslie Newbigin." *Trinity Journal for Theology & Ministry* 4.2 (2010) 85–98.

———. *Creation Regained: Biblical Basics for a Reformational Worldview*. Grand Rapids: Eerdmans, 1985.

Wolterstorff, Nicholas. *Divine Discourse: Philosophical Reflections on the Claim That God Speaks*. Cambridge: Cambridge University Press, 1995.

———. *Hearing the Call: Liturgy, Justice, Church, and World*. Edited by Mark R. Gornik and Gregory Thompson. Grand Rapids: Eerdmans, 2011.

———. *The Mighty and the Almighty: An Essay in Political Theology*. Cambridge: Cambridge Unviersity Press, 2012.

———. *Until Justice and Peace Embrace: The Kuyper Lectures for 1981 Delivered at the Free University of Amsterdam*. Grand Rapids: Eerdmans, 1983.

Woltjer, R. H. *Dr. A. Kuyper in Jezus Ontslapen Den Achsten November 1920*. Baarn: E. J. Bosch, 1920. Online. http://archive.org/stream/drakuyperinjezusooverw/drakuyperinjezusooverw_djvu.txt.

Wood, John Halsey. "Church, Sacrament, and Society: Abraham Kuyper's Early Baptismal Theology, 1859–1874." *Journal of Reformed Theology* 2 (2008) 275–96.

———. *Going Dutch in the Modern Age: Abraham Kuyper's Struggle for a Free Church in the Nineteenth-Century Netherlands*. Oxford: Oxford University Press, 2013.

Zuidema, Jason, ed. *Reformational Thought in Canada: Essays in Honor of Theodore Plantinga*. Toronto: Clements Academic, 2010.

Zwaanstra, Henry. "Abraham Kuyper's Conception of the Church." *Calvin Theological Journal* 9 (1974) 149–81.

OTHER SOURCES

Acton Institute. "About." Online. https://www.acton.org/about.

Acton, John Emerich Edward Dalberg. "Introduction." In *Essays on Freedom and Power*, edited by Gertrude Himmelfarb, xv–lxvi. Glencoe, IL: Free Press, 1948.

Alexander, Jeffrey C. *The Dark Side of Modernity*. Cambridge: Polity, 2013.

Aquinas, Thomas. *Summa Theologica*. 1485. Translated by Fathers of the English Dominican Province. New York: Benziger Brothers, 1947. Online. http://www.ccel.org/ccel/aquinas/summa.toc.html.

Aristotle. *Metaphysics*. Translated by W. D. Ross. Online. http://classics.mit.edu/Aristotle/metaphysics.mb.txt.

Arrington, French L. *The Acts of the Apostles: An Introduction and Commentary*. Peabody, MA: Hendrickson, 1988.

Ashford, Bruce. *Theology and Practice of Mission: God, the Church, and the Nations*. Nashville: B&H, 2011.

Ashford, Bruce, and Keith Whitfield. "Theological Method: An Introduction to the Task of Theology." In *A Theology for the Church*, edited by Daniel L. Akin, 3–66. Nashville: B&H Academic, 2014.

Augustine. *City of God*. In vol. 2 of *Nicene and Post-Nicene Fathers of the Christian Church*, Series 1, edited by Philip Schaff, 1–511. 14 vols. Edinburgh: T&T Clark, 1885.

———. *Confessions*. In vol. 1 of *Nicene and Post-Nicene Fathers of the Christian Church*, Series 1, edited by Philip Schaff, 1–208. Edinburgh: T&T Clark, 1885.

———. *Handbook on Faith, Hope, and Love [Enchiridion]*. 420. Translated by Albert C. Outler. Online. http://www.ccel.org/ccel/augustine/enchiridion.

———. "Sermon 341." In *The Works of Saint Augustine: A Translation for the Twenty-First Century*, edited by John E. Rotelle, 19–29. Translated by Edmund Hill. New York: New City, 1995.

Aulén, Gustaf. *Christus Victor: An Historical Study of the Three Main Types of the Idea of the Atonement*. London: SPCK, 1970.

Ávila Arteaga, Mariano. "The Hermeneutics of the Fraternidad Teoloógica Latinoamericana on its Fortieth Anniversary: Still Towards a Latin American

Evangelical Contextual Hermeneutics." *Journal of Latin American Theology* 6.1 (2011) 38–85.
Avis, Paul. *Authority, Leadership, and Conflict in the Church.* Philadelphia: Trinity, 1992.
Badcock, Gary D. *The House Where God Lives: Renewing the Doctrine of the Church for Today.* Grand Rapids: Eerdmans, 2009.
Balserak, Jon. *Divinity Compromised: A Study of Divine Accommodation in the Thought of John Calvin.* Dordrecht: Springer, 2006.
Barclay, William. *The Acts of the Apostles.* Philadelphia: Westminster, 1979.
———. "Men and Affairs." *The Expository Times* 79.4 (1968) 128.
Barnes, Michel René. *The Power of God: Dunamis in Gregory of Nyssa's Trinitarian Theology.* Washington, DC: Catholic University of America Press, 2001.
Barrett, C. K. *A Critical and Exegetical Commentary on the Acts of the Apostles.* Edinburgh: T&T Clark, 1994.
Barth, Karl. *The Church and the Churches.* Grand Rapids: Eerdmans, 2005.
———. *Church Dogmatics.* Edited by G. W. Bromiley and T. F. Torrance. Translated by G. W. Bromiley. 12 vols. Peabody: Hendrickson, 1932.
———. *Learning Jesus Christ through the Heidelberg Catechism.* Translated by Shirley C. Guthrie. Grand Rapids: Eerdmans, 1964.
Bauckham, Richard. *The Theology of Jürgen Moltmann.* Edinburgh: T&T Clark, 1995.
Beiser, Frederick. "Historicism." In *The Oxford Handbook of Continental Philosophy,* edited by Brian Leiter and Michael Rosen, 155–79. Oxford: Oxford University Press, 2007.
Bender, Kimlyn J. *Karl Barth's Christological Ecclesiology.* Burlington: Ashgate, 2005.
Berkovic, Danijel. "The Church and the Bible: In the Context of the Correlative Relationships of Power and Authority." *Kairos: Evangelical Journal of Theology* 1.1 (2007) 81–105.
Bess, Philip. *Till We Have Built Jerusalem: Architecture, Urbanism, and the Sacred.* Wilmington, DE: ISI, 2006.
Bibby, Reginald W. *A New Day: The Resilience & Restructuring of Religion in Canada.* Lethbridge: Project Canada, 2012.
Boff, Leonardo. *Church: Charism and Power: Liberation Theology and the Institutional Church.* Translated by J. W. Diercksmeier. New York: Crossroad, 1985.
Bond, L. Susan. "Between Text and Sermon: Acts 10:34–43." *Interpretation* 56.1 (2002) 80–83.
Bonhoeffer, Dietrich. *The Cost of Discipleship.* New York: Touchstone, 1995.
———. *Ethics.* New York: Touchstone, 1995.
———. *Letters and Papers from Prison.* New York: Touchstone, 1997.
———. *Life Together.* San Francisco: HarperSanFrancisco, 1993.
Bosch, David J. *Transforming Mission: Paradigm Shifts in Theology of Mission.* Maryknoll, NY: Orbis, 1991.
Brown, Alexandra R. "The Gospel Takes Place: Paul's Theology of Power-in-Weakness in 2 Corinthians." *Interpretation* 52.3 (1998) 271–85.
Bruce, F. F. *Commentary on the Book of Acts: The English Text With Introduction, Exposition and Notes.* Grand Rapids: Eerdmans, 1968.
Brueggemann, John. "Negotiating the Meaning of Power and the Power of Meaning." *Theology Today* 63.4 (2007) 485–92.
Brueggemann, Walter. *The Prophetic Imagination.* Minneapolis: Fortress, 2004.

———. *Reality, Grief, Hope: Three Urgent Prophetic Tasks.* Grand Rapids: Eerdmans, 2014.

Brunner, Emil. *The Church in the New Social Order: An Address Delivered to the National Congress of the Free Church Federal Council, Cardiff, on March 26, 1952.* London: SCM, 1952.

———. *The Misunderstanding of the Church.* Translated by Harold Knight. Philadelphia: Westminster, 1953.

Buckley, James Joseph, and David S. Yeago. *Knowing the Triune God: The Work of the Spirit in the Practices of the Church.* Grand Rapids: Eerdmans, 2001.

Campenhausen, Hans von. *Ecclesiastical Authority and Spiritual Power in the Church of the First Three Centuries.* Stanford: Stanford University Press, 1969.

Canetti, Elias. *Crowds and Power [Masse und Macht].* Translated by Carol Stewart. Middlesex: Penguin, 1973.

Capon, Robert Farrar. *The Foolishness of Preaching: Proclaiming the Gospel Against the Wisdom of the World.* Grand Rapids: Eerdmans, 1998.

Caputo, John. *The Weakness of God: A Theology of the Event.* Bloomington: Indiana University Press, 2006.

The Catholic Church and the World Alliance of Reformed Churches. "The Church as Community of Common Witness to the Kingdom of God." 2007. Online. http://www.vatican.va/roman_curia/pontifical_councils/chrstuni/alliance-reform-docs/rc_pc_chrstuni_doc_20070124_third-phase-dialogue_en.html.

Cavanaugh, William T. *Migrations of the Holy: God, State, and the Political Meaning of the Church.* Grand Rapids: Eerdmans, 2011.

Chadwick, Owen. *Professor Lord Acton.* Grand Rapids: Acton Institute, 1995.

Chesterton, G. K. *What's Wrong with the World.* London: Cassell and Co., 1912.

Clegg, Stewart. *Frameworks of Power.* London: SAGE, 1989.

———. *Power, Rule, and Domination: A Critical and Empirical Understanding of Power in Sociological Theory and Organizational Life.* London: Routledge & Kegan Paul, 1975.

———. *The Theory of Power and Organization.* London: Routledge & Kegan Paul, 1979.

Côté, James E., and Anton L Allahar. *Lowering Higher Education: The Rise of Corporate Universities and the Fall of Liberal Education.* Toronto: University of Toronto Press, 2011.

Council of Trent. "Seventh Session." In *The Canons and Decrees of the Sacred and Oecumenical Council of Trent*, edited by James Waterworth, 53–66. London: Dolman, 1848.

Crouch, Andy. *Culture Making: Recovering our Creative Calling.* Downers Grove, IL: InterVarsity, 2008.

———. *Playing God: Redeeming the Gift of Power.* Downers Grove, IL: InterVarsity, 2013.

D'Costa, Gavin. *Theology in the Public Square: Church, Academy, and Nation.* Oxford: Blackwell, 2005.

Dibelius, Martin. *Studies in the Acts of the Apostles.* Edited by Heinrich Greeven. London: SCM, 1973.

Donovan, Vincent J. *Christianity Rediscovered.* Maryknoll, NY: Orbis, 1983.

Dulles, Avery. "The Church as 'One, Holy, Catholic, and Apostolic.'" *One in Christ* 35 (1999) 12–26.

———. *A Church to Believe in: Discipleship and the Dynamics of Freedom.* New York: Crossroad, 1982.
———. "The Church, Sacrament and Ground of Faith." In *Problems and Perspectives of Fundamental Theology*, edited by Rene Latourelle and Gerald O'Collins, 259–73. New York: Paulist, 1982.
———. *Dimensions of the Church: A Post Concilliar Reflection.* Westminster: Newman, 1967.
———. "A Half a Century of Ecclesiology." *Theological Studies* 50 (1989) 419–29.
———. *Models of the Church.* Garden City: Doubleday, 1974.
Eijk, Ton van. "Sacrament of the Kingdom of God." *Exchange* 37.4 (2008) 508–16.
Ellul, Jacques. *On Freedom, Love, and Power.* Edited by Willem H. VanderBurg. Translated by Willem H. VanderBurg. Toronto: University of Toronto Press, 2010.
———. *Presence of the Kingdom.* Translated by Olive Wyon. Colorado Springs: Helmers & Howard, 1989.
———. *The Technological Society.* Translated by John Wilkinson. New York: Vintage, 1964.
Fackre, Gabriel. "Ecumenism and Atonement: A Critical Issue in Ecclesiology." In *Critical Issues in Ecclesiology: Essays in Honor of Carl E. Braaten*, edited by Alberto L. Garcia and Susan K. Wood, 6–22. Grand Rapids: Eerdmans, 2011.
Fairclough, Norman. *Language and Power.* Essex: Pearson Education, 2001.
Farrow, Douglas. *Ascension and Ecclesia: On the Significance of the Doctrine of the Ascension for Ecclesiology and Christian Cosmology.* Grand Rapids: Eerdmans, 1999.
Fee, Gordon. "Baptism in the Holy Spirit: The Issue of Separability and Subsequence." *Pneuma: The Journal of the Study for Pentecostal Studies* 7.2 (1985) 87–99.
Ferguson, Everett. *Backgrounds of Early Christianity.* Grand Rapids: Eerdmans, 1987.
Fitzmyer, Joseph A. *The Acts of the Apostles: A New Translation with Introduction and Commentary.* Edited by William Foxwell Albright and David Noel Freedman. The Anchor Bible. New York: Doubleday, 1998.
Flannery, Austin, ed. *Vatican Council II: Constitutions, Decrees, Declarations.* Northport: Costello, 1996.
Foakes-Jackson, F. J. *The Acts of the Apostles.* London: Hodder and Stoughton, 1960.
Foucault, Michel. "Disciplinary Power and Subjection." In *Power*, edited by Steven Lukes, 229–42. Oxford: Basil Blackwell, 1986.
Friedman, Edwin. *Generation to Generation: Family Process in Church and Synagogue.* New York: Guilford, 2011.
Garcia, Alberto L., and Susan K. Wood, ed. *Critical Issues in Ecclesiology: Essays in Honor of Carl E. Braaten.* Grand Rapids: Eerdmans, 2011.
Gaventa, Beverly Roberts. *The Acts of the Apostles.* Edited by Victor Paul Furnish. Abingdon New Testament Commentaries. Nashville: Abingdon, 2003.
George, Timothy. "John Calvin: Comeback Kid." *Christianity Today* 53.9 (2009) 26–32.
Gils, Pieterjan, and Arnout van Vaerenbergh. "Z-OUT." *Gijs Van Vaerenbergh.* Online. http://gijsvanvaerenbergh.com/z-out.
Gonzalez, Justo L. *Acts: The Gospel of the Spirit.* Maryknoll, NY: Orbis, 2001.
Gorman, Michael J. *Reading Revelation Responsibly: Uncivil Worship and Witness, Following the Lamb into the New Creation.* Eugene, OR: Cascade, 2011.
Grabowski, Stanislaus J. *The Church: An Introduction to the Theology of St. Augustine.* London: Herder, 1957.

Greenman, Jeffrey P., et al. *Understanding Jacques Ellul.* Eugene, OR: Cascade, 2012.

Gregory the Great. *Against Eunomius.* In vol. 5 of *Nicene and Post-Nicene Fathers of the Christian Church*, Series 2, edited by Philip Schaff. 1885. Online. http://www.ccel.org/ccel/schaff/npnf205.viii.i.i.html.

Grundmann, W. "Dunamai." In vol. 2 of *Theological Dictionary of the New Testament*, edited by Gerhard Kittel and Gerhard Friedrich Kittel, 295–313. Grand Rapids: Eerdmans, 1979.

Guder, Darrell L. *The Continuing Conversion of the Church.* Grand Rapids: Eerdmans, 2000.

———. *The Incarnation and the Church's Witness.* Christian Mission and Modern Culture Series. Harrisburg, PA: Trinity, 1999.

Guder, Darrell L., and Lois Barrett. *Missional Church: A Vision for the Sending of the Church in North America.* Grand Rapids: Eerdmans, 1998.

Habermas, Jürgen. "Hannah Arendt's Communications Concept of Power." *Social Research* 44.1 (1977) 3–24.

———. "Religion in the Public Sphere." *European Journal of Philosophy* 14.1 (2006) 1–25.

Hall, Douglas John. *The End of Christendom and the Future of Christianity.* Eugene, OR: Wipf and Stock, 2002.

———. "Metamorphosis: From Christendom to Diaspora." In *Confident Witness—Changing World: Rediscovering the Gospel in North America*, edited by Craig van Gelder, 67–79. Grand Rapids: Eerdmans, 1999.

———. *Waiting for Gospel: An Appeal to the Dispirited Remnants of Protestant "Establishment."* Eugene, OR: Wipf and Stock, 2012.

Hamill, Bruce. "Beyond Ecclesiocentricity: Navigating Between the Abstract and the Domesticated in Contemporary Ecclesiology." *International Journal of Systematic Theology* 14.3 (2012) 277–94.

Handy, David Allan. "The Gentile Pentecost: A Literary Study of the Story of Peter and Cornelius (Acts 10:1—11:18)." PhD diss., Union Theological Seminary, 1998.

Harink, Douglas Karel. *Paul Among the Postliberals: Pauline Theology Beyond Christendom and Modernity.* Grand Rapids: Brazos, 2003.

Hart, D. G. "Church Not State." *American Conservative* 11.2 (2012) 32.

Hauerwas, Stanley. *In Good Company: The Church as Polis.* Notre Dame: University of Notre Dame Press, 1995.

Hauerwas, Stanley, and William H. Willimon. *Resident Aliens: Life in the Christian Colony.* Nashville: Abingdon, 1989.

Hermann, Arnold. *To Think Like God: Pythagoras and Parmenides, the Origins of Philosophy.* Las Vegas: Parmenides, 2004.

Himmelfarb, Gertrude. *Lord Acton: A Study in Conscience and Politics.* Richmond: Institute for Contemporary Studies, 1993.

———. *The Roads to Modernity: The British, French, and American Enlightenments.* New York: Alfred A. Knopf, 2004.

Hippocrates. *On Ancient Medicine.* Translated by Francis Adams. Online. http://classics.mit.edu/Hippocrates/ancimed.mb.txt.

Hippolytus. *Against Noetus.* In vol. 5 of *Ante-Nicene Fathers*, edited by Alexander Roberts, et al. Translated by J.H. MacMahon. Buffalo, NY: Christian Literature, 1886. Online. http://www.newadvent.org/fathers/0521.htm.

Hughes, Philip Edgcumbe, ed. *Creative Minds in Contemporary Theology: A Guidebook to the Principal Teachings of Karl Barth, G. C. Berkouwer, Emil Brunner, Rudolf Bultmann, Oscar Cullmann, James Denney, C. H. Dodd, Herman Dooyeweerd, P. T. Forsyth, Charles Gore, Reinhold Niebuhr, Pierre Teilhard De Chardin, and Paul Tillich*. Grand Rapids: Eerdmans, 1966.

Hunter, James Davison. *To Change the World: The Irony, Tragedy, & Possibility of Christianity in the Late Modern World*. Oxford: Oxford University Press, 2010.

Hütter, Reinhard. *Suffering Divine Things: Theology as Church Practice*. Grand Rapids: Eerdmans, 2000.

Ineson, Emma Gwynneth. "Language and Authority in Christian Worship." PhD diss., University of Birmingham, 1998.

Jinkins, Michael. *The Church Faces Death: Ecclesiology in a Post-Modern Context*. Oxford: Oxford University Press, 1999.

———. "Unintended Consequences: Schism and Calvin's Ecclesiology." *Theology Today* 66 (2009) 217–33.

John Paul II. *Crossing the Threshold of Hope*. Edited by Vittorio Messori. Translated by Jenny McPhee and Martha McPhee. New York: Alfred A. Knopf, 1994.

Johnson, Allan G. *Privilege, Power, and Difference*. New York: McGraw-Hill, 2006.

Johnson, Luke Timothy. *Prophetic Jesus, Prophetic Church: The Challenge of Luke-Acts to Contemporary Christians*. Grand Rapids: Eerdmans, 2011.

Johnson, Phillip E. "The Swedish Syndrome." *First Things*, December 1993. Online. http://www.firstthings.com/article/1993/12/002-the-swedish-syndrome.

Karkkainen, Veli-Matti. *An Introduction to Ecclesiology: Ecumenical, Historical, and Global Perspectives*. Downers Grove, IL: InterVarsity, 2002.

Katongole, Emmanuel. *The Sacrifice of Africa: A Political Theology for Africa*. Grand Rapids: Eerdmans, 2011.

Kearsley, Roy. *Church, Community, and Power*. Surrey: Ashgate, 2008.

Kelly, Matthew J. "Aquinas on Power." *Thomist: A Speculative Quarterly Review* 43.3 (1979) 474–79.

Kim, Young C. "Authority: Some Conceptual and Empirical Notes." *The Western Political Quarterly* 19.2 (1966) 223–34.

Kinnamon, David. *UnChristian: What a New Generation Really Thinks About Christianity . . . and Why it Matters*. Grand Rapids: Baker, 2007.

———. *You Lost Me: Why Young Christians Are Leaving Church . . . and Rethinking Faith*. Grand Rapids: Baker, 2011.

Küng, Hans. *The Church*. New York: Sheed & Ward, 1968.

Leahy, Brendan. "'Christ Existing as Community': Dietrich Bonhoeffer's Notion of Church." *Irish Theological Quarterly* 73.1–2 (2008) 32–59.

Leeuw, Geerhardus van der. *Religion in Essence and Manifestation [Phanomenologie der Religion]*. Translated by J. E. Turner. New York: Harper & Row, 1963.

Legge, Marilyn J. "The Church in Solidarity: Liberation Ecclesiology." In *Liberation Theology: An Introductory Reader*, edited by Curt Cadorette et al., 159–69. Maryknoll, NY: Orbis, 1992.

Leo XIII. *Rerum Novarum*. Encyclical delivered May 15, 1891. Online. http://w2.vatican.va/content/leo-xiii/en/encyclicals/documents/hf_l-xiii_enc_15051891_rerum-novarum.html.

Lindsay, D. Michael. *Faith in the Halls of Power: How Evangelicals Joined the American Elite*. Oxford: Oxford University Press, 2008.

Lukes, Steven, ed. *Power*. Oxford: Basil Blackwell, 1986.

———. *Power: A Radical View*. Hampshire: Palgrave Macmillan, 2005.

Luther, Martin. *The Bondage of the Will*. Translated by Edward Thomas Vaughan. London: Paternoster, 1823.

Lynch, Chloe. "How Convincing Is Walter Wink's Interpretation of Paul's Language of the Powers?" *Evangelical Quarterly* 83.3 (2011) 251–66.

Macaulay, Thomas Babington. "Influence of the Church of Rome." *Christian Secretary*, March 15, 1850. 4.

Mackey, James. *Power and Christian Ethics*. Cambridge: Cambridge University Press, 1994.

Malas, William H. "The Literary Structure of Acts: A Narratological Investigation into Its Arrangement, Plot, and Primary Themes." PhD diss., Union Theological Seminary, 2001.

Marks, Darren C., ed. *Shaping a Global Theological Mind*. Hampshire: Ashgate, 2008.

Milbank, John. "Stale Expressions: The Management-Shaped Church." *Studies in Christian Ethics* 21.1 (2008) 117–28.

Moltmann, Jürgen. *The Church in the Power of the Spirit: A Contribution to Messianic Ecclesiology*. Minneapolis: Fortress, 1993.

———. *The Crucified God: The Cross of Christ as the Foundation and Criticism of Christian Theology*. Minneapolis: Fortress, 1993.

Newbigin, Leslie. *Foolishness to the Greeks: The Gospel and Western Culture*. Grand Rapids: Eerdmans, 1986.

———. *The Gospel in a Pluralistic Society*. Grand Rapids: Eerdmans, 1989.

———. *Sign of the Kingdom*. Grand Rapids: Eerdmans, 1981.

———. *Truth to Tell: The Gospel as Public Truth*. Grand Rapids: Eerdmans, 1991.

Novum Testamentum Graece. 27th ed. Stuttgart: Deutsche Bibelgesellschft, 1979.

O'Brien, John. "Ecclesiology as Narrative." *Ecclesiology* 4.2 (2008) 148–65.

O'Donovan, Oliver. *The Desire of the Nations: Rediscovering the Roots of Political Theology*. Cambridge: Cambridge University Press, 1996.

Origen. *De Principiis*. In vol. 4 of *Ante-Nicene Fathers*, edited by Alexander Roberts et al. Translated by Frederick Crombie. Buffalo, NY: Christian Literature, 1886. Online. http://www.ccel.org/ccel/schaff/anf04.vi.v.i.html.

Orr, James. *The Christian View of God and the World as Centering in the Incarnation*. New York: A. D. F. Randolph, 1893.

———. "The Value of the Idea of the Kingdom of God." *The Biblical World* 25.3 (1905) 196–200.

Padilla, C. Rene. *Mission Between the Times: Essays on the Kingdom*. Grand Rapids: Eerdmans, 1985.

"Pastor Arrested for Raping His Faithfuls After Convincing Them That His Eggplant Contained 'Sacred Milk.'" *News Chronicle*, September 3, 2015. Online. https://thenews-chronicle.com/pastor-arrested-for-raping-his-faithfuls-after-convincing-them-that-his-eggplant-contained-sacred-milk.

Penner, James, et al. *Hemorrhaging Faith: Why and When Canadian Young Adults Are Leaving, Staying, and Returning to Church*. Toronto: Evangelical Fellowship of Canada Youth and Young Adult Ministry Roundtable, 2011.

Percy, Martyn. *Words, Wonders and Power: Understanding Contemporary Christian Fundamentalism and Revivalism*. London: SPCK, 1996.

Pervo, Richard I. *Acts: A Commentary*. Hermeneia. Edited by Harold W. Attridge. Minneapolis: Fortress, 2009.

Piper, John. *The Future of Justification: A Response to N. T. Wright*. Wheaton: Crossway, 2007.

Pius XI. *Quadragesimo Anno*. Encyclical delivered May 15, 1931. Online. http://w2.vatican.va/content/pius-xi/en/encyclicals/documents/hf_p-xi_enc_19310515_quadragesimo-anno.html.

Plato. *Theaetetus*. 360. Translated by Benjamin Jowett. Online. http://classics.mit.edu/Plato/theatu.html.

Pohl, Christine D. *Living into Community: Cultivating Practices That Sustain Us*. Grand Rapids: Eerdmans, 2012.

Rahner, Karl. *The Church and the Sacraments*. Freiburg: Herder, 1963.

———. *Theological Investigations*. 23 vols. Baltimore: Helicon 1961–1979.

———. "The Theology of Power." In *More Recent Writings*, by Karl Rahner, 391–409. Translated by Kevin Smyth. Vol. 4 of *Theological Investigations*. Baltimore: Helicon, 1966.

———. "What Is a Sacrament?" *Worship* 47 (1973) 274–84.

Ratiner, Tracie. *Encyclopedia of World Biography*. 2nd ed. Gale Virtual Reference Library. Detroit: Thomson Gale, 2005.

Ratzinger, Joseph. *Principles of Catholic Theology: Building Stones for a Fundamental Theology*. Translated by Mary Frances McCarthy. San Francisco: Ignatius, 1987.

Reno, R. R. "Religious Freedom." *First Things* 240 (2014) 7.

Richardson, Alan, and John Stephen Bowden. *A New Dictionary of Christian Theology*. London: SCM, 1983.

Roscigno, Vincent J. "Power, Revisited." *Social Forces* 90.2 (2011) 349.

Runcie, Robert. *Authority in Crisis?: An Anglican Response*. London: SCM, 1988.

Sanks, Howland T. "Liberation Ecclesiology: Praxis, Theory, Praxis." *Theological Studies* 38.1 (1977) 3–38.

Schaff, Philip, ed. *The History of Creeds*. Vol. 1 of *Creeds of Christendom*. New York: Harper & Brothers, 1919.

Simon, Yves. *A General Theory of Authority*. Notre Dame: University of Notre Dame Press, 1962.

———. *Nature and Functions of Authority*. Milwaukee: Marquette University Press, 1948.

Smith, Christian. *Souls in Transition: The Religious and Spiritual Lives of Emerging Adults*. Oxford: Oxford University Press, 2009.

———. *Soul Searching: The Religious and Spiritual Lives of American Teenagers*. Oxford: Oxford University Press, 2005.

Smith, David W. *Transforming the World?: The Social Impact of British Evangelism*. Milton Keynes. Paternoster, 1998.

"Spurgeon, Charles Haddon." In *Son of Man—Tremellius*, edited by Samuel Macauley Jackson, 57–58. Vol. 11 of *New Schaff-Herzog Encyclopedia of Religious Knowledge*. Grand Rapids: Baker, 1953.

Stackhouse, John G. *Evangelical Ecclesiology: Reality Or Illusion?* Grand Rapids: Baker Academic, 2003.

Stockwell, Clinton. "Cathedrals of Power: Engaging the Powers in Urban North America." In *Confident Witness—Changing World: Rediscovering the Gospel in North America*, edited by Craig van Gelder, 80–93. Grand Rapids: Eerdmans, 1999.

Stott, John. *The Living Church: Convictions of a Lifelong Pastor.* Downers Grove, IL: InterVarsity, 2007.
Streufert, Mary J. "An Affinity for Difference: A Theology of Power." *Currents in Theology and Mission* 37.1 (2010) 28–39.
Sykes, Stephen. *The Identity of Christianity: Theologians and the Essence of Christianity from Schliermacher to Barth.* Minneapolis: Fortress, 1984.
———. *Power and Christian Theology.* London: Continuum, 2006.
———. *Unashamed Anglicanism.* Nashville: Abingdon, 1995.
Temple, William. *Christianity and Social Order.* New York: Seabury, 1977.
Tracy, Thomas F. *God, Action, and Embodiment.* Grand Rapids: Eerdmans, 1984.
Thompson, Daniel Speed. "The Church as Sacrament: Schillebeeckx's Contributions to the Construction of a Critical Ecclesiology." *Religious Studies and Theology* 17.1 (1998) 33–45.
Tillich, Paul. *Love, Power, and Justice: Ontological Analyses and Ethical Applications.* New York: Oxford University Press, 1966.
Veith, Gene Edward. *Postmodern Times: A Christian Guide to Contemporary Thought and Culture.* Wheaton: Crossway, 1994.
Ven, Johannes A. van der. *Ecclesiology in Context.* Grand Rapids: Eerdmans, 1993.
Volf, Miroslav. *A Public Faith: How Followers of Christ Should Serve the Common Good.* Grand Rapids: Brazos, 2011.
Walaskay, Paul R. *Acts.* Westminster Bible Companion Series. Louisville: Westminster John Knox, 1998.
Wall, Robert W. *The Acts of the Apostles: Introduction, Commentary, and Reflections.* Vol. 10 of *The New Interpreter's Bible: A Commentary in Twelve Volumes.* Nashville: Abingdon, 2002.
Ward, Graham. *The Politics of Discipleship: Becoming Postmaterial Citizens.* Grand Rapids: Baker Academic, 2009.
Watson, David Lowes. "Salt to the World: An Ecclesiology of Liberation." *Missiology* 12.4 (1984) 453–76.
Weber, Max. *The Protestant Ethic and the Spirit of Capitalism.* Translated by Talcott Parsons. London: George Allen & Unwin, 1976.
———. *The Theory of Social and Economic Organization.* Edited by Talcott Parsons. Translated by A. M. Henderson and Talcott Parsons. Oxford: Oxford University Press, 1947.
———. *The Vocation Lectures.* Edited by David Owen and Tracy B. Strong. Indianapolis: Hackett, 2004.
Webster, John. *The Grace of Truth.* Farmington Hills: Oil Lamp, 2011.
———. *Holy Scripture: A Dogmatic Sketch.* Cambridge: Cambridge University Press, 2003.
———. "On Evangelical Ecclesiology." *Ecclesiology* 1.1 (2004) 9–35.
———. "Purity and Plenitude: Evangelical Reflections on Congar's Tradition and Traditions." *International Journal of Systematic Theology* 7.4 (2005) 399–413.
Wells, David F. *Above All Earthly Pow'rs: Christ in a Postmodern World.* Grand Rapids: Eerdmans, 2005.
———. *The Courage to Be Protestant: Truth-Lovers, Marketers, and Emergents in the Postmodern World.* Grand Rapids: Eerdmans, 2008.
———. *God in the Wasteland: The Reality of Truth in a World of Fading Dreams.* Grand Rapids: Eerdmans, 1994.

———. "Reformational Theology: A New Paradigm for Doing Dogmatics." *Theology Today* 50.1 (1993) 136–38.
Wells, Ronald A. "Until the Trumpet Blows: Getting Personal with Kuyper Under the Cross." *Books and Culture* 19.2 (2013) 25.
Willer, David E. "Max Weber's Missing Authority Type." *Sociological Inquiry* 37.2 (1967) 231–40.
Willimon, William H. *Acts.* Interpretation: A Bible Commentary for Teaching and Preaching. Atlanta: John Knox, 1988.
Wink, Walter. *Engaging the Powers: Discernment and Resistance in a World of Domination.* Minneapolis: Fortress, 1992.
———. *Naming the Powers: The Language of Power in the New Testament.* Philadelphia: Fortress, 1984.
———. *Unmasking the Powers: The Invisible Forces that Determine Human Existence.* Philadelphia: Fortress, 1986.
Wolin, Sheldon S. "On the Theory and Practice of Power." In *After Foucault: Humanistic Knowledge, Postmodern Challenges*, edited by Jonathan Arac, 179–201. New Brunswick, NJ: Rutgers University Press, 1988.
Wood, James E., Jr. "A Theology of Power." *Journal of Church and State* 107.14 (1972) 107–24.
Wright, N. T. *Jesus and the Victory of God.* Vol. 2 of *Christian Origins and the Question of God.* Minneapolis: Fortress, 1996.
———. *Justification: God's Plan and Paul's Vision.* Downers Grove, IL: IVP Academic, 2009.
———. *The Last Word: Scripture and the Authority of God—Getting Beyond the Bible Wars.* New York: HarperSanFrancisco, 2005.
———. *The New Testament and the People of God.* Vol. 1 of *Christian Origins and the Question of God.* Minneapolis: Fortress, 1992.
Yong, Amos. "Radically Orthodox, Reformed, and Pentecostal: Rethinking the Intersection of Post/Modernity and the Religions in Conversation with James K. A. Smith." *Journal of Pentecostal Theology* 15.2 (2007) 233–50.

Index

Abuse of power (church), xiii, 3, 6, 11–13, 23, 47–48, 63, 131, 138, 141, 177, 202–3, 212, 259, 266, 270, 273, 275
Acton, Lord Emerich Edward Dalberg, 28, 74, 183
Acts, 10 26, 204–220, 224–25, 276
Anabaptist, 6, 8, 274
Anti-Revolutionary Party (ARP), xi, 10, 76, 78, 81–82, 105, 138–39, 282–88, 290–91, 293–95
Antithesis, 52, 116, 136, 139, 194, 218, 224, 285
Apartheid (South Africa), 184–86
Aquinas, Thomas, 38–41
"architechtonic critique," 112, 221, 276
Aristotle, 31–35, 39
Arminius, Jacob, 306
Authority, 7–9, 19–23, 39, 42–44, 47–48, 50, 55, 56–60, 62–67, 70, 73, 77, 86, 92–94, 98, 108–17, 119, 122, 124, 128, 132–34, 142–43, 145–46, 148, 158, 163, 165, 172, 174, 176, 187–88, 193, 204, 209–10, 212, 223, 132–32, 260, 274, 297–98, 301
Avis, Paul, 43, 48, 223

Badcock, Gary, 26, 169–70, 263, 266–67

Barth, Karl, 7, 155, 194, 201–2, 204, 219, 234
Bartholomew, Craig, 86, 109, 129, 135, 153, 254
Bavinck, Herman, 85, 90, 92, 105, 128, 171, 174, 291, 306
Bavinck, J. H., 105
Beesd, 98, 280
Belgic Confession, 167, 263, 297–302, 305, 307
Berkhof, Hendrikus, 46, 63, 98, 116, 248, 251, 304–5
Berkhof, Louis, 86
Berkouwer, G. C., 85, 105
Bess, Phillip, 253–54, 256
Bibby, Reginald, 4
de Bres, Guido, 298
Bosch, David, 116, 118, 249–51
Botman, H. Russel, 184–86, 189, 273

Calvin, John, 38, 41–43, 76, 79, 87, 92, 100, 120, 124, 156, 163–66, 183, 201, 227, 258, 279–80, 298–301
Calvinism, ix, 10, 14–15, 21, 23, 43, 55, 68, 75–80, 82–85, 87, 89, 92, 95, 98, 105–6, 110, 119–21, 124, 132–33, 145, 159, 161, 164, 168, 175, 179–80, 181, 183–84, 227, 287, 289, 297, 302, 304, 306

INDEX

Canada 4–5, 47, 81–82, 85
Canons of Dort, 297, 306–7
Congar, Yves, 235
Caputo, John, 189–92, 199, 218, 224–25, 246, 254
Chaplin, Jonathan, 41, 85, 92, 113–14, 124–25, 127–33, 141, 145, 153, 155–56, 159, 165
Chesterton, G. K., 272
Chicago, 108–9
Christian Labour Association of Canada, 85
Christian Reformed Church in North America, 85–86, 170, 297
Christocentrism/Christocentric, 13–15, 55, 157, 159, 176, 204, 239, 241–43, 259–60, 271
Civil society, 16–17, 21, 76, 91, 93–94, 123, 127, 133, 146, 152, 172, 180, 186, 230, 259–62, 297, 303
Clouser, Roy, 88–89, 92, 150, 154–55, 187–89
Coercion/coercive, 8, 29, 45–46, 48–50, 52–53, 56–57, 61, 64, 68, 73, 111–12, 125, 127–28, 136, 163, 177–78, 180, 183, 188–92, 194, 197–201, 203–5, 214, 217–20, 225, 260, 267, 269–71, 274, 276
Common Grace, 16, 18, 28, 101, 126, 148, 155, 166, 170–72, 259–61, 291
Common grace, 17, 139, 152, 159–60, 257–58, 260
Communication, 45, 192–193, 199–203, 227
Constantine/Constantinian, 5, 6, 97, 147, 163, 172, 182–83, 275
Council of Trent (1545–1563), 235

Derrida, Jacques, 191
Διάβολος (*diabolos*), 209–14, 216–19
Dolientie, 98
Dooyeweerd, Herman, 78, 92, 94, 123, 125, 128, 137, 145–47, 153–56, 165, 219
Dualism, 49–50, 112, 135–136, 139, 153, 169, 171, 176, 257, 270, 272

Dulles, Avery Cardinal, 84, 227, 229, 232–40, 242–47, 250
Δύναμις (*dunamis*), 30–31, 46, 210, 212–15
Dutch Reformed Church of South Africa, 184–86

Ecumenical, xiv, 26, 87, 105, 189, 249, 257
Election, 14, 100–101, 155–156, 160–161, 164, 197, 306
Ellul, Jacques, 26, 53, 112, 179, 192–205, 218–25, 248, 264, 270
Enlightenment, ix, xiv, 5, 9, 20, 56, 60, 71, 84, 115–19, 147, 179, 222, 230
Enlightenment (British), 221–22
Eschatology/Eschatological/Eschaton, 55, 116, 136, 178, 204, 211, 213–14, 218, 223–24, 237–38, 240, 242–43, 255, 274, 306
Evangelical Fellowship of Canada, 4

Fall (fallen), ix, 50–54, 63, 88, 95, 127, 135–136, 138, 142, 145, 147, 159–160, 174–175, 177, 181, 194–198, 204, 214, 219–220, 248, 253, 255, 257, 261, 263–264, 267, 271, 274, 277, 306
Foucault, Michel, 65, 68–72
Free University of Amsterdam (VU), 10, 19, 76, 79–82, 92, 112, 163, 221, 285–89, 292–93
French Revolution, 114–15, 118, 124, 162, 231

Gijs, Pieterjan ("Reading Between the Lines"), 1, 4, 266, 275
Gereformeerde Kerken Nederland (GKN), 11, 13, 16, 80, 95, 97–98, 105, 287–88, 297
Goheen, Michael, 86, 135, 172–73, 251–52
Gorman, Michael, 267
Gregory the Great, 36–37

Hall, Douglas John, 173–74, 220
Hauerwas, Stanley, 6, 196, 221

Heidelberg Catechism, 139, 167, 288, 297, 301-6
Heir of Redclyffe, 98, 280
Hellenism/Hellenistic, 210
Himmelfarb, Gertrude, 80, 221-22
Hippocrates, 32-33
Hippolytus of Rome, 34-36
Hunter, James Davison, 5, 6, 183

Ideology/ideological, 6, 18, 21, 29, 45, 48, 84, 105, 115, 119, 121, 126, 136, 182, 200, 230, 232, 274-75
Incarnation(al), 37-38, 89-91, 94, 100, 157-158, 160, 193, 198, 204, 218, 221-223, 225-226, 236, 239-240, 242, 245, 249, 253, 255, 257, 259-260, 265, 267, 271, 275
Institute for Christian Studies (Toronto), 85
Institutes of the Christian Religion, 15, 38, 41-42, 76, 92, 100, 156, 165, 300-301
Institutional (mode of church), ix, xiii-xiv, 12, 15, 16, 17, 18, 21, 24-25, 26, 29, 39, 41-43, 47, 48, 67, 88-104, 106-7, 117, 129, 143, 144-45, 148-66, 168-75, 177, 179-80, 181, 198-99, 201, 205-6, 217-18, 221, 223-25, 227-28, 230-31, 233-34, 238-65, 267-77, 299-300, 302, 307
International Roman Catholic-Reformed Dialogue, 249, 255, 257
Invitation (Latin: *vocare*), 190-92, 196, 199-204, 213-14, 218-20, 222, 254, 264-65, 267-68, 270-71, 274-76
Irenaeus, 172
Islam, 68, 292

Johnson, Luke Timothy, 205, 211-13
Justice, ix, 7, 51, 96, 100, 112, 125, 129, 131, 151, 168-71, 173-75, 177, 180, 188-89, 204, 216, 221, 223-24, 249, 258-62, 264-65, 267, 270-71, 273-74, 276

Kenosis/Kenotic, 53-55, 204, 220-23, 225-26, 249, 254-55, 259, 265, 267, 271, 275
Kerygma/kerygmatic, 144, 157, 169, 172, 174-81, 186-92, 195, 198, 201, 203-6, 208-10, 212-24, 227-28, 234, 247-49, 255-56, 258-65, 267, 270-71, 274-77
Keys (of the Kingdom) 8, 39, 42, 305
Kingdom of God, 53-55, 86, 90-91, 136, 142, 159, 162, 165, 172-73, 178, 191, 193-98, 200, 204, 211, 213-15, 219, 225, 237, 248-53, 255-58, 261, 265, 267-68, 271-72, 274, 276, 300-301, 305-6
King's University (Edmonton), 85
Koyzis, David, 19, 48, 60, 110-11, 122, 131, 260, 274

á Lasco, John, 79, 279-80
De Lubac, Henri, 235

Marks of the (true) church, 15, 164-66, 215, 258, 300-302, 305
Means of grace, 16-18, 173-74, 237, 244-46, 258, 260, 268, 299
  Direct, ix, 15-17, 20, 102, 170, 172-74, 258, 260-64, 272
  Indirect, ix, 16-18, 102, 170, 172, 258, 260-62, 272
Milbank, John, 248
missio Dei, 243, 250-53, 255-56
Missiology/missiologist, 173, 250-51
Missional, 83, 167, 172, 174, 237-39, 243, 246, 250, 256-57, 272, 276
Missionary, 26, 193, 205-6, 214, 238, 251-52
Moltmann, Jürgen, 52-55, 217-18
Mother Teresa, 186
Mouw, Richard, 21, 122, 124, 130, 132, 136, 139-40, 154, 165-68, 172-74, 182-83, 185-86, 269
Muller, Richard, 297

Neo-Calvinism, 14, 23, 83, 87, 155, 183
Newbigin, Leslie, 46, 173, 251-52, 261

Nederlandse Hervormde Kerk (NHK), 11–13, 80–81, 95, 97–98, 146, 176, 259, 279–80, 282–83, 286–87, 297
Nietzsche, Friedrich, 49, 70
Noll, Mark, 184, 220–221
nouvelle theologie, 235

Office (office-bearers), 11, 15–17, 22, 24–26, 39, 42–43, 56, 59–60, 80–81, 88–92, 95–104, 106, 113, 122, 146, 157, 167–69, 173, 175, 177, 180, 246, 274, 286
Olevianus, Caspar, 303
Organic (nature of human life), 123–34, 137, 242–43, 245
Organic/organism (mode of church), ix, 11, 16, 17, 22, 24–25, 26, 88–92, 95–104, 106, 158, 163, 165–66, 168, 170, 172–74, 180, 228, 231, 233, 242, 258–62, 264, 270, 272–73, 276–277, 299
Origen, 35–36
Orr, James, 109, 119
Otto, Rudolph, 253

Padilla, René, 252–253
Parmenides, 30–31
Penal Substitutionary Atonement, 214
Persecution, 171, 178, 195–97, 298, 301
Phenomenology/Phenomenological, 18, 29, 51–52, 73
Pillarization (Dutch: *verzuiling*), 126, 149, 185
Plato, 30–32
Pluralism, 93–94, 96, 229, 270, 272–73
Pope Benedict XVI (Cardinal Ratzinger), 236
Pope John Paul II, 238
van Prinsterer, Groen 84, 280–82, 284
Princeton 10, 14, 22, 78–79, 85, 109, 289
Proclamation(al), ix, 58, 84, 96, 104, 157, 164–66, 168–70, 172, 174–77, 183–84, 189, 191–92, 194, 198–99, 201–5, 207, 211, 213–20, 222, 224–25, 227, 234, 241, 243, 248–56, 258–65, 267–68, 270–72, 274–76, 305
Propaganda, 200–203, 220

Rahner, Karl, 7, 51–52, 238–44, 247, 250
"Reading Between the Lines," 4, 266, 275
Reconciliation, 175, 206–7, 214, 216–17, 236–37, 242
Redeemer University (Ontario), 85
(non-)Reductionism/reductionistic, 12, 25, 29–30, 46, 71–73, 110, 112, 139, 187, 190, 192, 225, 268–72
Royal Dutch Society, 80

Sacrament(s/al), ix, xiv, 3, 15, 17, 26, 38, 54, 84, 96, 102, 104, 156, 164–69, 172–75, 177, 179–80, 204, 223–25, 226–56, 257–65, 267–68, 271, 274–76, 300–301, 303, 305
Second Helvetic Confession, 297, 301–3
Second Temple Judaism, 210, 213
Shalom, 126, 210
Skillen, James, 73, 94, 123, 220, 268
Solidarity, 53, 204, 223
Sovereignty, 20–21, 60, 76, 83–84, 93–96, 108, 110, 112–14, 118–24, 126, 130, 132, 134, 138, 142–43, 151, 153, 159, 164, 167, 174, 221, 273–74
Special grace, 16–17, 95, 159–60, 260
Sphere sovereignty, ix, 20–21, 58, 60, 81, 83, 88–89, 91–95, 106, 111–14, 119–39, 141–44, 146–59, 166, 169, 175, 177, 181–83, 186–88, 219, 224, 229, 257, 259, 267, 269–70, 285
Sphere universality, 96, 149, 152
Spurgeon, Charles H., 75–77, 82, 107
Stockwell, Clinton, 108–9, 143
Stone Lectures, 10, 14–15, 83, 85, 102, 109, 113, 119–20, 128, 149, 161, 164, 257, 260, 289

Suffering, 13, 53, 55, 141, 157, 178, 186, 193, 195–196, 202, 204, 223, 261

Totalitarian, 69, 71, 187
Tract on the Reformation of the Churches, 81, 149, 158, 166, 169, 178, 286

Ursinus, Zacharius, 303

Vatican Council I (1869–1870), 235
Vatican Council II (1962–1965), 26, 179, 226–27, 233–43, 247–49, 257–58
Vocation, ix, xiv, 17, 20, 70, 83, 91, 118, 125–127, 134, 148, 167, 171, 197, 204, 215, 225, 259, 272, 276

Warfield, B. B., 79, 289–290
Weak(ness), 6, 13, 53, 58, 132, 179, 190–97, 199, 202–5, 212–13, 216, 218, 220–21, 224, 253, 263
Weber, Max, 43–45, 56–58, 60, 64–66, 118, 123–24, 128, 189
Webster, John, 226
Wells, David, 277
Wesley, John, 222
Westminster Shorter Catechism/ Confession, 287, 302
Wilhelmena, Queen, 81, 285, 289–292
William I, King, 84, 146
Wisdom of Solomon, 35
Wolters, Albert, 46, 86, 93, 109, 135–37
Wolterstorff, Nicholas, 24, 83–84, 96–97, 103, 112, 114, 121, 123–24, 127–29, 133, 154, 178, 183–84, 219, 260, 276
Wood, James E., 47–48
Wood, John H., 78, 81, 84, 89, 92, 94–96, 101, 104, 224, 227–35, 246–47, 256–57
Worldview, ix, xiv, 9, 18–21, 23, 25, 47, 65–67, 69, 71, 73–74, 77, 86, 88, 92, 107–12, 114–22, 124–26, 129, 133–36, 138, 142, 144–45, 147, 152–53, 180–81, 187, 189, 196–97, 248, 261–62, 268, 276, 297

Yale University, 290
Yonge, Charlotte M., 98, 280

Zwingli, Ulrich, 301
Zwinglian, 253

www.ingramcontent.com/pod-product-compliance
Lightning Source LLC
Chambersburg PA
CBHW061425300426
44114CB00014B/1546